WORLD WAR II

Tess Press

AMERICAN HERITAGE

WORLD WAR II

Revised and Updated by

STEPHEN E. AMBROSE

Original Text by C. L. SULZBERGER

 Tess Press

Library of Congress Cataloging-in-Publication Data available upon request.

Published by Tess Press, an imprint of
Black Dog & Leventhal Publishers, Inc.
151 West 19th Street, New York, NY 10011

Printed in China

ISBN: 978-1-60376-154-3

h g f e d c b a

CONTENTS

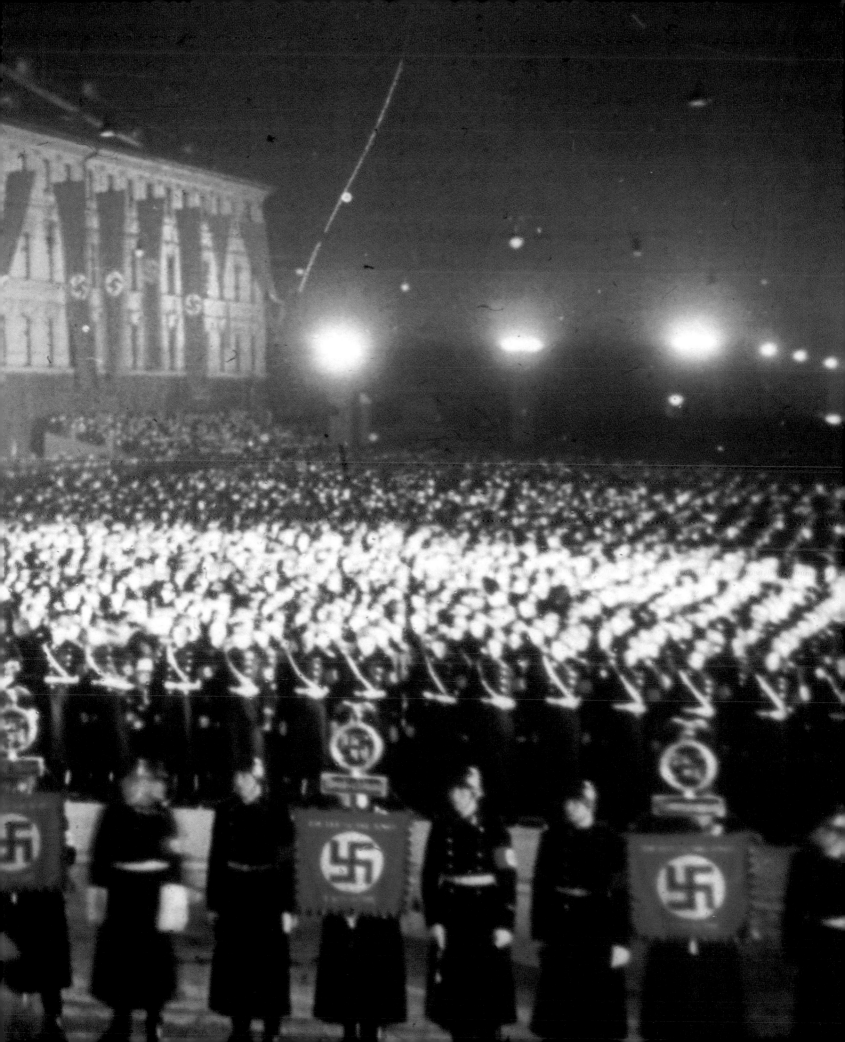

New History of
WORLD WAR II

INTRODUCTION

It was history's greatest catastrophe. More than five decades after it ended—years marked by constant conflict in at least some parts of the world and by enormous improvements in weaponry and firepower—World War II remains by far the most costly war of all time. As many as 50 million people died, a majority of them in their teens and early twenties. The destruction defies belief. In the summer of 1945, General Dwight Eisenhower flew from Berlin to Moscow at eight hundred feet, on a clear day. He could not see a single building still standing.

The war had a cataclysmic effect on world politics, economics, and social life. Empires disappeared, others sprang up. Allies became enemies, enemies turned into allies. A hundred years from now, students looking back at the first half of the twentieth century will find the shifts in alliances impossible to straighten out. But they will also have an overview: the great struggles of World War I and II were fought over ideology. In World War I it was autocracy vs. democracy. In World War II, there were three contenders: the fascists, the communists, and the democracies. Each dominated by turn: in the 1930s, the communists and fascists looked like sure winners; from 1940 to 1942 the fascists took the lead; by 1944 the democracies and communists had clearly come out on top.

World War II, for all its cost, did not settle the ideological issue. It took fifty years of Cold War to do that. Meanwhile, the various captive peoples in the Soviet Empire were consigned to a life as horrid as their lives under Nazi occupation from 1941 to 1944. So were the peoples of China and North Korea, where communist rule could be as brutal as the Japanese occupation.

In science and technology, the war saw the birth of the modern age. This was due to a tremendous burst of activity from physicists, chemists, engineers, and scientists around the world. Responding to the demands of war, governments gave scientists unlimited funding, and the payoff was spectacular. Radar, computers, jet aircraft, rocket-launched missiles, atomic weapons, and nuclear power all got their start in World War II. No innovation would have advanced as rapidly without war, and one might not have been realized at all: Minus the threat posed by Hitler, would the United States have put such a huge investment into so risky a project as an atomic bomb?

For everyone, everywhere, World War II had a deep impact. Today it continues to seize the imagination. The universal fascination with the war is all the greater because of its high drama, its titanic battles, its larger-than-life leading actors. Ultimately, the fascination becomes specific, directed toward both the individual people who lived and died in the war and the places where they fought. That is what makes photographs and illustrations so compelling.

The war made household names of places all but unknown in 1939. Iwo Jima, Monte Cassino, St. Mere Eglise, El Alamein, and so many others resonate today; thanks to the magic of the camera the mere mention of their names brings specific images instantly to mind. Examples follow in the pages of this volume.

This book is by no means the whole story of the war. No one book could contain the complete history. Our aim here is to cover, in words and pictures, the essential history of this greatest of human tragedies, and to recreate a feeling of what it meant in terms of the people who were swept up by it.

•

This revision was by all means a team effort: Michael Sagalyn convinced me to undertake the daunting task of revising the volume; Kathy Huck did an exemplary job of editing and cannot be thanked enough; the staff at Byron Preiss Visual Publications, Inc. did outstanding photographic and artistic research; Dr. Clayton Laurie at the U.S. Army Center of Military History read the manuscript and saved us from many embarrassing errors; the team at American Heritage gave expert advise, as usual; and the group at Penguin Putnam made sure that the book turned out beautifully.

STEPHEN E. AMBROSE

CHAPTER 1

THE DESCENT INTO HELL

The struggle for Europe that began in August 1914 did not conclude until November 1990 with the end of the Cold War. It was a struggle that took the shape of battles across Europe in World War I and throughout Europe, Asia, and North Africa in World War II. All the large nations, and nearly all the small ones, participated in the wars.

World War II was a direct consequence of the fighting and flawed peace making of World War I. Indeed, historians in later centuries will write of a world war that began in 1914, had a long armistice from 1919 to 1939, and was resumed and continued until 1945. What Woodrow Wilson hoped would be "the war to end all wars" turned out to be only a starting point for an even greater and more terrible war. Although World War I caused the disappearance of three great empires—the Austro-Hungarian Hapsburg Empire, the czarist Russian Romanov Empire, and the German Wilhelm's Imperial Empire—it lacked a decisive conclusion. Germany's war-making proclivities and capabilities were weakened but not destroyed, revolutionary Russia remained independent and fabulously wealthy in natural resources, and Japan was free to turn aggressive. The Allies imposed a so-called harsh peace on Germany but sent no permanent troops to occupy the country and uphold the Versailles Treaty.

Wilson thought the way to eliminate war was to "make the world safe for democracy," and he believed one way to do that was through the principle of "self-determination," leading toward "complete independence of various small nationalities now forming part of various empires." But self-determination proved to be a will-o'-the-wisp. Nowhere did stable democracies spring up; throughout the former German, Russian, and Austro-Hungarian empires, small wars followed the Great War as various ethnic and political

A Hitler Youth group holds its first Reichsmeeting in Hamburg (opposite). Strength through Joy dances brought a feeling of unity and a surge of patriotism to Germans of every age and class. The Nazis were masters of mass psychology. Symbols, especially the swastika (above), and medieval pageantry were integral to the process of getting young men and women to lose themselves in the group.

groups fought for control of their regions. In Asia and Africa, meanwhile, where Wilson never intended the principle to be applied, it set aflame the peoples of European-dominated colonies.

Almost everything done at the Versailles Conference was a colossal mistake. The treaty made Germany pay for the war—an enormous sum—which forced the Weimar Republic (named for the eastern German city where it was founded, it was the democratic government the Allies supported in Germany) to take such drastic economic measures that it had almost no support at home. Germany's colonies were taken from her, while the American, British, Dutch, and French empires stayed in place. The peoples of Central and Eastern Europe had boundaries created for them that made little ethnic, economic, or political sense. Wilson created a Poland free of German and Soviet occupation but without an outlet to the sea and without any protection from her rapacious neighbors to the east and west. And the League of Nations, supposed to enforce the treaty, never had a chance, because Wilson had misjudged his political support at home and was unable to lead the United States to membership in the League. Germany and the Soviet Union, the two most powerful states in Europe, were initially excluded from the

The victorious Big Four met in 1919 at the Versailles Conference—(left to right) David Lloyd George of Britain, Vittorio Orlando of Italy, Georges Clemenceau of France, and Woodrow Wilson of the United States. They came to make a fair peace that would last, but instead fashioned a vindictive settlement that left the Germans raging for revenge and their countries unwilling to enforce the various provisions of the treaty they wrote.

German artist Hans Grundig depicts the anger and discontent of German workers at a Communist meeting in the 1920s in his 1932 painting *KPD-Versammlung*. Thousands of Germans turned to Communism, Socialism, or Nazism in their frustration with Germany's faltering post-World War I economy.

League and thus eventually were thrown into each other's arms. In 1922, in the Treaty of Rapallo, they entered into a secret military alliance.

The economic consequences of Versailles were also a disaster. The new century's early economic expansion was totally disrupted. The revolution in the Soviet Union made European investments there worthless; tariffs rose; world trade was badly disrupted. Germany was engulfed by the worst inflation ever suffered by an industrialized economy. At the end of the war, the German mark was worth about twenty-five cents; by November 1923, its value had shrunk a billion times. Workers in Essen took their pay home in barrels, and some three hundred paper factories and one hundred fifty printing establishments were unable to turn out notes fast enough to keep the economy off a barter basis. Eventually, Hjalmar Schacht, later Hitler's minister of economy, introduced a device called the *Rentenmark,* based, theoretically, on a mortgage of all Germany. This device created a new currency but did not salvage the ruined and embittered middle class.

The man who profited most from this situation was Austrian-born Adolf Hitler, a former corporal in the German Army who had a fanatical belief in his own mission, a genius for rabble-rousing oratory, and an ability to articulate the resentments and fears of ordinary Germans. In September 1919, he joined the minuscule German Workers Party. Hitler later renamed it *Nationalsozialistische Deutsche Arbeiterpartei* (National Socialist German Workers Party—or Nazi, for short.) But the Nazi Party appeal was narrow; there were

WAR, NEVER AGAIN

Nobody wanted another war. Even that most bellicose of American presidents, Theodore Roosevelt, had had enough. Roosevelt had pushed President Woodrow Wilson to get into the First World War; Roosevelt had often contended that war improved a nation's moral fiber and built manly virtues. But in 1918 his beloved son, Quentin, was shot down over France. His romantic notion about war, perhaps appropriate to the Spanish-American War ("a splendid little war" as one of Roosevelt's friends called it), was destroyed with Quentin's plane.

One can multiply Roosevelt's experience by the millions. The faces in the crowds, whether in London, Paris, Berlin, Vienna, or St. Petersburg in August 1914—as the European nations announced that the war toward which they had been heading for decades was beginning—were full of joy, exuberance, patriotism, determination, pride, and anticipation. Four years and millions of deaths later, on the streets of the great capitals of Europe, the faces betrayed despair, sorrow, cynicism, resignation, shame, and fear.

In August 1914 the vast majority of Europeans had not the least idea what they were getting into. They anticipated a short, glorious war that would climax with their troops marching through the capital of their defeated enemy. Perhaps never before, or since, have expectations been so wrong. The ghastly business of the trenches in the eastern and western fronts came as a complete surprise.

So people vowed: Never again. That determination was reinforced by the awful knowledge that if there were to be another world war, it would be even more horrible than the Great War. By 1918 weapons improvements had greatly expanded the killing zone. That year saw bombing missions far behind the front lines, which meant that cities and civilians were now targets. Improved submarines meant that if there were another war, they would cause even greater losses. New weapons, along with expanded production capabilities, meant the next war would feature more and bigger bombs with better means of delivering them. At any cost, war had to be avoided. Never again.

On Memorial Day, 1919, in Saint-Nazaire cemetery (above) American soldiers pay tribute to comrades who died in action. World War I was a war like no other. Trench warfare and advances in weaponry that expanded the war zone to reach civilian targets made the death toll rise exponentially. Although United States forces were not sent "over there" until 1917, a year before the war ended, the devastating experiences of American soldiers like the one shown wounded in a trench in France in 1918 (opposite) made them, like their European allies, vow "never again."

A businessman draws his weekly payroll from the Reichbank in Berlin, August 15, 1923 (above right). Germany's 1923 inflation was the worst ever known in an industrial country and made the nation ripe for extremism of every kind. Due to the scarcity of food and increasing anger of the general public, the municipal government of Berlin opened food kitchens such as the one below to feed workers and children.

many right-wing parties far better known and supported. Hitler decided to seize power in Munich, capital of Bavaria, in the Beer Hall Putsch of 1923. The police opened fire, sixteen Nazis and three policemen were killed, Hitler ran. He was caught and sentenced to prison for five years but was out after nine months of being treated like an honored guest. In prison he wrote *Mein Kampf (My Struggle)*, a hodgepodge of philosophical musings loosely gathered under the umbrella of the superiority of the German race and its destiny to rule Europe and the world.

On his release, Hitler set himself to rebuild the party and to achieve power by constitutional means. He appealed to the German people by constantly reminding them of the humiliation of their defeat in the war, repeating the popular myth that the German armies had been "stabbed in the

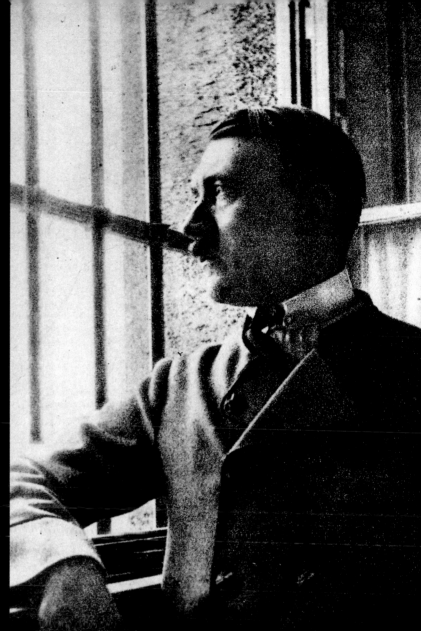

Hitler poses in lederhosen (left). He had been born in Austria but made Germany his adopted country. After fighting as a frontline soldier in France during World War I (for which he won an Iron Cross), he went into politics—or, more correctly, rabble-rousing. When he tried to overthrow the Bavarian government in the Beer Hall Putsch, he was taken prisoner, tried, and sentenced to Landsberg prison. He spent less than a year there (above), during which time he wrote *Mein Kampf* (*My Struggle*), a quasi-autobiography filled with dire warnings about Germany's need to overthrow the Versailles dictate.

Young Nazi students in 1933 prepare to throw armloads of non-German literature into a bonfire. Book burning was doubly appealing to them; it allowed them to destroy both the physical books and, symbolically, the ideas the books contained.

back" by the Jewish-dominated government. (Jews weren't the only group hated by the Nazi Party—they shared that honor with communists and socialists, among others.) He railed at the wrongs done Germany by the Treaty of Versailles. And he damned democracy and the ineffectiveness of the Weimar Republic. With these subjects for his tirades went a virulent anti-Semitism in which Hitler blamed the Jews for all ills of Germany and of the world, past and present. Interviewed by a reporter in 1925, he said his deepest desire was to see Jews hanging from every lamppost in Munich. His madness on the subject probably hurt more than it helped with the voters, and, despite Hitler's ability as a rabble-rouser, the Nazi Party remained small until the economic slump of 1929. Then, as unemployment rose, the Nazis skillfully exploited the growing despair. They had received fewer than a million votes in the elections of 1928, but in 1930 they got more than six million, and by 1932, almost fourteen million. The German Communist Party had also grown with hard times, but Hitler was more adept at intrigue. He made political alliances with the industrialists, with nationalist politicians, and with the army generals, and got himself named chancellor by President Hindenburg in January 1933. The next month, when a fire destroyed the Reichstag (Germany's national capitol in Berlin), the Nazis used it as an excuse to jail,

Two passersby examine the shattered window of a Jewish-owned store in Berlin, November 17, 1938. On the night of November 9–10, mobs all over Germany and Austria burned synagogues and vandalized more than 7,000 Jewish shops, businesses, and homes. *Kristallnacht,* or "Night of Broken Glass," was the first violent pogrom in Western Europe in hundreds of years and marked a new stage of the Nazi campaign against the Jews.

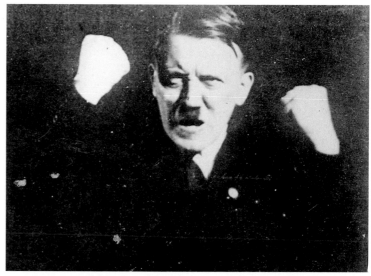

beat, and torture Jews and Communists wholesale. Other political parties were gagged, the churches made subservient. A bloodbath within the Nazi Party eliminated any internal opposition to Hitler.

The Nazis were masters of politics, and in the art of mass political rallies, unsurpassed. They could play many strings in the soul of Germany, which they did best at the annual Party Rally at Nuremberg. There, in a delirious round of music, parades, speeches, and pagan pageantry, all party members, from Hitler down to the shabbiest little village block leader, regenerated their enthusiasm and faith. The rallies were held in early September and lasted a week; the first was in 1933, after Hitler became chancellor, and thereafter they remained the high point of the Nazi calendar until the beginning of the war. Torchlight parades and other night spectacles were frequent, for Hitler believed that "in the evening the people's willpower more easily succumbs to the dominating force of a stronger will." The climactic finale of each rally was a speech by Hitler that sent both speaker and his hundreds of thousands of listeners into emotional frenzies. The theme was ancient German heroes and a sense of national unity. The Nazis—with filmmaker Leni Reifenstahl—produced a pathbreaking motion-picture documentary of the

A handsome Nordic youth with his flag brightens a recruiting poster for Hitler's National Student Organization (opposite). Young Germans were especially drawn to Hitler, shown above speaking to an audience in October 1930. Perhaps the greatest rabble-rouser of all time, Hitler all but hypnotized his listeners by voicing their resentments and fears. Those who saw him in action never forgot those eyes.

At the climax of the Nuremberg party rally in September 1934 (left), Hitler, in the middle, salutes the Nazis who perished during the period of struggle preceding his assumption of power in 1933. The man on the left is Heinrich Himmler, head of the Nazi SS troops; on the right is Chief of Staff Viktor Lutze. Above, Hitler is portrayed as a white knight by a German artist. Millions of Germans saw nothing ridiculous in such idolatry, and certainly it was not discouraged by Hitler, who had ranked himself with Alexander, Caesar, and Napoleon as a man of destiny. The picture was captured during the war, and in the process the head and the face were slashed by a GI who obviously was left unawed by the entire Hitler mystique.

rally entitled *Triumph of the Will* and a second entitled *Olympia*, about the 1936 Olympic Games in Berlin. They also led the world in their use of radio for propaganda purposes. Additionally, German scientists were ahead of the world in electronics, as were German designers of aircraft, tanks, and other weapons.

In the United States, meanwhile, through the 1920s, few people paid much attention to Hitler, or to just about anything happening beyond their borders. The country had had enough of world affairs. The Republican-dominated Senate rejected Wilson's League of Nations, and the constituency happily elected Warren Harding for his handsome face and his promise to "return to normalcy." But, except for the glad return to isolationism, there was no going back to prewar moods and tempos. Old verities had been questioned and old patterns were broken during the war and nothing could ever be the same again.

The twenties are remembered for Prohibition, the speakeasy, and home brew. It was the decade of jazz and the Charleston, when the collegian's coonskin coat and the flapper's rolled stockings symbolized a flaming youth that took advantage of relaxing moral standards, and the multiplying automobile, to discover sex. It was the heyday of Al Capone and rival gangster mobs, and it was the time of million-dollar boxing gates, home-run kings, and general sports mania. It was a period of prosperity, when thin-nosed Calvin Coolidge could say, "The business of America is business."

But fact and legend about the twenties are becoming blurred. The

In Berlin, August 3, 1936, Charles Lindbergh accepts a ceremonial sword from Luftwaffe commander Hermann Göring. Lindbergh had been touring German airfields, seeing the latest fighter aircraft, and he got on well with Göring, a fellow flyer. As a wave of isolationism swept over the United States during the 1920s and 1930s, Lindbergh, one of the leading isolationists, was suspected by some of being a Nazi sympathizer. This photo was used by his foes to discredit Lindbergh and, by extension, isolationism.

Franklin D. Roosevelt shakes hands with a coal miner during the 1932 presidential campaign. His platform promised immediate relief from the Depression.

decade was not universally prosperous; farmers were one conspicuous exception. Millions did not make bathtub gin and continued to support Prohibition. And the frantic speculation on the stock market and in Florida real estate involved only a minority of the people.

Insofar as the United States had a foreign policy in the twenties, it was to encourage worldwide disarmament. Washington took the lead in calling the Washington Conference of 1921–22, which put some limits to the big ship tonnage of the leading naval powers. It was the first successful arms reduction treaty in history—it led to the actual destruction of ships and weapons—and for seventy years remained the only such treaty. The United States unilaterally did to herself what Versailles required Germany to do, by demobilizing her army to under a hundred thousand men.

Overall, the decade was a time of frenetic—and often dogged—seeking after gaiety and thrills. It ended in October 1929 with the Wall Street Crash, and the country awoke to reality again. Within days, investors lost $30 billion—almost what the nation had spent on World War I. Men went to bed wealthy and awoke paupers. And prices kept on dropping until June 1932. By 1933 there were some twelve million unemployed, nearly a third of the labor force. Banks failed; mortgages were foreclosed; farm families evicted. Mines and factories ground to a halt. Shantytowns, known as Hoovervilles, grew like fungus around the edges of cities, and incredible as it may now seem *Business Week* reported that some one hundred thousand Americans were seeking jobs in the Soviet Union.

The effect of the Wall Street disaster was felt throughout Europe. On May 11, 1931, Vienna's powerful Credit-Anstalt bank collapsed. On September 21, England abandoned the gold standard. World trade dwindled. Wages shrank fantastically, and Europe's growing numbers of unemployed workers

Flappers (below) enjoy the high life in 1926, the heyday of the Roaring Twenties. The good times came to an abrupt end as the stock market crashed on "Black Tuesday," October 29, 1929 (right). After the crash, a man who lost everything tries to sell his car (opposite bottom). Not until President Roosevelt came to office in 1933 did the nation slowly and fitfully begin to pull itself out of the economic emergency. One of the president's first acts was to close all the banks, then re-open them on a sounder basis. Customers at a Detroit bank line up (opposite top) to recover 30 percent on their deposits, April 25, 1933, after the banks re-opened.

Hard times in America wore many faces. The photographer Dorothea Lange captured the despair of a man down on his luck in San Francisco (below) and a Missouri family on U.S. Highway 99 in Tracy, California (opposite). Bread lines (right) became a familiar sight across the country. Many families, especially in the drought-stricken Midwest, pulled up stakes and left home to find work and a better life elsewhere.

The new German Army (above) was tough, well-disciplined, professional, and fanatical—everything Hitler wanted in his army. The ambitious Hitler (opposite) speaks on the final day of the party rally, September 24, 1935. He had great plans for his new military machine.

joined the ruined bourgeoisie in following the Italian Fascist, German National Socialist, and Soviet Communist movements, which thrived on despair. In America, however, there was no turn away from democracy, although the Republican Party was repudiated. In November 1932, New York Governor Franklin D. Roosevelt decisively defeated President Herbert Hoover. He took office in March 1933, bringing new policies and enthusiasm to the task of recovery.

Thus in 1933, the pattern of leadership among the world's three most powerful nations was set for the next dozen years with the arrival in office of Roosevelt in Washington and Hitler in Berlin and Joseph Stalin in Moscow.

Roosevelt came in on promises of immediate relief, recovery, and reform. He lowered tariffs, repealed Prohibition, relieved pressure on the farmers, revalued gold. He launched vast public works to take up the employment slack. Exuding self-confidence and galvanizing national faith, Roosevelt got much of America back to work. By the end of the decade the United States, though still not fully cured of its economic illness, was struggling to its feet.

By 1939, Hitler's rearmament program was producing state-of-the-art planes and tanks in impressive numbers. Above, the Stuka dive-bomber soon became the terror of Europe. The formidable Mark IV tank (opposite) would roll through Europe in a massive, organized blitzkrieg.

Germany, however, was doing far better in dealing with the economic crisis. Using Schacht's *Rentenmark* and the essential fact that, while it had lost the war, its territory had remained unravaged, it had recaptured much of its industrial and trading position. However, it harbored bitter psychological complexes of defeat and thirsted for revenge. Hitler denounced Versailles and vowed to overthrow the system it created; his unremitting attack on the treaty was his single strongest issue. In addition, by playing on middle-class resentments, the ambitions of the industrialists, and a fear of Communism that was fanned by monarchists, officers, and the church, Hitler and his National Socialist (Nazi) Party used power in a dynamic, dedicated way. Hitler was a builder. His public works—most of all the autobahn—were on a far greater scale than Roosevelt's. He built schools and swimming pools in nearly every German village. He restored German pride as he brought into the open the remilitarization program that the German General Staff (intact despite being forbidden in the Versailles Treaty) had started secretly in 1921, putting the unemployed and discontented into uniforms. Hitler also smashed democracy, dispossessed Germany's Jews, and crushed party dissidents through terror or sometimes outright murder. He silenced the General Staff when moderate German officers questioned his policies.

During the astonishing six years between his accession in 1933 and the outbreak of World War II, Hitler made himself dictator and made Germany Europe's strongest military power, while the victors of World War I looked on in confusion. His main goal was to rewrite Versailles. The treaty allowed Germany a hundred-thousand-man army only, with no air force or General Staff. In 1935 Hitler boldly and officially proclaimed Germany would no longer be so constrained. The treaty forbade the entry of German troops into a demilitarized Rhineland. On March 7, 1936, Hitler sent his troops into the Rhineland and began to fortify it. France and Britain said they would enforce the treaty if the United States would lead the way. Roosevelt would not;

his country was strongly isolationist and struggling with the Great Depression. The treaty also forbade a union between Austria and Germany. In March 1938, Hitler—born in Austria—marched into Vienna, to the hysterical delight of a multitude of Austrians. He was on the move.

Hitler reckoned that France and Britain would leave Germany alone so long as their interests were not directly threatened. The world's third great democracy, meanwhile, worried Hitler not at all. The United States had no army to speak of, nor any foreign policy. President Roosevelt seemed almost indifferent to the rest of the world. It was not just that domestic worries were so many and so pressing that they left no time for other concerns. It was also that Roosevelt, like his compatriots, was steeped in the old isolationist tradition that the only proper business of the United States lay right at home. During this decade, isolationism reached what was probably an all-time peak. It was a time for being cynical about war and patriotism; it was commonly accepted that the country had become involved in the First World War only because of shrewd Allied propaganda and because of American

In March of 1938, Hitler triumphantly returns home to Austria (above), and his German troops are welcomed by crowds of Nazi supporters. Adolf Hitler, born in Austria, first went to Vienna when he was nineteen. There he spent four years as an impoverished vagrant, sleeping in flophouses, doing odd jobs, often eating in charity soup kitchens, and turning out hundreds of mediocre watercolors (right), which was as close as he got to achieving his dream of becoming an artist.

bankers and arms makers who wanted to protect their loans and sales on credit to the Allies. In the search for scapegoats for war guilt, the investigations of munitions makers by the Nye committee in the Senate offered one of the most popular; it was believed that these "merchants of death" deliberately fomented wars to increase the market for their wares. As soon as the sound of aggression from across the seas—in Manchuria, Ethiopia, and Spain—began to be disturbing, Americans insulated themselves with neutrality laws that forbade trade with either side in a conflict and forbade the "cash and carry" policy of selling weapons on credit or transporting them to Europe in American vessels. At the same time, Roosevelt slashed the budget of the already pitifully small armed forces.

Unconcerned with, even contemptuous of, the democracies, Hitler was more concerned with Italy and the Soviet Union. In 1921, Benito Mussolini, a renegade Socialist, had developed an antidemocratic party from restless elements and, dressing them in black shirts, had used them to take over Rome from a flabby parliamentary regime. Mussolini was personally more colorful than Hitler. He was flamboyant, cultivated, with a literary flair and a way with women; but, like Hitler, he dreamed of empire. However, the huge army he created was backed neither by economic sinews and national will nor by modern weapons.

There was a formal military alliance between Berlin and Rome (the October 1936 Rome-Berlin Axis) when Hitler seized Austria on Italy's frontier. He forced an Austrian showdown despite Mussolini's vaunted "8,000,000 bayonets," which failed to protect a country whose independence was vitally important to Rome. After that, Hitler knew he could bind Italy to the German juggernaut. On March 11, 1938, he explained to Mussolini why he had grabbed Austria, and on September 29, they signed an agreement that gave Hitler a free hand in Eastern Europe, and gave Mussolini nothing except an alliance with a devil who was threatening to drag Italy into a war for which it was not prepared.

Stalin, meanwhile, was consolidating his power by purging Soviet peasants, army officers, and intellectual elite. A rocklike personality, devoid of humanity or fear, he was sustained by the same icy faith as the Spanish inquisitor Torquemada, who could do horrible things and then sleep like a child. Stalin's small frame, his withered left arm and pocked face, concealed a mixture of strength, vision, and murderous intent. He wrote dismally and spoke dully in heavy Georgian accents. Stalin was a brutal realist. After he had liquidated or starved millions of peasants, he remarked: "It is ridiculous to expatiate today on the expropriation of the kulaks. We do not lament the loss of the hair of one who has been beheaded."

While Stalin murdered and repressed, he also molded the apparatus for eventual war. He feared Germany, but even more he feared a German alliance with the West. In 1933 he proclaimed, "The conquest of power by Hitler does not signify a defeat for the Communist Party." It is possible this assertion contained the first hint that Stalin wished to renew the old German-Soviet ties, despite the clash of ideologies. There is evidence that Stalin tried in 1936 to discuss a partition of Poland with Hitler. But of course the dictators could not trust one another. Each side prepared war plans even while negotiating.

Mussolini—the man who invented Fascism—in 1936. His pomposity, like his ambition, was unlimited.

Joseph Stalin (above) takes a walk in Moscow, June 27, 1925. He had recently seized full control of the Communist Party, following the death of Lenin, seen above right speaking in Red Square, May 1, 1919.

"The world must be made safe for democracy," President Wilson had told Congress in his war message. But war-prostrated Europe proved sterile ground for the growth of democracy and produced instead the new tyranny of totalitarianism. Hitler, Stalin, Mussolini—they were the dynamic leaders, welcomed by many because of their promise of law, order, and jobs, never mind that totalitarianism was antithetical to everything democracy stood for. In the Soviet Union, in Germany, and in Italy, a police state, answerable to but one man, controlled the economic, political, and cultural lives of its citizens. Americans, generally, chose to ignore the obvious and instead openly expressed admiration for Mussolini, who had "made the trains run on time."

Japan, too, became a totalitarian state, when the military seized control and embarked on aggression. During the 1920s the political parties and commercial interests in Japan had tried to assert themselves in support of a rational, nonaggressive foreign policy, but with the coming of hard times after 1929 the military offered the tempting panacea of conquest abroad. In September 1931, the Japanese Army used a minor incident as a pretext for seizing Manchuria; five months later, the huge province was proclaimed the puppet nation of Manchukuo, while divided China stood by helplessly, the League of Nations debated, and the United States expressed disapproval but did nothing. More of North China was occupied in 1933, and in Japan, by terror and political pressure (which included assassination of its opponents on a regular basis), the military took complete control of the government.

U.S. Secretary of State Henry Stimson denounced the Japanese aggression and issued the Stimson Doctrine, which refused to recognize Manchukuo, specifically, and gains made by aggression, in general. As the doctrine had no enforcement power and Stimson was unable to persuade the other democracies to join in opposition, it had no effect on the Japanese.

This scene of Japanese samurai warriors was painted at the time of Admiral Matthew Perry's visit to Japan in 1853. The samurai, whose code of *Bushido*, or honor, had dominated the nation for centuries, were intensely brave and utterly loyal. These legendary warriors disappeared as Japan was modernized in the late nineteenth century.

Japanese soldiers symbolize the resurgence of the samurai spirit with their bulletproof armor during an incident in Shanghai in 1932.

The army had taken control of politics in Japan. Its policy was to expand into China. In 1937, Japan invaded China proper, capturing its principal cities. In the summer of 1938, Japan's headstrong army even clashed with the Soviet Union on the Manchukuo frontier. These Asiatic incursions saw brutal fighting and vicious savagery by the Japanese Army. They also exposed the frailty of international peace machinery. The democracies were paralyzed. The American people were horrified by the pictures and stories coming out of China, but the majority remained resolutely isolationist.

With a population of 450 million in 1939, China was the world's most populous nation (India was second with 359 million; the Soviet Union, third with 194 million; the United States, fourth with 129 million). China had immense national resources and an ancient culture, but no political or military unity. The Japanese did. Her 72 million people followed one leader. The Chinese, meanwhile, were fighting both a nationwide civil war and a bewildering set of regional conflicts between rival warlords.

The Chinese Civil War, which began in 1927 and continued to 1949, pitted Chiang Kai-shek's Nationalist Government against Mao Tse-tung's Communist Party. When Japan invaded China, Mao resisted while Chiang tried to appease the Japanese in order to concentrate on fighting the Communists.

Then, in December of 1936, Chiang was kidnapped by Mao's army and given the choice of joining the Communists in a united front against the Japanese or of being killed. Chiang took the prudent choice, and from that time the two armies joined in fighting the common enemy. As resistance grew, the Japanese blows became more widespread. The invading armies took the coastal cities and territories first, then moved up the rivers and spread inland. But the giant was too big to swallow. The Chinese armies always slipped away, and though they won virtually no victories they continued to tie down a large number of Japanese troops throughout the war.

In October 1935, Mussolini, anxious to show off his new Fascist troops and to expand his new Roman Empire in Africa, provoked a war with Ethiopia. Emperor Haile Selassie made a dramatic appeal for help to the League of Nations, but since France and Britain refused to act, and the United States was not even a member, the ineffectual League could only level economic sanctions—which Standard Oil refused to honor. The Italians, unhindered, proceeded to slaughter Ethiopians. Mussolini's son-in-law, Count Galeazzo Ciano, led a bombing raid against tribesmen on horseback, armed only with spears. Vittorio Mussolini, the conqueror's son, wrote enthusiasti-

In 1937, Chiang Kai-shek (below left) and Mao Tse-tung (below right) were the principals in a titanic struggle for power in the world's most populous nation. Chiang's Nationalists and Mao's Communists carried out a war within a war even as the Japanese advanced through China.

Between the Chinese Civil War and the Japanese invasion, China was torn by strife throughout the 1930s and 1940s: a Nationalist Chinese soldier (above) stands guard; in Shanghai, a Japanese armored car (above right) pummels shells into buildings while Japanese troops wait to shoot anything that might be left over after the tank finishes its deadly mission; in one of the most famous photographs from the Sino-Japanese war, a child cries amid the Shanghai ruins after a Japanese bombing raid on August 28, 1937 (right).

cally of an air attack: "One group of horsemen gave me the impression of a budding rose unfolding as the bomb fell in their midst and blew them up." Britain left the Suez Canal open to Italian troop ships. Italian forces, helped by a remarkable engineering corps, marched across mosquitoed swamps and craggy mountains to Addis Ababa; Haile Selassie fled the country.

The wildest, bloodiest, and most heartrending of these lesser conflicts was the civil war in Spain, where Germany, Italy, and the Soviet Union tested weapons, tactics, and commanders. On July 18, 1936, a handful of well-financed right-wing generals, headed by forty-four-year-old Francisco Franco, led a military revolt against the weak Republic. Communists and liberal groups throughout the world joined to support the Republican militia, while Fascists, the Spanish Catholic Church, and conservatives backed Franco. The Germans sent him tanks, planes, and twenty thousand men; the Italians, another forty to sixty thousand men. A full 40 percent of Franco's forces were German or Italian. Meanwhile the Soviets sent planes, tanks, and ammunition to the Republican forces, plus some of their best officers, operating under aliases. The Soviet and pro-Republic volunteers numbered approximately 50,000 men.

Spain aroused infinite passions and came to represent, in some weird prevision, the ideological fanaticism of Communists and Fascists that would characterize World War II, so soon to explode. Before their own bodies and souls were torn on far greater battlefields, millions of people were caught up in the emotional and symbolic Spanish vortex. Picasso painted his greatest picture, *Guernica*, after Hitler's Luftwaffe first practiced mass bombing on that city. Hemingway wrote *For Whom the Bell Tolls*, one of his finest novels, about Republican guerrillas. Miguel de Unamuno, Spain's famous author, died of a broken heart, and the poet García Lorca was murdered. Georgi Dimitrov,

In his picture of a Loyalist soldier caught at the instant of death (above), *Life* magazine photographer Robert Capa achieved one of the great portrayals of the ultimate meaning of battle. While in Spain, Capa learned a saying he repeated on Omaha Beach on D-Day in 1944: *Es una cosa muy seria. Es una cosa muy seria.* ("This is a very serious business.") General Francisco Franco (opposite top) was the leader of the Fascist forces that fought Republican Loyalists in the Spanish Civil War of 1936–39. Pablo Picasso began work on his *Guernica* (opposite bottom) in 1937, only two days after German planes had bombed the Basque city of Guernica, with casualties of over 2,500. It became one of the artist's most famous paintings.

later head of the Comintern, and Josip Broz of Yugoslavia, later called Marshal Tito, gained conspiratorial experience working for the Republican cause. André Malraux led an air squadron against Franco. Yet what the Spanish War lacked was another Goya. Only a Goya could describe the horrors committed by both sides: burned churches, raped nuns, massacred labor leaders, tortured intellectuals; the slaughter in a bull ring, the shooting of prisoners on the cold Castilian killing ground of Cuenca; the savagery of Spaniards against Spaniards, in the name of ideologies that were foreign to Spain.

While German tanks, bombers, and tacticians were being tested, Hitler turned his attention to the great Slavic plains that the Germans long had coveted as living space, or *Lebensraum*. By seizing Austria, he had managed to outflank a ring of fortifications erected by conglomerate Czechoslovakia—a nation created by Versailles that contained not only Czechs and Slovaks but also a sizable ethnic German minority. Turning the principle of self-determination to his own uses, the Führer applied massive new pressures on the Czechs to turn over the Sudetenland to Germany. When Eduard Beneš, the solemn little soccer-playing Czechoslovak president, turned for help to his French allies and British friends, they cynically ignored him and their pledged word.

Initially, Beneš was resolute. C. L. Sulzberger was in Prague as a newspaperman much of that fateful summer of 1938, and he remembered how, on one hot afternoon in his baroque palace, Beneš unrolled a large map and with a pointer showed Sulzberger which German cities he intended to bomb if Hitler invaded. He recited impressive military production figures from his famous Skoda and Tatra ordnance works. But Paris and London feared Hitler and were more than willing to allow him to expand in Eastern Europe if he would leave them alone. Unctuous French statesmen, cautious generals who hoped to gain strength with time, and pressure groups in the British establishment persuaded French Premier Daladier and British Prime Minister Chamberlain to sell out the Czechs (with whom France had a mutual defense treaty) and proclaim that they had preserved peace. What they did was give away Czechoslovakia, because the country was indefensible without the mountainous, fortified Sudetenland. British politician Winston Churchill, not then in government, put it perfectly: "You have gained shame and you will get war."

The Munich Conference of 1938 has come to symbolize the prewar policies of the democracies, policies of appeasement bordering on abject surrender. The conference had been called by Mussolini, who feared war in Europe (as opposed to in Ethiopia), and was attended by Hitler, Chamberlain, and Daladier. Neither the United States nor the Soviet Union were present. The United States did not want to be involved; the French and British were unwilling to make an alliance with Stalin, perhaps the only move that could have saved Czechoslovakia. Munich was the last time for almost fifty years that the Europeans dealt with their own border disputes; in all subsequent Cold War summit meetings of heads of government, it was the United States and the Soviets who made the decisions.

Hitler's bold, aggressive moves had paid off. He was more contemptuous of the democracies than ever, certain they would never act. After the acquisition of the Sudetenland, he announced he had no more territorial demands in Europe, an obvious lie given his stance on Versailles, as the part of the

We, the German Führer and Chancellor and the British Prime Minister, have had a further meeting today and are agreed in recognising that the question of Anglo-German relations is of the first importance for the two countries and for Europe.

We regard the agreement signed last night and the Anglo-German Naval Agreement as symbolic of the desire of our two peoples never to go to war with one another again.

We are resolved that the method of consultation shall be the method adopted to deal with any other questions that may concern our two countries, and we are determined to continue our efforts to remove possible sources of difference and thus to contribute to assure the peace of Europe.

Neville Chamberlain

September 30, 1938.

At the Munich Conference, on September 30, 1938, British Prime Minister Neville Chamberlain and Hitler shake hands (above) before signing the Munich Agreement. Chamberlain returns to England (right) holding a copy of the agreement in his hand. He proclaimed it meant "peace in our time." The agreement (above right) was so vague it was meaningless. Months afterward, Hitler arrives in Czechoslovakia (opposite), ignoring the promises made at Munich.

Czech Nazis and ethnic Germans guard and worship Hitler as he enters Prague, above, on March 15, 1939, the day of annexation of the Czech nation to Germany. Opposite, young Germans train for combat during the same period in which Hitler was talking about peace. This special iron structure trained men in jumping and climbing for their parachute assignments.

treaty that most stuck in his craw was the creation of Poland and the cutting off of East Prussia from the rest of Germany by the Polish Corridor.

In March 1939, Hitler broke his pledge to make no further claims on the Czechs. He partitioned the rest of the country, installing his own satraps. Chamberlain refused even to censure Hitler in the House of Commons for the rape of Czechoslovakia, but the national outcry was so loud that the astonished prime minister quickly reversed himself. And so, after having spinelessly yielded every position where Hitler might have been turned back, Great Britain, with France reluctantly concurring, announced at last that they would defend the integrity of Poland against any threat from outside. British and French warnings were meaningless, however, as neither country could in any way come to Poland's aid, except by attacking German from the west, and they had neither the will nor the means to do that.

The obvious course was to enlist the Soviet Union in an anti-Nazi alliance. The British and French did ask the Soviet Union to help stop Germany, but Stalin was still angered at the way he had been ignored during the Munich crisis; moreover, he had little faith in the Allies after their record of appeasement. Even more important, as a result of Stalin's purge of the officer corps of the Red Army, it was in a state of near chaos. The Soviet air force, meanwhile, was no match for the Luftwaffe. Worst of all, Stalin suspected with good cause that Daladier's and Chamberlain's policy was to encourage Hitler's embroilment with the Soviet Union by urging his attentions eastward across Czechoslovakia. Stalin wanted to urge Hitler westward, hoping to see his capitalistic enemies destroy each other. Free to choose, Stalin chose Germany.

Hitler made it possible. He was attracted by the thought of another German-Soviet deal, in the tradition of Rapallo. He could eliminate potential threats from Eastern Europe by partitioning it with Stalin, and then invade the West. On August 23, 1939, Molotov and Joachim von Ribbentrop, Hitler's foreign minister, signed a nonaggression pact in Moscow that arranged to divide Poland between Germany and the Soviet Union, gave the Baltic nations to the Soviets, conceded a potential Soviet sphere in Finland, and gave Moscow a free hand to take Bessarabia from Romania when it wished. Under a further secret protocol, the Soviet Union promised to supply Germany with raw materials and food in exchange for manufactured goods.

In Moscow, August 23, 1939, German Foreign Minister von Ribbentrop and Joseph Stalin smile (below) after signing the nonaggression pact that made Germany and the Soviet Union allies. Their first victim would be Poland. That these two totalitarian states, one politically on the far right and the other on the far left, had joined together came as a great shock to everyone in the world; the Nazi-Soviet pact was one of the greatest political surprises of all time. A French cartoonist of the period made his cynical comment (right) on the treaty. Hitler and a buxom Göring depicted as prostitutes, snuggle up against Stalin as Hitler coaxes, "Now, then, you are going to pay us, eh?"

In 1939, crack German troops demonstrate the goose-step march that will come to symbolize a reign of tyranny.

The Nazi-Soviet pact stunned the world. One day Nazis and Communists were the bitterest enemies; the next they were allies. In a century full of political surprises, this was the greatest. Free from the threat of the Red Army, Hitler's demands for the return of the Polish Corridor increased. The French mobilized, sending their troops into the Maginot Line fortifications on their border with Germany. Britain also mobilized and finally began to re-arm. But gloom and disappointment swept London and Paris. Without the help of the United States and the Soviets, the British and French felt, rightly, that they could not match Germany's armed forces, the *Wehrmacht*.

In the United States, the cynosure for most eyes was the 1939 New York World's Fair, with its trylon and perisphere, its "Town of Tomorrow," its General Motors show, and a Japanese Shinto shrine enclosing a replica of the American Liberty Bell, made of diamonds and pearls. The news from Europe was indeed dark, but most Americans felt Europe was far away, a distant continent from which the United States had sensibly withdrawn.

CHAPTER 2

BLITZKRIEG

No one man can be blamed for the greatest cataclysm in history, but the man who started the war in Europe in 1939 was Adolf Hitler, and although he hardly did it on his own, it would not have happened without him. His generals were opposed; they wanted more time to recruit, train, and equip the *Wehrmacht,* and they remembered the Great War all too well. His economists were opposed; they knew what the Great War had done to the German economy, and they, too, wanted time to produce and build. His diplomats were opposed; they warned that if he continued his aggressive course against Poland, England and France would declare war on Germany. His people, including some of the Nazi Party, were opposed; like the generals, they remembered the Great War. And everyone feared a two-front war.

Hitler avoided this last threat with his August 23 alliance with Stalin. Then he plunged ahead. His action was predetermined. The whole point to his moves in the Rhineland, Austria, and Czechoslovakia, of rebuilding the *Wehrmacht,* of walking out of the League of Nations, was to rewrite the Versailles Treaty. (Appeasement as a policy had the same goal; by the 1930s, the Allies had decided the treaty was unfair to Germany and were willing to modify it.) One part of Versailles that Hitler and his people hated was the creation of the Polish Corridor, a strip of land that ran through Germany, separating East Prussia from the rest, and the taking of Danzig from Germany to give the Poles a seaport.

But Hitler wanted more than just the revision of Versailles. He was a conqueror, a risktaker, who lusted for power and used it ruthlessly to create a mobile, offensive-oriented army. Like Napoleon, he soon became too fond of war, of booty, of adulation, of the sweet taste of victory, of occupying and exploiting rich foreign lands. Like Napoleon, he came to believe himself an infallible genius. Like Napoleon, he was born outside the nation he led into world war, asserting as he did so that he was the greatest patriot of all, only

German infantrymen advance through a burning Norwegian village in May of 1940. The *Wehrmacht* at this time was running like a well-designed and quite irresistible machine.

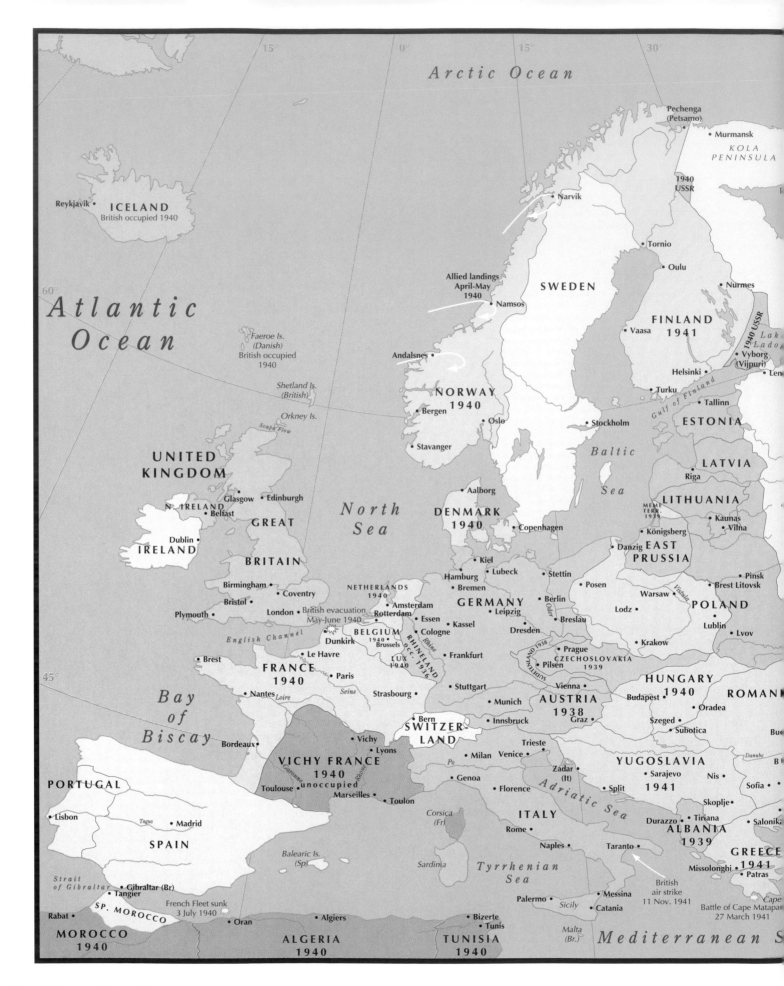

Arctic Ocean

Pechenga
(Petsamo)
• Murmansk

KOLA
PENINSULA

Reykjavik • ICELAND
British occupied 1940

1940
USSR

• Narvik

• Tornio

Atlantic
Ocean

Faeroe Is.
(Danish)
British occupied
1940

SWEDEN

Allied landings
April-May
1940

• Namsos

FINLAND
1941

• Vaasa

• Nurmes

1940 USSR

Lake
Lado

Shetland Is.
(British)

Andalsnes •

• Vyborg
(Vijpuri)

• Len

Helsinki •

60°

Orkney Is.

Scapa Flow

NORWAY
1940

• Bergen

• Oslo

• Turku

Gulf of Finland

• Tallinn

ESTONIA

• Stavanger

• Stockholm

Baltic

UNITED
KINGDOM

• Aalborg

Sea

LATVIA

• Glasgow • Edinburgh

• Riga

N. IRELAND
• Belfast

GREAT

DENMARK
1940

• Copenhagen

LITHUANIA

MEME
TERR.
1939

Dublin •
IRELAND

North
Sea

• Kiel

• Lubeck

• Kaunas
• Vilna

BRITAIN

• Stettin

• Königsberg

Birmingham •

• Coventry

Hamburg
• Bremen

• Posen

• Danzig EAST
PRUSSIA

• Pinsk
• Brest Litovsk

Bristol •

NETHERLANDS
1940

• Berlin

Warsaw •

Vistula

Plymouth •

London • British evacuation
May-June 1940

• Amsterdam
Rotterdam •

GERMANY
• Leipzig

• Essen

• Breslau

Lodz •

POLAND

• Lublin

• Brest

English Channel

BELGIUM
1940
occ. 1936
Brussels •

Dunkirk •

RHINELAND

• Cologne

• Kassel

• Dresden

• Krakow

• Lvov

Rhine

• Le Havre
LUX.
1940

Oder

• Frankfurt

SUDETENLAND 1938

• Prague
CZECHOSLOVAKIA
1939
Pilsen •

FRANCE
1940

• Paris

Seine

• Stuttgart

45°

• Nantes

Loire

Strasbourg •

• Munich

Vienna •

AUSTRIA
1938

HUNGARY
1940

Budapest •

ROMAN

Bay

• Innsbruck

Graz •

• Oradea

of

• Bern

SWITZER-
LAND

Biscay

Bordeaux •

• Vichy
• Lyons

Trieste •

• Milan Venice •

Szeged •

• Subotica

Bu

VICHY FRANCE
1940
unoccupied

Po

• Genoa

Zadar
(It)

YUGOSLAVIA
1941

Danube

B

Garonne

PORTUGAL

Toulouse •

Rhône

Marseilles •

• Florence

Adriatic Sea

• Split

• Sarajevo

Nis •

• Toulon

Corsica
(Fr)

ITALY

• Sofia

Skoplje •

• Lisbon

Tagus

• Madrid

Balearic Is.
(Sp)

Sardinia

Rome •

Naples •

Tyrrhenian
Sea

Durazzo •
• Tiriana
ALBANIA
1939

• Salonika

GREECE
1941

SPAIN

Taranto •

Missolonghi •

Strait
of Gibraltar

• Gibraltar (Br)

• Tangier

French Fleet sunk
3 July 1940

• Oran

• Algiers

• Bizerte
• Tunis

Palermo •

Sicily

• Messina

• Catania

British
air strike
11 Nov. 1941

• Patras

Cape

Battle of Cape Matapan
27 March 1941

Rabat •

SP. MOROCCO

Malta
(Br.)

Mediterranean S

MOROCCO
1940

ALGERIA
1940

TUNISIA
1940

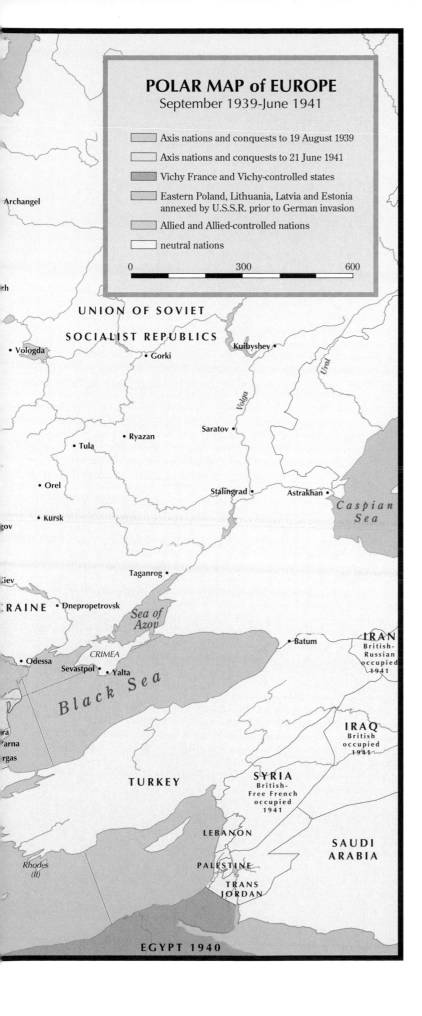

POLAR MAP of EUROPE
September 1939-June 1941

- Axis nations and conquests to 19 August 1939
- Axis nations and conquests to 21 June 1941
- Vichy France and Vichy-controlled states
- Eastern Poland, Lithuania, Latvia and Estonia annexed by U.S.S.R. prior to German invasion
- Allied and Allied-controlled nations
- neutral nations

0   300   600

Archangel

UNION OF SOVIET
SOCIALIST REPUBLICS

• Vologda
• Gorki
Kuibyshev •

zh

Ural

Volga

• Ryazan
Saratov •
• Tula

• Orel
Stalingrad •   Astrakhan •

Caspian Sea

• Kursk

gov

Taganrog •

Kiev

RAINE   • Dnepropetrovsk

Sea of Azov

IRAN
British-
Russian
occupied
1941

• Batum

• Odessa   *CRIMEA*
Sevastpol •   • Yalta

Black Sea

IRAQ
British
occupied
1941

ra
arna
rgas

TURKEY   SYRIA
British-
Free French
occupied
1941

LEBANON
SAUDI
ARABIA

*Rhodes
(It)*

PALESTINE
TRANS
JORDAN

EGYPT 1940

By the eve of his Russian adventure, Adolf Hitler had already achieved domination over an incredible amount of territory in a short period of time. By threats, subterfuge, broken pledges, and open warfare, he had overrun lands and peoples so extensive and so numerous as to rank him with Napoleon, Caesar, and history's other famous conquerors.

to reveal in the end that he always put his needs ahead of the needs of his adopted country. And like Napoleon, he was lucky in the ineptness of his enemies, whether in Moscow, Paris, London—or Washington.

Hitler boasted that he had "an army such as the world has never seen." He didn't really. Even Hitler's generals told him that not until 1942–3 would the *Wehrmacht* be as totally prepared as he claimed it was in 1939. But his claim was believed, which was what counted, and his boasts terrified the British and French, while the Americans had unilaterally disarmed and were incapable of playing even a minor role in European affairs.

One of the great myths of the war is that England slept while Hitler rearmed. In fact the British and French spent as much as the Germans on rearmament. It was just that they bought the wrong weapons and had inferior doctrines for employing them. The mystique of the *Wehrmacht* was symbolized by two new weapons, the Stuka dive-bomber and the tank.

They made possible a new kind of war: blitzkrieg, or lightning war. The Stukas could protect the flanks of tank columns penetrating far behind the enemy front lines. When the columns joined, the enemy was surrounded and had to surrender. This use of tanks in an independent role was first developed by English officers, especially J. F. C. Fuller, but was rejected by the British and French armies, which held that the role of tanks was to support infantry.

New weapons, new doctrines—Hitler was confident they would cow the British and French. So through the summer of 1939 he continued to bully

In early September 1939, Warsaw's civilians work with soldiers to erect barricades in the city streets. It was to no avail; Warsaw fell at the end of the month. This photograph was taken by Julien Bryan, a noted lecturer and photographer who was the last American to leave the besieged city.

The Poles. With the completion of the Nazi-Soviet alliance, he was ready to strike. When Paris and London finally gave a guarantee to the Poles and warned Hitler that if he invaded Poland they would declare war on Germany, Hitler didn't believe them. Had they stiffened before Munich, Czechoslovakia could have been defended; the Czechs had a well-trained, well-equipped army and a defensible, mountainous border, while the Poles had a badly equipped army and no defensible border.

Hitler called his generals together just before the invasion of Poland to brief them on the political situation and to fire them up for the job ahead. Be harsh and remorseless, he told them. They were to act with brutality, close their hearts to pity. It was, he said, the stronger man who was always right.

At 4:45 A.M., September 1, Hitler struck. Two hundred fifty thousand men in sixty German divisions, nine of them armored, rumbled toward Warsaw, Bialystok, Kraków, and Lvov, under a galaxy of generals whose names were soon to be feared from the Caspian to the Channel: Von Küchler, Guderian, von Kluge, von Reichenau, List, von Bock. The brave but antiquated forces of Marshal Edward Smigly-Rydz, the Polish commander, were encircled by German tanks, then squeezed. Sixteen hundred Luftwaffe planes, including the Stuka dive-bombers with their terrifying whistles, smashed Polish towns and cities. The Poles fought bravely, but their old-fashioned infantry, lancers, and armor proved useless.

On September 3, France and Britain declared war on Germany. They went to full mobilization, but failed to do the one thing they could have done to help Poland: immediately invade Germany from the west and force Hitler into a two-front war. That same day, German Foreign Minister Ribbentrop invited the Soviet government to move into Poland from the east, binding

The Polish cavalry perform prewar maneuvers. It was later said that the Poles charged tanks on horseback, but nothing of the kind ever happened.

German tanks and infantry (above) move into Poland, their flanks protected by Stukas. German forces on the outskirts of Warsaw watch the city burn (right).

On October 5, 1939, the victorious Germans held a parade in the center of Warsaw, a virtually deserted city. For the fourth time in its history, Poland was divided between the Germans and the Russians.

the Hitler-Stalin relationship in blood. The Polish government fled Warsaw to Lublin on September 6. On the seventeenth, surrounded by thousands of refugees riding everything from handbarrows to fire engines, the government crossed the Romanian border. Eventually it established itself in Paris and then London, the first of those pitiful exile cabinets to become so commonplace in World War II.

On September 17, the Red Army moved into eastern Poland. That same day, the German pincer snapped shut south of Warsaw, the Polish ambassador in Moscow was handed a note announcing that the Soviet-Polish nonaggression pact was void. The explanation was curt. "A Polish state no longer exists," and the Red Army was moving in "to protect White Russian and Ukrainian minorities in Poland."

Isolated Warsaw fought with exemplary fortitude. There was no bread; the bakers had been mobilized. A few barrage balloons were hoisted above the smoking city, and trenches were dug in the outskirts. Surrounding roads were encumbered by peasant carts and by corpses. Day after day the radio broadcast Chopin's "Military Polonaise" and appeals for "the quickest aid" from France and Britain.

The end came on September 28 when Warsaw, Modlin, and a few scattered military units in the hinterland gave up. That same day, in Moscow, Ribbentrop and Soviet Foreign Minister Molotov signed a treaty, completing Poland's fourth partition in two centuries. Germany took some 71,000 square miles; the Soviet Union, about 75,000. The Germans admitted to having 10,572 killed and claimed 450,000 prisoners. The Soviets suffered almost no losses. They rounded up a huge Polish force, whose officers were incarcerated. Stalin ordered them murdered, which was done in the spring of 1940 at Katyn Forest, near Smolensk. This eliminated 15,000 young Polish leaders, all of them as anti-Communist as they were anti-Nazi.

A reign of terror descended on Poland the likes of which the world has seldom seen. The Nazis were worse than the Communists, but only because they were in occupation of Poland for five years and the Red Army for just one and a half. While Stalin was murdering Polish officers, Hitler was slaughtering Polish Jews, Gypsies, Socialists, and democrats. Between September 1939 and May 1945, Poland suffered 5.5 million dead, overwhelmingly civilian, about 16 percent of the population (Yugoslavia was the second worst hit by the war, with 10 percent dead; the Soviet Union lost about 5 percent dead).

In October, Stalin, who was Hitler's ally but potential victim, moved to strengthen his defenses in the north by taking territory from Finland. Provocation was nonexistent, and the formula was blunt. The Soviets invited Helsinki to send a negotiator to the Kremlin, October 5, 1939, to discuss Moscow's demand for cession of territory on the Karelian Isthmus, exchange of woodlands in the north, and the right to establish a Soviet naval base in the Finnish gulf. The Finns said no. On November 30, Soviet planes bombed

New York newspaper headlines spread the news of the outbreak of war in Europe, September 3, 1939. (right). Meanwhile, the Germans overran western Poland, where the shooting of "undesirables"—Jews, Communists, Gypsies, Socialists, Polish patriots—began to take on a systematic shape (opposite). Such scenes soon became commonplace.

Finnish troops, dressed in white camouflage, hold their own at the Salla front in the winter of 1940. Trench digging was impossible, so snow-covered ditches provided the only protection.

Helsinki and Vyborg. The Red Army rumbled across Finland's border at five different points. The vapid League of Nations responded by expelling the Soviet Union.

It was evident from the start that the Red Army would eventually overwhelm the tiny Finnish Army, but the Finns proved to be hardy warriors, while the enormous Soviet Army was badly trained, ill equipped, and above all, poorly led. Stalin's purges of his officer corps had eliminated almost every Red Army general and caused chaos in the command structure. Furthermore, the Soviets, deceived by their own propaganda, had expected to be hailed as liberators by an enthusiastic proletariat. Instead, they were slaughtered by careful artillery barrages and expert marksmanship. Their loosely organized supply lines were easily severed by Finnish ski patrols. White-uniformed Finnish infantry knifed Soviet patrols in the long nights and blocked off entire battalions on the edges of frozen lakes. There the Soviet troops congealed into awkward agonies of death. One eyewitness wrote: "For four miles the road and forest were strewn with the bodies of men and horses. . . . The corpses were frozen as hard as petrified wood."

Despite their valor, the Finns could expect but limited aid from the slow-moving Allies and the wary Scandinavian neutrals. The Swedes transgressed their neutral affirmations by sending eager but limited numbers of volunteers; the British and French permitted a few adventurous handfuls to par-

As fires rage in the Finnish city of Vaasa after a February 1940 Soviet bombing raid, civilians drag their belongings onto the streets in a desperate attempt to salvage some of their possessions.

ticipate; the Americans cheered lustily; and the Soviets won. The sheer weight of their matériel, of their massive if clumsy gunnery and their aerial onslaught, plus the bravery of their bewildered infantry, managed an ultimate penetration. Helsinki capitulated. It forced the Finns to concede far more than those originally asked.

The Soviets both lost and gained by this dismal experience. They lost prestige, but acquired hard-won understanding of their own defects. Old-fashioned officer ranks were restored, after years of experimentation with less formalized discipline. Attention was paid to the need for modernizing equipment and training and, above all, for revising fundamental concepts of strategy. The costly and humiliating Finnish campaign in a sense could be said to have saved the Soviet Union from absolute disaster when the final German onslaught came in 1941. The Winter War also showed Hitler what a "paper tiger" the Red Army supposedly was. This, perhaps, convinced him that a total military defeat of the USSR was possible and could be obtained with relative ease at low cost.

By treaty, France had promised to launch a major offensive against Germany within days of an attack on Poland. Hitler's Siegfried Line facing France was largely a fraud, constructed of a minimum of concrete and a maximum of propaganda. Its garrison was fighting in Poland, and only 23 second-class divisions faced the Maginot Line, where there were 110 Allied

A lone French soldier stands atop a section of the Maginot Line (above). There was much more to it below the earth, where a maze of tunnels ran under the fortification (opposite).

divisions, mainly French. But the French, grown timid with memories of their losses in the First World War, did not attack.

Through the late summer and fall of 1939, and the winter of 1939–40, the French Army sat in the Maginot Line, a state-of-the-art fortification that ran the length of the Franco-German border. Nor did the Germans act at all aggressive, and so the fall and winter of 1939–40 produced one of the strangest interludes of the war. An American senator dubbed it the Phony War; to the Germans it was the *Sitzkrieg*. Opposing troops often worked and rested in plain sight of each other; outposts were reduced to tokens; German supplies moved up the Rhine railroad system undisturbed by French big guns just across the river. But while Hitler was only pausing to repair the wear and tear of the Polish campaign, the French and British seemed to think that somehow they might still find a way out without actual fighting. Field Marshal (then General) Montgomery told how Chamberlain came to France in December and asked Montgomery hopefully if he did not agree that the Germans really had no intention of attacking. The Royal Air Force, meanwhile, was sending bombers over Germany, many of which dropped not bombs but propaganda leaflets carrying the improbable message that Hitler was leading the Germans to disaster.

With the coming of spring in 1940, Hitler struck again, this time to forestall the British. The Norwegian port of Narvik, linked by a railroad over the mountains to Sweden's iron mines, was the prize. German industry was dependent on these mines, and the British studied means of blockading the route, unaware that Hitler had been tentatively planning the occupation of Norwegian bases as early as October of 1939. By April 8, when London and Paris proclaimed they had mined the area south of Narvik, a Nazi invasion was already secretly under way. The very next night, Hitler's forces landed in Norway—spearheaded by paratroopers, in Germany's first use of airborne troops—while the *Wehrmacht* rolled unopposed across Denmark—as usual without a declaration of war.

Although the German fleet was no match for the Royal Navy, by stealth and efficiency it succeeded in landing sufficient troops in Norway, and the Luftwaffe achieved prompt superiority, enabling it to offset British naval power. The Norwegians showed an intense will to resist, fighting vigorously and sinking several Nazi vessels. But the Allies came late with little. Vidkun Quisling, a local Norwegian Nazi, arose to help the insidious aggression, thereby adding his name to history's leaden roll of traitors.

The notable but miniature campaigns fought by British and French expeditionary forces at Namsos, Åndalsnes, and Trondheim are today, outside Norway itself, hardly remembered. The Royal Navy managed to land a considerable army around Narvik, but the RAF was based too far away to provide the desperately needed air cover. Resolute German defenses succeeded

in first discouraging and then repulsing inexperienced Allied troops, who were pinned against the sea and eventually evacuated.

The king of Norway, Haakon VII, fled with his government to London. And the few French and British, aided by disorganized Norwegian bands, found themselves doomed along the northern fjords. Winston Churchill concluded: "We, who had the command of the sea and could pounce anywhere on an undefended coast, were outpaced by the enemy moving by land across very large distances in the face of every obstacle." Hitler's ruthless audacity succeeded in sealing off Europe's northern flank, insuring access to Sweden's invaluable iron, closing off the Baltic, and providing the German Navy with port facilities and air fields that gave them domination of the North Sea. It also put the Luftwaffe within bombing distance of the British Isles.

From late summer 1939 until late spring 1940, the British and French gave the appearance of being removed from the conflict they had accepted. Britain, with all its sea power, mustered only small overseas land expeditions, for which it was able to grant only marginal air support. The French, comfortable in their casemates, sent a gallant group to Norway, talked of their audacious army, and waited for the inevitable showdown. President Roosevelt watched helplessly as one democracy after another went down.

On May 10, the hapless Chamberlain resigned. The proximate cause was the Norwegian fiasco, for which Winston Churchill, the First Lord of the Admiralty, was most responsible. Yet after some intense political maneuvering King George VI chose Churchill to form a wartime coalition government. The new prime minister was then sixty-six years old. A fabulous figure for almost half a century, he had been a political outsider through the interwar years, considered an unstable alarmist by his peers. Now he was no longer the leading critic of pusillanimous policies, but the maker of new policies. His self-confidence ran high: he later wrote that on assuming the position of prime minister, "I was conscious of a profound sense of relief. At last I had authority to give direction over the whole scene." Three days later he told the House of Commons, "I have nothing to offer but blood, toil, tears, and sweat."

On May 10, the day Churchill came to power, the so-called Phony War came to a sudden end. Hitler attacked Holland, Belgium, and Luxembourg. Despite what had happened to Denmark and Norway, the Low Countries had gone on hoping Hitler might respect their neutrality. But about three hours after midnight on May 10, 1940, the Nazi blitzkrieg swept across the borders of Belgium, the Netherlands, and Luxembourg. The Germans announced that they were coming to protect the three victims from an invasion planned by Great Britain and France and gave an ultimatum that any resistance would be ruthlessly crushed. The attack was well under way before the ultimatums were delivered.

In the Netherlands, the assault initially came from the sky, by glider and parachute troops. The Germans at once seized bridges intact, enabling panzer units (tanks) to penetrate deep into the country, unhindered by the water defenses on which the Dutch had depended so heavily. But the defenders rallied surprisingly well. At The Hague they threw back a Nazi force that had landed on the airfields expressly to capture Queen Wilhemina and the government. And they resisted so stoutly before Rotterdam that Hitler ordered a mass bombing of the city even while negotiations for its surrender were

Allied ships blaze in the harbor at Narvik as the Germans complete their invasion of Norway.

Winston Churchill, the First Lord of the Admiralty, arrives at his office in 1939. A few months later, he will become Prime Minister of Great Britain, during one of the darkest times in the country's history.

On an improvised bridge (opposite), German infantrymen cross the Maas River from Holland into Belgium during the early hours of the lowlands invasion on May 10, 1940.

under way. Rotterdam's heart was wiped out, some eight hundred were killed, several thousand injured. This was the beginning of a policy eventually adopted by every side in the war, the mass bombing of cities.

That same evening, May 14, all Dutch troops were ordered to stop fighting, and the next day the surrender was officially signed. But Queen Wilhelmina had escaped to England, and her government-in-exile remained in the war. In Belgium, the fortresses around Liège were captured with surprising ease by Nazi engineers and paratroopers. At Fort Eben Emael, the most vital of these strongholds, some twelve hundred Belgian defenders capitulated to only eighty Germans. Britain and France sent forces to join the Belgian Army on a strong defense line between Antwerp and Namur. Over most of this front they outnumbered the Germans, but they were immobile and ineptly led. German columns forced crossings of the difficult Meuse River. Then, as the Allies struggled desperately to plug the gap by sending armed formations into Belgium, King Leopold III surrendered the Belgian Army on May 28 with virtually no warning to his allies. The German panzers pushed onward to the Channel, and the Allied forces in the north, now cut off, retreated toward the one remaining port of Dunkirk.

Simultaneous with the assault on the Low Countries, Hitler moved against France. He had spent four years in the western front trenches in the Great War; he knew the futility of pounding against prepared defenses. He directed his tanks to avoid the Maginot Line by going north, through the undefended Ardennes of Belgium (considered to be too rugged for tanks), to reach the English Channel at Abbeville and cut off the British and French forces in Belgium. Tanks, followed by motorized infantry and protected by Stuka dive-bombers, drove through the Ardennes virtually unopposed.

Seventy-five divisions took part in the initial attack under generals Fedor von Bock and Gerd von Rundstedt. The offensive stunned the world. For four years in the Great War, the British and French had held back massive German thrusts. The carnage had been awful. Nothing like a decisive advance had been achieved by either side, despite millions of casualties. In May 1940, just twenty-two years later, the Germans got a clean breakthrough with casualties measured in the dozens rather than in the tens of thousands. The French Army, widely considered to be the best in the world, was simply pathetic. Despite its 2.5 million men, it was immobilized in the Maginot Line and hardly fired a weapon.

The German panzers, meanwhile, led by Erwin Rommel, had reached the coast. When the Belgians surrendered unconditionally, the entire left flank of the Anglo-French defenses was exposed. France was crumbling fast.

The British decided to evacuate. On May 28, Churchill pulled the RAF out of France, to preserve it for the defense of Britain. That decision all but severed the Anglo-French alliance; from the end of May on, it was each country for itself. Britain's retreat from the Continent via the small port and beach at Dunkirk left the French abandoned and broke whatever spirit the French Army and government still had. France felt betrayed, with cause, as their alliance contained a pledge to fight it out side by side. They made last-second pleas to President Roosevelt: Where was the United States?

Roosevelt commanded an army of 160,000 men, ranked sixteenth in the world. The Army Air Forces was a fledgling. He had to stand by, uninvolved, as the democracies of Western Europe fell one by one. In an era of Depression,

A three-man German crew (above) inches forward with a light machine gun in Holland, May 1940. Despite the lack of cover of any kind, the Germans kept advancing. Opposite, a German patrol rows down a Flemish watercourse.

OVERLEAF: Rotterdam smolders in the aftermath of the German onslaught. Hitler ordered Rotterdam destroyed not for military reasons but for *Schrecklichkeit* ("frightfulness"), the doctrine that the deliberate use of terror tactics could break a people's will to resist.

German troops advance on Antwerp in late spring 1940 against a background of burning oil tanks ignited by the Belgians (left). King Leopold of Belgium (opposite) ignored his cabinet's plea not to surrender and refused to go to London to head a government-in-exile. The Germans kept him a prisoner during the war. A soldier in Ostend, Belgium, sits on a bridge cluttered with furniture damaged by air attacks (below). A Belgian mother with her children flee the consequences of a German air bombardment (right).

On the beach at Dunkirk, a long line of men, still maintaining perfect discipline under enemy attack, wind out toward the water to meet the rescuing boats (below). And off the coast of Dunkirk in the North Sea, a group of soldiers (opposite) try to save themselves in the wreck of a half-sunken vessel and on the wing of a German airplane. The German officer who drove the British from the Continent was Field Marshal Gerd von Rundstedt (right), who commanded the offensive in the West.

A tumultuous scene, *Retreat, May 1940,* by the French artist Jean Delpech, illustrates the confusion as hundreds of thousands of British and French soldiers escape from Dunkirk. Many have compared it to Picasso's masterpiece of the Spanish Civil War, *Guernica.*

when defense spending would have been a great help to the economy, not to mention to the nation's ability to help her friends and defend herself, Roosevelt kept the military budget at absolutely minimal levels. He did so right on through the late 1930s, when the rest of the world was arming itself to the teeth. His defenders argue that the isolationist majority of the public tied his hands. True, but it is also true that he never chose to use his persuasive powers to tell the American people that Western civilization was at stake and that the United States had to participate in its defense. France felt understandably let down by the U.S. failure to help. With a single stroke Hitler had

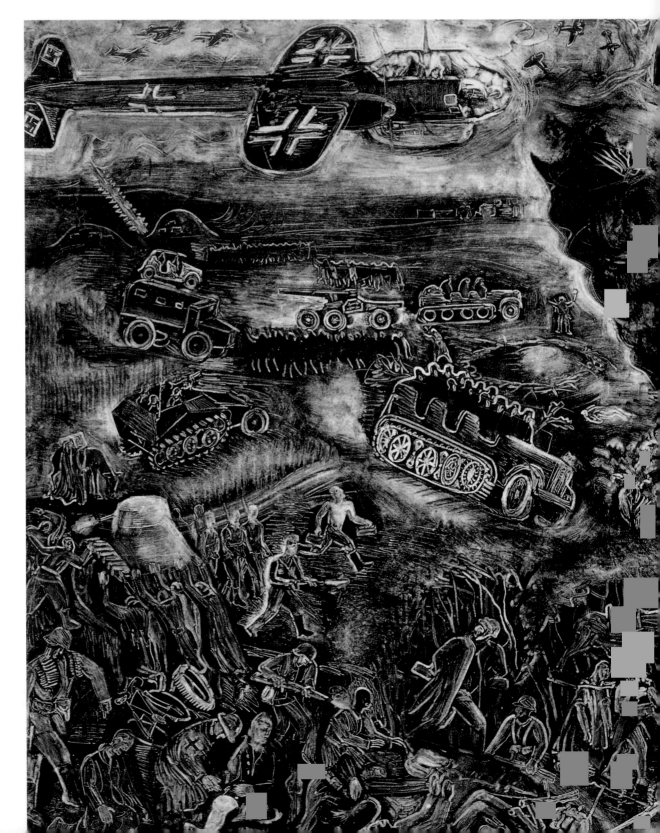

achieved what the kaiser had not. He had splintered the alliance of his enemies, driven Britain off the Continent, defeated the French Army, rewritten Versailles. Had he died at that moment he would be remembered today in Germany as the greatest German of all, greater even than Frederick the Great or Bismarck.

The British, meanwhile, managed to cheer themselves up over Dunkirk. They had good reason. The evacuation had been one of the remarkable moments of British history. By a miracle of improvisation an Allied army of 338,226, which appeared to be hopelessly cut off on the French Channel

coast, was taken away by more than a thousand hastily mustered boats. Dunkirk was typical of a British strategy that specialized in losing battles and winning wars. It was a dreadful affair, but the survivors—and their number was astonishing—became the heart of a new army that would one day march through London in the Victory Parade.

The total British casualties were 68,111. On May 26, it had looked as if the total might be more like 300,000. Field Marshal von Rundstedt, whose Army Group A held the British in its grasp, later said: "If I had had my way the English would not have got off so lightly at Dunkirk." Hitler had consigned the Dunkirk annihilation task to Göring's Luftwaffe for several reasons. He feared the cost to his straining tanks of direct ground assault over difficult terrain while the French armies to the south had not yet been destroyed. He overrated the destructive power of air bombardment, especially against troops on a sand beach protected by anti-aircraft fire. And finally, he seems to have had vague thoughts that perhaps, once France had fallen, he could force a swift peace upon the British.

Hitler's misjudgments concerning Britain were profound. He didn't think they would fight in 1939; he didn't think they would persevere in 1940; and until late 1942, it never occurred to him that the British might actually win.

Meanwhile France dissolved, militarily and morally. General Maxime Weygand, then seventy-three years old, replaced General Maurice Gamelin as supreme commander. Weygand came too late. He attempted to stand on the Somme and Aisne rivers, but on June 5, the Germans broke through this feeble line and drove on to the Seine. Nazi propaganda encouraged tales of terror and a mass flight of civilians, who blocked important roads to both the retreating French and the pursuing German armies. On June 13, Paris was declared an open city. The next day, the German forces entered.

Hitler himself came to Paris, where he had the unique pleasure of seeing the city from the only car allowed to drive in the streets that day. At Napoleon's tomb he was transfixed. Afterward, he told Albert Speer, his official architect, "It is magnificent. You must build me a bigger one in Berlin." (Fifteen years earlier, Major Dwight D. Eisenhower had told his wife, Mamie, after seeing the tomb, "That's disgusting." Today, no one knows where Hitler's grave is, while Eisenhower is buried in a modest chapel on the Kansas prairie.)

Hitler had obliterated the army he supposed to be his greatest enemy, at a cost of only 27,074 German dead. And in Rome, on June 10, on a balcony above the Piazza Venezia, protruding his jaw, Mussolini announced to the cheers of a huge crowd carefully assembled below that Italy had declared war on France and England. President Roosevelt said in a speech at the University of Virginia, "The hand that held the dagger has struck it into the back of its neighbor." A huge new army and a sizable navy and air force thus entered the war.

Once the Germans took Paris, it was evident that the conflict in Western Europe was over. Premier Paul Reynaud and his government fled south to Bordeaux and sent a junior cabinet official, Brigadier General Charles de Gaulle, to London to discuss ways of transporting forces to North Africa. De Gaulle was much impressed by the vigor of British resolve and even brought back to France an offer from Churchill for a Franco-British union with a joint defense program, joint economy, and joint citizenship for all Englishmen and Frenchmen.

The remarkable offer was ignored. Perhaps the French felt the British could not be trusted. The Reynaud Cabinet resigned on June 16, and Marshal Philippe Pétain, the hero of Verdun, took power. He was backed by the fleet commander, Admiral Jean Louis Darlan, and by Pierre Laval, a brilliant but unscrupulously ambitious politician who saw a future for France only as triumphant Germany's mistress. Pétain asked for an armistice, later claiming that he had thus "performed an act of salvation."

On June 22, 1940, the French surrender was formally signed at the same clearing in Compiegne forest, north of Paris, where Marshal Ferdinand Foch had dictated terms to Germany in November 1918. The identical railway car, hitherto kept as a museum piece, was wheeled out of its shed to serve as the parlor for France's funeral. The armistice provided that German troops would occupy more than half of France, including the entire Atlantic coastline. The French Army was demobilized and its fleet rendered immobile. France yielded its German prisoners and any German refugees Berlin wanted. French prisoners were left in the Reich. As compared to Hitler's occupation policies in the East, this settlement was relatively lenient. Hitler allowed the French to have their own government in the unoccupied zone. Obviously, as he held two million French POWs, it was a government that would do as he said. Under his orders, the French economy was integrated into a single European system dominated by Germany. He hoped to enlist the French in the upcoming anti-Communist crusade. On a shorter-term basis, he wanted to prevent the French fleet from joining Britain. What he feared was that it would sail for North Africa from its Toulon port and the French would continue the struggle from Algiers.

The British were resolute in carrying on, resolved to go it alone if necessary. Churchill expressed to the House of Commons "brotherly sentiment for the French people" but promised to fight on without mercy. Like Hitler, his eyes were on the French fleet and the possibility of France continuing the war from Algiers. He turned to a man who emerged as one of the most dramatic and consequential figures of the war, and who was to cause Churchill great difficulties in the process.

Charles de Gaulle refused to accept the armistice. He flew to London, where he planned to gather up the French troops evacuated from Dunkirk, induce the navy to sail to Algiers, and continue the war. Churchill gave de Gaulle the use of the facilities of the BBC to broadcast an appeal to the French people. As de Gaulle boarded the small plane to return home, Churchill wrote: "He carried his bag in one hand and the honor of France in the other."

On June 18 a text of less than three hundred words was read aloud by "Moi, le general de Gaulle," summoning Frenchmen and Frenchwomen throughout the world to carry on the fight. "This war has not been settled by the Battle of France. This war is a world war . . . whatever happens the flame of resistance must not and will not be extinguished."

De Gaulle's message was basically the same as Churchill's: Hang on until the United States mobilizes and enters the war. But in the United States, Roosevelt was running for an unprecedented third term. He dared not

Hitler, at his headquarters in Belgium, stamps his foot in exultation on being told that Marshal Pétain had asked for an armistice. American film editors were able, through clever splicing of the film of the event, to make it appear that Hitler was doing a victory dance.

A diverse group of leaders saw France through the agony of war: General Maxime Weygand (far left), who surrendered to the Germans; General Charles de Gaulle (top left), shown broadcasting to the French people on the facilities of the BBC, June 18, 1940, who insisted on continuing the fight; Marshal Philippe Pétain (bottom left), who came out of retirement to make a deal with the Nazis; Paul Reynaud (below), the prime minister who lost his nerve; Pierre Laval (right, with U.S. Secretary of State Henry Stimson, at right), who served Pétain as prime minister of the government in Vichy, and became the most hated man in France.

THE GERMANS AS OCCUPIERS

Of Hitler's many mistakes, his occupation policy looms especially large. At the beginning of the war, Hitler and the Nazis had many admirers and potential allies, because anti-Communism and anti-Semitism were deep and widespread throughout Europe. Here was an opportunity for Hitler to appeal to idealistic Poles and Frenchmen and to the peoples of the western reaches of the Soviet Union—Ukraine, Lithuania, Latvia, Estonia, Belorussia—who hated Stalin and Communism. But instead of encouraging and building on this potential asset, Hitler adopted occupation policies that made him and the Nazis even more hated than Stalin. In so doing, he encouraged the growth of resistance movements throughout his conquered empire.

It began in Poland. The Germans incorporated the western half of Poland into the Reich and administered the remainder as an occupied country under SS officer Hans Frank. He decreed that Poles would be made "the slaves of the Greater German Empire." During his regime more than 6 million people, about half of them Jews, were killed in mass murders, in the Warsaw Ghetto, and in concentration camps. An underground Polish Army, responsible to the Polish government in exile in London, continually harassed the Germans, who retaliated by executing randomly selected Poles at a rate of a hundred civilians for each German soldier killed. Such savagery only provoked more Poles to join the resistance.

At first the Danes did not suffer as much, but in the fall of 1942 the Nazis attempted to incorporate Denmark into the Reich. A Danish guerrilla movement arose and harassed the Germans with hundreds of acts of sabotage. The Germans responded by sending the SS into Denmark, arresting thousands of Danes, summarily executing saboteurs, and rounding up all Danish policemen. Some two thousand of them went to concentration camps. This led to more resistance. When the Germans tried to round up Denmark's Jews, thousands of Jews were ferried to Sweden in an operation that involved almost the entire population.

Norway was ruled by a Reich commissioner, who declared that the only legal party was the pro-Nazi National Unity Party headed by Vidkun Quisling, the leading Norwegian collaborator (his name became synonymous with treason). Quisling tried to turn Norway into a Fascist state. He sent thousands of his opponents to concentration camps in Germany. Still, resistance was all but universal; for example, teachers resigned their posts and refused to work for the state, so did bishops and clergymen. After the war, Quisling was arrested, tried, and shot by a firing squad.

In Holland, Artur von Seyss-Inquart became Reich commissioner. He had served as deputy to Hans Frank in Poland. Seyss-Inquart promised the Dutch he would not try to make Nazis of them, but his economic and labor policies, combined with newspaper and radio censorship, put the lie to the promise. In February 1941, he began rounding up Jews. To protest, the Dutch people went on a general strike, one that Seyss-Inquart ruthlessly suppressed. Still, the Dutch tried to hide their Jews from the Gestapo—the most famous being Anne Frank in her attic in Amsterdam. She was eventually discovered and sent to her death in Bergen-Belsen.

In Belgium, as in Holland, the Germans pillaged the countryside. They

Hitler's racism comes to Paris: the writing on the door of a popular cafe reads, "Only for Aryans."

confiscated such vast amounts of food that by the fall of 1940 an estimated one-fifth of the Belgian population was starving. Thousands of Belgians were sent to concentration camps for supporting the resistance. Tens of thousands were deported to Germany for slave labor.

In France, the Germans imposed a tough, swaggering conquest. They incorporated Alsace-Lorraine into the Reich. They ran northern and western France as a conquered territory. Southern France was left unoccupied and was administrated by the collaborationist Vichy government. Like the other occupied countries, France was forced to pay "occupation costs," which came to about $2 billion a year (four times the annual reparation Germany had paid the victors after World War I). And, as elsewhere, the Nazis looted the national museums and shipped back to Germany some 140 railroad cars stuffed with the works of Rembrandt, Rubens, and other masters. French POWs, numbering more than one million, were held in Germany as slave labor. Tens of thousands of young French boys were sent to Germany to work in factories.

The French resistance, headed by Jean Moulin, began small but grew steadily in response to Nazi oppression. The German response, as always, was to get tougher. One hundred French civilians were executed for each German soldier killed by the resistance; altogether, the Germans killed 30,000 French hostages.

The amazing thing is that in comparison with the policies Hitler later instituted in Eastern Europe, the Nazi occupation policies toward the nations of Western Europe were mild, almost generous. There was a semblance of law. In many ways the Germans tried to behave correctly; for example, army officials came down hard on German soldiers guilty of rape or theft, and at least a pretense was made of paying Frenchmen forced to work for the Germans. Following the Allied invasion of North Africa, in November 1942, the Germans occupied the southern part of France; although the Vichy government remained, it was powerless. Thereafter, the Germans held France in a grip of steel.

The Nazis ruled Poland by terror. This is a September 1942 *Lapanka*, or mass roundup. Such roundups happened daily. Jews, Communists, or patriots were put into trucks and driven away, some to a mass grave they would dig themselves, others to a factory in a concentration camp, where they would become slave labor.

The man in this *Movietone News* photo is generally believed to be a French citizen weeping at the sight of historic French battle flags being paraded through Marseilles on June 14, 1940 (they were sent across the Mediterranean to forestall capture). However, the subject has also been identified as a black marketeer, a uniform manufacturer, and an emotional Italian visitor. This shot has become one of the most famous of World War II photos.

offend the isolationists. There would be no mobilization, no declaration of war. The European democracies were on their own.

As were the remaining tiny republics in Eastern Europe. The dramatic events in the West allowed Stalin to carry out acts of aggression that were hardly noticed by the rest of the world. He ordered his troops into Latvia, Lithuania, and Estonia, all of which he annexed to the Soviet Union. In the wake of a hasty ultimatum, he took Romania's Bessarabia and north Bukovina provinces. From the Black Sea across Poland to Finland and the Arctic, a huge band of territory, once czarist, was returned to Soviet control.

At the midpoint of 1940, the two dictators stood atop the world. Hitler had surpassed every German leader. And Stalin had equaled the greatest of the czars.

In the three-way struggle for domination of the twentieth century, it seemed certain in June 1940 that the future belonged to the two totalitarians, while the democracies appeared finished. Britain stood alone, America was unprepared, while the Communists and the Nazis had divided Europe between themselves and were everywhere on the march.

Hitler poses triumphantly at the Eiffel Tower. On June 23, during his first and only visit to Paris, the German occupiers kept all Parisians indoors and the streets clear, so that Hitler could drive around a Paris completely free of traffic.

Hitler and his entourage cross the French frontier in June 1940. On the morning of June 14, the Parisians who did not flee woke up to a German loudspeaker announcing an eight o'clock curfew. A swastika flag was hung beneath the Arc de Triomphe.

CHAPTER 3

ENGLAND ALONE

Remember him, for he saved all of you: pudgy and not very large but somehow massive and indomitable; baby-faced, with snub nose, square chin, rheumy eyes on occasion given to tears; a thwarted actor's taste for clothes that would have looked ridiculous on a less splendid man. He wore the quaintest hats of anyone: tinted square bowlers; great flat sombreros squashed down on his head; naval officer's caps rendered just slightly comic by the huge cigar protruding beneath the peak. On grave and critical occasions he sported highly practical teddy-bear suits few grown men would dare to wear in public. He fancied oil painting, at which he was good, writing, at which he was excellent, and oratory, at which he was magnificent. His habits were somewhat owlish (a bird he faintly resembled), and he stayed up late at night, often working mornings in bed with a lap tray for his desk.

This was the man who guided Britain to victory in World War II—and, one might add, who was the guiding spirit for the whole free world. For had Britain succumbed, as it had every logical reason to do in 1940, probably no successful coalition could have formed.

Winston Churchill once complained that democracy is the worst system of government—except for all the others that had been tried. And it was democracy, with its curious and lethargic workings, that, allied with its Russian antithesis, produced Hitler's defeat. One may argue that the Führer's strategic errors caused his ultimate downfall: that he allowed Britain's Army to escape him at Dunkirk; that he misjudged Germany's strength in attacking the Soviet Union; that he overextended himself both at El Alamein and at Stalingrad. It was not in the end the negative factor of Nazi miscalculation but, rather, the positive factor of democratic vigor that brought the German

The hat, the cane, the bulk were known around the world in 1941. Winston Churchill had made himself into a symbol of resistance to tyranny. It was his unbreakable will that provided hope and a rallying point for lovers of freedom everywhere.

This was Britain's defense force, in the event the Germans got across the Channel. Called the Home Guard, for the most part these World War I veterans were without weapons. This is the Sheffield Group on parade, being inspected by the commander in chief of the Fifth Battalion.

Götterdämmerung. This democratic vigor, freely voiced in a moment of bleak despair, produced Churchill as prime minister and a government resolved to win the war.

Even before France collapsed, an irate House of Commons had summoned the irresolute and gullible Neville Chamberlain to defend the conduct of the Norwegian debacle. It was no longer a party matter; the nation's life was at stake. Clement Attlee, the Labor leader, said: "We cannot afford to leave our destinies in the hands of failures." Arthur Greenwood added: "Wars are not won by masterly withdrawals." The retired Fleet Admiral, Sir Roger Keyes, appearing in full uniform, thundered that the Norwegian disaster was "a shocking story of ineptitude which I assure the House ought never to have happened." And spry little Leopold Amery, a staunch Conservative, told the government, in Cromwell's famous words: "You have sat too long here for any good you have been doing. Depart, I say, and let us have done with you. In the name of God, go!"

Churchill had loyally served Chamberlain as First Lord of the Admiralty and accepted ministerial responsibility for his share of the Norway mess.

But even old Lloyd George, arising as it were from the grave of an earlier Great War, urged that "Mr. Churchill will not allow himself to be converted into an air-raid shelter to keep the splinters from hitting his colleagues." Chamberlain won an initial vote of confidence, but two days later, on May 10, as the Nazis launched their attack on the Low Countries, he resigned and designated Churchill to succeed him. Churchill named a national coalition government of all three parties and set his jaw in the bulldog expression that was to become so famous. Thus was the stage set for the epic Battle of Britain.

It was one of the great moments in world history, the finest hour in Britain's history. She stood alone, defending western civilization, while Hitler held all of Western and Central Europe, Stalin provided Hitler with foodstuffs and raw materials, and the United States slept. At stake was the future of mankind. On the front line of defense stood the Royal Navy, the Royal Air Force, and Britain's scientific genius.

The presence of the home fleet, intact, shaped the Battle of Britain. Before the *Wehrmacht* could cross the Channel to invade England, the Germans had to win control of the Channel. They couldn't get it in a head-to-head Jutland-type naval battle—the British fleet was much too massive—so they turned to control by the air. If the Luftwaffe could achieve air supremacy over the Channel, the Royal Navy could be pinned down in port, or harassed so badly as to be ineffective for the twenty-four hours the Germans needed to ferry their army across to the British Isles. So the point to the Battle of Britain was to gain command of the air over the Channel.

The battle that raged over Britain in the summer and fall of 1940 was a titanic struggle for the highest possible stakes. It brought into play every aspect of German and British life, including productivity, management techniques, organizational structure, scientific capability, and the skills, dash, bravery, and vigor of the young men the nations put into the cockpits. At the end of the day, it was British scientists and pilots who excelled.

When Churchill said in his famous tribute to the RAF pilots that "never in the field of human conflict was so much owed by so many to so few," he was not able to include the scientists as a crucial part of those "few," because they made their contributions in the secret war of code-breaking and surveillance. Without them, Britain surely would have gone down, but because of the nature of their work, their names are hardly known. R. V. Jones was one of them, along with Sir Henry Tizard, Sir Robert Watson-Watt, and many others. Their contribution gave the British radar superiority, critical to the RAF. With radar, the RAF knew about each incoming wave of bombers without wasting fuel and flying time scouting for them. Radar gave a fifteen- to twenty-minute warning when German aircraft was approaching the English coast as well as a relatively accurate prediction as to size of formation and direction of flight. Thus, radar was the source of victory—the first time electronic devices were the decisive factor in a battle.

On July 16, Hitler ordered secret preparations for Operation Sea Lion, a landing on England's southern coast. Planning for it required a leap of imagination into the future—"triphibious" warfare. The German Army had neither training in amphibious operations, beyond crossing rivers, nor any landing

craft; the Luftwaffe had no training in harassing naval vessels. These were problems that Hitler's generals felt were insolvable. To prove to them that the problems had to be faced and solved, and apparently with the hope that the British might sue for peace, on July 19, Hitler delivered a speech to the Reichstag that seemed to imply he was ready to cut a deal: the British could keep their independence and their empire if they would sign an armistice that recognized German conquests in Poland and Western Europe. Churchill refused.

Hitler sent the Luftwaffe to pound the British into submission. Initially the targets were military ones, the ports of southern England and their surrounding radar stations. Thus was the battle joined. Each side had certain advantages. The Luftwaffe had more planes, 1,892 bombers and 1,290 fighters to the RAF's 620 fighters. The Germans knew where and when they were going to attack, but thanks to radar the RAF knew the strength and direction of the German planes soon after they took off from their airfields in France. RAF fighters—Hurricanes and Spitfires—were better armed and more maneuverable than those of the Luftwaffe, which were speedier and climbed faster. The Luftwaffe had veteran pilots, while the RAF suffered from a shortage of pilots. But the RAF pilots were fighting for their homes, whether in occupied Europe (10 percent of the RAF pilots were Polish, another 10 percent were from the Western European nations). They were young—overwhelmingly between eighteen and twenty-two years of age—and daredevils.

Perhaps the greatest advantage to the RAF was Hermann Göring's impatience. He kept switching targets, hoping to find the right mechanism to

A barrage balloon floats above London's Tower Bridge in the summer of 1940 (opposite). The steel cable holding the balloon prevented low-flying German planes from strafing the streets. Churchill (above) inspects the southern coastal defenses in July 1940. The defenses were not much, but the publicity Churchill garnered from the visit helped boost spirits and keep hope alive. He was the real defense. Photographs like this one showed his determination and helped strengthen the British will to resist.

Field Marshal Hermann Göring and his staff gaze across the English Channel at the white cliffs of Dover on July 1, 1940 (opposite top; Göring is sixth from right). During the summer of 1940, Germany was poised to take Britain—but unless Göring won air superiority over the Channel, there would be no invasion. Britain's defense depended on her air force, like the RAF pilots (opposite bottom) scrambling to get to their Hurricanes and the flight of British Beaufighters (above) circling over a German convoy. (Two ships have been hit.) On such planes and pilots rested the fate of Britain—and the world.

A motion picture camera in a RAF fighter captures the moment the pilot hit a Focke-Wulf 190 Luftwaffe fighter in the tail (below). The use of wing cameras was adopted by the RAF to verify the wildly exaggerated number of "kills" claimed by young and over-enthusiastic pilots.

force Churchill to his knees. First it was ports, then after Göring realized how valuable radar was to the RAF it was radar stations. But after an August 12 strike of a thousand bombers destroyed one station and damaged five, Göring decided the plan had been rendered useless (the RAF figured that two more such attacks would have rendered radar blind). His next target was the airfields and their communication facilities. On August 15, up to a thousand bombers opened Operation Eagle. Losses were heavy on both sides, the Luftwaffe losing sixty-five planes, the RAF thirty-four.

Beginning August 24, the Luftwaffe sent an average of a thousand planes per day against RAF Fighter Command. British pilots, operating on adrenalin, went up again and again after landing only long enough to refuel and replenish ammunition. They suffered fearfully, for the first time taking losses greater than the Germans. In two weeks some 25 percent of the RAF pilots were casualties. But the Germans, too, were losing planes and pilots at a rate they could not afford.

Daylight bombing was too costly, Göring decided, so he shifted the Luftwaffe to nighttime bombing on September 7. Meanwhile, on August 24, the first German bombs had dropped on London. Churchill ordered a retaliation raid on Berlin. Hitler furiously announced: "If they attack our cities, we will simply rub out theirs." So Göring blundered again. On September 7, he responded to Hitler's demands by switching targets and tactics two weeks before the RAF figured it would run out of planes and pilots. Now Göring was going after nothing less than London itself, initiating terror bombing on an unprecedented scale. The British turned from the Battle of Britain to what they dubbed "the Blitz," a thunderous, brutal assault primarily on civilians. Göring's purpose was to destroy not military targets but the British spirit.

The Blitz was one of the great mistakes of the war and left the worst legacy. Göring's merciless campaign against London and other British cities backfired; rather than cowing the British into submission, it raised their determination to resist. It also opened the way for terror bombing by all sides in the conflict. The civilian as target became commonplace, culminating with Hiroshima. (The civilian as hostage later became the principal characteristic of the Cold War.) Terror bombing caused immense destruction and countless deaths. Whether it shortened the war cannot be said; according to critics, the enormous effort that went into building the bombers, training the crews, and sending them on missions over Berlin or Tokyo or Moscow was not cost effective.

It certainly wasn't for Göring. His attacks brought about destruction, desolation, death, but they did not force Britain to her knees and they helped prod the United States into a stronger pro-British stance, which was about the worst thing that could happen to the then-triumphant Nazi Germany. In large part, the American reaction was due to one man, Edward R. Murrow, and to the technological advance in radio that made it possible for him to give eyewitness accounts of the Blitz. When Murrow opened his broadcast from England with his deep, portentous voice—"This . . . is London"—listeners from New York to San Francisco paid attention. His vivid descriptions shocked them; his personal faith in the British ability to withstand the assault caused many Americans who had expected Churchill to cut a deal

Luftwaffe pilots in the cockpit of their bomber (left) make last minute preparations just before takeoff on a mission to Britain. Note the Iron Cross on the pilot on the right. The British artist Paul Nash conveys the power and menace of the Luftwaffe in his painting *Follow the Führer* (below).

with Hitler, and others who figured Britain was finished in any case, to change their minds.

In response to the terror from the air, Churchill gave voice to the British lion. "This wicked man," he said of Hitler, "this monstrous product of former wrongs and shame, has now resolved to break our famous island race by a process of indiscriminate slaughter and destruction." He vowed, "We can take it." London did. Hundreds were killed each night, thousands injured, but neither the British government nor the economic machinery of London was paralyzed. Churchill himself had an elaborate underground headquarters under Whitehall, the naval ministry, near 10 Downing Street.

On September 15, Churchill went to the underground headquarters of No. 11 Group, Fighter Command, at Uxbridge. At the combat center, huge maps and a vast electric tableau showed incoming German bombers and available RAF fighters. That day the Germans launched one of their greatest raids. RAF Vice-Marshal Keith Park strode through the command post, barking out directions, reinforcing some areas, moving fighters to defend new zones. He asked for and got reinforcements from No. 12 Group.

"What other reserves have we?" Churchill asked.

"There are none" was Park's reply.

Churchill winced. It was of this moment that he later wrote: "The odds were great; our margins small; the stakes infinite."

Hitler gloried in the destruction the Luftwaffe was raining on London and was glad to make the British suffer, but by the end of September the Luftwaffe was suffering more (2,698 Luftwaffe planes down in 1940 over Britain, compared with 915 RAF fighters lost). Rather than gaining air superiority over the Channel, the Luftwaffe had lost it. On September 17, Hitler acknowledged the indefinite postponement of Sea Lion. Although increasingly sporadic nighttime raids over London continued through the fall into the spring of 1941, they were of nuisance value only. Fighter Command of RAF, with the indispensable help of radar and the British people, had won the Battle of Britain.

Like the evacuation at Dunkirk, the victory over the skies of Britain was a defensive one, and wars are not won by successful retreats or defensive measures. But Britain had no way of going over to the offensive in conventional warfare. Her exhausted army had left its artillery and many of its vehicles in France, and it badly needed refitting and retraining.

The summer of 1940 was an historic moment for Europe. The abandonment of Operation Sea Lion, leaving an undefeated German Army stranded on the Channel beaches, marked the beginning of Hitler's defeat. The example and the success of Churchill served as a glowing reminder to the people of occupied Europe that, as in the days of Napoleon, a dictatorial land power need not succeed in ultimately triumphing over an intact sea power. And in secret, underground fashion, a Continental resistance to the Nazis started.

To help the resisters, the British in 1940 established an organization known as the Special Operations Executive. It engaged in subversion and sabotage in German-occupied lands, aided by skillful propaganda broadcast by the BBC with its clever Morse code signal, V—for Victory—dot, dot, dot, dash. Slowly but remorselessly, in Poland, France, Belgium, Holland, and Norway, a collection of agents and adventurers, mostly amateur, threw back

Londoners take shelter in the Elephant and Castle underground station on November 11, 1940 (opposite). Up to 177,000 citizens used the shelters each night. Above ground, the Blitz continues as firemen fight a blaze on London's Victoria Street (above) during the great firebomb raid of the night of December 29–30, 1940. This was London's worst conflagration since the Great Fire of 1666.

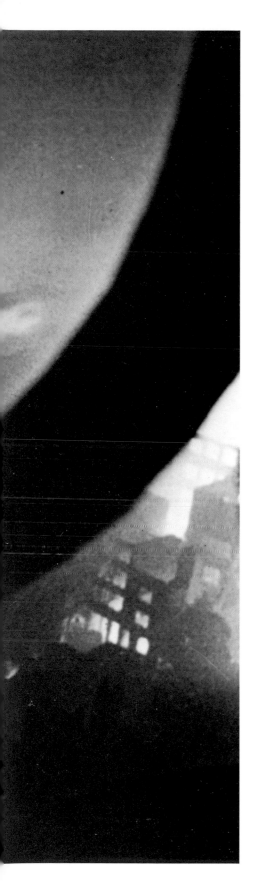

A view from the dome of St. Paul's Cathedral (left) on December 29, 1940, reveals the devastation of the German bombing raids. Although the cathedral was hit a number of times, it stood through the Blitz (below).

Coventry's city streets (above) and its famed cathedral (opposite) were completely gutted by a German raid on the historic city on November 14–15, 1940. Coventry, which had aircraft and machine-tool factories, was the first victim of the new tactics of Göring, who wanted to destroy the industrial centers that produced much of Britain's war materials. The Germans bombed indiscriminately; 800 civilians died; operation of the factories was not halted, but 70,000 homes were laid waste, and most of the city's ancient churches were destroyed or damaged.

Lieutenant R. Davies looks for the fuse on a 1,200-pound time bomb, dropped in the grounds of the German Hospital in London on November 25, 1941. Davies, in command of the Bomb Disposal Unit, was given credit for saving St. Paul's Cathedral by defusing a bomb.

into the teeth of the German General Staff the cautionary words of the great Prussian military theorist, General Karl von Clausewitz: "Armed civilians cannot and should not be employed against the main force of the enemy, or even against sizable units. They should not try to crack the core, but only nibble along the surface and on the edges." And, as another reminder of Napoleonic days, the first of Lord Louis Mountbatten's famous Combined Operations and Commando units began to experiment with the tactics and mechanics of small amphibious assaults.

During this summer of Hitler's first frustration, Stalin decided to collect what was left on the bill for his German pact. In June he successively completed the annexation of the three little Baltic states—Lithuania, Latvia, and Estonia—and five days after notifying Germany of his intention he seized Bessarabia from Romania. Sir Stafford Cripps, Churchill's new ambassador to Moscow, sought to convince the master of the Kremlin that Hitler was a danger "to the Soviet Union as well as England." He urged that the two countries "agree on a common policy of self-protection," and he secretly offered a bribe: the promise to recognize the Soviet Union's claims in the Dardanelles and to give her a leading role in the Balkans. But Stalin turned a deaf ear.

It soon became evident that Germany was also looking to that part of eastern Europe it had not already conquered, where the Soviet Union was inching forward and where Italy, having entered the war without Hitler's permission and somewhat to his dismay, had staked its own claim. On August 30, 1940, Ribbentrop and Ciano signed an agreement in Vienna awarding 40 percent of Romania's Transylvania province to Hungary and the southern part of Romanian Dobruja to Bulgaria. King Carol, the dissolute Romanian monarch, loaded a train with his mistress, his closest friends and courtiers, and all the valuables he could pack, and fled.

On October 28, again without asking Hitler's advice, Mussolini attacked Greece from Albania, expecting a swift and easy victory. But the courageous Greeks forgot their political differences and astonished the world by beating back the Italians and invading Albania themselves. The gallantry and conceit of the Greek Army were formidable. Rickety trucks bounced to the front over impossible roads, bearing Hellenic fishermen and farmers. They rode to death and glory with garlands over their ears and their rifle muzzles stuffed with flowers, shouting: "On to Rome." Antiquated mountain artillery was trundled along ridge combs to shell the Fascists in the valleys. Evzone guard patrols attacked with their knives and teeth, biting the scared Italian infantrymen. The Duce's highly touted air force, furthermore, proved inaccurate and timid and was soon largely offset by a handful of British planes rushed to Greece from the Middle East. Churchill sent advisers to Athens to investigate the possibility of opening a land front against the Axis in Europe. He cautioned them: "Do not consider yourselves obligated to a Greek enterprise if in your hearts you feel it will only be another Norwegian fiasco. If no

A man is injured by a V-I bomb on a London street, 1940. Scenes like this one were commonplace during the Blitz.

WAR OVER THE RADIO

The following excerpts are taken from two of Edward Murrow's broadcasts during the height of the Blitz.

September 10, 1940. . . . We are told today that the Germans believe Londoners, after a while, will rise up and demand a new government, one that will make peace with Germany. It's more probable that they'll rise up and murder a few German pilots who come down by parachute. The life of a parachutist would not be worth much in the East End of London tonight.

The politicians who called this a "people's war" were right, probably more right than they knew at the time. I've seen some horrible sights in this city during these days and nights, but not once have I heard man, woman, or child suggest that Britain should throw in her hand. These people are angry. How much they can stand, I don't know. The strain is very great. The prospect for the winter, when some way must be found to keep water out of the shelters and a little heat inside, is not pleasant. Nor will it be any more pleasant in Germany, where winters are generally more severe than on this green island. After four days and nights of this air blitzkrieg, I think the people here are rapidly becoming veterans, even as their army was hardened in the fire of Dunkirk.

Many people have already got over the panicky feeling that hit everyone in the nerve centers when they realized they were being bombed. Those people I talked to in long queues in front of the big public shelters tonight were cheerful and somewhat resigned. They'd been waiting in line for an hour or more, waiting for the shelters to open at the first wail of the sirens. They had no private shelters of their own, but they carried blankets to throw over the chairs in this public underground refuge. Their sleep tonight will be as fitful as you could expect in such quarters without beds. Of course, they don't like the situation, but most of them feel that even this underground existence is preferable to what they'd get under German domination.

All the while strong efforts are being made to remind the British subjects who live underground that RAF bombers are flying in the other direction and that the Germans are having rather a rough time of it, too. For instance, tonight's British news broadcast led off with a long and detailed statement about last night's RAF air raids against Germany: the docks at Wilhelmshaven, Hamburg, Bremen, and Kiel were bombed again; a power station in Brussels, wrecked; and a gasworks on the outskirts of Lorraine set afire; Docks and shipping at Calais, Ostend, Flushing, and Boulogne were also bombed.

October 10, 1940. . . . This is London, ten minutes before five in the morning. Tonight's raid has been widespread. London is again the main target. Bombs have been reported from more than fifty districts. Raiders have been over Wales in the west, the Midlands, Liverpool, the southwest, and northeast. So far as London is concerned, the outskirts appear to have suffered the heaviest pounding. The attack has decreased in intensity since the moon faded from the sky.

All the fires were quickly brought under control. That's a common phrase in the morning communiques. I've seen how it's done; spent a night with the London fire brigade. For three hours after the night attack got going, I shivered in a sandbag crow's nest atop a tall building near the Thames. It was one of the many fire-observation posts. There was an old gun barrel mounted above a round table marked off like a compass. A stick of incendiaries bounced off rooftops about three miles away. The observer took a sight on a point where the first one fell, swung his gun sight along the line of bombs, and took another reading at the end of the line of fire. Then he picked up his telephone and shouted above the half gale that was blowing up there, "Stick of incendiaries—between 190 and 220—about three miles away." Five minutes later a German bomber came boring down the river. We could see his exhaust trail like a pale ribbon stretched straight across the sky. Half a mile downstream there were two eruptions and then a third, close together. The first two looked like some giant had thrown a huge basket of flaming golden oranges high in the air. The third was just a balloon of fire enclosed in black smoke above the housetops. The observer didn't bother with his gun sight and indicator for that one. Just reached for his night glasses, took one quick look, picked up his telephone, and said, "Two high explosives and one oil bomb," and named the street where they had fallen. . . .

There was peace and quiet inside for twenty minutes. Then a shower of incendiaries came down far in the distance. They didn't fall in a line. It looked like flashes from an electric train on a wet night, only the engineer was drunk and driving his train in circles through the streets. . . . Half an hour later a string of firebombs fell right beside the Thames. Their white glare was reflected in the black, lazy water near the banks and faded out in midstream where the moon cut a golden swathe broken only by the arches of famous bridges.

We could see little men shoveling those firebombs into the river. One burned for a few minutes like a beacon right in the middle of a bridge. Finally those white flames all went out. No one bothers about the white light, it's only when it turns yellow that a real fire has started.

I must have seen well over a hundred firebombs come down and only three small fires were started. The incendiaries aren't so bad if there is someone there to deal with them, but those oil bombs present more difficulties.

As I watched those white fires flame up and die down, watched the yellow blazes grow dull and disappear, I thought, what a puny effort is this to burn a great city. Finally, we went below to a big room underground. It was quiet. Women spoke softly into telephones. There was a big map of London on the wall. Little colored pins were being moved from one point to another and every time a pin was moved it meant that fire pumps were on their way through the black streets of London to a fire. One district had asked for reinforcements from another, just as an army reinforces its front lines in the sector bearing the brunt of the attack. On another map all the observation posts, like the one I just left, were marked. . . .

We picked a fire from the map and drove to it. And the map was right. It was a small fire in a warehouse near the river. Not much of a fire; only ten pumps working on it, but still big enough to be seen from the air. The searchlights were bunched overhead and as we approached we could hear the drone of a German plane and see the burst of anti-aircraft fire directly overhead. Two pieces of shrapnel slapped down in the water and then everything was drowned in the hum of the pumps and the sound of hissing water. Those firemen in their oilskins and tin hats appeared oblivious to everything but the fire. We went to another blaze—just a small two-story house down on the East End. An incendiary had gone through the roof and the place was being gutted. A woman stood on a corner, clutching a rather dirty pillow. A policeman was trying to comfort her. And a fireman said, "You'd be surprised what strange things people pick up when they run out of a burning house."

And back at headquarters I saw a man laboriously and carefully copying names in a big ledger—the list of firemen killed in action during the last month. There were about a hundred names. . . .

Edward R. Murrow was among the best of a new generation of radio newsmen, and one of the most courageous. Before the war ended, he would fly as an observer on twenty-five combat missions over Germany. Murrow was thirty-two years old in 1940, when his CBS broadcasts from London made him famous and brought home the war in Europe to millions of Americans.

Prime Minister Churchill makes one of his frequent walking tours of London streets, inspecting bomb damage and giving a boost to morale. "We can take it," he would say on these occasions. Children were evacuated from London during the Blitz, but adults stayed and regular work went on. Hitler, by way of contrast, refused to visit bomb sites.

A convoy of vehicles of the defending Yugoslavia Army, caught by the air-ground onslaught, burns on one side of a village street while a German armored column moves down the other (opposite top). The lightning speed of the conquest amazed military experts in other countries because Yugoslavia's precipitous mountain terrain had been considered completely unsuitable for blitzkrieg operations. The front page of the *New York Herald Tribune* (opposite bottom) announces Germany's most recent conquests, April 6, 1941.

good plan can be made, please say so." They were sufficiently impressed by the chances to take the gamble. Early in 1941, Britain began to move troops from Egypt into Greece.

In the long run, this decision was to have a profound and helpful strategic effect on the war, even though the British expeditionary force was smashed successively in Greece and Crete. Hitler had already reached the basic conclusion that since he could not use his army directly against England he would strike at the Soviet Union. As an initial step, he had begun moving divisions eastward from France into Poland and had signed a "transit agreement" allowing him to send troops into Finland, although that country had been cynically allotted to the Soviet sphere. The Führer then sent Romania what was called a military mission. The Romanian "mission" was followed by an accord permitting Germany to send troops into Bulgaria. This surrounding pressure understandably frightened the Yugoslavs. Their cultivated and gentlemanly regent, Prince Paul, sought to stave off trouble by permitting his government to sign an accord with Hitler. But army officers forged the boy King Peter's name to a declaration assuming power and ordering resistance. This was read on the radio amidst wide rejoicing by the warlike Serbs.

Hitler was infuriated at this insult to his prestige. He ordered a swift assault on Yugoslavia and embattled Greece. The invasion began early in the morning of April 6, 1941. C. L. Sulzberger, in Yugoslavia at the time, had watched peasant boys march into the old fortress at the tip of Belgrade, where the Danube and Sava rivers meet, pick up their uniforms and guns, and trundle out behind oxcarts, singing: "Oh my love, the German is again at our frontiers and there again he will meet the Serbian bayonet." Within hours the capital was shattered by the Luftwaffe. German tanks and motorized infantry rolled in, aided by the Hungarians and Bulgarians, who had been bought by the Vienna award; the Italians launched their own offensive from Albania.

Yugoslavia was riddled with fifth-column movements among its Croatian, Albanian, and German Volksdeutsch minorities. Defections among the non-Serbs were manifold, and the Yugoslav armies were torn apart before they had even been deployed. The Germans captured Skopje and poured across the undefended Monastir Gap into Greece. From Bulgaria they hammered southward against Greek pillbox positions in Thrace. The colonel commanding one of these, Fort Rupel, summoned his garrison and told them: "We will hold them with our teeth." When the Germans finally broke in, they found, written with chalk on a wall above the dead: "At Thermopylae, the three hundred were killed. Here the eighty will fall defending their country."

Greece, in an agony of despair and bitter confusion, collapsed. The government fled to Cairo. British Army units in Greece defended themselves stubbornly, especially—and appropriately—in the area of Thermopylae, and managed to salvage a considerable part of their expeditionary force. But on April 17, 1941, Yugoslavia capitulated; Greece did the same six days later.

Initially, this seemed but another dreadful Nazi victory. The British suffered 11,480 casualties while the Germans lost only 5,058. The Germans imprisoned 270,000 Greeks and 300,000 Yugoslavs. They partitioned

Yugoslavia, taking some bits and giving pieces to Hungary, Italy, and Bulgaria, while establishing puppet states in Croatia and Serbia. They allowed Mussolini, in theory, to take over Greece, after awarding a portion to the Bulgarians.

And on May 20, 1941, history's first fully airborne invasion was launched against Crete with remarkable efficiency. The combined British, Commonwealth, and Greek forces on Crete made the Germans pay a heavy price; yet by the end of the month, the legendary island was in German hands. All the Mediterranean's northern shore and central bastions now were under Axis control, save for Gibraltar and beleaguered Malta, which at one time was defended principally by three old Gladiator biplanes called Faith, Hope, and Charity. The Balkans had been lost, Turkey was trembling, and there were rumors of an impending invasion of Cyprus and the Middle Eastern Arab states.

Nevertheless, Hitler paid dearly for this improvised and impressive Balkan victory. It has been argued by his own generals that the time lost in conquering Greece and Yugoslavia delayed by two or three critical weeks the eventual assault on the Soviet Union. As a consequence, despite the mauling they suffered in June and early July, the Soviets were able to check the *Wehrmacht*

The body of a Yugoslavian civilian (opposite), guilty of some offense against the Nazi occupation and summarily executed as a warning to the populace, hangs from a lamppost. Extreme Nazi ruthlessness gave rise to a bitter guerrilla campaign that soon cost the occupation forces very heavily in human lives and matériel.

Mussolini (below), who loved to pilot aircraft himself, followed the campaign in Greece closely. He even went to the front lines to give his troops encouragement—without much success.

The Luftwaffe flies over Athens while the Nazi flag flies over the Acropolis—a modern barbarian invasion of Greece. Although conquered and occupied, Greece never lost the spirit that the Acropolis symbolized. Resistance groups sprang up around the country to redeem the birthplace of democracy.

at Smolensk, to hold them at Moscow, and then to drive them backward into the most awful winter the Soviet Union had known for years. Had Hitler not run up a swastika on the Acropolis, he might have succeeded in draping it upon the Kremlin.

At approximately this point, a curious incident occurred. Forty-seven-year-old Rudolf Hess, the number three man in the Nazi hierarchy, flew secretly to England in an unarmed plane that he had persuaded aircraft designer Willy Messerschmitt to lend him. Hess was seeking out the Duke of Hamilton, whom he had met at the Berlin Olympic Games in 1936. He hoped the duke would help him get in touch with British leaders so that he could propose conclusion of a peace that would guarantee the integrity of Britain's empire and leave Hitler free to attack the Soviet Union, thereby bringing about the end of bolshevism. Hess broke his ankle while parachuting to Scotland, was captured by a farmer with a pitchfork, and then was locked up as a prisoner of war. Hitler was baffled and furious. He denounced Hess as being in "a state of hallucination," which was perhaps not wholly inaccurate. Hess was known to have been ill and psychologically disturbed. British

German paratroopers on the ground attack as more descend onto the island of Crete.

German paratroops land around the British hospital at Canea, Crete, as painted by Peter McIntyre. The Germans captured the island in May 1941 but their paratroopers took such catastrophic losses that this was their last big parachute drop for the duration of the war.

Peter McIntyre

propaganda made the most of this unexpected opportunity to create the impression of confusion in the highest Nazi ranks. The arrival of this haunted-looking enemy at a moment of bleak despair was a heaven-sent gift to England.

None of these dramatic events, including a new Axis offensive in North Africa and the failure of German efforts to hold Syria with Vichy French collaboration and to seize Iraq in a conspiracy, served to deflect Hitler from his main preoccupation, the forthcoming Soviet campaign. Once he realized that his enormous army, perched on the Channel, was doomed to an indefinite period of idleness, he decided to march it eastward against Stalin.

Hitler's decision to invade the Soviet Union was prompted by more than military stalemate in the West. Not only did he hate both bolshevism and the Slavs; in July 1940, he summed up his credo: "Russia is the factor by which England sets the greatest store. . . . If Russia is beaten, England's last hope is gone. Germany is then master of Europe and the Balkans. . . . Decision: As a result of this argument, Russia must be dealt with. Spring 1941."

On July 29, 1940, General (later Field Marshal) Alfred Gustav Jodl, chief of staff of the Armed Forces High Command, informed a select group of *Wehrmacht* planners of the Führer's "expressed wishes" for an attack on Russia. On August 9 the first directive for an offensive was issued. And so Hitler decided to defeat England by defeating the Soviet Union—a decision forced on him by the RAF.

Hitler confers with General Field Marshal Walter von Brauchitsch and General Franz Halder over a map of the Soviet Union (above). Having lost the Battle of Britain, Hitler decided to invade the Soviet Union—surely one of the great mistakes of all time.

Rudolf Hess (opposite), number three man in the Nazi Party, shakes hands with his Führer at a Nazi congress in Nuremberg at the height of their power. On May 10, 1941, Hess flew a small plane to England. His purpose remains a mystery. Some believe he went with an offer from Hitler to Churchill: make peace and Britain can keep her empire. Others believe he was insane enough to believe that he could make contact with pro-Nazi Englishmen and overthrow the Churchill government. Still others say that the British deliberately lured Hess to Scotland by secretly communicating to him that the British were willing to negotiate a peace but would only do so face-to-face with Hess.

CHAPTER 4

ARSENAL OF DEMOCRACY

T he American people's obsession for avoiding entanglements with the countries from which their forefathers escaped has its roots in both history and philosophy. In 1794 the new republic passed its first neutrality act to escape involvement in a continental war between England and France. Two years later, George Washington warned in his Farewell Address against "interweaving our destiny with that of any part of Europe." Americans considered their nation a noble and moral experiment, removed from the corruption and decay of other lands; and they wished to preserve it untarnished. But the consequent desire for total isolation did not become a real problem until the early twentieth century, when the United States became a world power.

During World War I, most Americans supported the Allies. There were, to be sure, many who did not, especially among those of German, Irish, and Jewish ancestry who cherished anti-British or anti-Soviet sentiments. Thousands of such Americans actually left the United States to fight for the kaiser. Nevertheless, the nation as a whole fervently hoped to stay out of the conflict, even though many leaders clearly saw that should the Allies lose, the United States might become an island of democracy in a militaristic world.

In the interwar period, the American people had come to believe that their participation in the Great War had been a huge mistake. To stay out of the next war, it was felt, the United States had to adopt policies of neutrality and unilateral disarmament. In the 1920s and 1930s, the army demobilized and Congress passed a series of bills, together known as the neutrality acts, well designed to keep the United States out of World War I but entirely unsuited to the situation on the eve of World War II. In 1935, Congress passed a law authorizing the president to stop arms shipments and to prohibit U.S.

American productivity was critical to victory, and it increased tenfold during the war. Henry Kaiser's shipyards cut the average time to deliver a ship from 355 days in 1940 to 69 days in early 1942 and to less than two months by 1944. At this Kaiser yard (opposite), workers are assembling the SS *Joseph Teal*. America's farmers, too, increased their productivity dramatically (above), and did so with aging machinery that had to be patched together, petted, and pampered.

citizens from traveling on foreign ships except at their own risk. The next year, Congress declared all loans to belligerent nations illegal. Another neutrality act in 1939 repealed the arms embargo but authorized a so-called "cash-and-carry" system, designed to allow American manufacturers to sell arms to Britain and France, but only if they paid cash and sent their own ships to pick up the goods.

When war began in September 1939, the U.S. Army hardly existed. As the enemies of democracy armed themselves, America slept. After Poland was overrun, President Roosevelt asked for an increase in appropriations to $853 million for the armed services. Congress cut the figure by 10 percent. These paltry sums constituted an announcement to the world that the United States did not intend to fight anytime in the near future. Washington gave Berlin and Tokyo nothing to worry about.

The nation was taking great risks. If the Soviet Union remained a Nazi ally, and if the Germans overran France and Britain, the United States would be the sole democracy left in a hostile, heavily armed world. The risks were all the greater because the world was on the verge of a huge leap forward in destructive weapons. On October 11, 1939, world-renowned physicist Albert Einstein, a Jewish refugee from Nazi Germany, warned Roosevelt that the Germans were working on the problem of harnessing atomic energy into a bomb. If Hitler had the atomic bomb and no one else did, he would surely conquer the world. Impressed by the warning, Roosevelt conferred privately with congressional leaders; together they created the Office of Scientific Research and Development (OSRD). Under the leadership of Dr. Vannevar Bush as director, OSRD set up the Manhattan Project to develop an atomic bomb capable of being dropped from an airplane and to get it built before the Germans did. This was the beginning of the marriage between science and government in the United States, one of the most important legacies of World War II.

The German spring offensive in 1940 further awakened the United States. With France overrun, two unspoken assumptions were shattered: that, as in 1914–17, the British and French could hold and bleed the German Army, and that the United States could safely land troops in France whenever she felt like it to become the decisive factor in the war. On June 10, 1940, as the Germans raced unopposed across France, Roosevelt told the graduating class of the University of Virginia that the United States would follow "two obvious and simultaneous courses," extending to Britain and France "the material resources of this nation" and speeding up the development of these resources so that the U.S. armed forces would also be strengthened. But four days later, when Premier Paul Reynaud of France appealed to Roosevelt to send U.S. troops and weapons to Europe in France's hour of need, Roosevelt refused. Even if he had wanted to act, he had no forces available. A few days later, France capitulated.

Roosevelt's caution in this crisis was a consequence of the divisions among the American people. Some wanted to fight the Nazis immediately; others wanted to support Britain but stay out of the war; many wanted no part of another European war in any form whatsoever. The debate cut through all levels of American life, and the arguments went on in Congress, on the radio, at public forums, in bars, wherever people gathered. Some seven hundred

Some of the men who would lead American scientific efforts in the war (above) meet in 1940: (left to right) Ernest Lawrence, Arthur Compton, Vannevar Bush, James Bryant Conant, Karl Compton, Alfred Loomis. It was Albert Einstein (right) who wrote the 1939 letter to President Roosevelt reporting the possibility of German atomic research and spurring FDR to start the Manhattan Project. The scientists on the project came from around the world, and only the United States was rich enough to simultaneously build and equip the largest conventional forces in existence and undertake the atomic bomb project.

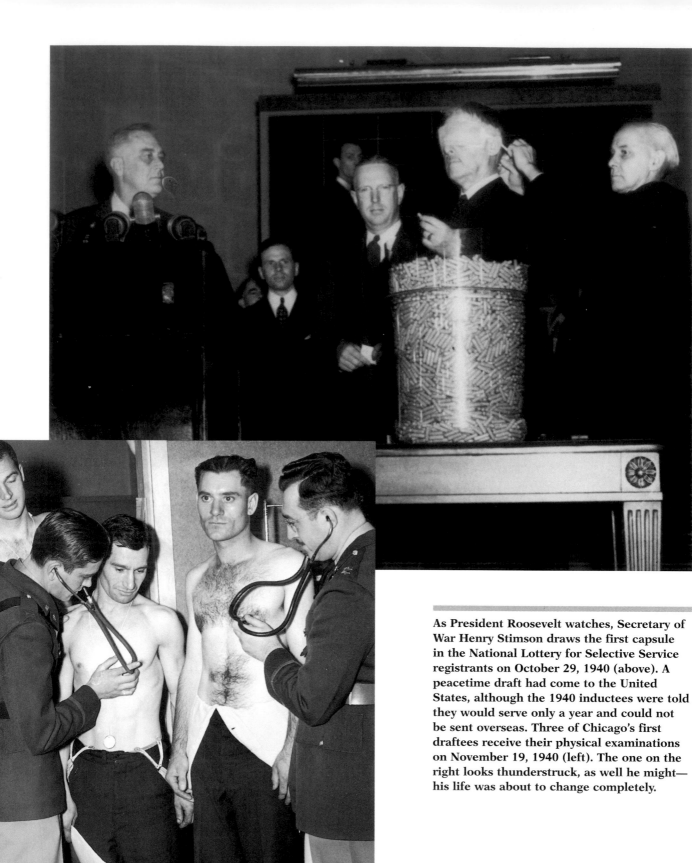

As President Roosevelt watches, Secretary of War Henry Stimson draws the first capsule in the National Lottery for Selective Service registrants on October 29, 1940 (above). A peacetime draft had come to the United States, although the 1940 inductees were told they would serve only a year and could not be sent overseas. Three of Chicago's first draftees receive their physical examinations on November 19, 1940 (left). The one on the right looks thunderstruck, as well he might—his life was about to change completely.

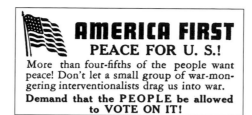

organizations became involved, most of them isolationist. There were various hate groups, fascist organizations of differing degrees of rabidness, and communist groups that supported isolation because Hitler was Stalin's friend. The largest isolationist group was the America First Committee, which was pacifist, Anglophobic, stained with anti-Semitism, and primarily midwestern. Charles Lindbergh was a leading member.

Roosevelt did give Britain limited help. On July 21, 1940, Churchill made an eloquent plea for U.S. destroyers: "Mr. President, with great respect I must tell you that in the long history of the world this is a thing to do NOW." The British were losing merchant ships in appalling numbers and the Battle of Britain was on. In September, Roosevelt responded in a destroyers-for-bases deal, which gave the Royal Navy fifty overage destroyers in return for U.S. bases on British possessions, from Bermuda to British Guiana (now Guyana).

Congress, meanwhile, authorized the president to call the National Guard and Army Reserves to active duty for one year and to institute a draft, but with a one-year time limit. Further, both measures limited the employment of troops to the Western Hemisphere. But it was a start, and the first peacetime conscription in U.S. history.

The year was 1940—a presidential election year—and Roosevelt was running for an unprecedented third term. The Republicans nominated businessman Wendell Willkie, who was more pro-British than was Roosevelt, on a platform plank that mirrored the Democratic plank on the subject of foreign policy, which was to continue to aid Britain and strengthen U.S. armed forces, but to keep out of the war.

In a famous election-eve speech in Boston on October 30, Roosevelt responded to those sentiments when he declared, "And while I am talking to you mothers and fathers, I give you one more assurance. I have said this

The posters of the America First Committee (above left) try to rally isolationists against the war. Roosevelt had just won his third term, but by no means had he turned the country around on the question of involvement. As the Willkie campaign button and card (above) illustrate, the Republican candidate did not take an isolotionist position. Even so, the polls indicated that a majority of Americans wanted to stay out of the war. Roosevelt had pandered to that mood with his promise that American boys would not be sent into foreign wars.

Crates containing knocked-down fighter planes and motors are slung from the deck of a freighter alongside an American cargo carrier ready to leave for Europe (right). Workmen stack cases of gunpowder (below right) 100 feet underground in a tunnel dug out of solid rock in western England. Shipments like these, part of the Lend-Lease program, kept Britain in the war. Lend-Lease aid totaled more than $50 billion in the course of the war. Some $32 billion went to Britain, $11 billion to the Soviet Union. Most of it consisted of U.S.-made munitions, aircraft, and ships. Churchill called Lend-Lease "Hitler's death warrant."

before, but I shall say it again and again and again: Your boys are not going to be sent into any foreign wars."

Roosevelt won the election handily. Churchill, counting on the newly re-elected president to do more than he had, sent Roosevelt a bleak description of the British situation, emphasizing that the United Kingdom was running out of money. Cash-and-carry would no longer suffice, for "the moment approaches when we shall no longer be able to pay cash for shipping and supplies."

Roosevelt responded quickly. On December 7, 1940, he declared he believed that "the best defense of Great Britain is the best defense of the United States." Seeking to avoid the mistakes of Woodrow Wilson and the long controversy over World War I war debts, Roosevelt said he wanted to simply lend or lease to England the supplies she needed. He compared his scheme

to the idea of lending a garden hose to a neighbor whose house was on fire. But he also repeated that he had no intention of sending American boys to Europe; his sole purpose was to "keep war away from our country and our people." He would do this by making America "the great arsenal of democracy."

Churchill called Lend-Lease, as it came to be known, the most unsordid act in human history. Of course he wanted much more—a full-scale American intervention—but at least he now had the United States as an ally, openly committed, as Stalin was to Hitler.

The isolationists were furious. They charged that Lend-Lease was a most unneutral act and would bring the United States into the war. But the program was too beguiling for them to stop it. "Give us the tools," Churchill declared, "and we will finish the job." America could support democracy without shedding any American blood. Then Hitler invaded the Soviet Union (June 1941), which gave the isolationists another argument for America staying out—let Nazis kill Communists and vice versa. Roosevelt moved ahead and helped Britain anyway. In July, he sent U.S. troops to occupy Iceland, freeing the British troops there for the Middle East, and the U.S. Navy began escorting convoys as far as Iceland.

The isolationists opposed the policy of Lend-Lease and any involvement in a foreign war. Here members of the Mothers' Crusade Against Lend-Lease kneel in prayer near the nation's Capitol to plead with Congress to repeal the legislation in March 1941.

BUILDING AN ARMY

Germany and Japan began re-arming in the mid-1930s. In the late thirties, Britain, France, and the Soviet Union struggled to catch up. Meanwhile, the United States stayed out of the arms race. In numbers and quality, the U.S. armed forces lagged woefully behind the world. Their rifles and machine guns were inferior. So were their boots and radios, the tanks and airplanes. The United States didn't even have a design for landing craft. Only in aircraft carriers did America excel, in quality if not in numbers.

Yet there was a certain benefit to being behind. If the Americans could gain enough time, they could outproduce the Axis ten to one. The potential power of the country was enormous: one-third of the factories were idle, one-third of the skilled workers were unemployed. The latent genius of the country was unprecedented: hundreds of thousands of skilled technicians, thousands of engineers whose creative talents had been stifled during the Depression, hundreds of scientists from around the world, hundreds of capitalists who knew how to think big, act big, all of them men who couldn't wait to get going.

But it would take time to design new weapons and get them into production. Meanwhile the United States was going to have to get along with a make-believe army armed with broomsticks. The nation was at peril and incapable of defending itself. Lend-Lease was a great morale booster, but in the main Britain held out alone with her own resources. In the summer of 1940, America's defense began at the English Channel, yet she could contribute almost nothing to the battle raging there. Had Britain fallen, the world would be a very different place today—and every scenario that comes to mind is worse than the previous one.

But Britain held, and America went to work. While the Germans stuck with the Stuka and other war-winning weapons from the 1940–41 battles, and the Japanese stayed with the Zero, the Americans designed and built such planes as the P-51 and B-29, which were at the cutting edge of tech-

Members of the West Virginia National Guard, called into active duty, climb aboard a train in Clarksburg that will take them to they know not where. The scene looks more like 1917 than 1940.

Captain Paul Brown puts volunteers in Garden City, Long Island, through the manual of arms, using the only rifles available in 1940—wooden ones.

nology and far superior to the Stuka and the Zero. That theme ran through almost all weaponry: at the end of the war, save only for the German 88 artillery piece, the Soviet T-34 tank, and the German Tiger, U.S. weapons and equipment were generally the best in the world, and they were there in staggering numbers.

But it had been a close call. The photographs of U.S. Army life from 1939 to 1941 look more like the eve of World War I, or even of the Spanish-American War, than like the second year of World War II. This is why the generation of American leaders who came out of the Second World War vowed, "Never again." Never again would America fall behind anyone in weapons technology, never again would America neglect to maintain strong armed forces, never again would America fail to make binding alliances with her fellow democracies. Those were the great lessons of American unpreparedness.

Lieutenant John Kimbrough (at left, center), former Texas A & M football star, gives recruits instruction at Camp Roberts, California, in firing a Springfield rifle. This was the basic rifle of World War I, badly outdated even before 1940—but until American industry got rolling the old rifles were all the army had.

Harry Hopkins meets with Joseph Stalin in Moscow, July 1941. A month after Hitler invaded the Soviet Union, Roosevelt sent Hopkins, his most trusted adviser, to see Stalin and find out what the Soviet Union needed in the way of Lend-Lease. Tanks, planes, fuel, and food led the list. Stalin demanded more than even America—already giving all-out support to Britain and getting started on building the American armed forces almost from scratch—could give. Further, anti-Communist sympathies among voters and members of Congress were strong enough to keep Roosevelt from extending Lend-Lease to the Soviet Union until November 1941, five months after Germany's invasion.

Roosevelt's most decisive act, however, came in response to the German invasion of the Soviet Union. In July, he sent his special envoy Harry Hopkins to Moscow to consult with Stalin. Hopkins carried a letter from the president, asking what Stalin needed that the United States could supply "in its magnificent resistance to the treacherous aggression by Hitlerite Germany." Stalin's immediate answer was the same as Churchill's: declare war on Germany. He had to settle for a trade mission in October that authorized a Soviet Lend-Lease credit of $1 billion.

In view of the need, it wasn't much. And in view of Stalin's past support of Hitler, not to mention his Communist dictatorship, the credit represented a momentous change in national policy. Thus was the strange alliance born, uniting Great Britain, the Soviet Union, and the United States.

But it was the Anglo-American alliance that had a rough affinity of political views and thus a solid partnership. In August, Churchill and Roosevelt spent four days together at Argentia Bay, Newfoundland. Afterward, they issued a joint statement, known at the Atlantic Charter, outlining the principles for which the war was being fought. The principles were Wilsonian in form—freedom of the seas, the right of people to choose their own form of government, a united nations organization to keep the peace. Plus, the charter included a pledge that neither the United States nor the United Kingdom would seek any territory for itself.

By September 1941, the U.S. Navy was fully engaged with Germany in the Atlantic, in the first "presidential war" entered into by the chief executive without the constitutionally required congressional declaration of war. And not only was it undeclared, it was also unknown to the American people. When a German submarine fired a torpedo at the U.S. destroyer stalking it, Roosevelt brazenly denounced the "rattlesnakes of the Atlantic" for the supposedly unprovoked act, and he ordered the navy to shoot on sight at all German submarines they encountered. In October, he persuaded Congress to remove nearly all restrictions on U.S. merchant vessels; they were now free to carry weapons and supplies to British ports.

Roosevelt never asked for a declaration of war. He did not want to lead a divided nation into the war. Instead, he wanted the Germans to take the final step, apparently reasoning that Hitler could not long permit U.S. ships to transport goods to Britain. If sufficiently provoked, the Germans would have to order their submarine captains to sink American vessels. The attacks could be presented as an outrage and unite the country behind a declaration of war. But Hitler ordered his captains to avoid U.S. ships and to hold their fire unless absolutely necessary. Roosevelt had done all he could to goad Hitler into war. By late fall of 1941, he had run out of options.

In a sense, it was the Japanese who came to Roosevelt's rescue, and solved his dilemma of how to get America fully involved in the war. When the war broke out in Europe, Japan was already on the march in China. The fall of France in 1940 and Britain's preoccupation with Germany opened the door to Southeast Asia for Japan. Roosevelt moved to cripple the Japanese military through an economic blockade, beginning an on-and-off oil and strategic material embargo. Japan decided to overcome her oil shortage through a program of southward expansion. Only the Soviet Union and the United States were potentially strong enough in the Pacific to interfere; Japan moved politically to minimize these threats. On September 27, 1940, she joined Germany and Italy in the Tripartite Pact that obliged the signatories to come to each other's aid should one be attacked. Six months later she signed a five-year nonaggression pact with the Soviets, an agreement that Stalin, fearing Hitler might turn on him next, was eager to sign. Thus for a short period it looked as if World War II would pit the Axis nations (Japan, Germany, and Italy) supported by the Soviet Union against Britain and the United States.

In August 1941, Winston Churchill and Franklin Roosevelt met on HMS *Prince of Wales* in Argentia Bay, Newfoundland. Here, Churchill and Roosevelt, with Admiral Ernest J. King and General George C. Marshall standing behind, join in shipboard church services on August 10. At the conclusion of their meetings, Churchill and Roosevelt issued the Atlantic Charter. America was clearly Britain's ally; the charter proclaimed that Britain and the United States were fighting the Axis "to ensure life, liberty, independence, and religious freedom and to preserve the rights of man and justice." The charter's principles laid the foundation for the United Nations.

That possibility dissolved in June 1941 with the German invasion of the Soviet Union. The new situation prompted a great debate in Tokyo: Should Japan take advantage of the Soviet Union's desperate position vis-à-vis Germany and attack the Soviet Union through Siberia? Some military leaders thought so. Others argued that because of Hitler's involvement in the Soviet Union, Germany no longer posed a serious threat to Britain; this strengthened the Anglo-American position in the Pacific because Churchill was now free to send part of the Royal Navy from the home isles to Britain's Asian colonies (as he in fact did do in the second half of 1941). Japan therefore should seek to reach an agreement with the United States, making such concessions as were necessary to prevent war. The majority of military leaders, however, held out for the long-planned conquest of Southeast Asia.

Roosevelt listened in on the debate through the medium of Magic, the code name applied to intercepted and decoded Japanese radio messages, and characterized it as "a real drag-down and knock-out fight to decide which way they were going to jump." The decision was to shun war with the Soviet Union and instead move south immediately, meanwhile trying to avoid war with the United States by carrying on negotiations as long as possible. The first step was the unresisted occupation of French Indochina (Vietnam, Cambodia, and Laos), giving Japan possession of air and naval bases stretching from Hanoi to Saigon, from which she could launch attacks on Singapore, the Philippines, and the Dutch East Indies.

Roosevelt's response was to tighten the oil embargo and to freeze all Japanese assets in the United States. The British and Dutch supported this move. The effect was to create an economic blockade of Japan. She could not buy oil, steel, or other necessities. The embargo made it clear to the Japanese that they either had to pull back from Indochina and even China itself, thereby reaching an agreement with the United States that would provide them with access to oil, or go to war. The one slim hope remaining was that America's fear of a two-ocean war would impel Roosevelt to compromise. From August until November of 1941, the Japanese sought some form of acceptable political compromise, all the while sharpening their military plans and preparations. If the diplomatic offensive worked, the military offensive could be called off, including the planned attack on the U.S. fleet at Pearl Harbor.

In essence, the Japanese demanded from the United States a free hand in Asia. The central points included an end to American support for China, an Anglo-American promise not to "meddle in nor interrupt" a settlement between Japan and China, a Western recognition of Japan's "special position" in French Indochina, an Anglo-American agreement not to reinforce their bases in the Far East, and a resumption of commercial relations with Japan. Granting these demands would have been a humiliating defeat for Roosevelt and the United States. In October, when the United States made it clear that these concessions were unacceptable and the Japanese military refused a partial withdrawal from China, moderate Prime Minister Fumimaro Konoye resigned, hoping that his action would "save us from the crisis of a Japanese-American war." His successor was General Hideki Tojo, who was willing to continue the negotiations with the United States but only until late November. If no progress was made by then, Japan would strike.

The United States, meanwhile, had gotten started on becoming the arsenal of democracy in fact as well as in self-proclaimed name. By mid-1941 Congress had appropriated $37 billion for rearmament and aid to the Allies, a sum larger than the total cost of World War I. Deficit financing, which had seemed out of hand during the New Deal, grew by a factor of ten. Unemployment, still a major problem in 1939, all but disappeared in 1940, as orders for weapons and goods of all types, including food, got the economy moving again, after a full decade of Depression.

The New Deal had created a bewildering variety of new government agencies; the world war accelerated that trend. In September 1940, Roosevelt declared a state of emergency and created the Office for Emergency Management, followed in January 1941 by the Office of Production Management. In April, the Office of Price Administration began its work. In June, OSRD was launched. In July, the Office of the Coordinator of Information was formed; it soon became the Office of Strategic Services, which eventually was transformed into the Central Intelligence Agency. Other agencies followed, including the Office of War Information (June 1942) and the Office of War Mobilization (April 1943), but the basic pattern of government control of the economy in wartime had been set even before Pearl Harbor.

Much had been done. Much needed to be done. In December 1941, the generals and admirals in charge of America's pell-mell mobilization believed that by late 1943 the nation would reach the strength U.S. commitments required. If the Axis powers were going to win the war, they would have to do it before that time. The sleeping giant was waking up.

Scrap metal piles up on a dock in Portland, Oregon, awaiting shipment to Japan. American metal and gasoline fueled the Japanese war machine until scrap and oil were embargoed by the United States government in mid-1941. Roosevelt also froze Japanese assets in the United States. The Japanese regarded these measures as provocative and felt the embargo left them no choice but to conquer Malaya and the Dutch East Indies and take possession of supplies of metal and oil there.

...*we here highly resolve that these dead shall not have died in vain*...

REMEMBER DEC. 7th!

CHAPTER 5

JAPAN STRIKES

The businessmen, generals, and admirals who ran Japan during World War II were perhaps the most irresponsible leaders in a war characterized by irresponsibility. They initiated a war they could not hope to win if their foes fought to the end, because those opponents had twenty times the productivity and a hundred times more natural resources than did Japan. And they started it with a brilliant victory so humiliating to the vanquished that the Americans vowed to fight on until retribution was total, thereby sealing Japan's fate. Three and a half years later, those same Japanese leaders fought to the finish a war that had been lost a year or more earlier, thereby bringing down on the Japanese people a rain of ruin the likes of which the world had never seen. It was as if the country had been taken over by madmen.

In the summer of 1941, the Japanese military had only enough fuel on hand for a few months of hard flying and hard sailing. They either had to back out of Indochina and China, so that Roosevelt would lift the embargo, or find their own oil. Oil fields were located to the south, principally in the Dutch East Indies. But the Philippines lay directly athwart their line of advance. Roosevelt had already sent some fifty B-17 heavy bombers to the Philippines as a deterrent to the Japanese. The Japanese took this as proof that the United States was determined to keep them a second-class power. They decided to destroy the bombers on the ground in a surprise attack, thus securing their supply line to the south. Admiral Isoroku Yamamoto insisted on a second surprise attack, this time against the U.S. fleet at Pearl Harbor (also sent to the Pacific in May by Roosevelt to deter the Japanese). He reasoned that if he could destroy the fleet, Japan would have two years of control of the Pacific, during which time she could build an impenetrable

A 1942 government poster (opposite) captures the humiliation and shame of Pearl Harbor, invoking Lincoln's Gettysburg Address to spur the nation to retaliatory action. Pearl Harbor drew the American people together like nothing else could have. Above, a matchbox demonstrates the lengths to which anti-Japanese propaganda could go.

The mood of the Japanese armed forces on the eve of Pearl Harbor was one of wild enthusiasm and reckless abandon, as this captured photograph of a carrier crew waving good-bye to one of the attacking planes suggests. The Japanese military led their nation into a war they had little chance of winning. It was General Hideki Tojo (opposite top), the front man for the military dictatorship, who directed unprovoked attacks on more countries than even Hitler. General Tomoyuki Yamashita (opposite bottom) was in command of a series of impressive Japanese victories in the first half year of the war. After taking Singapore, he commanded in the Philippines and captured Bataan and Corregidor. After the war he was executed for war crimes.

defensive ring, based on airfields throughout the various island groups. The United States, Yamamoto felt, would be unwilling to pay the cost of breaking through the ring and might negotiate a peace that would leave Japan in possession of her conquests. What he did not realize was that a surprise attack on Pearl Harbor would so completely unite the American people that no negotiated settlement would ever be considered. He won a big victory but made one of the biggest mistakes of the war.

By November, the Japanese carrier fleet was ready. Yamamoto assembled his commanders on the *Nagato* and told them that without a triumph at Honolulu, Japan could neither make war nor aspire to great-power rank. But he warned his subordinates: "The Americans are adversaries worthy of you." On December 2, the fleet received the coded message ("Climb Mount Niitaka") that irrevocably ordered the attack. Officers and pilots listened to their instructions, then bowed in prayer before the Shinto shrines aboard their carriers. On December 7, they struck.

What was especially galling about the surprise attack was the deliberate duplicity of the Japanese diplomats in Washington. Even as the carriers sailed to their launch point, Tojo's special envoy Saburo Kurusu and Ambassador Kichisaburo Nomura were seeking a negotiated settlement. (They had not been told that an attack on Pearl Harbor was underway.) At 2:05 P.M., December 7, Kurusu and Nomura called upon Secretary Hull—twenty minutes late for their appointment. They arrived just after Roosevelt had telephoned Hull to tell him of the attack on Honolulu. The Secretary coldly accepted the document presented by his visitors, which outlined the Japanese formula for a Pacific settlement. When he had finished reading it, he said: "In all my fifty years of public service I have never seen a document that was more crowded with infamous falsehoods and distortions—infamous falsehoods and distortions on a scale so huge that I never imagined that any government on this planet was capable of uttering them."

At that moment, early in the morning by Pearl Harbor time, the U.S. fleet was smoking in disaster. Three hundred fifty-three Japanese bombers, torpedo bombers, and fighters had within a few hours knocked out half of the U.S. Navy.

The surprise was total. Soldiers were taking their Sunday ease outside their billets; sailors were sauntering along the decks of their moored vessels. When the first enemy aircraft swept out of the morning haze above Diamond Head, few people paid attention. Passengers on an incoming U.S. liner were pleased to be able to witness what they thought to be remarkably realistic preparatory exercises. Then the intruders leveled off. The torpedo planes, armed with special shallow-running devices, headed for the moored battleships, their prime targets. High-flying bombers blasted crowded Hickam Field. Six great battleships—*West Virginia, Tennessee, Arizona, Nevada, Oklahoma,* and *California*—were sunk or seriously damaged. The Army Air Corps was left with only sixteen serviceable bombers.

The Japanese had achieved one of the great surprises in naval history. U.S. striking power in the Pacific was virtually paralyzed. The U.S. Army and Navy had been badly damaged and seriously humiliated. Tokyo newspapers proclaimed that the United States had been reduced to a third-class power. But the Japanese had achieved surprise only by doing something that made no sense—starting a war with the United States—and they made some mistakes of their own. The first was to neglect the oil storage depots. The second was to forego a series of strikes: Pearl Harbor from December 8 to the end of the year had virtually no defenses. The third was to not have prepared an occupying force that could have taken Hawaii. In addition, the Japanese had some bad luck; the U.S. carriers were not in port that Sunday morning.

Their absence was accidental; the carriers were carrying some B-17s to Midway Island. But the fact that the carriers were spared has helped keep alive one of the most persistent myths in American history: that Roosevelt knew the attack on Pearl Harbor was coming but refused to give the commanders in Hawaii advance notice. According to the myth, Roosevelt needed a Pearl Harbor to unite the country behind war. He knew that the aircraft carrier, not the battleship, was the dominate naval ship of the day, so he sacrificed the battleships while ordering the carriers out of port. In fact, neither he nor anyone else knew the battleship was "obsolete" (actually, battleships

Two remarkable photographs record Japanese fighters at dawn, December 7, 1941, on a mission to attack Pearl Harbor. In one photograph (top), captured by American troops on the island of Attu and apparently taken from a Japanese motion picture, dive-bombers rev up their engines. In the other (bottom), a Zero fighter plane rises from the flight deck. There were fifty Zeros providing protection for the bombers and torpedo planes in the first wave, forty in the second. In its carrier form, with folding wing tips, the Zero was called the "Zeke" by the Allies. It was faster and more maneuverable than anything the Americans had in service at the time.

participated fully and effectively in the war) or anticipated the role of the carrier. Further, Washington gave the military in Hawaii plenty of warning about the imminent outbreak of hostilities. One December 2 message opened: "This is a war warning." But there was no specific warning about an attack on Pearl Harbor because no one imagined the Japanese were capable of such a daring raid. Magic was no help because the Japanese carrier fleet maintained radio silence.

The American people were stunned. The next day, President Roosevelt told a joint session of Congress that December 7 was "a date which will live in infamy." With a single dissenting vote, Congress voted to recognize that a

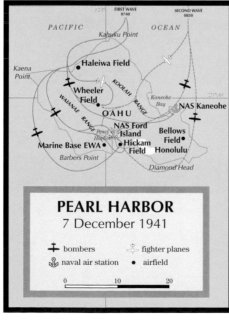

PEARL HARBOR
7 December 1941

Another captured Japanese photograph (above) shows an aerial view of Ford Island at Pearl Harbor on the morning of December 7, 1941. The U.S. ships are lined up like ducks in a shooting gallery. The Japanese attack plan was simple, as the map (left) illustrates; the results were costly to the Americans, although luckily aircraft carriers were not in the harbor that morning.

The Japanese blow was skillfully carried out, as is evident in this view of the U.S. battleships (above, left to right) *West Virginia, Tennessee,* and *Arizona,* the pride of the fleet. So ill-prepared were the Americans that soldiers such as these at right, firing a machine gun and rifles, were about all there was in the way of defense. Very few American fighter aircraft got into the air that morning, nor did the anti-aircraft guns on the fleet get into full operation.

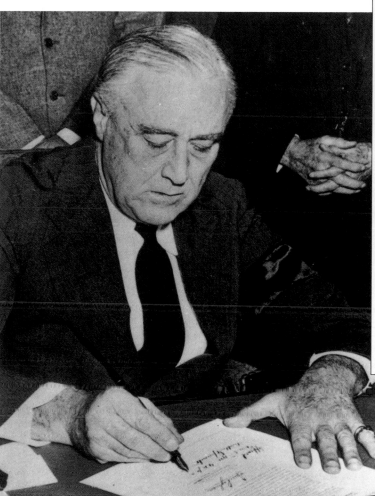

The headline of *The New York Times* gives the somber news to millions of Americans (right). Shortly before 5 P.M., Sunday, December 7, President Roosevelt called his secretary, Grace Tully, to his study and began dictating the message (above right) he wanted to give to Congress the following day. This address referred to December 7 as "a date which will live in infamy" and asked for a declaration of war against Japan, which was signed that day (above).

Young Americans, full of resolve to avenge Pearl Harbor, line up at the U.S. Navy recruiting station in Boston on December 8, 1941. Navy enlistments had been slow, but not on this day. Patriotism was a primary motive, but it helped the Navy recruiting effort that for these young men, joining the Navy meant avoiding the Army—which was almost sure otherwise to get most of them.

state of war now existed between the United States and Japan. The resolution, however, said nothing about Germany and Italy. It had never occurred to anyone that America might go to war with Japan without also going to war with her Axis partners. The United States military had held staff talks with the British High Command throughout 1941 into 1942, and agreed that when America got into the war she would direct her major effort against Germany, holding a defensive position in the Pacific until after victory in Europe. But Pearl Harbor had riveted all eyes on Japan, and the cry for revenge was sweeping the country. What Roosevelt might have done cannot be known, but he never had to face the issue of fighting Japan and not Germany because Hitler declared war on the United States on December 10; Mussolini fell into line and did the same.

This was an inexplicable action on Hitler's part. He was not required to do so by the terms of the Tripartite Pact (Japan had not come to his aid when he attacked the Soviet Union, something he very much wanted), and he did not discuss his action with his own military leaders or foreign office. He just did it. Thus Hitler, after a long string of successes, made two fatal errors between June and December of 1941—going to war with both the Soviet Union and the United States. Of course, on December 10 the United States had no military force available for Europe, and her Pacific fleet, save the carriers, and her air base in the Philippines were all but destroyed.

Pearl Harbor ended the debate between isolationists and interventionists. Leading isolationist Senator Burton Wheeler said: "The only thing now to do is to lick the hell out of them." Lindbergh asked to be reinstated in the air corps; since Hitler had attacked the Soviet Union, Communists and other left-wing pacifists were now enthusiastic warriors. The government saw to it that the pro-Nazi German-American Bund organization was dissolved, but a wholly unjust penalty was paid by the Nisei, Americans of Japanese ancestry, who were forcibly relocated from their West Coast homes because of exaggerated spy fears.

As Hitler's armies fought the Battle of Moscow in December 1941, the Japanese onslaught continued with simultaneous attacks against Hong Kong, Malaya, and the Philippines, where the U.S. Far East Air Corps was crippled in a catastrophe almost as bad as that of Pearl Harbor and one for which there was even less excuse, for there had been sufficient and accurate advance notice. General MacArthur had reason to expect an assault on at least Luzon. Nevertheless, just a few hours after Pearl Harbor, Japanese planes succeeded in destroying eighteen of the thirty-five B-17s at Clark Field, as well as fifty-six fighters and twenty-five other planes. They lost only seven aircraft in the process. Within three weeks, strong amphibious forces under Lieutenant General Masaharu Homma had landed on the northern and southern shores of Luzon and were driving on to Manila. The U.S. Asiatic Fleet withdrew with large convoys of merchant shipping to safer and more southerly waters. By January 2, 1942, Manila had fallen, and American and Philippine troops were retreating to the Bataan Peninsula.

People quickly grew tired of the war. By 1944 blood donations had fallen drastically, despite every form of public appeal. But in late 1944 when a commercial laboratory in San Francisco opened a blood bank and offered $4 a pint for plasma, the lines stretched around the block in both directions. By way of comparison, the combat infantrymen—the ones who would need that blood—got paid $2.50, before deductions, for a twenty-four-hour day.

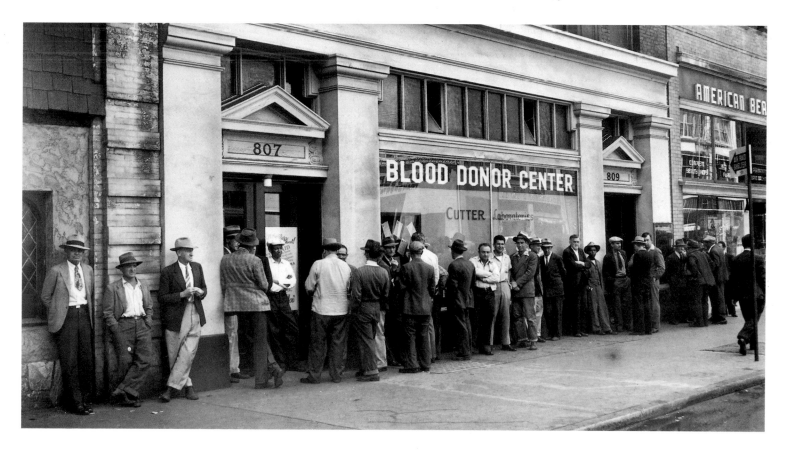

JAPANESE-AMERICANS

There were 127,000 people of Japanese ancestry in the United States in 1941, 80,000 of them native-born American citizens, or Nisei. Most Nisei were simple truck farmers in California. This tiny group caused the greatest panic. They were suspected of sabotage—every forest fire on the West Coast was blamed on them—of sending signals by bonfires or automobile headlights to Japanese submarines, and of espionage. A demand arose, fed by politicians, led by California Governor Earl Warren, to evacuate them to camps in the interior.

That most of them were American citizens made no difference; as one official put it, "A Jap is a Jap." That not one single act of sabotage had been charged, much less proved, made no difference. Yet in Hawaii, where Japanese-Americans made up a quarter of the population, and where at least a few had engaged in espionage, there was no demand to remove them, because to do so would have disrupted the economy and thus the war effort.

In February 1942, President Franklin Roosevelt responded to the demands of West Coast politicians and ordered the War Department to move the Nisei out. General John DeWitt, who oversaw the evacuation, defended the policy with a curious logic: "The very fact that no sabotage has taken place to date is a disturbing and confirming indication that such action will be taken."

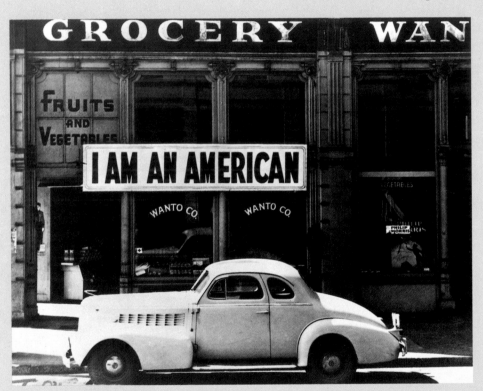

The owner of this Oakland, California, store, a graduate of the University of California, put the sign up on December 8, 1941. But in March of 1942 he was ordered to close his store and be "relocated" to an internment camp in the desert.

The Nisei were rounded up, forced to sell their property at outrageously low prices, and shipped off to camps in the desert, or as far away as the Arkansas Delta. They were put to work as farm laborers, harvesting crops by day, living in camps surrounded by barbed wire at night. These were not concentration camps in the Nazi sense—physical conditions were fairly good, with shelter, ample food, clothing, an opportunity to conduct classes or to have concerts, and other touches—but they were bad enough. Milton Eisenhower, the general's younger brother and the number two man at the Department of Agriculture, was in charge of the camps. He did what he could for the Nisei. For example, he wrote every college president in the Ivy League, Big Ten, and other prestigious institutions, saying that there were many young Nisei who were excellent students. Wouldn't the president be willing to take one or two of them on his campus? Without exception, the answer was no.

In 1944, the Supreme Court ruled the evacuation and concentration into camps of the Nisei was constitutional. Forty years later Congress condemned the relocation policy as a product of "war hysteria, racial prejudice, and failure of political leadership," and compensated internees with a payment of $20,000 each. It was too little, too late.

Private Herrett Wilson, in a letter to his mother written from the Pacific, put the whole business in context: "I fought and killed so that the enemy might not invade our land and I ask is it all for naught when red, white and blue fascists drive Nisei about like coyotes and plague the fathers, mothers, and relatives of our colored comrades that fight by our side."

Under the relocation policy, no Japanese-American on the West Coast was safe from internment. Even a decorated World War I veteran (above) was subject to question and confinement. At the relocation camps, people had to live in cramped quarters for the duration of the war; the one at left was photographed by Dorothea Lange. Below, a new contingent has just arrived at the Salinas, California, camp. For the most part the Nisei did labor in the agricultural fields stretching from California across the mountains and plains to Arkansas. Conditions were bad, but it should be noted that they were nothing to compare to German, Japanese, and Russian slave labor camps.

While the United States reeled from these savage blows, the Japanese had unleashed a multiple offensive on the Asian mainland. The Indochinese colonies of defeated France had already been occupied; now it was Britain's turn. As the hitherto dominant Western nations faltered, the Asiatic peoples were subjected to Japanese propaganda. The Royal Navy adhered to obsolete tactics. Hong Kong was entirely isolated and fell on Christmas Day. Singapore, vaunted island citadel of the East, had all its guns and fortifications facing seaward and lay open to the Malayan land side, from which the attack developed. Wearing sneakers, carrying small sacks of rice and riding bicycles, venerating their emperor, and believing implicitly in their commanders, some two hundred thousand Japanese soldiers rushed through the Malayan jungle.

The British kept falling back, only to find their enemy already installed behind them. "It's like trying to build a wall out of quicksand," said one despairing officer. Within six weeks the Japanese had taken the peninsula. The British withdrew into Singapore, swarming with refugees, but Sir Arthur Percival, the commanding general, found himself outnumbered, outmaneuvered,

Japanese artist Sato Kai interviewed combat veterans before painting famous victories, such as Clark Field (opposite), where the Japanese caught General MacArthur's air force on the ground and destroyed it. Kohei Ezaki also used soldiers' accounts to give a Japanese perspective in a detailed painting of the landings on Guam (above).

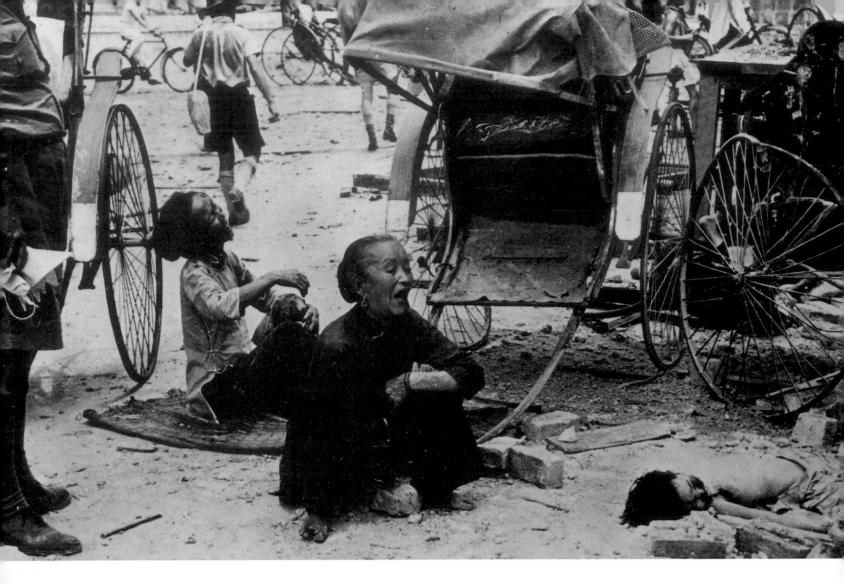

In the first half year of the war, Japanese troops swarmed across Asia, well-armed, well-equipped, tightly disciplined. Troops like these (left) on the move in the Philippines in early 1942 were the terror of the countryside. Destruction also rained from the skies. A Chinese mother and grandmother weep for a child killed in a bombing raid on Singapore in February 1942 (above). A photograph (opposite bottom), taken on January 2, 1942, shows tanks rolling through Manila, past the Philippine legislature, after MacArthur declared Manila an open city. General Homma (opposite top) was in charge of the amphibious forces that landed on Luzon and driven onto Manila. He was relieved of his command, however, because he insisted on treating the Filipinos with respect. (After the war he was nevertheless tried as a war criminal and found guilty. The man he had humiliated, MacArthur, ordered him shot.)

and out of nerve. With more than seventy thousand men, he surrendered on February 15, 1942. It was the worst military disaster ever suffered by any European nation in Southeast Asia.

Even before that great island city fell, Britain had suffered an unmitigated naval catastrophe. A flotilla of six ships, including the heavy cruiser *Repulse* and the powerful new battleship *Prince of Wales,* was cruising openly in Malayan waters, hoping to deter Japan. There was no aircraft carrier in the flotilla, and its commander, Sir Tom Phillips, an old-fashioned "battlewagon admiral," easily reconciled himself to the lack of support from land-based planes. When the Royal Air Force notified him, "Regret fighter protection impossible," Phillips merely remarked to an officer on the bridge, "Well, we must get on without it." Soon he found himself being shadowed by Japanese observation planes. By the time he turned back, it was too late. On December 10, the *Prince of Wales* and the *Repulse* were both sunk by Japanese bombers and low-flying torpedo planes. Phillips went down with his ships. Churchill told Parliament: "In my whole experience I do not remember any naval blow so heavy or so painful. . . ."

The Japanese swarmed southward across Malaya toward the Dutch East Indies and far-off Australia and westward over Thailand to Burma and the edge of India. In Burma, the British were aided by a Chinese force under Chiang Kai-shek's chief of staff, the redoubtable U.S. general Joe Stilwell. But his troops were soon cut off and had to make a difficult forced march

Although MacArthur had declared Manila an open city and the Japanese had acknowledged the declaration, they nonetheless continued to bomb the city until their troops had completed its occupation (left). Eventually, the Japanese flag was raised over Manila in May of 1942 (opposite page) and they proceeded to humiliate their conquest, as seen below, holding a Japanese military parade using a Filipino band.

The Japanese artist Nakamura painted this scene of Japanese planes attacking the heavy cruiser HMS *Repulse* on December 10, 1941. On this day, the British had sallied forth convinced that airplanes could not damage major warships. They paid for their hubris: both *Repulse* and the battleship *Prince of Wales* were sunk. In a single day Britain's naval presence in the Far East was all but eliminated.

out of Burma to northeast India. Stilwell confessed in his usual unabashed fashion: "The Japs ran us out of Burma. We took a hell of a beating!" The Burmese, like many other Asians, were pleased to see the Western overlords defeated. A Tokyo newspaper, commenting on the extent of collaboration in Mandalay, observed: "We do not have to reward our friends with posts in the government. They had taken them before we arrived."

One of the principal objectives of the Japanese strategic plan was the Dutch East Indies (now Indonesia). Japan desperately needed petroleum, and after Holland's occupation by the Nazis, Tokyo had applied increasing pressure on the Dutch colonial administration in Java. Even before the fall of Singapore, the Japanese landed troops near the Borneo oil fields, and shortly afterward the invasion of Java began. To oppose this, the Allies assembled a small flotilla of American, Australian, and Dutch ships, which met the Japanese on February 27, 1942, in the three-day Battle of the Java Sea. The

Allied force was entirely destroyed. By March 9, the whole archipelago was gone, and nearly one hundred thousand prisoners were marching off to Japanese POW camps. In four weeks the Dutch lost an empire that they had owned for nearly four centuries.

One consequence of this sensational advance was to expose the entire continent of Australia to invasion. The Japanese pushed across the mountains of neighboring New Guinea and bombed Darwin, the northern Australian port. A landing seemed imminent. A member of parliament at Canberra warned: "We are facing the vile abomination of a Jap invasion." The country was placed on a total-war footing, but there was a dangerous shortage of troops because of the units sent to North Africa.

Australia looked to the United States for help, but the Americans couldn't defend their own Pacific installations. Pearl Harbor was paralyzed, and Wake and Guam islands, deep in the Pacific, had been lost to amphibious assault in December. In the Philippines, a tough, efficiently commanded Japanese force had bottled up MacArthur's defenders on the peninsula of Bataan. His first line of defense was crushed by a redoubtable infantry thrust in which Japanese hurled themselves on barbed-wire entanglements, permitting their comrades to cross upon their writhing bodies. Then, as MacArthur fell back on a second line, a Japanese battalion landed behind him.

On February 22, 1942, Roosevelt ordered MacArthur to abandon his force and go to Australia, there to prepare a counteroffensive. Placing MacArthur in command in the Southwest Pacific was an appeasement of the right wing of the Republican Party, the core of the isolationists; to them, MacArthur was a hero. But many officers in the War Department—including Eisenhower and Chief of Staff George Marshall—felt he had failed miserably in the Philippines from December 7 onward and should have been relieved of command.

On March 11, General MacArthur, his wife, son, and staff quit Corregidor by PT boats. At Mindanao they transferred to two B-17s that flew them to Darwin, Australia, where MacArthur issued his famous statement, "I came through and I shall return." The public relations people rather liked the line, but thought it should be changed to "We shall return." MacArthur insisted on the original version.

The troops he had left behind were now commanded by General Jonathan Wainwright. The defenders of Bataan fought on with great courage but small hope. Their rations had been halved in early January. Now they were foraging for any kind of flesh: dogs, pack mules, monkeys, iguanas, snakes. Ill fed, ravaged by tropical diseases, totally isolated, the troops composed their own war song:

We're the battling bastards of Bataan;
No mama, no papa, no Uncle Sam;
No aunts, no uncles, no nephews, no nieces;
No pills, no planes, no artillery pieces . . .
and nobody gives a damn!

On April 8, Wainwright ordered the withdrawal from Bataan. When informed by radio of this, MacArthur, from Australia, sent Wainwright a Hitler- or Stalin-like order. The troops were barely able to hold their weapons,

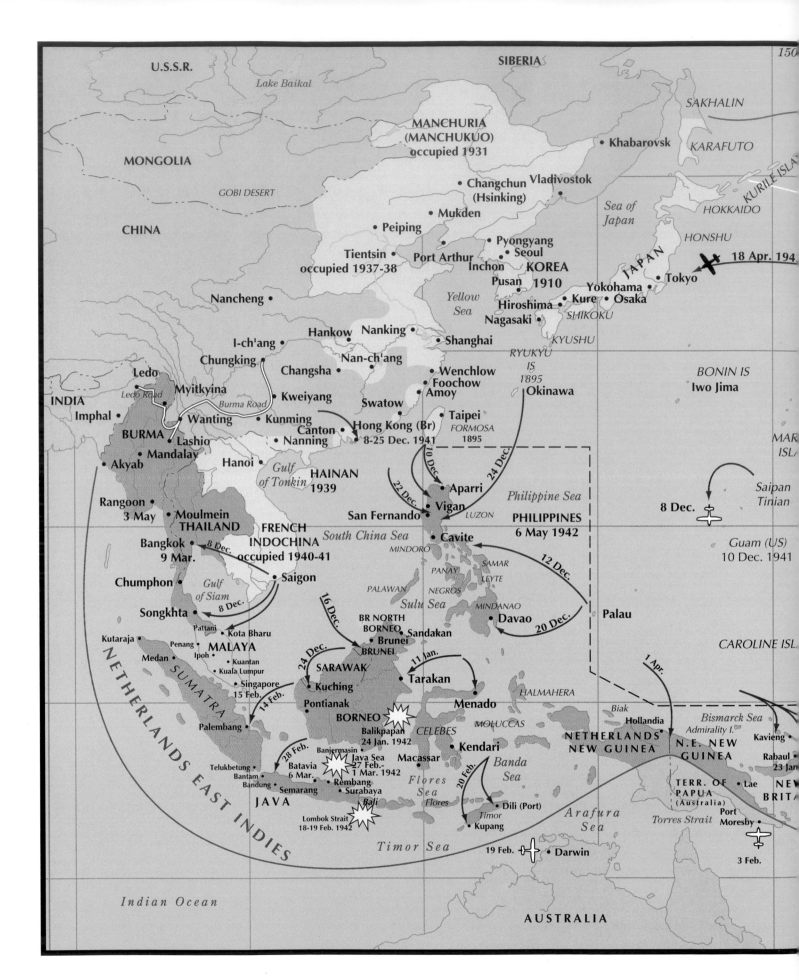

150

U.S.S.R.

SIBERIA

SAKHALIN

Lake Baikal

MANCHURIA
(MANCHUKUO)
occupied 1931

• Khabarovsk

KARAFUTO

MONGOLIA

GOBI DESERT

• Changchun
(Hsinking)

Vladivostok

Sea of
Japan

HOKKAIDO

CHINA

• Mukden

• Peiping

Tientsin •
occupied 1937-38

Port Arthur •

• Pyongyang
Seoul
Inchon
Pusan

KOREA
1910

HONSHU

KURILE ISLA

✕ 18 Apr. 194

• Tokyo

Nancheng •

Yokohama •
Hiroshima •
Nagasaki •

• Kure • Osaka

JAPAN

SHIKOKU

Hankow • Nanking •

• Shanghai

KYUSHU

BONIN IS

I-ch'ang •
Chungking •

Changsha • Nan-ch'ang •

RYUKYU
IS
1895

Iwo Jima

Ledo •
Myitkyina •

Kweiyang •

Swatow •

• Wenchlow
• Foochow
Amoy

Okinawa

MAR
ISL

Ledo Road

Burma Road

Kunming •

Canton •

• Taipei

INDIA

Wanting •

• Nanning

Hong Kong (Br)
8-25 Dec. 1941

FORMOSA
1895

10 Dec.

24 Dec.

Saipan
Tinian

Imphal •

BURMA

• Lashio

Hanoi •

Gulf
of Tonkin

HAINAN
1939

22 Dec.

• Aparri

Philippine Sea

8 Dec.

• Mandalay
Akyab •

• Vigan

San Fernando •

LUZON

PHILIPPINES
6 May 1942

Guam (US)
10 Dec. 1941

Rangoon
3 May

• Moulmein
THAILAND

FRENCH
INDOCHINA
occupied 1940-41

South China Sea

• Cavite

MINDORO

12 Dec.

Bangkok •
9 Mar.

8 Dec.

SAMAR

PANAY

LEYTE

Chumphon •

Gulf
of Siam

Saigon •

PALAWAN

NEGROS

Palau

Songkhta •

8 Dec.

Sulu Sea

MINDANAO

• Davao

20 Dec.

CAROLINE ISL

Pattani •
Kutaraja •

• Kota Bharu

BR NORTH
BORNEO

• Sandakan

Penang •
Medan •

Ipoh •

MALAYA

• Kuantan

24 Dec.

• Brunei

BRUNEI

16 Dec.

11 Jan.

1 Apr.

• Kuala Lumpur

SARAWAK

• Tarakan

HALMAHERA

Biak

Bismarck Sea

• Singapore
15 Feb.

14 Feb.

• Kuching

• Menado

Hollandia

Admirality I.

• Kavieng

Palembang •

Pontianak •

BORNEO

MOLUCCAS

NETHERLANDS
NEW GUINEA

N.E. NEW
GUINEA

Rabaul
23 Jan

Balikpapan
24 Jan. 1942

CELEBES

• Kendari

Banda
Sea

Telukbetung •

28 Feb.

Banjermasin •

Java Sea
27 Feb.-
1 Mar. 1942

Macassar •

NEW
BRIT

Bantam •
Bandung •

Batavia
6 Mar.

• Rembang

Semarang •

• Surabaya

20 Feb.

Flores
Sea

Flores

TERR. OF
PAPUA
(Australia)

• Lae

JAVA

Bali

Lombok Strait
18-19 Feb. 1942

Dili (Port) •

Timor

Arafura
Sea

Torres Strait

Port
Moresby •

Kupang •

Timor Sea

19 Feb. ✈ • Darwin

NETHERLANDS EAST INDIES

Indian Ocean

AUSTRALIA

3 Feb.

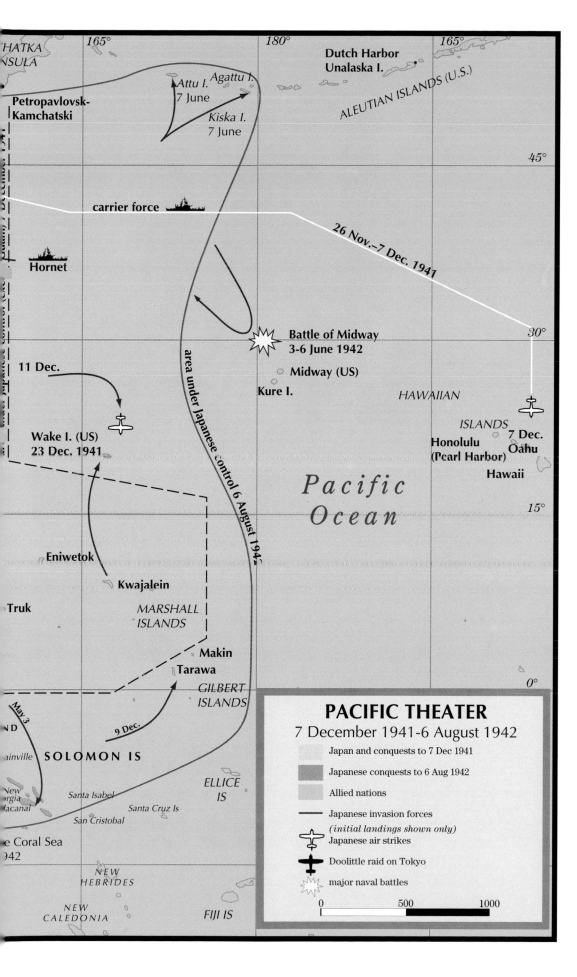

HATKA
NSULA

165°

Petropavlovsk-Kamchatski

180°

165°

Dutch Harbor
Unalaska I.

45°

Attu I. *Agattu I.*
7 June

ALEUTIAN ISLANDS (U.S.)

Kiska I.
7 June

carrier force

26 Nov.–7 Dec. 1941

Hornet

area under Japanese control 6 August 1942

Battle of Midway
3-6 June 1942

30°

Midway (US)

Kure I.

HAWAIIAN

11 Dec.

Wake I. (US)
23 Dec. 1941

ISLANDS

7 Dec.
Oahu

Honolulu
(Pearl Harbor)

Hawaii

15°

Pacific Ocean

Eniwetok

Kwajalein

Truk

MARSHALL
ISLANDS

Makin

Tarawa

GILBERT
ISLANDS

0°

May 3

9 Dec.

ND

SOLOMON IS

ainville

New
rgia
acanal

Santa Isabel

ELLICE
IS

Santa Cruz Is

San Cristobal

e Coral Sea
942

NEW
HEBRIDES

NEW
CALEDONIA

FIJI IS

PACIFIC THEATER
7 December 1941-6 August 1942

Japan and conquests to 7 Dec 1941

Japanese conquests to 6 Aug 1942

Allied nations

Japanese invasion forces
(initial landings shown only)
Japanese air strikes

Doolittle raid on Tokyo

major naval battles

0   500   1000

This is the Japanese Empire at its fullest extent. By the summer of 1942, the Japanese controlled more of the earth's surface than any previous empire had. Although most of it was water, the empire contained immensely valuable natural resources, strategic locations, and millions of inhabitants. The Japanese wanted even more—all of New Guinea first, then Australia and New Zealand. Next would come Midway, then Honolulu. Why not? Look what they had already conquered.

General Douglas MacArthur and family escape from Corregidor. They retreat to Adelaide, Australia, by train (right). Senior military advisers had urged President Roosevelt to fire MacArthur because of the debacle at Clark Field and the loss of the Bataan Peninsula. Roosevelt decided instead to keep MacArthur in the war and ordered him to Australia, to begin the buildup for a counteroffensive. Some saw this as an appeasement of the Republican right wing by Roosevelt, others as one of his better decisions.

Some 76,000 prisoners, 12,000 of them American, line up four abreast and start off on the Bataan Death March (opposite). In poor health when they began in April 1942, the prisoners suffered terribly from a lack of food, water, and medicine on the sixty-five-mile trek to prison camp. An estimated 5,200 Americans died on the march.

so emaciated and disease-racked were they, and unable to hike, much less run. But MacArthur told Wainwright, "If food fails you will prepare and execute an attack upon the enemy." Wainwright ignored the order. After detroying Bataan's ammunition dumps, the general and a few others retreated to the island fort of Corregidor; the rest of the troops surrendered.

The Japanese displayed particular callousness toward the American and Filipino soldiers they captured at Bataan, marching them sixty-five miles to a railway junction from which they were to entrain for an internment camp. Dazed and weak from thirst and starvation, the prisoners were formed into columns of fours, then driven forward under a blinding sun. Thousands of them died from disease and exhaustion or from Japanese brutality in what became known as "the Bataan Death March."

After the withdrawal from Bataan, the Japanese assault turned on Corregidor, where some thirteen thousand defenders braced themselves. The island fortress, like all American outposts in the Pacific, was a formidable work. Called "the Rock," there had been driven through its central height, Melinta Hill, a long tunnel whose many laterals provided living quarters, storage, hospitals, and other necessities of life under siege. Barracks and other outside quarters were abandoned as everyone moved underground.

Only those who manned artillery positions or other defense posts went into the open to face the enemy bombardment. Dust and dirt constantly sifted down into the tunnels as the earth shook from shell explosions. The air was bad; hunger was constant because rations had long since been cut in half; quarrels flared over trifles in the tense atmosphere. Some men were so terrified of the dangers outside that they refused to take their tours of duty there; they became known as tunnel rats and were bitterly resented by those who did go out.

By May 4, enemy shells were falling at the rate of one every five seconds, sixteen thousand in twenty-four hours. Corregidor's big guns were wrecked; little more than the beach defenses remained. Japanese landing forces came ashore on the night of the fifth, and, after terrible losses, moved toward the tunnel. General Wainwright, fearful the enemy might advance with guns firing into the tunnels among the nurses and wounded, had his men lay down their arms. But he had previously released other commanders in the Philippines from further compliance with his orders, and General Homma refused to accept surrender under these conditions. Wainwright, almost distraught and with visions of the Japanese reopening hostilities against his now disarmed troops, took to the radio to plead with commanders elsewhere to lay down their arms. After weeks of uncertainty, all surrendered, although many of their men took to the hills to continue the war as guerrilla fighters.

Despite the immense emotional pressures engendered by successive blows to American prestige in the Pacific, President Roosevelt and his chiefs of staff held to the strategy that had been fixed with Churchill just after Pearl Harbor. The first objective was still the defeat of Nazi Germany. In the Paci-

A soldier on the Bataan Death March used a piece of cigarette paper (above) to write a letter. A scene (right) in May 1942 shows a few of the thousands of deaths caused by the long and arduous march. MacArthur wrongly blamed General Homma for the atrocity, and his public relations staff put out the first information on it. Bit by bit, over the next months, the staff revealed more details, keeping the outrage boiling hot.

In lateral No. 12 of the Melinta Tunnel on the island of Corregidor on April 24, 1942, the men of the U.S. Army Signal Corps share their tight space with the Finance Office. At right is an encoding machine. The troops were safe from shelling here, but without incoming supplies they were doomed.

fic, American planners emphasized the strategic triangle embracing Alaska, Hawaii, and Panama, thus implicitly accepting the loss of Wake, Guam, and the Philippines.

The summer of 1942 was a very dark time. The Germans were on the offensive in the Soviet Union again, this time headed for Stalingrad and the Caucasus oil fields. In the North Africa desert, the Afrika Korps was threatening Egypt. On the Atlantic, the German submarines seemed unbeatable. In the Pacific, the Americans and their allies had taken a terrible beating. In six months the Japanese had occupied a huge area; it covered more of the surface of the globe than any other empire in history. The Japanese armed forces were everywhere triumphant. Their armies had beaten the Americans in the Philippines, the British in Malaya, and the Dutch in Java. Their ships had

A Japanese photographer captures General Jonathan Wainwright (left), MacArthur's successor, as he announces the surrender of all American forces in the Philippines on May 6, 1942. U.S. soldiers and sailors (below) surrender at Corregidor. It had been a long and bitter campaign for the Americans (opposite).

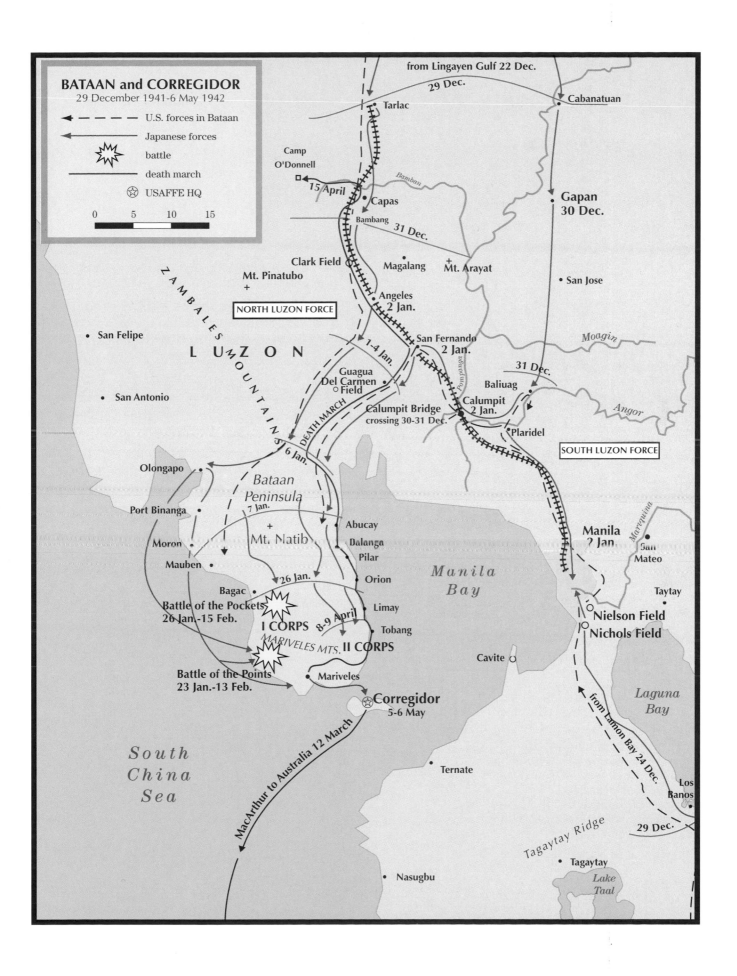

BATAAN and CORREGIDOR
29 December 1941-6 May 1942

- ◀━ ━ ━ ━ U.S. forces in Bataan
- ◀━━━ Japanese forces
- ✦ battle
- ━━━ death march
- ✪ USAFFE HQ

0   5   10   15

from Lingayen Gulf 22 Dec.

29 Dec.

Cabanatuan

Tarlac

Camp
O'Donnell

15 April

Capas

Bamban

Gapan
30 Dec.

Bambang   31 Dec.

San Jose

Clark Field

Magalang

Mt. Arayat

Mt. Pinatubo

Angeles
2 Jan.

Moagin

NORTH LUZON FORCE

San Felipe

L U Z O N

San Fernando
2 Jan.

1-4 Jan.

Pompanga

31 Dec.

Baliuag

San Antonio

Guagua
Del Carmen
Field

Angor

Calumpit
2 Jan.

SOUTH LUZON FORCE

DEATH MARCH

Calumpit Bridge
crossing 30-31 Dec.

Plaridel

6 Jan.

Olongapo

*Bataan
Peninsula*
7 Jan.

Port Binanga

Mt. Natib

Abucay

Manila
? Jan.

Marquina

San
Mateo

Moron

Dalanga

Pilar

*Manila
Bay*

Taytay

Mauben

Orion

Nielson Field

Bagac

26 Jan.

Nichols Field

Battle of the Pockets
26 Jan.-15 Feb.

I CORPS   8-9 April

Limay

MARIVELES MTS. **II CORPS**

Tobang

Cavite

Battle of the Points
23 Jan.-13 Feb.

Mariveles

*Laguna
Bay*

✪ **Corregidor**
5-6 May

from Lamon Bay 24 Dec.

*South
China
Sea*

MacArthur to Australia 12 March

Ternate

Los
Banos

29 Dec.

Tagaytay Ridge

Nasugbu

Tagaytay

*Lake
Taal*

Colonel James Doolittle (above) led the bombing raid on Tokyo, Nagoya, and Yokohama. On April 18, 1942, a B-25 (opposite), one of the many attacking planes in the Doolittle raid, takes off from the deck of the aircraft carrier USS *Hornet*. The raid was the first time enemy bombs had been dropped on Japan. It did little military damage but did a great deal to raise American morale. In September 1942, after leading his famous raid, Doolittle went to North Africa, where he commanded the Twelfth Air Force. In January 1944, he took command of the Eighth Air Force in England. Doolittle was one of the most popular and best respected generals in the Air Corps (after 1942 the Army Air Force).

defeated every American and Allied ship that dared to fight. Their air force had destroyed a fleet at Pearl Harbor, America's biggest bomber fleet at Clark Field, and two British battleships.

But they had failed to get the U.S. aircraft carriers operating out of Pearl Harbor. One of these, *Hornet*, made possible the first American counterattack of the war. The idea originated with a submarine staff officer, Captain Francis S. Low, who submitted a plan for using army bombers from aircraft carriers. General "Hap" Arnold, head of the Army Air Corps, asked Lieutenant Colonel James Doolittle to study the project. Doolittle ascertained that, properly modified, B-25 medium bombers could carry one-ton bomb loads and still manage the risky, short takeoff. Sixteen planes with specially selected five-man crews were prepared for the dangerous mission and loaded aboard the carrier *Hornet*. On April 18, 1942, some 670 miles from Tokyo, they flew off one by one, in a strong wind that helped lift them from the short deck. Their orders were to strike the enemy capital and head for a small airfield deep inside unoccupied China. The resolute bombers swung in over Japan, spending some six minutes over the target, where, ironically, a practice air-raid drill was going on. All but one of the planes later crashed or were abandoned in China or off the coast of China; one landed at Vladivostok, and its crew was interned by the Soviets; two came down inside enemy territory, and three of their crewmen were later shot in reprisal for American bombing of Japanese residential areas. Of the eighty flyers on the mission, seventy-one eventually returned to the United States.

The other two carriers—*Lexington* and *Yorktown*—played the critical role in one of the most historic naval battles in history, Coral Sea, May 7–8. It was historic not because it was decisive—it was a draw—but because for the first time two opposing fleets fought a battle without any ships seeing each other. And even though a draw, it contributed to the Japanese admirals' decision to withdraw from the Southwest Pacific in order to fight in the Central Pacific.

Doolittle's raid, although in military terms far more expensive to the Americans than to the Japanese, had a momentous effect on Yamamoto and his senior naval officers. They were humiliated by bombs dropping in Tokyo. Rather than continuing to support the army in its drive for New Guinea, the admirals decided to eliminate those troublesome American carriers by a bold stroke in the Central Pacific, designed to force the Americans to come out and fight at a time when Japan's strength was at its peak and America's was mostly potential. Yamamoto believed the time had arrived to fight the great naval battle for the control of the Pacific that the Japanese had been dreaming about and practicing for for decades.

CHAPTER 6

WAR AT SEA

German strategist Karl Haushofer believed that he who controlled the heartland—central Europe—controlled the world. To a large extent the Germans and Soviets, the great land powers of Europe, believed him. But American strategist Alfred Thayer Mahan argued that he who controlled the seas controlled the world. The British, Americans, and Japanese, all maritime powers, believed him.

None of the countries, of course, put all its eggs in one basket: the Germans had a considerable fleet of warships, including battleships and submarines (U-boats); the British and Japanese had large armies; the Americans by 1944 had both a two-ocean fleet and a two-continent army. The truth was that Haushofer and Mahan were both right and wrong. World War II was a war fought on land, at sea, and in the air. Only on the eastern front, in the titanic struggles between the *Wehrmacht* and the Red Army, was sea power relatively unimportant (although still necessary to get Lend-Lease supplies to the Soviet Union); only in the central Pacific was land supremacy relatively unimportant (although still necessary to hold island bases). And on land and sea, air power was critical. But the British and Americans could neither mount nor support land and air operations in the Mediterranean, in Europe, and in the Pacific without control of the sea. So for them, sea power came first. How to achieve it?

Going into the war, the admirals and political leaders who were veterans of World War I had Jutland—the greatest naval battle in history—on their minds. They wanted battleships, the bigger the better. But only once in the war did these behemoths hurl their 12-, 14-, and 16-inch shells at each other. The fighting ship that was responsible for keeping the main battle fleets out of sight of one another was the aircraft carrier. It brought a whole new

British seamen use steam jets to clear ice from the anchor chains and winches on the HMS *Scylla* in the northern Atlantic, February 1943. The conditions under which the Battle of the Atlantic was fought were brutal. During the long winter nights so far north, weather could be as dangerous as the enemy.

BATTLE of the ATLANTIC
1939-43

Allied and Allied-controlled nations
Axis nations   Axis occupied
Vichy France and Vichy-controlled colonies
nonbelligerent nations
■ U.S. bases leased from Great Britain 1940
□ Allied bases
■ German U-boat bases
→ typical convoy routes

Sinking of Allied merchant ships by U-boats:
(each symbol represents 10 ships)
September 1939-December 1941
December 1941-May 1943

0   400   800

GREENLAND
U.S. Protectorate
1941   • Angmag

Godthaab •

Davis Strait

Ivigtut •   • Narsarssauk
Julianehaab □
Cape Farewell

Goose Bay □

LABRADOR

CANADA   transatlantic route

Quebec •   NEWFOUNDLAND • Gander
                        Argentia ■ • St. John's
Montreal •   Sydney •
            Halifax □

Portland •

Boston •
    • New York

UNITED STATES
        Philadelphia •
        Washington •

        Norfolk •
        Cape Hatteras

        Wilmington •
        Charleston •
        Savannah •   Atlantic Ocean
                Jacksonville •
    Mobile
New • • Pensacola
Orleans •
    • Tampa   The Bahamas

Houston   Port
•   Arthur •
Galveston •

        Gulf of Mexico   • Miami
                    Key West •
                        • Great Exhuma I.
        Havana •
MEXICO   CUBA
                Guantanamo Bay □
            Galleon   DOM. PUERTO
            Harbor   HAITI REP. RICO
    BR.   JAMAICA ■   San Juan □   □Virgin Is.
HONDURAS   Antigua
    HONDURAS   Guadeloupe ■ joined Allies 1942
GUATEMALA   Martinique
EL SALVADOR   *Caribbean Sea*   St. Lucia■ joined Allies 1942
    NICARAGUA   Aruba
                        Trinidad ■
COSTA RICA   VENEZUELA
    Panama Canal □   Georgetown
PANAMA   BR. GUIANA
            joined Allies 1942   FRENCH GUIANA
COLOMBIA   DUTCH   joined Allies 1942
                GUIANA
                US occupied 1941

ECUADOR   □Belem
                        to Natal, Middle East

PERU   BRAZIL

15°

0°

15°

    BOLIVIA

U.S.   BRITISH
STRATEGIC   STRATEGIC
ZONE   ZONE

90°   75°

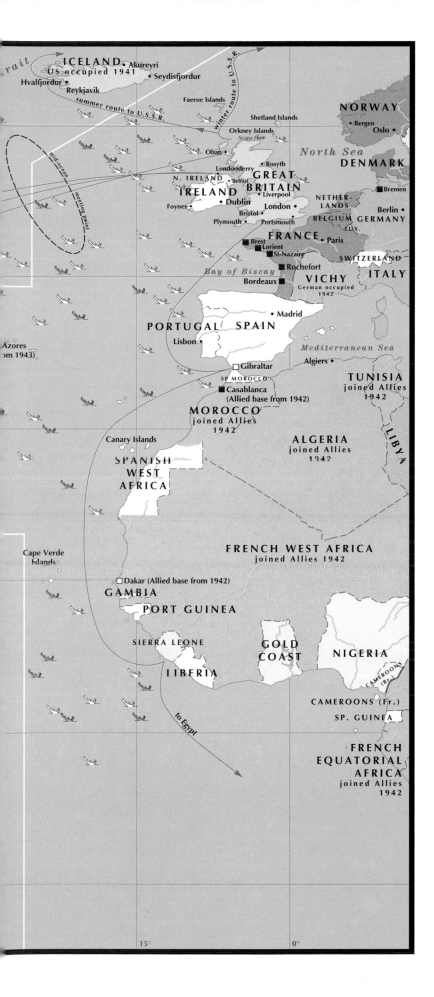

The North Atlantic was the scene of the longest, most crucial battle of the war. All hopes for an Allied victory over Nazi Germany depended on Britain; the air offensive would be mounted from there, and so would the second front. But Britain depended on supply from the sea. The three-thousand-mile-long shipping lanes from North America were her lifeline. Cut that lifeline, Hitler said, and Britain would soon be starved into surrendering.

For a long time it looked as though Hitler might succeed in his mission. It was not until well into 1943 that the crisis passed. But by then, millions of tons of vital goods, thousands of ships, and many thousands of brave men had vanished into the icy depths of the Atlantic. The map at left shows the general pattern of those sinkings. What it does not show, of course, is the way men died at sea, or the hours upon hours of terrible boredom, the strain and cold and unbelievable fatigue they endured—on both sides.

A German U-boat like the one shown here under construction at the Dachsmag Submarine Factory, in Bremen, Germany, could fire a spread of six torpedoes from its bow. From 1939 through 1944, this shark-like image was the terror of Neptune's world. Of all Hitler's "secret weapons," this was the one that had the potential to win the war. But he never built enough of them.

dimension to war at sea. Under the sea, the weapon that almost had been decisive in World War I, the submarine, was much improved and more deadly. Together, the carriers and the submarines dominated the war.

When Hitler began his onslaught in 1939, he reckoned that sea power was not a crucial military matter. Unlike the favored Luftwaffe, the German Navy was ill prepared. Not even Germany's redoubtable U-boat fleet was ready for a long campaign. But it was the sea—the narrow English Channel—that inevitably thwarted Hitler's ambitions for total domination of Europe and led him to turn his armies eastward into the disastrous Soviet snows. In North Africa, where Rommel almost broke the British on the verges of the Nile, failure to control the Mediterranean narrows cost the Germans still another important triumph. And ultimately, from across the seas, came a huge U.S. armada. As time passed, even the U-boats began to lose their efficacy.

Japan made no such basic miscalculation. As a sea people, the Japanese were instinctively aware of the maritime key to victory, and they boasted a massive fleet that included the world's two largest battleships, the 72,908-ton *Yamato* and the *Musashi*. The flaw in Tokyo's thinking was the belief that an initial advantage attained at Pearl Harbor would gain sufficient time to insure an impregnable economic and military position, and that this in turn could ward off eventual counterattack. As General Marshall reported in 1945, such assumptions proved erroneous because "the Japanese had reckoned without the shipyards of America and the fighting tradition of the United States Navy."

In 1939, when the conflict started, the world was accustomed to regarding Britain as the great maritime power, but the Royal Navy was no longer that Queen of the Seas that had dominated the nineteenth century. Its command had gradually succumbed to a hierarchy of class and was more preoccupied with tradition than with technology, despite admirable equipment made available by British scientists. Its tactics often were outdated. And the Royal Navy was not sufficiently strong for the immense combination of duties it had to face.

Had the Germans produced a rational and consistent strategy, they might have capitalized upon British weakness, but Hitler began full-scale naval preparations only in 1939. Admiral Erich Raeder, commander in chief of Hitler's Navy, had hoped there would be no conflict before 1942, by which date he planned to have ready a prodigious fleet that would include 250 U-boats, 13 battleships, and 4 aircraft carriers. When the Führer precipitated war, Raeder was forced to abandon this program and concentrate on the immediate construction of submarines.

Because the British were spread so thin and because the German fleet was inadequate, the naval potential of Italy and France assumed heightened importance. The Italians had fast ships but showed more dash in maneuvers than in battle. They were never able to control the eastern Mediterranean, even when British power was at its ebb. Had the Axis gained the use of the French Navy, however, the balance might have been dangerously turned. Its main strength lay in Toulon, with substantial forces also anchored at the Mers-el-Kebir base of Oran in Algeria. On July 3, 1940, unwilling to risk the possibility that Hitler might force the French Navy to turn over the ships to

him, the British sent an ultimatum to the Oran flotilla. When the French commander failed to respond within six hours, the British then attacked and seriously damaged three French battleships, a seaplane carrier, and two destroyers.

The Oran battle between the vessels of Britain and France was a difficult and heartrending affair (more than a thousand French sailors were killed), but it was made necessary by British determination to retain the upper hand at sea. Inflammatory Nazi propaganda sought to persuade the French to join the campaign against Britain. Nevertheless, as Churchill later recalled in his history of the war: "The genius of France enabled her people to comprehend the whole significance of Oran, and in her agony to draw new hope and strength from this additional bitter pang. General de Gaulle, whom I did not consult beforehand, was magnificent in his demeanour, and France liberated and restored has ratified his conduct."

The first dramatic confrontations of the war at sea were between conventional surface vessels. The earliest of these was the hunting down of the *Graf Spee*, third and last of those German pocket battleships so neatly designed to get around the regulations of the Versailles Treaty: fast, light, heavily gunned. Like the U-boats, its purpose was not to challenge the British battle fleet but rather to engage in commerce raiding, always the strategy of the nation with inferior fighting ships. When hostilities started, *Graf Spee* dashed for the South Atlantic to prey on Allied shipping and soon sank nine cargo vessels off the coast of Latin America.

The French battleship *Bretagne* is struck when the Mers-el-Kebir base of Oran, Algeria, is attacked by the British Royal Navy, July 3, 1940. The last time British ships fired on French ships was at the Battle of Trafalgar in 1805.

On December 13, 1939, the *Graf Spee* appeared near Uruguay, where it was surprised by three British cruisers, *Exeter*, *Achilles*, and *Ajax*. For fourteen hours the ships pounded away at one another. Then the *Graf Spee* turned away to seek haven in Montevideo. It was summarily ordered out by the neutral Uruguayans. On December 17, the *Graf Spee* blew itself up in the broad River Plate while three hundred thousand spectators lined the shore to watch. Captain Hans Langsdorff, a veteran of Jutland, was interned in Argentina with his crew. Three days later, he draped around him the old German Imperial Navy flag, ignoring Hitler's swastika, and shot himself dead.

A second great sea encounter came in the spring of 1941, when the German battleship *Bismarck*, accompanied by the cruiser *Prinz Eugen*, sailed from occupied Poland through the British blockade, intent on sinking as much tonnage as possible on the cold, gray North Atlantic. Six U-boats were assigned to help the mighty surface raider. The British first spotted the *Bismarck* when it was refueling at Bergen, Norway, on May 21 and began to mark its passage through fog and clouds. Three days later, in clear weather, the powerful *Hood* and *Prince of Wales* found their enemy and opened fire. The *Hood* was sunk by a formidable salvo; the *Prince of Wales*, badly damaged, limped

The German battleship *Graf Spee* burns after being scuttled on December 17, 1939, off Montevideo, Uruguay. This great British victory, so in keeping with the traditions of the Royal Navy, marked the beginning of the end of the German attempt to use surface raiders to cut enemy commerce.

away. But the *Bismarck,* also seriously wounded and leaving a steady oil trail, turned back, at reduced speed, to seek haven at Saint-Nazaire in occupied France.

Without air cover, the *Bismarck* was a toothless tiger. On the morning of May 26, a Royal Air Force flying boat spotted the great ship, still seven hundred miles from the French coast, much too far out for land-based airplanes to reach. The British sent carrier-based torpedo planes to delay its escape. *Bismarck* was struck twice, once in the rudder. The next morning a squadron of British ships encircled their victim like yapping hounds and opened concentrated fire. They were unable to pierce the *Bismarck*'s armored deck or destroy its engines, but one by one they smashed the machinery of its turrets. Finally, unable to proceed, the German captain scuttled. In a strategic sense this was a British naval triumph because Hitler lost his greatest and irreplaceable battleship. But in the process Britain also lost the *Hood* and suffered damage to two other battleships, a destroyer, and many planes. Furthermore, much of the British fleet had been diverted from important Mediterranean assignments in order to encompass the elusive *Bismarck*'s

On May 24, 1941, just south of the Denmark Strait, the German battleship *Bismarck*—the fastest in the world at that time—attacks the HMS *Hood.* The *Bismarck*'s eight 15-inch guns had a range of 25,000 yards. The ship fired a shell that penetrated to the *Hood*'s magazines.

The *Hood* goes down in Somitz Westerholt's painting *The* Bismarck *Sinking the* Hood. She took 1,338 crewmen to their deaths; there were but three survivors. But the end to German commerce raiding hopes came three days later, when the relentless British pursuit finally sent *Bismarck* to the bottom.

end, and this weakened the defense of Crete at the moment of its invasion on June 1. The victory proved to be an expensive one.

Second only in naval importance to the home fleet's task of supplying and guarding the United Kingdom itself was Britain's Mediterranean role. The sea served as a lifeline to British possessions in the Middle East, to Suez and the route to India, and to the Army of the Nile, which had been concentrated in Egypt in 1939. From Gibraltar to Malta and on to Alexandria, their bases were now directly menaced. German land-based air power denied the Mediterranean to British convoys; to supply its Middle East forces, Britain sent convoys by the long and costly route around the Cape of Good Hope. The Royal Navy was further weakened during the Battle of Crete and the consequent need to evacuate British and Greek troops when that island

The British finally sink the elusive *Bismarck* on May 26, 1941, some seven hundred of miles west of the French port of Brest (below). Around 1100 hours, May 27, 1941, a British ship picks up survivors from the *Bismarck* (left), which had gone down at 1036 hours. There were 110 survivors from a crew of some 1,900.

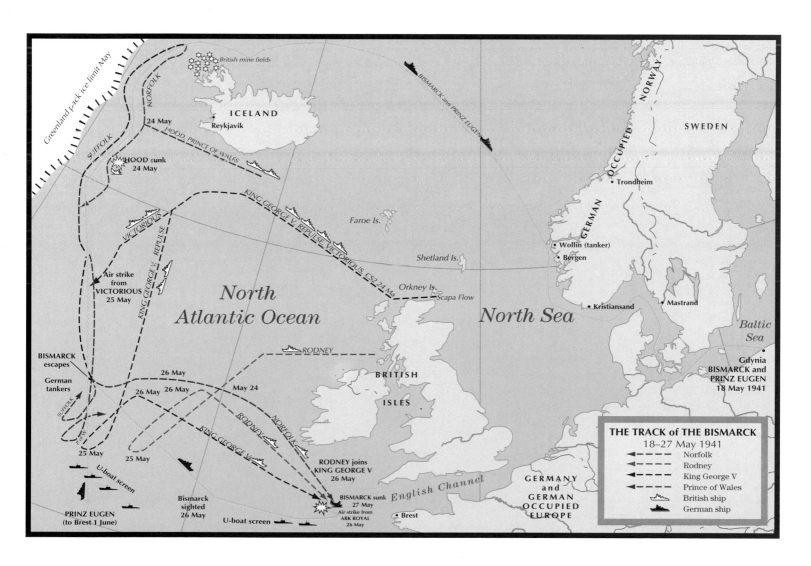

THE TRACK of THE BISMARCK
18–27 May 1941

◄─ ─ ─	Norfolk
◄─ ─ ─	Rodney
◄─ ─ ─	King George V
◄─ ─ ─	Prince of Wales
🚢	British ship
🚢	German ship

United States Army infantrymen arrive in Reykjavik, Iceland, in the fall of 1941. Roosevelt had sent them there to relieve British troops and take over defense of the island, while the British went off to North Africa to fight. In the Atlantic by that fall, America was fully involved in the war against Germany and was neutral in name only.

fell. But the British were able to hold on in Malta, and, although the island suffered terribly, planes from its airstrip continued to hamper the flow of supplies from southern Italy to Rommel's Afrika Korps in the desert.

The Mediterranean naval war was a desperate and hemmed-in affair in which land-based aircraft played an increasingly prominent role. But at least it had the advantage of being fought in an agreeable arena. When men jumped from their sinking ships, they stood a chance of surviving. The war in the Atlantic was another story. There a dreary, lengthy, and far more strategically vital battle on a much bigger scale was fought to decide whether Britain would survive and become the marshaling point and base for the ultimate European assault. Britain was the node between triumph and disaster, and its safety, as it had for centuries past, relied on its ships.

The Battle of the Atlantic endured through two stages. In the first, before

Pearl Harbor, Britain—with increasing United States support—fought to keep supply lines open against the savage and expert U-boat hunters and to track down any German surface vessels that ventured out to open water. During the latter part of this stage, U.S. warships, violating all technical definitions of neutrality, helped to escort convoys across the northern arc from Newfoundland to the Irish Sea. U.S. vessels were torpedoed, and American lives were lost. The situation had come about by degrees as Roosevelt moved carefully to aid Britain without arousing the nation's isolationist sentiment. There had been the destroyers-for-bases agreement, and then Lend-Lease, and in July of 1941 the sending of U.S. troops to Iceland.

Then, in a step barely short of war, U.S. naval units went on convoy duty. Roosevelt and Churchill had divided the Atlantic between them. The ocean west of Iceland was the American defense zone, and through its waters the U.S. Navy shepherded the convoys; east of the line the Royal Navy was responsible. On September 4 the destroyer USS *Greer* exchanged torpedoes for depth charges with a submarine; both vessels were unharmed, but Roosevelt ordered the navy to shoot on sight German warships in the west Atlantic. In mid-October, the *Kearny* was torpedoed, with eleven killed, but did

In 1941, President Roosevelt tore a map from *National Geographic* and drew a line to show how Britain and the United States should divide Atlantic defense. Harry Hopkins carried the map to Churchill, who approved. Roosevelt thereupon put the U.S. Navy into the Battle of the Atlantic.

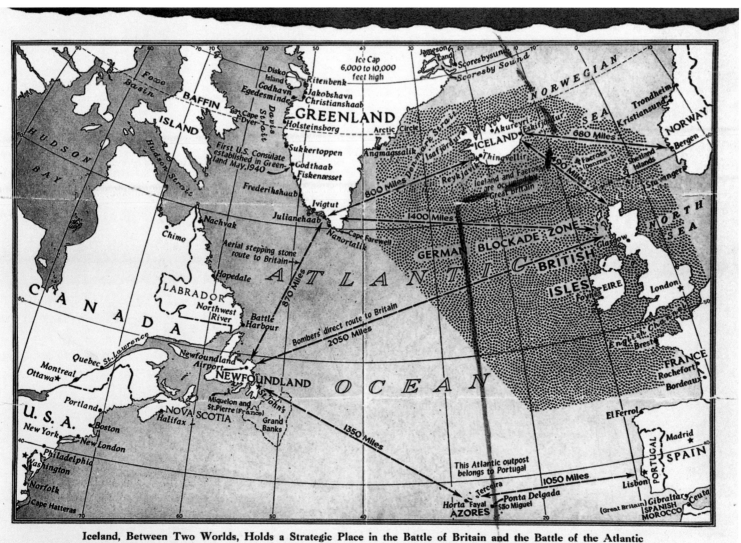

Iceland, Between Two Worlds, Holds a Strategic Place in the Battle of Britain and the Battle of the Atlantic

not sink, and just after dawn on October 31 the first United States warship was sunk: the *Reuben James*. A trim but obsolete U.S. destroyer, "the Rube" was helping out the shorthanded British in the protection of a convoy west of Ireland when its direction finder locked on U-boat signals. Moments later, it was hit by a torpedo. The magazine exploded, and the ship was blown in two. One hundred fifteen men, including the captain and all the officers, were lost. Robert E. Sherwood, a Roosevelt adviser, observed that the public seemed more interested in the Army–Notre Dame football game. Roosevelt hardly needed to hide the secret war from a public so indifferent to world events.

With the fall of France in June 1940, Germany became a power in the Atlantic. Suddenly, Hitler had a 2,500-mile coastline to launch his U-boats from, and his reach into the Atlantic had been extended some 450 miles. Now even his smallest 250-ton subs could prowl the Atlantic shipping lanes.

In the fall of 1941, three American destroyers engaged German submarines. The *Greer* exchanged torpedoes with a submarine; the *Kearny* (below) was torpedoed with eleven killed but did not sink, and the *Reuben James* was hit and sank at once.

German submarine pens, shown here under construction on the west coast of France in March 1942, gave the U-boats easy access to the open Atlantic; these pens were about the toughest target in the war. The British and later the Americans bombed them over and over, without ever inflicting serious damage.

All that summer and fall, while Britain fought for its life against the Luftwaffe, the U-boats had their best hunting season of the whole war. The threat of invasion kept British destroyer forces close to home; convoys went out virtually without escort. As a result, between July and October of 1940, the U-boats sank 217 ships. On average, each U-boat sank eight ships per month. German submariners would later call this the "Happy Time." But the number of U-boats in operation was relatively small, and despite the urging of his top naval commander, Erich Raeder, Hitler had refused to step up submarine production. The subs he had were doing very well, and there was still hope that Britain might come to its senses and make peace. It was one of Hitler's crucial mistakes. Although he had lifted all restrictions on submarine production in July 1940, it was not until the following summer that the building program was really under way.

By then, the British had worked out more effective defenses, especially in code-breaking. The Ultra enabled them to read Admiral Karl Dönitz's orders to his captains at sea and gave the British a great advantage, but one that was lost for the first few days of each month, following Germany's change in the Enigma settings. But the Germans were also breaking Royal Navy codes. The result was a direct correlation between how the battle was going—how many

A German skipper (right) looks through the periscope of his ship. Nearly 90 percent of the German submariners perished in the war, but they exacted a toll. Among the hundreds of Allied vessels sunk by U-boats in 1941 and 1942 was the British armed merchant cruiser HMS *Rajputa* (below). Crippled by two torpedoes, it slips beneath the water.

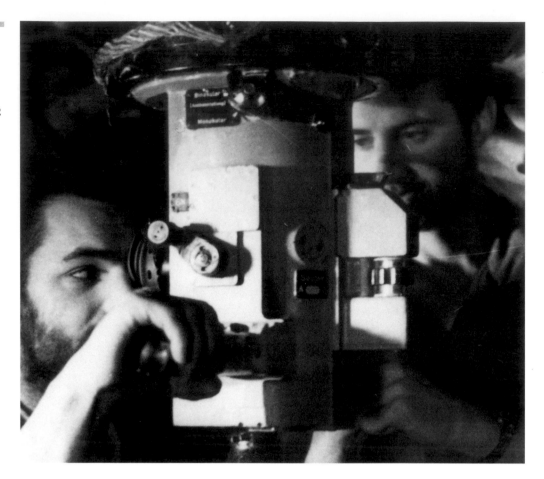

This Navy seaman's destroyer, USS *Lansdale,* was sunk by German bombers off the coast of North Africa. The seaman was rescued by the Coast Guard. Medical personnel are scraping a thick coating of oil from his body.

subs lost, how many cargo vessels, how many destroyers—and who had most recently broken the other guy's code. Through 1941 first one side, then the other, was winning the Battle of the Atlantic.

In early 1942, the Battle of the Atlantic came to America's shores, where the German skippers found an inexcusably unprepared U.S. Navy and an abundance of fat targets—many of them oil tankers sailing along the Gulf and Atlantic coastlines of North America, easy marks at night thanks to the lights on shore. This was a second "Happy Time" for the U-boats.

Eastern ports such as New York, Boston, and Norfolk had to be protected with mines, nets, and booms. Coastal convoys were established, blackouts ordered, and ship radios restricted after U-boat packs, operating initially in northern waters off Newfoundland and then moving south to warmer bases in the Caribbean, achieved astonishing initial successes. Insofar as the Americans had given any thought to the possibility of combat operations on their shores, they had thought of the Pacific Coast. The surprise achieved by the German U-boats in early 1942 was almost as great and costly as Pearl Harbor. In the first four months of 1942, eighty-seven ships went to the bottom off the Atlantic Coast. When the U.S. Navy finally got convoys organized along the Atlantic line, the German subs moved into the Gulf, where they sank another forty-one ships.

Eventually the Americans won this phase of the Battle of the Atlantic by building enough destroyers and escorts to make convoys possible everywhere and by putting together an air-sea team to search for and destroy U-boats. Allied merchant ship production was so great that the available

Ice covers a twenty-inch signal projector on board the cruiser HMS *Sheffield*. The convoy was on its way to the Soviet Union via the northern route of the Arctic Sea, bringing desperately needed supplies to the Red Army.

U-boats could not sink them fast enough. The big, ungainly PBY naval aircraft was a mainstay in the effort.

In the first seven months of 1942, German submarines sank an appalling total of 681 Allied ships, at small cost. This was the year in which Admiral Dönitz devised his wolf-pack tactics. A number of U-boats would lay in wait across the shipping lanes; the first to locate a convoy gave the signal, and all closed in for the kill. Beset from all sides, its protecting escorts unable to fend off so many simultaneous attacks, a convoy thus struck suffered heavy losses.

Nevertheless, as U.S. radar improved and U.S. planes came increasingly into play, the ratio changed to Germany's disadvantage. Long-range aircraft operating from Newfoundland, Northern Ireland, and Iceland hunted down enemy raiders and blasted them into the depths. As the Germans lost their best submarine commanders, replacements proved less expert and less resolute. By late spring 1943, Dönitz was forced to conclude: "Losses, even heavy losses, must be borne when they are accompanied by corresponding sinkings. But in May in the Atlantic the destruction of every 10,000 tons was paid for by the loss of one U-boat. . . . The losses have therefore reached an unbearable height." They had indeed; by mid-1943 nearly three-quarters of the original submarine force had perished at sea. Churchill proudly reported to the House of Commons that, at sea, June 1943 "was the best month from every point of view we have ever known in the whole forty-six months of the war." German submarine losses were at 80 percent.

Moreover, Roosevelt and Churchill, honoring their promises to Stalin, managed to start convoying vast amounts of matériel along the so-called Murmansk Run, a dangerous route from Scotland, north of Nazi-occupied Norway, and on to the northern Soviet ports of Murmansk and Archangel.

Nowhere was the Battle of the Atlantic worse than on the Murmansk Run. The most direct route between Britain and the Soviet Union was by convoy around the northern tip of Norway to Murmansk. But to get there, convoys had to run a gauntlet of U-boats, surface raiders, and aircraft based in Norway as well as appalling seas and cold. During the period June 1941 to September 1943, more than a fifth of all ships making the Murmansk Run went down. Soviet convoy PQ 17, sailing from Iceland to northern Soviet Union in July 1942, lost twenty-four of thirty-five ships. PQ 17, sailing in September, lost ten of its thirty-nine merchant ships, but its destroyer escorts managed to shoot down forty-one enemy aircraft and sink three U-boats.

The Atlantic Battle was a dirty, cold, grueling business. Nerves were constantly on edge, whether in the quivering, claustrophobic submarines, dodging among depth bombs, or aboard the destroyers zigzagging overhead, always on the alert for telltale sonar signals. Vessels were generally sunk by submarine shell fire if they had not been finished off by the first torpedo salvos, and at times during the early part of the Atlantic Battle, before the Allies had perfected their defenses, U-boats even attacked from the surface. In those days, when crews escaped in lifeboats, they were sometimes overtaken, questioned on their destinations and cargoes, offered provisions and cigarettes, and told with bluff bonhomie to send the bill for damages to Roosevelt or Churchill. But such good cheer was soon to disappear. Sometimes U-boat crews machine-gunned survivors as they tried to swim through viscous oil slicks, ducking to escape the searing flames, or as they floundered about, clinging to rafts or life preservers. The Battle of the Atlantic became brutal and merciless.

Losses had to be replaced, and when they were the numbers had to be doubled, then doubled again, in ships of war and cargo ships. Shipyards all over the world worked around the clock, turning out ships in record numbers. But it was in the United States that the greatest burst of activity took place.

In July 1940, Congress had passed a "Two-Ocean Navy" bill, designed to

The American public was told to avoid loose talk that could give information to the enemy; the poster above warned of what careless gossip could lead to. In another effort to keep the public aware of the gravity of the war, the poster below advises the public on the blackouts in the coastal towns of the Atlantic.

A British seaman (left) manages to take a catnap between submarine alerts. The Germans were not the only enemy on the high seas; bad weather was a dangerous threat as well. High winds make for a difficult travel on the American destroyer on patrol in the North Altantic (below) and officers on the bridge of the HMS *Sheffield* (right), battling a hurricane-force storm, look out on fifty-foot waves. The high seas stove in the starboard whaler, and the depth charge smoke floats and Carley rafts went overboard. After three days the storm abated with surprising suddenness, and the *Sheffield* was able to get to port for repairs.

The first months of 1942 were the "Happy Time" for Admiral Karl Dönitz (above) and his crews, as they caught the Americans woefully unprepared. A number of tankers were lost: (right, top to bottom) the tanker *Dixie Arrow* falls victim to a U-boat off Cape Hattaras, March 26, 1942; the tanker *R. P. Roser* gushes smoke and flames off the Atlantic Coast, February 27, 1942; the tanker *Bensen* burns off the Gulf Coast after being hit, early 1942; the tanker *Republic* founders after being torpedoed off the Atlantic Coast, March 1, 1942.

Shipbuilders work day and night at the Oregon Shipyard in Portland, Oregon. American production techniques were the wonder of the world. Neither Hitler nor Tojo had the slightest idea of what American industry was capable of. Despite being ranked almost at the bottom in military power among the nations of the world in 1939, the United States by 1945 had more weapons and firepower than the rest of the world put together.

make the U.S. fleet all-powerful by 1944. The country was far from that goal in early 1942, yet productive capacity was able to keep well ahead of the initial losses. Shipyards began turning out a destroyer in five months instead of twelve. Big carriers were launched within fifteen months instead of three years. By the end of World War II, despite heavy casualties, the United States had 6 more battleships, 21 more aircraft carriers, 70 more escort carriers, and 127 more submarines than in 1941. By 1945 an astonishing one-half of all the ships afloat in the world had been built in the United States.

At Mare Island shipyard in California, the longest assembly line in the United States was established. More than twelve hundred miles inland, in Denver, Colorado, vessels were constructed in sections and sent by rail to the sea. Prefabricated landing craft were shipped in pieces and assembled abroad for attacks on distant shores. Andrew Higgins in New Orleans developed an amphibious assault boat that was used on almost every invasion beach from Guadalcanal to Normandy. His workforce numbered 800 in 1940; in 1944 it reached 30,000. He built the Higgins Boats at assembly lines under canvas cover. In 1939 there wasn't even a blueprint of the boat; by 1944 some 20,000 had been built and sent to war.

In the course of the war, the Allies lost 22 million tons of shipping (slightly more than 5,000 ships). But the Americans alone built 34 million tons of new shipping (5,400 cargo ships); the Allied total was 43 million tons. This was production such as the world had never seen.

But even in America it took time to build, and that time had to be bought for the shipyards by warships already afloat in the Pacific. There were not many of them in early 1942 when General MacArthur began building a base at the little town of Port Moresby on New Guinea. The Japanese had tried to take Port Moresby by land, but New Guinea's treacherous mountains seemed impassable. Therefore they decided to attack by water and sent an invasion fleet down past the Solomon Islands and into the Coral Sea. To insure success, they ordered in a carrier force commanded by Vice Admiral Shigeyoshi Inouye.

Rear Admiral Frank Fletcher, commanding a combined fleet of Australian and U.S. Navy vessels, intercepted the Japanese fleet in the Coral Sea. Fletcher's fleet included the two big flattops *Yorktown* and *Lexington*. Almost as if blindfolded, the two admirals groped for each other with scout planes. The result was the first of those famous sea-air confrontations that became a phenomenon peculiar to the Pacific between 1942 and 1945, in which the fleets at battle never saw one another. On May 7 and 8, 1942, the planes of each force flew through fog and mist to attack their enemy's ships. U.S. planes sank the light carrier *Shoho* in minutes ("Scratch one flattop!" the flight commander radioed back to the *Lexington*) and an enemy destroyer. American losses were a destroyer, an oiler, and, most grievous of all, the *Lexington*, which was so badly damaged it had to be sunk after the battle. Although losses were roughly equal, Coral Sea was an important strategic victory for the Allies because the invasion force was turned back.

Goaded by the Doolittle raid, Admiral Yamamoto convinced his colleagues at Imperial Headquarters that a single major naval engagement would prove to be a decisive course for the rest of the war. He selected the

The carrier USS *Lexington* burns after the Battle of Coral Sea on May 8, 1942 (above). After she was hit by two torpedoes and three bombs, fires below deck got out of control and she had to be abandoned. Some 2,700 seamen on the ship were rescued by accompanying destroyers (left), only 216 were lost. After *"Lex"* was abandoned, the destroyer *Phelps* fired two torpedoes into her to sink the gallant lady. She was the first American carrier sunk in the war.

LANDING CRAFT

Specialized landing craft capable of a variety of functions were new to World War II and limited exclusively to the British and Americans. Hitler had none; it was one of the reasons he could not cross the English Channel in the summer of 1940.

The U.S. Navy wasn't much interested in landing craft; aircraft carriers and battleships were more their thing. But in 1939, the U.S. Marines, anticipating island battles in the Pacific, forced the U.S. Navy to sponsor a competition. What the Marine Corps was looking for was a boat that could take a rifle platoon off troop transports straight onto the beach. Andrew Higgins, a small-boat builder in New Orleans, had the perfect answer. He designed a flat-bottomed boat 36 feet long and 10 1/2 feet wide, propelled by a diesel engine. It could carry a platoon or a squad and a jeep. The ramp was metal but the sides and square stern were plywood. Even in a moderate sea it would bounce and shake while swells broke over the ramp and sides. It was called Landing Craft Vehicle and Personnel (LCVP) by the services; the "Higgins Boat" by the marines and GIs.

The massive jaws of an LST open to discharge its cargo, here onto a low-riding ferry called a Rhino, for the last push onto the beach. Very quickly, LST skippers figured out that they could run right to the waterline during low tides, disgorge directly onto land, and float off on the next high tide.

Higgins was as much a genius at mass production as he was at design. His factory began with 80 employees in 1940 and swelled to 30,000 workers by 1944. He produced 20,000 LCVPs, which carried fighting men ashore in the Pacific, North Africa, Sicily, Italy, and Normandy. Eisenhower said of Higgins, "He is the man who won the war for us."

Higgins also built Landing Craft Tanks (LCTs), Landing Ship Tanks (LSTs), Patrol Boats (PTs), and others. The LCT and LST were of British design; when the United States entered the war, it took on the task of all LST and most LCT production, in the process considerably improving the designs.

The LCT (in U.S. Navy parlance, a "ship" was more than 200 feet in long, while a "craft" less than that) was a flat-bottomed craft 110 feet long, capable of carrying from four to eight tanks (eventually there were four types of LCTs) across relatively wide bodies of water, such as the English Channel, even in rough seas, and discharging its cargo over a ramp.

The LST was a big ship, as big as a light cruiser, 327 feet long, displacing 4,000 tons, but it was flat bottomed and thus hard to control in any kind of sea. It was agonizingly slow; the crews said LST stood for "Long, Slow Target." But it was capable of crossing the ocean, then grounding at the beach, and discharging tanks or trucks; when it beached, two bow doors opened to the sides and a ramp was lowered to allow the vehicles to drive ashore. It could carry dozens of tanks and trucks in its cavernous hold, with Higgins Boats on its deck.

The Landing Craft, Infantry (LCI) was a sea-going troop-landing craft of 160 feet in length capable of carrying a reinforced company of infantry—nearly 200 men—and discharging them down ramps on each side of the bow.

Taken together, these and other craft made it possible for the Allies to exploit their control of the seas to the maximum. Their enemies never knew where to expect them; any open beach was a potential target. Thus Hitler had to build his Atlantic Wall all the way from the north German ports to Brittany, because the Allies did not have to cross the Channel at its narrowest point.

Hitler assumed the Allies would need port facilities immediately on landing, so he concentrated his defenses around the ports. The Allies tended to agree on the need for ports. Churchill put a tremendous national effort into building two experimental artificial harbors to meet the need. They were towed across the Channel and set up off the invasion beaches. As experiments, the harbors were moderately successful (the American one was destroyed by a storm on June 19; the British one was badly damaged but repaired and soon functioning again). But as it turned out, their contribution to the total tonnage unloaded over the Normandy beaches was only about 15 percent.

It was the LSTs, supported by a myriad specialized landing craft, that did the most carrying and unloading. It was a hodgepodge fleet: a British crew of old salts on a Higgins Boat in the Canadian Navy taking GIs ashore at Utah Beach; LSTs commanded by a twenty-two-year-old American lieutenant carrying British troops to Gold Beach; LSTs at every beach, their great jaws yawning open, disgorging tanks and trucks and jeeps and bulldozers and big cannons and small guns and mountains of cases of rations and ammunition, thousands of jerry cans, crates of radios and telephones, typewriters and forms and all else that men at war required.

The LSTs came onto the beaches to supply the fighting divisions with their needs. The LST was as critical to the battle in northwest Europe as to the Pacific battles. It was far more valuable to the Allies than Hitler's secret weapon, revealed a week after D-Day Normandy, the V-1. Without the LST and its little cousin, the LCVP, the Allies could not have gotten ashore on any Pacific Island or European beach.

GIs climb from an LCI into a Higgins Boat (LCVP) for the run onto shore at Normandy, France (above). The armada of LCIs stretches to the horizon under its umbrella of barrage ballons. An LCT unloads troops onto Normandy Beach (below).

U.S. planes on the prowl for the Japanese fleet fly over Midway Island on June 4, 1942 (opposite). These are Douglas Devastators (TBD-1), slow, antiquated, and difficult to maneuver. Three squadrons made courageous but fruitless attacks on the Japanese carrier force, taking heavy losses. But in the end the battle was won thanks to some very good luck, the skill of American pilots, and bold leadership from the U.S. Navy high command.

little-known island of Midway, situated some one thousand miles northwest of Honolulu, as the focal point for the attack and marshaled an armada of more than a hundred warships plus transport and supply vessels to deal the knockout blow. Yamamoto reasoned that the capture of Midway would mean Japanese penetration of Hawaiian waters, giving Japan a base in the eastern Pacific from which to harry and shake the American people. Even more, he lusted for the great naval battle he had been preparing for all his adult life.

The force assigned to Midway was the most powerful in Japan's naval history. It included eight carriers and eleven battleships. Yamamoto himself took command of this combined fleet. Vice Admiral Chuichi Nagumo was given the vital carrier striking force. Yamamoto was relying once again on secrecy and surprise, but he was still unaware that the United States had broken the Japanese code.

Gathering together the huge fleet required extensive use of radio signals. The U.S. cryptanalysts in Hawaii were able to read some parts of many of those messages. They could tell that the Japanese were getting ready for their biggest strike of the war, but they couldn't tell where: to the north, in the Aleutians? in the central Pacific, at Midway? or once again into the Coral Sea? All the analysts knew was that the target was designated "AF." One analyst, certain that AF was Midway, used a secure telegraphic link between Hawaii and Midway to instruct the Midway people to send a radio message in clear saying the island was running short of fresh water. The following day a Japanese radio signal was broken; it said that AF was running short of fresh water. Thus Admiral Chester Nimitz in Honolulu knew of Yamamoto's intentions and began his countermeasures. Later he admitted: "Had we lacked early information of the Japanese movements, and had we been caught with carrier forces dispersed, . . . the Battle of Midway would have ended differently."

The Japanese thought it was merely a matter of bad luck that an American seaplane spotted the enormous fleet as it gathered up a convoy of assault troops from Saipan, some twenty-six hundred miles west of Midway. But Nimitz had ordered that sweeping searches be made, and two task forces under admirals Spruance and Fletcher were deployed to meet the armada. Their strength, even in carriers, was not equal to the Japanese; but they relied on the support of land-based planes from Midway itself and ultimately from Honolulu.

The fighting started June 4, 1942. Japanese planes swept off from their carriers to hit the little island target, and U.S. planes retaliated by seeking out the invasion force. For four days the fighting raged. Again, as in the Coral Sea, aircraft battered ships that were always too distant from each other to fire their customary broadsides. One group of fifteen U.S. torpedo bombers continued to press home their attack until all had been shot down by a curtain of anti-aircraft fire thrown up around the huge Japanese carriers. Only one man survived to tell the tale.

For a very brief time, it looked as though the Japanese had triumphed. Then, from 14,000 feet up, U.S. dive-bombers roared down on their targets, catching the Japanese carriers at their most vulnerable moment, when the flight decks were crowded with planes refueling for another strike. In a matter

of minutes those dive-bombers changed the course of the war which has come to be known as "the fatal five minutes." They sank three Japanese carriers (*Soryu*, *Kaga*, and *Akagi*), and the next morning a fourth (*Hiryu*). It was the planes that did all the fighting (Yamamoto's dozen battleships, held in reserve, never engaged).

Yamamoto finally decided to turn homeward before his entire force vanished. As it was, he had suffered a smashing defeat, losing four carriers and a heavy cruiser plus many damaged vessels. The Americans lost one carrier,

A Japanese heavy cruiser is on fire after an attack by U.S. planes off Midway Island. Japanese losses in the battle were steep: four aircraft carriers and one cruiser sunk, a cruiser and two destroyers badly damaged. The U.S. Navy lost the carrier *Yorktown*.

the *Yorktown*, one destroyer, and more than one hundred planes. But this was a small price to pay. The Japanese Navy had forced a showdown with superior strength, and it was decisively beaten. Instead of threatening Hawaii and the West Coast, Japan suddenly found itself up on the defensive for the first time.

From that historic instant, the U.S. counteroffensive began to gather force and to move relentlessly toward the home islands of Japan. Midway—

named so for being the Pacific's midpoint between Japan and the United States—was one of World War II's critical battles and one of history's greatest naval battles. The tiny atoll group was, indeed, properly named, for the contest marked a dividing line in strategy if not in time. Everything before Midway was an immense Japanese success, and everything afterward, a failure. At Midway the Rising Sun that had shone so suddenly and so ferociously over all Asia slowly began to set. The Japanese had suffered their first naval defeat in history. Their long, impressive sea offensive had ended.

Midway Island burns under attack from Japanese carrier-based planes. The Japanese strike leader reported that Midway needed another pounding, so the Japanese aircraft on board the carriers swapped torpedoes (used against U.S. carriers) for bombs. In the midst of the switch, with fuel lines all over the decks, the American dive-bombers swooped down on them.

CHAPTER 7

THE DESERT WAR

The war in North Africa, 1940–1943, was fought over a featureless desert, where the waves of sand sparkled in the sunlight like white caps at sea, and indeed the tactics employed in the great tank and infantry battles that were fought there resembled naval warfare more than any traditional land campaign. Away from the coast there were no roads. Ports were few and small on the southern coast of the Mediterranean, which made them critical, just as in a sea war. Tanks and trucks needed to refuel, like ships at sea. The tanks swept around their foes in long, looping encirclement maneuvers, threatening to get between the enemy and his supply depots. Places other than ports had no strategic significance; only the enemy force mattered. And the whole reason for the campaign was to protect one of the world's most important waterways, the Suez Canal. The canal was Britain's lifeline to India and the Far East, and it was in Egypt that the British made their biggest commitment of men and matériel after the fall of France.

When the war began, Britain had assembled in Egypt a force vaingloriously named the Army of the Nile, under the overall command of Sir Archibald Wavell, a one-eyed general who boasted diplomatic skill and strategic talents more lavishly admired by his contemporaries than by history. It was Wavell who planned the first success in the famous Western Desert campaign.

In September 1940, Marshal Rodolfo Graziani had penetrated Egypt at Sidi Barrâni, but the Western Desert campaign really began that December, when the vastly outnumbered British attacked the Italian Army and drove it into Libya. It was an unqualified British victory. While the Greeks were making mockery of Mussolini's invasion from Albania, Wavell took a series of Libyan citadels from the Duce's badly commanded African Army, penetrating

The German war artist Helmut Georg painted an armored column coming under fire from hidden enemy troops amidst the terrible heat and swirling dust of North Africa in the spring of 1941. The desert war is often compared to war at sea: vistas stretched for miles; there were few strategic spots, except for the ports along the Mediterranean coastline; movement was rapid, mobility great.

Italian POWs are herded to a British base after surrendering in December of 1940. More than 35,000 were captured that month. In January, another 55,000 surrendered, including the garrison at Tobruk.

deep into Cyrenaica and capturing enormous quantities of matériel and some 130,000 prisoners.

As a result of Italy's humiliations in Albania and Libya, Hitler was forced to spread his forces by dispatching aid. General Marshall later concluded that this overextension "subsequently became one of the principal factors in Germany's defeat." The Führer sent his paratroopers to stiffen the Italian Air Force. Then, in command of a German armored corps, he sent in Rommel.

Field Marshal Erwin Rommel was one of the great figures of the war. A brilliant tactician, he became the acknowledged master of armored warfare in a desert campaign (U.S. tankers in the Persian Gulf War of 1991 avidly studied his tactics and techniques). Rommel imposed his personality on the Afrika Korps and on his opponents, leading his units into combat from the turret of his tank, exploiting the slightest opening presented. His men idolized him, and, to the dismay of British officers, when the Tommies approved of or were delighted by something, they would say, "That's a Rommel!" Even Churchill said, "His ardor and daring inflicted grievous disasters upon us. . . . [He was] a great general."

Although Hitler only wanted Rommel to hold the line in the desert, Rommel opened his first offensive on March 24, 1941, a few weeks before Hitler overran the Balkans. The British hardly knew what hit them. Their lines had been thinned down to about half strength in order to send aid to Greece. In a matter of days they were outflanked, outfought, and chased clear back to Egypt, leaving an isolated British garrison sealed off in the Libyan port of Tobruk. From bases in Tripolitania and Sicily, the Luftwaffe

started to raid Alexandria, Port Said, and Suez where they intensively mined the canal, thus cutting off the main route to India and hampering Wavell's normal supply lines. But the improvised fortress of Tobruk held out on Rommel's flank. It was reinforced by General Sir Alan Cunningham of the newly named Eighth Army. (The overall commander for the Middle East was now General Sir Claude Auchinleck. In June, Churchill had decided that Wavell needed a rest from desert campaigning and had sent him to India.) All through the summer and autumn of 1941, coastal ships from Alexandria scurried along the dangerous North African shore to strengthen Tobruk.

During the fourteen months following Rommel's arrival in Libya, the Desert War was a seesaw affair. There were lengthy advances and retreats but no crucial victory in what the Tommies called, "miles and miles and bloody miles of absolutely damn all." Soldiers learned to navigate like sailors, reckoning the featureless spaces by map, compass, speedometer, and stars. At night, formations of each side would encamp, unsure just where the other's hull-down tanks lay. Acres of flatness were marked by countless tracks left by the treads and tires of past battles, littered with piles of Jerry cans and discarded tins of food swarming with insects. Drivers sought to steer to the windward of each other and thus escape the dust. From desert boots to goggles, they were generally covered by a beige coating compounded of sand, dust, and sweat. Supply services were hard pressed to provide enough water for the thirsty vehicles and men.

From the start of this extraordinary campaign, the naval-minded British realized the critical importance of Malta to the desert fighting. They kept the

Italian tanks—seen here retreating in Libya—were no match for the heavier British Crusader tanks. The Italians, ill-equipped, ill-trained, and poorly led, had little interest in Mussolini's ambitions. Like Mussolini himself, the Italian Army hid genuine incompetence behind a belligerent false front.

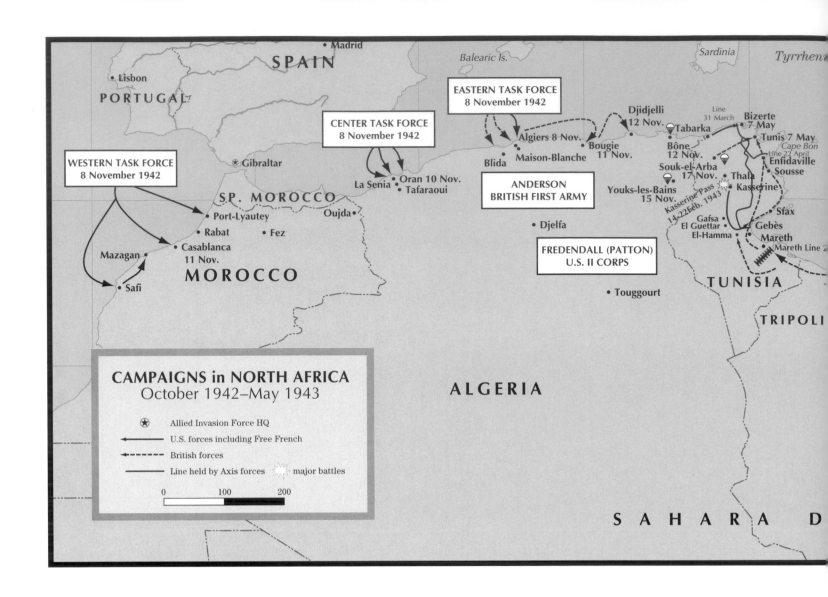

CAMPAIGNS in NORTH AFRICA
October 1942–May 1943

⊛   Allied Invasion Force HQ

←——   U.S. forces including Free French

←-----   British forces

———   Line held by Axis forces   ✳ major battles

0   100   200

island bastion alive, losing vast shipping tonnage in the process. But the price was not too heavy; Rommel's need for supplies and reinforcements could not be satisfied so long as Axis convoys were being smashed from Malta. The British pilots were enormously helped by Ultra, which picked up and read the Enigma-coded radio signals flashing across the Mediterranean from German supply bases in Italy to Rommel in North Africa, making it possible for the RAF to intercept slow-moving ship convoys or heavily laden transport planes carrying fuel to Rommel.

In the desert, victory went to the side with the most gasoline. The war ran on gasoline, and, like nearly everything else, it had to be brought from a long way off and at great cost. The main British supply route to North Africa ran three thousand miles around the Cape of Good Hope, while the Axis only had to cross three hundred miles of Mediterranean. This should have given Rommel a big advantage, but Malta and Ultra negated it. Hitler and Mussolini agreed that the British air and naval bases there had to be destroyed and the island taken before Rommel made another and, they hoped, final drive on Egypt. Churchill and his high command agreed that Malta had to be held at all cost. The Luftwaffe gave the island a merciless pounding. In

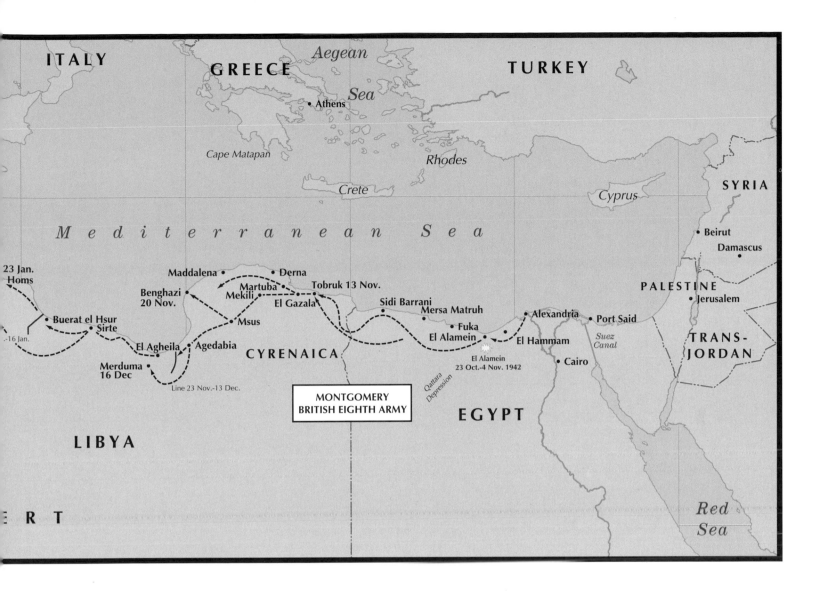

The map shows place names including: ITALY, GREECE, Aegean Sea, TURKEY, Athens, Cape Matapan, Rhodes, Crete, Cyprus, SYRIA, Beirut, Damascus, Mediterranean Sea, 23 Jan. Homs, Maddalena, Derna, Tobruk 13 Nov., PALESTINE, Jerusalem, Benghazi 20 Nov., Martuba, Mekili, El Gazala, Sidi Barrani, Mersa Matruh, Alexandria, Port Said, Buerat el Hsur, Sirte, Msus, Fuka, El Alamein, El Hammam, TRANS-JORDAN, El Agheila, Agedabia, CYRENAICA, El Alamein 23 Oct.-4 Nov. 1942, Cairo, Merduma 16 Dec., Line 23 Nov.-13 Dec., Suez Canal, Qattara Depression, EGYPT, LIBYA, Red Sea, -16 Jan.

MONTGOMERY
BRITISH EIGHTH ARMY

In the fall of 1942, the British and Americans invaded Morocco and Algeria while the British Eighth Army struck at El Alamein and sent the Axis armies reeling back on one of the longest retreats in history (above). In eighty days Rommel traveled 1,750 miles. Behind him he left a desert strewn with burned-out tanks and thousands of dead and wounded. At the end of his retreat, he ran into the British First Army and the Americans coming in from the west. This success was built in part on the breaking of the Enigma machine code (opposite); the Germans were sure the code was unbreakable. The Desert War was also won and lost on the flow of gasoline to the frontline tankers. It took many four-gallon containers like this one (left, held by a British Tommy) to fill a Crusader.

THE DESERT FOX

Erwin Rommel was one of the best known and most capable German generals of the war. Winston Churchill paid him a unique compliment when in January 1942, in the House of Commons, he said of Rommel: "We have a very daring and skillful opponent against us, and, may I say across the havoc of war, a great general."

Born in 1889, Rommel grew up in Swabia, where his father was a schoolteacher. Rommel was active in cycling, tennis, skating, rowing and skiing. Although his family had no military tradition, in 1910 Rommel entered the Royal Officer Cadet School in Danzig. In World War I he was a highly decorated combat leader in France and Italy. One of his sergeants recalled, "When I first saw him in 1915 he was slightly built, almost schoolboyish, inspired by a holy zeal, always eager and anxious to act. Everybody was inspired by his initiative, his courage, his dazzling acts of gallantry. His men idolized him and had boundless faith in him."

General Rommel rides to the front in Libya in 1941. A man of mercurial temperament and tremendous energy, he often displayed brilliance in the tactical handling of his forces. He led from the front and was on the move constantly. The men of the Afrika Korps loved and respected him and would follow him anywhere.

In the interwar years, Rommel remained a line officer. His regimental commander wrote in 1934 that he was "head and shoulders above the average battalion commander in every respect." In 1940 Rommel proved him right when he led the way through France and became one of the first panzer division commanders to reach the Channel. As commander of the Afrika Korps in North Africa in 1941–42, he added enormous luster to his reputation and became a world figure.

Despite his spectacular victories in the desert, after Rommel lost the Battle of El Alamein in the late fall of 1942 he became what Hitler called a defeatist, what others called a realist. He urged Hitler to end the war, to no avail. So Rommel did his duty and fought on. In February 1943, he surprised Eisenhower and the Americans with a counterattack at Kasserine Pass in Tunisia. He scored impressive initial gains but lacked the fuel and resources to follow them up. Suffering from high blood pressure, violent headaches, nervous exhaustion, and rheumatism, Rommel left North Africa for good, shortly before the German surrender.

Rommel spent the rest of 1943 recuperating. At the end of the year he took command of the German forces in France. His immediate task was to make the Atlantic Wall a reality. He put his tremendous energy into the task, convinced that if his men did not stop the Allies on the beaches, the war was lost. But on D-Day, he wasn't present to inspire his men or to shape the battle, because he had gone to Germany to celebrate his wife's birthday (his weatherman assured him conditions in the Channel precluded an invasion) and to go to Hitler's headquarters to persuade Hitler to let him have more tanks.

Rommel hurried back to Normandy, and through the month of June and on into July he managed to impose a stalemate on the Allies. But he knew that the Allies would inevitably prevail and urged Hitler to make peace, again with no success. On July 17, he was badly wounded when his car crashed after being shot up by British fighter aircraft. Rommel went to the hospital. Three days later the July 20 assassination attempt against Hitler failed. Rommel was implicated. He knew the conspirators and agreed with them about the need to end the war, but he disagreed with their judgment that Hitler had to be assassinated. Rommel feared that assasination would make Hitler a martyr and urged instead that Hitler be arrested by the army and put on trial. But to Hitler such distinctions did not matter: he regarded Rommel as just another conspirator.

By October, Rommel was at his home, recuperating from his wounds. On October 14, SS troops surrounded his house and a German general confronted him with a choice of suicide or trial. Rommel accepted the proffered poison, told his wife and fourteen-year-old-son, Manfred (a private in anti-aircraft, later mayor of Stuttgart), that Hitler was charging him with treason, and said he would be dead within fifteen minutes. Publicly, his death was attributed to his wounds, and Hitler gave him a state funeral, not neglecting to send his condolences to Frau Rommel. (Had Rommel not taken the poison and instead demanded a public trial, Hitler had promised retribution against his wife and son after his sentencing execution.)

Rommel was also an amateur photographer. Here are three scenes he took in the desert: (clockwise from the top) a carefully composed close-up of a dead British soldier; two panzer warriors taking a break from the business at hand; and four of Rommel's comrades-in-arms smiling for their commanding officer.

These German Ju-52 transport aircraft have just been blasted by British planes, which found them on the ground at El Aquina airfield in Tunis. Almost certainly the British were acting on information picked up from the Enigma machines. Of all the German armed services, the Luftwaffe was the most lax in security, seldom bothering to change the code settings on the Enigma once a month, and thus allowing the British to crack the current code on a regular basis.

December 1941, the Germans flew 169 bombing raids on Malta; the next month, there were 262 raids. The British did everything possible to keep Malta supplied, at a terrible cost in men and ships. The situation grew desperate. Axis convoys began getting through, and, as a result, Rommel set off on a new offensive toward the end of January 1942, driving the Eighth Army back to the Gazala-Bir Hacheim line. Churchill urged a strong counteroffensive to stop Rommel and to relieve pressure on Malta, but Auchinleck did not think his army was ready yet.

Then, in May, Rommel struck again. By the nineteenth of June, he was outside Tobruk. Two days later, Tobruk fell. For Churchill it was one of the worst moments of the war. Rommel was made a field marshal, and his army took possession of huge dumps of ammunition, food, and, best of all, gasoline. His supply problems, it appeared, were suddenly solved. Why stop now for an invasion of Malta, he argued. Hitler agreed. The invasion was canceled, and Rommel pushed on toward Egypt. But Auchinleck was fighting back with terrific determination now, and by July, near El Alamein, Rommel called a halt "for the time being."

In August 1942, Churchill flew to Cairo in order to weigh the military prospects before meeting Stalin for the first time. Rommel by then had established a new forward position deep inside Egypt. The British prime minister, in one of his most significant military decisions, reorganized his command. He named General Sir Harold Alexander to replace Auchinleck as head of all Middle Eastern forces. Then, to take over the Eighth Army after the officer slated for that post, W. H. E. ("Strafer") Gott, had been killed in an airplane crash, he picked Lieutenant General Bernard L. Montgomery.

"Monty," as he became known to his soldiers, was a highly unlikable figure,

In the spring of 1942 the island of Malta came under almost continuous attack (above). The HMS *Euryalus,* with a convoy traveling from Egypt to Malta (right), meets and engages Italian warships on March 22, 1942. In an unprecedented gesture, King George VI bestowed upon all residents of Malta the George Cross for valor. Rommel later blamed his ultimate defeat in North Africa on the failure to neutralize Malta.

Prime Minister Churchill inspects the front lines at El Alamein in August 1942. He had grown impatient with his generals, and it shows. Out of the shake-up he ordered came General Bernard Law Montgomery to assume command of the British Eighth Army. Then Churchill began pestering Montgomery to take the offensive. Montgomery stood up to him, saying he would drive the Germans from the Egyptian border when he was ready, and only then.

detested by many officers, yet deeply admired by others. He was lean, tough, conceited, insolent, often supercilious. His tastes were plain; he was a stern disciplinarian who forced his staff to keep strenuously fit, frowned on smoking and drinking, fired many of the commanders he had inherited, and injected into his dispirited army a sudden surge of confidence. His troops began to cherish the label "Desert Rats," first accorded with contempt, and took for their own the Afrika Korps's favorite song, "Lili Marlene." Because his soldiers soon came to know their new leader, who visited and talked to every unit, they came also to have personal faith in his craft and wisdom. He insisted on refraining from the offensive until he had overwhelming weapons superiority. And with such superiority, his army soon presented him with a massive string of victories.

A lonely man and in some respects a priggish puritan, Monty was a latter-day Cromwell. He was fascinated by his own homilies and had a habit of repeating them at least twice for the sake of stress. "There are only two rules of war," he would say. "Only two rules of war. Never invade Russia. Never invade China. Never invade Russia or China." General Hans Speidel, at one time Rommel's chief of staff, insisted that Montgomery understood only two maneuvers—a left hook and a thrust through the center—and that because he always telegraphed his punches the Germans knew in advance what he planned to do. But he was a superb trainer of troops and he gave heart to a disheartened army at a critical moment.

In the fall of 1942, Montgomery was aware that Rommel was preparing his final push toward Alexandria and the Nile, but he was not dismayed. He propped Rommel's photograph in his headquarters and, with characteristic immodesty, remarked: "Give me a fortnight and I can resist the German attack. Give me three weeks and I can defeat the Boche. Give me a month and I can chase him out of Africa." As it was, Monty spent two months just getting ready for the chase.

Fate threw these two great captains against each other fifty miles west of Alexandria, in an ugly, arid patch of a village named El Alamein. To the north lay the Mediterranean flank, covered by the Royal Navy, and to the south gaped an impassable rock canyon named the Qattara Depression. Thus the battlefield was a narrow passage that restricted the customary wide, high-speed flanking movements of desert warfare so often used by Rommel. The passage itself was strewn with mines and packed densely with guns and tanks. It was difficult for infantry to dig in on the rock-studded terrain. Rommel was intent on punching through this gap before his opponent could thicken his own defenses. In August he said: "We hold the gateway to Egypt with full intention to act. We did not go there with the intention of being flung back sooner or later."

And indeed, his power seemed inexorable. Were he to penetrate, the entire Nile Valley would have been exposed to the fanning out of his tanks and

Montgomery poses for a news shot in the desert in the fall of 1942. He had his shortcomings, but he was a great trainer of troops and was able to restore morale in the Eighth Army when it was badly needed. Publicity like this helped.

British soldiers move forward in the desert in the opening stages of the El Alamein battle on October 23, 1942. They were to sweep on through North Africa to Tunis. As this was Britain's first victory after three years of war, it was celebrated throughout the empire with a joy out of all proportion to its significance.

self-propelled guns. The British moved masses of stores out of Cairo, flew out dependents, and established distant contingency headquarters. Hitler ordered medals struck to honor the expected triumph of his Afrika Korps; Mussolini sent his favorite white charger to Libya so he could ride through Cairo in a victory parade. But the British lines held. In September, Rommel flew to Germany to report to Hitler, complaining at the Führer's East Prussian headquarters that RAF bombers were destroying his panzers with U.S. 40-millimeter shells. "Quite impossible," Göring observed. "Nothing but latrine rumors. All the Americans can make are razor blades and refrigerators." Rommel replied: "I only wish, Herr Reichsmarschall, that we were issued similar razor blades!"

Rommel was resting at a German sanatorium when, in late October 1942, Montgomery at last felt strong enough to launch his own offensive. On October 23, Montgomery announced to his troops: "When I assumed command of the Eighth Army I said that the mandate was to destroy Rommel and his army, and that it would be done as soon as we were ready. We are ready NOW!"

Thunderous artillery pieces, to the clattering counterpoint of mortars and machine guns, suddenly smothered the advance German positions with their blast, and that night, under a shining moon, the famous foot soldiers—Britons, Australians, New Zealanders, Indians, South Africans, Highlanders probing forward beside their kilted pipers—began to move into the mine fields. When these were partly cleared, the British tanks rumbled through.

America's most famous World War II photographer, Robert Capa, took this shot (above) of a convoy of guns and ammunition being moved to the front along a road guarded by Arabs commanded by Free French officers. A 1943 picture (left) of an American-made truck swinging onto the dock at Casablanca was also taken by Capa. The flow of supplies from the United States to North Africa appeared to be never-ending. American productivity was becoming the chief factor in the war around the world.

After the successful battle at El Alamein (opposite), the Eighth Army juggernaut moves forward in November 1942 (above). Advancing British infantry, wearing shorts, take cover behind a knocked-out panzer in the Libyan desert. Many usable panzers had to be abandoned because they ran out of fuel. Fuel supplies were always Rommel's single greatest worry.

The Germans were outnumbered, outweaponed, and overwhelmed. General Georg von Stumme, Rommel's replacement, fell dead of a heart attack. Two days after the assault started, Rommel was back, surveying the wreckage of his burned-out panzers. Hitler sent him a desperate message: "In the situation in which you now find yourself, there can be no other consideration than to hold fast, never retreat, hurl every gun and every man into the fray. . . . You can show your troops no other way than that which leads to victory or death." Rommel protested, to no avail. He tried to carry out the order, but it was impossible, and after suffering heavy and needless casualties he started a massive retreat. General Ritter von Thoma, when captured in full uniform by the British, expressed the feeling of the entire Afrika Korps command by assailing Hitler's order as "unsurpassed madness."

After Axis forces began withdrawing on November 2, Montgomery sent armor sweeping around behind them, and two days later Rommel's escape road was blocked; yet somehow he managed to slip his forces through the barrier. Sudden heavy rains, which bogged down vehicles in mud were all,

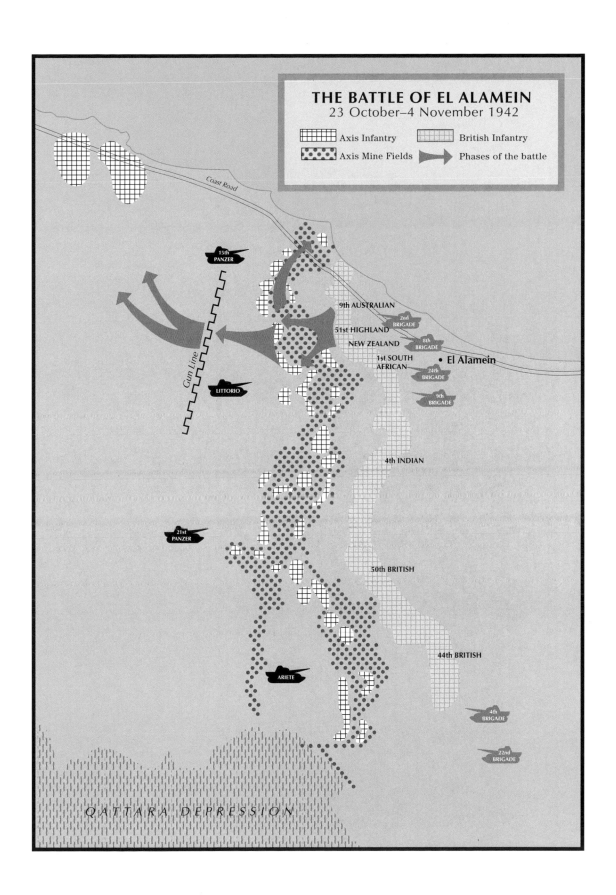

THE BATTLE OF EL ALAMEIN
23 October–4 November 1942

Axis Infantry   British Infantry
Axis Mine Fields   Phases of the battle

Coast Road

15th PANZER

9th AUSTRALIAN

2nd BRIGADE

51st HIGHLAND

8th BRIGADE

NEW ZEALAND

1st SOUTH AFRICAN

El Alamein

24th BRIGADE

LITTORIO

9th BRIGADE

Gun Line

4th INDIAN

21st PANZER

50th BRITISH

44th BRITISH

ARIETE

4th BRIGADE

22nd BRIGADE

QATTARA DEPRESSION

according to Montgomery, that saved his foe from annihilation. The RAF constantly bombed Rommel; Montgomery's armor slashed at his columns. Rommel abandoned every nonessential as well as the Italian infantry, after taking all their motorized vehicles. His route was littered with burned-out vehicles and other debris of war.

In the long rout from Egypt westward across the Libyan frontier, Rommel helped protect his disciplined German troops by posting Italian rear guards and using their transport for evacuation. He lost approximately sixty thousand men as well as most of his guns and tanks before, under cover of a rainstorm, he managed to establish a temporary holding position. And then, on November 8, came word of an Allied landing in French North Africa. Not only was Egypt irrevocably lost, but now an enormous pincer started to close in on the Afrika Korps.

Rommel's forces were trapped just as it became clear that another huge German army was caught in the snowy wastes of the Volga bend at Stalingrad and that the Americans were striking back against Japan in far-off Guadalcanal. Late autumn of 1942 was the turning point of the war. As Churchill said, "Before Alamein we survived, after Alamein we conquered."

Up to this point the U.S. Army, which had been at war with Germany for eleven months, had yet to fire a shot at a German soldier. Only a couple of infantry divisions had gone to Britain. But the army was building and the American High Command was eager to get into the battle in order to imple-

German motorized troops and armored vehicles make the long retreat across North Africa in November of 1942. This was not a rout: Montgomery took care to stay close behind the retreating Germans, but not too close. With some important exceptions, the Germans managed to get out of Libya in good order.

ment the Germany-first strategy. In June 1942 Marshall had sent Brigadier General Dwight Eisenhower to take command of U.S. forces in England. Unknown at the time, "Ike," as he was called, was an immediate hit with the British. They liked his professional competency, his rugged good looks, his optimism, his determination, his apparently simple manner—and they liked even more the promise his appointment implied, that the Americans were about to send dozens of divisions to the European Theater of Operations (ETO).

But the British did not like the strategy Eisenhower was propounding. He and Marshall wanted to spend the next six months building up the assault force in Britain, then launch an cross-channel invasion of France in the spring of 1943, code-named Roundup. Churchill and his generals were absolutely opposed.

They argued that the Allies were not ready to fight the *Wehrmacht* in France and refused to participate in Roundup. Instead, they proposed a fall 1942 invasion of French North Africa, code-named Torch, with the aim of driving the Germans off the African continent. As the British were the stronger partner at this time, they got their way. When he learned of the final decision, Eisenhower wrote in his diary that July 28 could well go down as "the blackest day in history." What he and Marshall feared was that Torch would fail to help the besieged Red Army, and if a desperate Stalin made a separate peace with Hitler the Western Allies would never get back on the European continent. Whether Roundup could have worked remains one of the great controversies of the war. Marshall and Eisenhower remained convinced that it would have succeeded and ended the war much sooner. As it was not tried, no one can ever know.

There was a stiff political price to pay for Torch. Ever since Hitler's invasion of the Soviet Union, Stalin had been demanding that the Allies mount a second front in France, so as to take the pressure off the Red Army. Roosevelt had promised Molotov that the second front would be opened in 1942. Torch was no second front. The invading forces would not even be fighting Germans, only French colonial troops defending France's North African empire, troops they hoped would come over to the Allied side. Torch therefore strengthened Stalin's already great suspicion of his capitalist partners.

In early August, the serious planning for Torch, featuring joint Anglo-American landings in Morocco and Algeria, began. Marshall insisted that Eisenhower be given overall command of the expedition. A formal directive to proceed was sent to him only on August 13, after full consideration had been made of the strain the operation would place on Allied resources. Endorsement of Torch meant that in the Pacific the United States would be confined to holding a Hawaii-Midway line and preserving communications to Australia. In Europe it meant cancellation of Roundup and of Operation Sledgehammer, a diversionary attack across the Channel into France in 1942 that was to be put into operation in the event of a sudden Red Army collapse. The Torch invasion was made up of three separate forces: thirty-five thousand Americans embarked from Norfolk, Virginia, to cross the Atlantic and assault French Morocco; thirty-nine thousand Americans embarked from England to take Oran in western Algeria; and a third force of ten thousand Americans and twenty-three thousand British also sailed from Britain to

U.S. landing craft were shot up by the French on November 8, 1942, during the invasion in Casablanca. The fleet had sailed from Virginia a month earlier, the landing craft riding on the decks of Higgins Boats. These were the first Higgins Boats to carry troops ashore on a hostile coast. Eventually some 20,000 of the boats participated in invasions around the world.

seize Algiers. All were transported and protected by the U.S. and Royal navies. Eisenhower wrote of this extraordinary undertaking: "The venture was new. . . . Up to that moment no government had ever attempted to carry out an overseas expedition involving a journey of thousands of miles from its bases and terminating in a major attack."

The operation was further complicated by the confused situation of France itself, part occupied, part under Pétain's Vichy regime, part in a colonial limbo. Some French officers in North Africa were longing to join General de Gaulle's movement in England; others were conspiring to back General Henri-Honoré Giraud, who had just escaped to France from a German prison camp; still others were pledged to their Pétainist commanders, especially the Vichy commander in chief, Admiral Jean Darlan; and there were those who were merely waiting to see how the war would go. In October 1942, Eisenhower sent his deputy, Major General Mark W. Clark, with a handful of specialists, to visit Algeria secretly by submarine and confer with the State Department's Robert Murphy, who had spread an intelligence network throughout North Africa on direct orders from Roosevelt. De Gaulle, who was disliked in Washington and suspected in London of indiscretion by incautious talk, was excluded from all planning, an insult he never forgave.

Clark and Murphy believed they had so arranged things with the French colonial forces that there would be no resistance to Torch.

At 3 A.M. on November 8, 1942, a series of convoys numbering more than eight hundred war vessels and transports began to assemble along the African coast between Morocco to the south and Algeria to the west, disembarking troops on the Atlantic and Mediterranean shores. To their surprise, the French fought back at Casablanca and Oran. Pétain, senile and embittered, ordered French North African forces to resist and severed diplomatic relations with Washington. Despite these actions, Hitler used the landings as an excuse to occupy the southern parts of France and take absolute control of the Vichy government. For a brief time the position of the fourteen French divisions in Africa remained uncertain. In the hope of finding a figure to whom the French would rally, the Allies had smuggled General Giraud out of France to Gibraltar, where he agreed to take part in the operation but at the same time arrogantly demanded command of the entire expeditionary force. Instead he was flown to Algiers, where it was immediately apparent that the French Army in Africa was not going to follow him. Meanwhile Admiral Darlan had arrived in Algiers and was caught by the invasion. On November 10, Eisenhower, seeking to establish some kind of order, offered Darlan the post of political chief for all French North Africa, with Giraud the military chief, if they could persuade the French soldiers to lay down their arms. Darlan quickly accepted the deal and the fighting ended.

There was a storm of protest from Britain and the United States. Darlan was an archcollaborationist, an avid fascist, who represented everything the Allies said they were fighting against. Yet Eisenhower had elevated him to

General George S. Patton Jr., inspects a shell fragment in Casablanca. He commanded the invasion at Casablanca, then moved onto Tunisia, before taking charge of the American forces invading Sicily. He relished his roles and handled his publicity so well that he became America's most popular and admired field commander.

American troops head inland after disembarking on the beaches of Surcouf, outside Algiers, on November 8, 1942 (above). The man kneeling behind the sandbank carries a flag, for it was hoped that the French would not want to fight the Americans. For the most part, they didn't; after a couple of days of ineffectual resistance, the French switched sides. At right, General Dwight Eisenhower confers with Admiral Jean Darlan and General Mark Clark in French Morocco, November 13, 1942. Eisenhower had just put his stamp of approval on a deal Clark had made with Darlan; for ordering the French colonial army in Algeria to lay down its arms, Darlan was made the governor general of French North Africa (until he was assassinated on December 24). The "Darlan Deal" excited great controversy in Washington, London, and Moscow; it seemed to indicate that the Western Allies were prepared to deal with Fascist generals and admirals, if not with Hitler himself.

the top post. Political criticism of the "Darlan deal" threatened to destroy Ike before he got well started in the war. Fortunately for him, and for the Allies, on Christmas Eve, Darlan was assassinated by a young French royalist. Giraud, a brave, vain, but somewhat inept and politically inexperienced officer, was soon outmaneuvered by the cunning and furious de Gaulle and found himself gradually stripped of all but the costume of authority. De Gaulle assumed real power over the gathering elements of Free France in North Africa.

The Germans reacted swiftly and effectively to the landings. Long before Eisenhower managed to get his inexperienced forces moving, the Germans and Italians occupied Tunisia and, benefiting from its proximity to Sicily,

American troops advance over typical terrain in Algeria. These men felt they were in top physical condition and well trained for modern battle. They found out they were not. Eisenhower ordered his commanders, not only in North Africa but those in England and the States, to toughen up the training process. The need for more and constant training was perhaps the single most important lesson the Americans learned in their first contact with the Germans.

Free French Legionnaires (above) attack in North Africa in June 1942. General Charles de Gaulle (below) played a large role in reviving the French nation, beginning with the building of the Free French forces.

built up impressive strength, especially in aircraft. Winter rains turned the roads into quagmires, bogging down the Allied eastward advance, and for the first time the Americans were pounded by Stuka dive-bombers and the remarkable German 88 artillery piece, which astonished the Allies by its deadly effect against troops, tanks, and planes. On November 23, Eisenhower transferred his headquarters to Algiers. Through December and January, the rains continued, precluding offensive action. Eisenhower built up his forces, while Rommel arrived from Libya and joined the German forces in Tunisia.

Before he could accomplish much else in the Tunisian campaign, General Eisenhower had the basic problem of creating an efficient fighting force. There was the fundamental matter of welding British, American, and French units into a functioning army, for there were problems not only of communications but also of national pride and prestige—some serious, such as the bitterness of French toward British. As for the U.S. forces, they were green, their training was not always all it might have been, and coordination between service branches was faulty, as when fighter planes sent to hit the enemy badly mauled a U.S. tank destroyer unit instead. The winter's fighting in Tunisia, most of it on a small scale, began the process of making the U.S. troops realize that, in Ike's words, "war is a tough, dirty business."

But the GIs were still complacent and unprepared when, on St. Valentine's Day in 1943, Rommel made a sudden thrust at the uncoordinated Allied advance and hurled the Americans back through the Kasserine Pass. The GIs fled the battlefield or surrendered. They were clearly not capable of fighting the Afrika Korps. Major General George S. Patton Jr., a formidable United States commander whose name, genius, and eccentricities were soon to become renowned, was blocked further to the south near El Guettar, where his troops met unexpectedly stubborn resistance from Italian infantry. At this point Eisenhower summoned an old West Point classmate, Brigadier General Omar Bradley, to serve as his "eyes and ears" and to stimulate the faltering United States Army. Ike meanwhile dismissed incompetent American officers.

The American fighting man soon proved, however, that he could be competent, crafty, and courageous if given skilled commanders. He learned the art of camouflage, the value of digging, and the need for coordinated patrolling. Professional officers, National Guard divisions, and drafted replacements were slowly welded into an efficient, weather-beaten force. On Eisenhower's orders, Patton began to look forward to a new invasion, this time against Sicily, and, before the North African campaign ended in the summer of 1943, General Clark had been assigned to develop and train a new Fifth Army in Morocco for the eventual assault on Italy itself.

By March it was apparent even in Berlin and Rome that the Allied pincer arms extending toward each other from Cairo and Casablanca could not be kept apart. Rommel, in ill health, was recalled by Hitler so as to spare the most popular German general from the humiliation of surrender. The British under Montgomery moved on Tunisia from the east, aided by Jaques Philippe Leclerc's tiny, glamorous French force that had fought its way up from Chad, and the British and Americans closed in on Tunisia from the

The universally feared and universally envied German 88-millimeter gun could shoot at a flat trajectory as an antitank gun or as an anti-aircraft weapon (and was the best in the war at that role).

west. On April 23, the final attack began. Montgomery had already pierced the Mareth Line between Libya and Tunisia and now swept up toward Tunis as the United States II Corps overran Hill 609, blocking the road to Bizerte, and the British First Army took bloody Longstop Hill, the last great natural barrier. On May 7, Tunis and Bizerte fell, and the final line of Axis retreat on the Cape Bon peninsula was severed. Only a few hundred German troops escaped; some 275,000 German and Italian soldiers became POWs. Eisenhower complained to Marshall that they had never taught him at West Point how to deal with so many prisoners.

Torch had been a success but at a heavy price in lives and opportunities lost. Because of the huge buildup of men and supplies in Algiers, there were only a handful of American troops in Britain, which meant Hitler felt no threat of an invasion through France. That freed him to send additional forces into the Soviet Union. The Allies decided to follow up the victory in North Africa with offensive operations in the Mediterranean in 1943, which in practice meant another year's delay in opening the second front.

There were many positive attributes, however. The North African campaign was the largest pincers movement ever successfully applied in war, joining forces from the Nile Valley to the Atlantic. Its timing was superb. The coincidence between Montgomery's El Alamein breakthrough and the Moroccan-Algerian landings was carefully foreseen, but that impact, already immense, was enhanced by the simultaneity of triumphs at Stalingrad and Guadalcanal, the latter being of special political and morale importance to the United States.

All told, North Africa cost the Germans and Italians 349,206 in dead and prisoners. Apart from extensive losses at sea, they were deprived of nearly

General Dwight D. Eisenhower sits for a publicity shot in Algiers, January 1943 (opposite). Two years earlier he had been an unknown colonel about to retire. Now he was the commander of the Allied Forces in North Africa and world famous. But this was his first command, and he still had a lot to learn about making war.

At the Kasserine Pass (below), Rommel, reinforced with new armor, drove a "bulge" into the Allied lines and gave the U.S. Army its first real taste of German fire. The weight of the attack caught the Allies by surprise, and some 2,400 green GIs surrendered. Hundreds of tanks and trucks were destroyed and the Americans suffered 3,300 casualties. Rommel's losses were less than 1,000, but he had insufficient fuel to drive onto the coast in the rear of the Allied armies and failed to demoralize the Americans, who were learning fast.

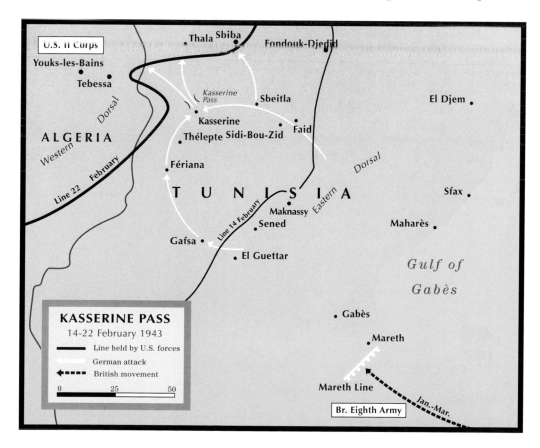

KASSERINE PASS
14-22 February 1943

—— Line held by U.S. forces
⟶ German attack
◀---- British movement

0   25   50

Generals Patton and Eisenhower confer in Tunisia, March 1943. They had a lot to worry about: The American soldiers had not done well in the Kasserine Pass battle. They were determined to have the GIs perform better next time.

two hundred thousand tons of matériel. Italy's Field Marshal Alessandro Messe and Germany's General Jürgen von Arnim were among those taken. When it was suggested to Eisenhower that he receive the latter, Eisenhower refused, believing himself engaged in a "crusade" against "a completely evil conspiracy." (It was a policy he would stick to for the rest of the war.) Mussolini's vision of a new Roman Empire dissolved in blood where Rome had once obliterated its Carthaginian enemy; soon the Duce would lose Italy itself. And for Hitler it was a catastrophe. Montgomery analyzed the Führer's strategic error accordingly: "From a purely military point of view, the holding out in North Africa once the Mareth Line had been broken through could never be justified. I suppose Hitler ordered it for political reasons; it may sometimes be necessary, but they will generally end in disaster."

Rommel commented on the crucial El Alamein battle with justifiable acerbity: "The fact is that there were men in high places who, though not without the capacity to grasp the facts of the situation, simply did not have the courage to look them in the face and draw the proper conclusions. They preferred to put their heads in the sand, live in a sort of military pipe dream and look for scapegoats whom they usually found in the troops or field commanders. Looking back, I am conscious of only one mistake—that I did not circumvent the 'Victory or Death' order twenty-four hours earlier [at Alamein]."

Eisenhower, with General Omar Bradley, makes a jeep sweep inspection of the American positions in Tunisia, April 1943. Bradley had recently been appointed commander of the U.S. Second Corps, which was marching victoriously on Bizerte. Ike's mood was now considerably better than it had been in March.

The African victory gave resurgent confidence to the weary British. The experience proved the effectiveness of a new team of United States commanders and broke in an American army. It forged an alliance that, at Eisenhower's insistence, was led by an integrated, international staff. It prepared the foundation for a liberated Gaullist France. For de Gaulle, ignored in planning the invasion, then thrust aside in favor of Darlan and Giraud, forced his way by willpower and artful maneuver to the leadership of French North Africa. From there he moved into France, carrying all his bitter memories.

Most of all, it was in North Africa that the U.S. Army gained invaluable experience, from the lowliest private to the highest commander. Leaders emerged, at the noncommisioned officer, junior officer, and general levels. Incompetents were weeded out, while the men who would lead the drive in Europe were discovered—Eisenhower, with his amazing ability to get men from different nations and traditions to pull together; Patton, with his swashbuckling style; and Bradley, quiet, competent, a "soldier's general."

Captured Afrika Korps troops show obvious relief that their war is over. And well they should; they were shipped to the States and put to work on America's farms—the best place for a German young man to be in 1943–45.

Units of African-French troops and American troops march past
General Eisenhower on a victory parade in Tunis on May 20,
1943. From this moment, North Africa was cleared of Axis forces.
The total count of prisoners was 250,000.

CHAPTER 8

THE WAR IN THE SOVIET UNION

From August 1939 to June 1941, Stalin and Hitler were allies. The Soviet Union sent large quantities of minerals, oil, food, and other materials to Germany in an apparently endless line of trains. But despite the advantages to the Nazis, Hitler wanted more. He wanted direct control of the vast resources of the Soviet Union; he wanted *Lebensraum* for the German people in the east; he feared and detested Communism and was determined to destroy it; he regarded the Slavs as subhuman and intended to make them into slave labor for Germany. Never did he doubt that he would one day invade the U.S.S.R. His question was when. The loss of the Battle of Britain and cancellation of Sea Lion answered the question.

What else was he to do? He had the best army in the world—and no place to send it. He couldn't get across the English Channel. He already controlled Western and Central Europe. Demobilization of his army was unthinkable. The Red Army was in sad shape as a result of Stalin's purges. It all made sense to Hitler.

Hitler had made only a few minor mistakes in his conduct of the war up to June 1941, and he was full of himself ("the greatest general who ever lived," German officers said scornfully of him—but only behind his back). The first lesson of military history is "Don't invade Russia," his generals told him when he outlined his strategy of conquest. But he was sure he could attain what had eluded Napoleon. Thus was set in motion the greatest campaign ever waged, involving millions of men, tens of thousands of planes and tanks, and a front line that stretched from Leningrad on the Baltic Sea to Sevastopol on the Black Sea, a distance of well over a thousand miles.

The first preparations were made even as the Battle of Britain raged, on July 29, 1940. Colonel General Alfred Jodl, chief of German operations, told

The war on the eastern front was waged on a titanic scale, but as always it all came down to individuals, especially frontline infantry. The conditions under which men like these Red Army troops outside Moscow in January 1941 (opposite) lived and fought defy description. It was as bad for the *Wehrmacht*, as attested by German artist Ernst Widmann's sketch of an infantryman (above) drawn during that terrible winter.

215

a conference of staff officers that the Führer had decided "to attack the U.S.S.R. in the spring of 1941." Two days later, Hitler himself revealed this plan to his leading generals. Colonel General Franz Halder took down Hitler's words at the briefing: "Wiping out the very power to exist of Russia! That is the goal!" That November, Stalin sent Molotov to Berlin to demand further extension of Soviet influence in Eastern Europe. The request only reaffirmed Hitler's decision to double-cross his partner. On December 18, he issued military Directive No. 21, outlining Operation Barbarossa, named in honor of the medieval German emperor who had won great victories in the East.

The object of Barbarossa was not merely to occupy the Soviet Union but to destroy the Red Army in huge battles of annihilation along a fantastically large front. Assuming his panzers would advance as rapidly as in France, the Führer reckoned that within eight weeks they could capture Leningrad, Moscow, and the Ukraine, putting an end to organized resistance. He decided the campaign could not be "conducted in a knightly fashion" and authorized Gestapo chief Heinrich Himmler to use his SS troops independent of the army in conquered territories, to terrorize and slaughter civilians. And on

In the first stages of Barbarossa, the German Army appeared unstoppable. First the panzers then the infantry advanced with virtually no opposition. Below, German soldiers burn a village in Belorussia, probably in retaliation for some act of sabotage. But Stalin recovered from his initial shock and rallied the Soviet people. Getting better generals, such as Marshal Semyon Timoshenko (opposite), helped.

March 21, 1941, Hitler drafted his infamous Commissar Order: all Soviet commissars (political officers) who were captured would be shot.

In the original timetable, Barbarossa was to begin in May to insure the conquest of Moscow and Leningrad before the first Soviet snows set in. But Mussolini's misfortunes in Greece and the Belgrade coup d'état caused Hitler to postpone the date by one month. This distressed many German generals and has been cited as one of Hitler's big mistakes, but it may have been lucky for the Germans, because by the time they did attack the unpaved roads of the Soviet Union had dried out, making blitzkrieg possible. In May, columns would have been hip-deep in mud; in late June, they sped ahead.

German soldiering genius accomplished miracles in preparing this unprecedented offensive. The *Wehrmacht* deployed 207 divisions, 25 of them armored, fleshing out gaps with more than 50 satellite divisions, largely Finnish, Romanian, Italian, and Hungarian. The two-thousand-mile front was divided into three main thrusts under Field Marshal Wilhelm von Leeb, aiming at Leningrad; Field Marshal Fedor von Bock, aiming at Moscow; and Field Marshal Gerd von Rundstedt, aiming across the Ukraine.

At 6 A.M., June 22, after initial bombings and barrages had begun, Count Werner von der Schulenburg, Hitler's ambassador in Moscow, handed Molotov a note officially declaring war. Pale, tense, silent, the commissar for foreign affairs took the document, spat on it, tore it up, and then rang for his secretary. "Show this gentleman out through the back door," he said.

Despite some indications of Hitler's decision, Stalin had made few moves to meet an attack. The onslaught came with terrible surprise, smashing an incompetently led Red Army that was still engaged in routine border exercises. The speed of the Nazi advance was impressive on all fronts. Hundreds of Soviet aircraft were destroyed on the ground. Siege guns were trundled up to demolish fortresses of the so-called Stalin Line as they were successively isolated by German panzers. Three Red Army marshals, Kliment Efremovich Voroshilov in the north, Semyon Mikhailovich Budenny in the south, and Semyon Konstantinovich Timoshenko in the center, faced Leeb, Rundstedt, and Bock. Of the three, only Timoshenko showed any ability. Indeed officer competence at any level was lacking in the Red Army, a consequence of Stalin's purges.

Early on, Brest-Litovsk, key to Soviet central defenses, fell. Confused, cutoff Soviet units radioed each other: "We are being fired on. What shall we do?" They received such answers as: "You must be insane. Why is your signal not in code?" On June 27, Minsk fell, and Bock crossed the Berezina, heading for Smolensk. Leeb raced along the Baltic toward Leningrad; Rundstedt paraded into the Ukraine against Budenny's inept cavalry.

Stalin, apparently, was in a daze. During the first week of the campaign he made no public appearance and gave no orders. His being caught by surprise was inexcusable, but understandable: like the Japanese at Pearl Harbor, the Germans surprised the Soviets because what they did made no sense. Stalin knew as well as Hitler the historical consequences of invading the Soviet Union.

Willy-nilly, Stalin was now a partner of Churchill and Roosevelt. Both democratic leaders embraced him and his cause within hours of the invasion.

German infantry march on their relentless drive eastward (above), July 1941. Their progress, as indicated on the map at right, was unprecedented. But as the map also illustrates, the Soviets had a lot of space to trade for time, time in which they could bring in reinforcements from Siberia and rebuild the Red Army. Meanwhile, however, they were losing hundreds of thousands of troops in the German encirclements, from Leningrad in the north to the Caucasus Mountains in the south.

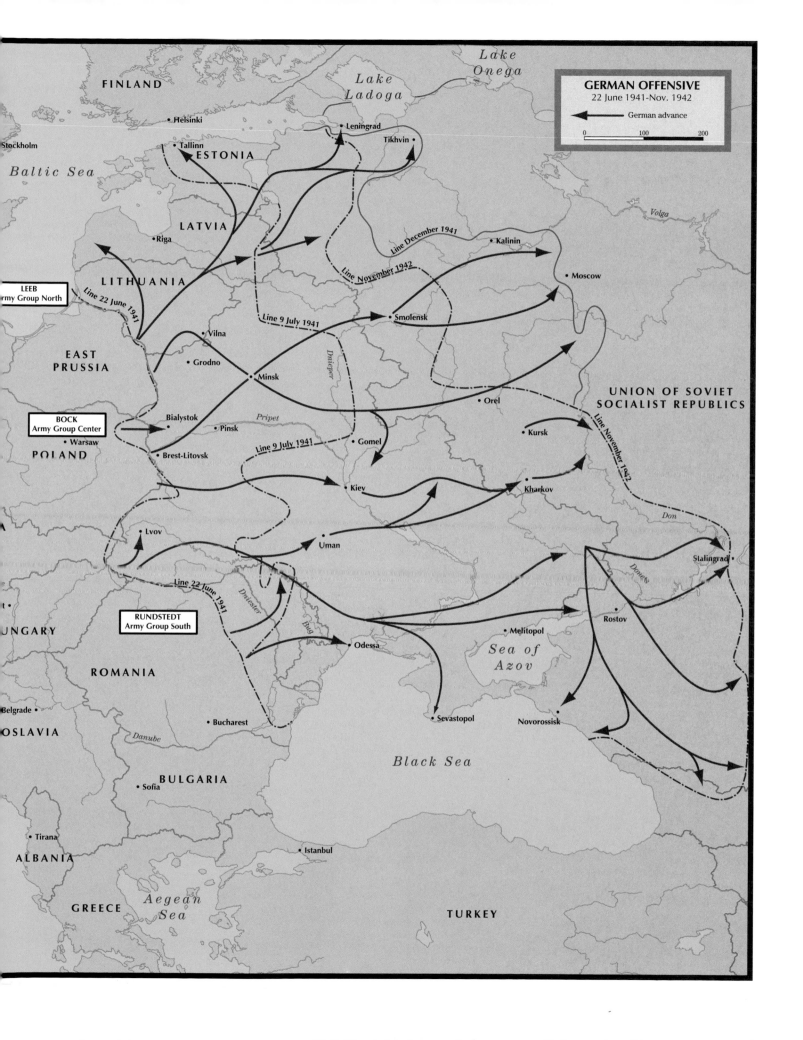

GERMAN OFFENSIVE
22 June 1941–Nov. 1942

← German advance

0   100   200

FINLAND

Lake Onega

Lake Ladoga

• Helsinki

Stockholm •

Baltic Sea

• Tallinn
ESTONIA

• Leningrad

Tikhvin •

Volga

LATVIA

• Riga

Line December 1941

• Kalinin

Line November 1942

LITHUANIA

┌─────────────────┐
│ **LEEB**   │
│ rmy Group North │
└─────────────────┘

Line 22 June 1941

• Vilna

Line 9 July 1941

• Smolensk

• Moscow

EAST PRUSSIA

• Grodno

Dnieper

• Minsk

UNION OF SOVIET SOCIALIST REPUBLICS

┌──────────────────┐
│ **BOCK**   │
│ Army Group Center│
└──────────────────┘

Bialystok •

Pripet

• Orel

• Kursk

• Warsaw

• Pinsk

Line 9 July 1941

• Gomel

Line November 1942

POLAND

• Brest-Litovsk

• Kiev

• Kharkov

Don

• Lvov

• Uman

Donets

Stalingrad •

┌─────────────────┐
│ **RUNDSTEDT**   │
│ Army Group South│
└─────────────────┘

Line 22 June 1941

Dniester

Bug

• Rostov

NGARY

• Melitopol

ROMANIA

• Odessa

Sea of Azov

Belgrade •

OSLAVIA

• Bucharest

• Sevastopol

• Novorossisk

Danube

BULGARIA

• Sofia

Black Sea

• Tirana

ALBANIA

• Istanbul

GREECE

Aegean Sea

TURKEY

Although the Germans suffered ten percent casualties during the summer of 1941, this stage of the invasion was a good one. They were free to liberate whatever they wanted or could carry. And as they advanced, they had many victories to celebrate: Opposite, the crew of a German antitank gun cheer after hitting a Soviet tank, July 1941. Below, German soldiers who had sacked a village show off some of their loot, August 1941. These frontline soldiers, however, were well-behaved and disciplined compared to the SS groups coming behind them.

This came as a surprise to Hitler. The Soviet Union was the only communist nation in the world. It had no natural allies, and Hitler could not imagine the capitalist West coming to the aid of the Communists. "When Barbarossa commences," he predicted, "the world will hold its breath and make no comment." But Churchill and Roosevelt took the commonsense view that "the enemy of my enemy is my friend"; Churchill remarked that if Hitler invaded hell, he would go to the House of Commons to say a kind word about the devil. America and Britain committed themselves to all-out aid for the U.S.S.R. and began to send tanks, trucks, planes, food and other contraband to Murmansk.

Thus was the Big Three formed. Only Hitler could have brought together this strange alliance, whose members had little in common except for their determination to destroy Hitler and his party. Once that was accomplished they could—and in the end they did—go separate, antagonistic ways. But first they had to hang together. No member of the Big Three was powerful enough to defeat Hitler on its own; indeed, no two of the members could do that. Final victory would require supreme effort from all three, as Stalin knew perfectly well. When he was assured of both Churchill's and Roosevelt's support, he began to recover from his initial shock.

On July 3, Stalin spoke over the radio to his people for the first time. To their amazement, he called them "brothers and sisters," or "friends," rather

Initially the people of the western republics of the Soviet Union greeted the Germans as liberators, including these Ukrainians in July 1941 (opposite). The German soldiers plucking fowl (left) have a wonderfully innocent, wholesome look, and do indeed appear to have been sent to free the Ukrainians from that devil Stalin. But the Germans showed their true face when their rear-area convoys began to roll into the villages (above). In one of his biggest mistakes, Hitler imposed a terribly cruel regime on the occupied republics, thereby throwing away a potentially advantageous political asset.

In Russia, as opposed to the western republics of the Soviet Union, there was no question of a full commitment on everyone's part to defeat Hitler. Every citizen strained, suffered, and showed a toughness of spirit and strength of soul that can only be marveled at. They worked twelve hours and more, in many cases every day of the war. Yet they still found more to give for Mother Russia. Here Moscow workers, after a day in the fields or factories, turn out to dig antitank trenches outside the city. It is notable that no one is holding any guns on them.

than "comrades." Nor did he call on them to make a supreme effort to save Communism, which after twenty-three years in power was widely hated. Instead he appealed to their nationalism, urging everyone to do everything possible to save the Motherland from the horror of a German occupation. He gave the conflict its official Soviet name, the Great Patriotic War. This was perhaps his single greatest contribution to the ultimate Soviet victory. A wave of patriotism sprang up all across the country. No sacrifice was too great to save Mother Russia.

Moscow itself, basking in the summer sun, had been draped in camouflage. The Bolshoi Theater and other buildings easily identified from the air were hung with huge scenic curtains depicting woodland villages. Principal squares were painted to give the wholly unsuccessful impression of rural countryside. When the Luftwaffe came over the capital, it was met by thunderous anti-aircraft barrages, whose fragments clattered down upon the streets. A few bombs struck the Kremlin compound, and one knocked a corner off the Bolshoi, leaving its pitiful camouflage curtain flapping like a torn dress.

Moscow's fears were realistic. Nothing seemed to slow the Germans. Even as Stalin spoke they came on. For here was panzer warfare in the grand style. Armored columns raced forward along parallel roads, then converged, trapping great masses of Soviet troops, sometimes even entire armies. The war appeared so clearly won only three weeks after the opening attack that, on July 14, Hitler issued a directive to prepare for reducing the size of the army in the near future. But the German generals, in all the flush of victory, began to feel the cold chill of doubt. Instead of the Soviets' losing heart in defeat, their resistance was actually increasing. Moreover, if German military intelligence evaluations at the beginning of the war of the size of the Red Army were correct, there should have been no Red Army left after the losses it had taken. And yet fresh Soviet divisions that German intelligence had never heard of kept appearing in battle. An even bigger shock came with the appearance of the Soviet T-34 tank, which no one had a hint of and which proved to be as good as anything the Germans possessed.

It was not until mid-July that the Germans met their first serious opposition. At Smolensk heavy fighting developed as Timoshenko threw in trained reserves, and, by the time that city fell three weeks later, it was in ruins. Hitler's plan to encircle and destroy the Red Army had achieved considerable

In one of the great feats of the war, the Soviets managed to extract much of their defense industry from the German path and get it operating in the Urals far to the east in just a few weeks. Here a tank assembly plant in the Urals is completing construction of some T-34 tanks. These thirty-ton machines were described by Rommel thus: "The Russian tank designers understand their job thoroughly; they cut out refinements and concentrate on essentials—gun power, armor, and cross-country performance." Rommel and many others rated the T-34 the best tank of the war.

VEHICLES

The first use of the internal combustion engine in war was in 1914, when the taxicabs of Paris carried the some two thousand troops of the French Army to the Battle of Marne. In 1916, the French supplied their army at Verdun with trucks, another first. And by 1917 the British had developed the first tanks. These vehicles and weapons pointed the way to the future, primitive though they were by World War II standards.

One of the miracles of the war was the American production of jeeps, trucks, and tanks. The United States beat the rest of the world combined in numbers (half of all the weapons in the world in 1945 had been made in the United States), and in most areas was far ahead in design and quality. The U.S. jeep was the envy of the world's armies; Germans loved the captured jeeps they used. The home of Mercedes and Volkswagen could produce nothing as good. The jeep was a quarter-ton vehicle that could carry five passengers or 800 pounds of payload and tow an antitank gun at the same time. Most jeeps had a pedestal-mounted .50-caliber machine gun. With four-wheel drive, they could go almost anywhere. Wherever Americans fought, the jeep was there, and dearly loved.

Detroit also beat the world in the design, quality, and production of trucks. The two-and-a-half-ton truck, called "the Deuce and a Half" by the GIs, was unattractive to the eye and uncomfortable to the driver and passengers, but it was a marvel of utility. The Deuce and a Half made the Red Ball Express possible; it carried supplies from the Normandy beaches to the German border in round-the-clock operations. And it gave the U.S. Army an unequaled mobility. During the Battle of the Bulge, Eisenhower turned to the Red Ball to get his reinforcements into the fight. In one week, the Americans moved 250,000 men with 50,000 vehicles. Not even in Vietnam or the Persian Gulf was the U.S. Army capable of moving so many men and so much equipment so quickly.

The DUKW (D, the code letter for the year of design (1942); U for amphibian; K for all-wheel drive; and W for dual rear axles)—the GIs called it a "Duck"—was another American innovation. It could carry twenty fully equipped riflemen in considerable comfort. It could make five knots in a moderate sea and fifty miles per hour on land riding on over-sized rubber tires, without the bounce of the Deuce and a Half or the spring-less jarring of the jeep. Sergeant Ken Webster of the 101st Airborne said the DUKW "rides softly up and down, like a sailboat in a gentle swell." No other country had anything to compare to it.

With its transportation capabilities, the U.S. Army was able to accomplish many things. One of the most important was the bridging of rivers. The combat engineers could get their pontoons, Bailey bridges (prefabricated of steel, British designed), and other equipment to a crossing site and throw up a bridge with amazing speed, often under fire.

America also made a bewildering variety of tracked vehicles, ranging from self-propelled guns to tank destroyers (basically tanks without a turret) to armored personnel carriers. So did all the other combatants. But in the tracked vehicle that mattered most, the tank, it was the opinion of every American tanker that his Sherman was woefully inferior to German and

The jeep (above) was much-loved by the GIs, and envied by the enemies. The Deuce and a Half (below) carried the bulk of the weapons and supplies from the beaches to the front. The DUKW (bottom) could go almost anywhere a jeep could go and could swim as well.

Russian tanks and not much better than the poorly designed and poorly constructed Japanese tank.

The Sherman was a 32-ton tank with a 75-millimeter cannon and a .50-caliber machine gun. It was no match for the 1944 German models, the Panther (43 tons) and the Tiger (56 tons), mounting a 75-millimeter cannon and much heavier armor than the Sherman. One on one the Sherman had no chance. But seldom did Shermans have to fight one on one, because there were so many of them. By the end of 1944 German industry had produced 24,630 tanks, the British 24,843. The Americans, meanwhile, turned out 88,410 tanks.

For all their shortcomings, the Shermans were a triumph of U.S. mass production techniques. They were far more reliable than the competition. The Sherman had a top speed of 40 kilometers an hour, with a range of 230 kilometers. For the Tiger, the figures were 32 and 168 kilometers, respectively. A Sherman's tracks lasted for 4,000 kilometers, the Tiger's for 900. The Sherman had a faster-turning turret and was much more maneuverable.

The reason the United States did not have the biggest, best-armored tank was that the tanks had to cross the oceans before they could go into battle, and the number one strategic shortage of the Allies was shipping. You could get two Shermans on the deck of an LST for every heavier tank. General Marshall made the decision to concentrate on lighter, faster, easier-to-ship tanks. Further, U.S. preference was to avoid tank-against-tank battles in order to exploit a breakthrough.

The Russian T-34, generally regarded as the best tank of the era, was American-designed but built in the Soviet Union. It was a 32-ton vehicle with an 85-millimeter cannon and two light machine guns. Its top speed was 55 kilometers per hour, its range 300 kilometers, and it was even more maneuverable than the Sherman. Its depressed silhouette contrasted with the high-profile Sherman and made it a poor target, while the slanted surfaces of its armor caused projectiles to glance off. And the T-34s were present in great numbers; by the end of 1944 the Soviet Union had produced 105,251 tanks and self-propelled guns, more than half of them T-34s.

The Japanese tank, designed in 1937 and hardly upgraded, was 15 tons, with a top speed of 42 kilometers per hour and a 47-millimeter cannon. Japan produced only 2,580 of them.

A major U.S. advantage was the skill of the GI when it came to vehicles. The armored divisions had their own maintenance battalions. Within two days of being put out of action by German shells, maintenance battalions had about half the damaged Shermans repaired and back on the line. GIs who had been working at gas stations and body shops two years earlier had brought their mechanical skills to Normandy, where they replaced damaged tank tracks, welded patches on the armor, and repaired engines. They stripped tanks beyond repair for parts. The U.S. maintenance battalions operated like a shop floor back in the States. The men made their own decisions, got out their tools, and got after the job. The Germans and Russians just left their damaged tanks where they were.

The U.S. Sherman tank (top) was reliable and versatile, but undergunned and underarmored. The German Panther (above), a medium tank, carried the best cannon of the war, the 88-millimeter. The British Churchill (below) was well armored, but also heavy and cumbersome.

success. There were huge losses all along the front. At Kiev the Germans claimed to have captured 600,000 Soviets. (Even Soviet historians admit to 200,000.) At Smolensk the Germans claimed 348,000 prisoners. By the end of September, Stalin had lost 2,500,000 men, 22,000 guns, 18,000 tanks, and 14,000 planes.

Nevertheless, the German advance was slowing down. Soviet resistance hardened. Nazi brutality, the ravaging of towns and hamlets, the torture and execution had combined to turn against the invaders a population that had welcomed the Germans as their liberators from Communist terror. What the Soviets discovered was that the Nazis were worse than Stalin. Gangs of SS troops roved behind German lines, murdering Jews and others in incredible numbers with unbelievable brutality. This was one of Hitler's worst mistakes of the war. Had he chosen to bring to the Ukraine and other areas the kind of mild occupation policies he followed in Western Europe, millions of Soviet citizens would have rallied to the Nazi cause. Instead, he turned the populace against him.

When Smolensk fell, Major Hans von Luck, commanding a reconnais-

Hitler called it "an army such as the world has never seen." These scenes of the Germans on the march in the Soviet Union capture the apparently irresistible tide of their advance. But the distances were so vast that it seemed to soldiers such as these that the long march would never end, that after each village or town was taken, there was another one to take farther east.

German soldiers pull a car stuck in the mud, somewhere in the Soviet Union, June 28, 1941. The Soviet roads—made from dirt or gravel—were nearly impossible to travel after a heavy rain.

sance unit, was the first German officer into the city. He was approached by a priest who was the caretaker for Smolensk's cathedral. It had lost the roof and suffered other damage, but the walls and altar were intact. The priest told Luck that he had not been allowed to celebrate mass in the church for twenty-three years. Could he do so tomorrow? Of course, Luck replied. The next day Luck went to the cathedral, where he saw tens of thousands of worshipers, crowded into every available space inside and outside, praying and singing hymns. But their joy at liberation quickly turned to tears for, as Luck and the combat troops moved out, SS groups moved in.

Nazi conduct guaranteed the growth of resistance groups, often formed around encircled units far to the German rear. And in occupied Poland and France, local Communists—who had been pro-German up to Barbarossa—responded to a Moscow summons to sabotage German bases and supply lines. The deeper the Germans got into the Soviet Union, the longer and more vulnerable their supply lines became. It was a man-wasting job for the Germans to defend their rail and road lines.

When Barbarossa came the U.S.S.R. was incompletely mobilized, with but 150 understrength divisions deployed. The Soviets possessed some

21,000 tanks—more than four times the number opposing them—but few were of recent manufacture. The new medium model, T-34, was not thrown against the Germans until Smolensk. Yet the traditional soldiering qualities of the Soviets and the traditional Soviet strategy of trading space for time slowly rectified the balance. Moreover, manpower was ever plentiful. The Germans began to realize that the Soviets could afford to trade lives at a rate of five to one, making up their losses from a population that was three times the size of Germany's—and the Soviets were fighting for their homeland and were on one front only. Further, the Soviets fully mobilized women, while Hitler insisted that a woman's job was to have blond-haired babies and raise them to be good Nazis. Soviet women worked in the factories, which had been moved east of the Ural Mountains, twelve hours a day, seven days a week—for four years. Women and old men did the farming, and did it well enough to feed as many as 20 million young men a year.

For the first time in his dictatorship, Stalin gave the people things they deeply yearned for. He accorded religion a new role. Privileges and honors that had not existed since the Revolution were returned to officers. He sponsored the film *Alexander Nevsky*, one of the classics of moviemaking. It depicted the triumph of the Russians over the Teutonic knights in 1410. The film was seen by almost all Russians; it ran continuously in Moscow through the war, and there were always lines, day and night. People came away inspired, not to be better Communists but to be better Soviets. Guderian, the German panzer general, recalled meeting a former czarist general at Orel

A German infantryman leads the way while a runner follows, bringing telephone wire to the forward positions. In addition to the inadequate roads, the Germans were hampered by the primitive Soviet communications system. They had to build their own.

A German soldier on the Leningrad front is caught in the open during a Soviet artillery bombardment. For all its shortcomings, the Soviet system was able to provide shells and guns to the Red Army in numbers that far exceeded anything the *Wehrmacht* anticipated. By the late fall of 1941 the Germans had won tremendous victories and taken an immense amount of ground, but it had not destroyed the Red Army.

who said: "If only you had come twenty years ago we should have welcomed you with open arms. But now it's too late. We were just beginning to get on our feet and now you arrive and throw us back twenty years so that we will have to start from the beginning all over again. Now we are fighting for the Soviet Union and in that cause we are all united."

German losses were both heavy and hard to replace. Halder estimated that by the end of November 1941, Hitler had forfeited 743,112 men, or 23 percent of the total originally thrown into the Soviet campaign. And as the German advance lost momentum, the Soviets managed to assemble quantities of artillery. Since 1936, a new series had been under mass production: guns of 76, 122, and 152 millimeters; tremendous 280-, 305-, and even 406-millimeter howitzers; the famous katyusha rockets, which rolled up to the line on trucks for the first time on September 12, 1941, at Khandrov, outside Leningrad, and harassed the Germans with their multiple whistling explosions. "Stalin organs," the Red Army called them. The infantry was reequipped with Degtyarev and Goriunov machine guns and Shpagin machine pistols. And the Soviets maintained a cavalry force of six hundred thousand men, which, though it took terrible losses, disheartened the Germans by filtering through snowbound forests or suddenly sweeping out of dawn fogs. To support this complex apparatus, on August 25, 1941, Stalin created a "Command of the Rear of the Red Army" to assure logistical support, and an "Army of the Interior" to maintain absolute internal security.

Still, the Germans might well have taken Moscow in 1941 if Hitler had not decided to play the military genius. (Of course, Napoleon did take Moscow, for all the good it did him.) Ignoring his generals' advice, Hitler transferred forces from the Moscow front for use against Leningrad and the Ukraine. By the time the Moscow offensive could be resumed, it was October, and a great deal of valuable fall weather had been lost. But even so, the German offensive, named "Typhoon," took a terrible toll. In the first two weeks of October, two entire Soviet armies were encircled with a loss of 650,000 prisoners, according to German claims (Soviet figures are much lower).

By October 20, Bock was within forty miles of Moscow. A week earlier, Stalin had decided to evacuate his main ministries and the diplomatic corps to Kuibyshev, a ramshackle provincial town 550 miles to the southeast on the Volga, although he himself, with his chief lieutenants, remained in the Kremlin. The evacuees drove to the Kazan railway station through a city consumed by panic. The usual police units had been taken from the streets and rushed into line to plug a gap on the main highway from Vyazma. Families with bundles were hurrying to rail depots. Trucks loaded down with old men, women, children, and deserting bureaucrats were heading eastward. Crowds were looting bakeries and food stores as the usual stern order crumbled into chaos. At the Kazan station, every inch of the platform and track sidings was littered with huddled families and their pitiful belongings.

Fortunately, the first heavy snow was feathering down, obscuring the evacuation from the Luftwaffe. Boxcars and flatcars moved westward with silent troops and eastward with rusty machinery from Ukrainian and Soviet factories, which, with astonishing success, were being reassembled in distant Soviet Asia. By November, some two million people had either been shifted from the capital or had somehow managed to flee; many were later ashamed of their desertion.

This was the Soviet Union's moment of truth. A Red Army communiqué admitted: "During the night of October 14–15, the position of the western front became worse. The German-Fascist troops hurled against our troops large quantities of tanks and motorized infantry and in one sector broke through our defenses." German soldiers came close enough to Moscow to set their watches by the bells of the Kremlin. The official Soviet history of the war later said: "It was the lowest point reached throughout the war."

From the Kremlin itself, Stalin personally conducted the battle on his doorstep. He dispatched the dogged Timoshenko to take over from Budenny on the southern front, where Rundstedt was now hammering at the gateway to the Caucasus, and replaced him with General Georgi Zhukov, who painstakingly built up his reserves and waited for his ally, "General Winter." Snow alternated with rain, ice with mud, and gradually the Germans bogged down to the west, southeast, and north of Moscow. Hitler's generals pleaded with him to establish a winter line, but he refused, ordering them to press on.

German soldiers advance in a blizzard, their dark forms silhouetted against the white snow. The Red Army had white camouflage uniforms, but Hitler had thought he would have Moscow and Leningrad in hand before the onset of winter and failed to provide adequate winter gear for his troops. They suffered, as did their vehicles and weapons—oil congealed in motors, weapons froze—in the bitter cold of a Soviet winter.

Toward the end of October 1941, Germans outside Moscow were still on the attack (below). By now, the *Wehrmacht* was running out of energy. German casualties numbered three-quarters of a million by November, and still there was no end in sight. On November 7, meanwhile, the Red Army paraded in Red Square (right). In his speech Stalin evoked the picture of Mother Russia, an ancient land of heroes that had routed all previous barbarian invaders.

Sandbag barricades line a Moscow street in December 1941 (opposite). Many of the bureaucrats had fled, the diplomatic corps had fled, whole factories had been moved east to the Urals, but the citizens remained. If the *Wehrmacht* ever got into their city, the Muscovites were prepared to fight for it house by house. In Leningrad, too, the determination to resist was complete. Siberian troops came all the way from Soviet Asia via the trans-Siberian railroad—that is, almost halfway around the world—to participate in the relief of Moscow. These are among the few captured by the Germans (below). They nonetheless retain a look of determination that typified the revived Red Army.

The Germans resumed their offensive on November 16. Zhukov carried on a flexible defense, retreating to avoid encirclement, then striking back. The German armor became active again as the ground froze. Major von Luck's armored reconnaissance unit crossed the Moscow-Leningrad canal and for a day was actually east of Moscow.

But temperatures continued to drop, German equipment was immobilized by bitter cold, and, worst of all for the Germans, the snows came. A beaming Stalin told his aides, "General Winter has arrived." The danger to Moscow was past.

As the battle raged through November, Stalin took one of the great gambles of all time. He ordered the Red Army in Siberia, his only deterrent to a Japanese Army that was on the move—who knew where?—to come by the trans-Siberian railroad to Moscow. Had the Japanese invaded the denuded Soviet Asia, the course of history would have been changed. But they went south instead and Stalin's gamble worked.

On December 6, Zhukov used the reinforcements from Siberia to go over to the offensive. After he threw one hundred divisions into a sudden counterassault, the German lines faltered and dissolved. As Halder was to write:

**Outside the city of Moscow, thousands of
German dead were hastily buried in a
makeshift cemetery.**

"The myth of the invincibility of the German Army was broken." Droves of German soldiers were taken prisoner and displayed in newspaper photographs wearing women's furs and silk underclothing to supplement their inadequate uniforms against the cold. The German front started to crumble, but Hitler adamantly refused to permit the slightest retreat. Men died miserably and hopelessly. Field commanders forced to pull back were relieved and publicly disgraced. And on December 19, Hitler took over personal control of the army by making himself the commander in chief.

Hitler's commanders were bitter about his fanatical demand that they die rather than retreat; withdrawal to better positions, they said, could have saved tens of thousands of men. But some argued later that the dictator's adamant stand had saved the army, because a retreat, once begun, would have become a rout like the one that wrecked Napoleon's army. In any event, the German forces, although badly mauled, did not collapse; though the morale of the German soldier was often low, he was not yet beaten. The extreme cold hampered the Soviet armies, too; attempts to encircle large German forces failed. But by the time a late March 1942 thaw with its mud ended the Soviet offensive, total Nazi casualties on the eastern front had passed well over a million.

In those heroic days outside Moscow, one of the first publicized Soviet war heroes was the gigantic General Andrei Andreyevitch Vlasov, a dramatic and inspiring figure and one of Zhukov's most successful field commanders. Vlasov was later seized by the Germans and promptly switched sides, becoming the highest-ranking Soviet traitor of World War II. He recruited an army of Soviet prisoners and led them for Hitler until May 1945. General

Patton captured him in Czechoslovakia, handed him over to Stalin, and he was hanged.

Snow lay all along the Moscow front, even under birch copses and pine groves. The cold was savage. Everything froze totally and suddenly. Dead horses balanced stiffly on the edge of drifts as ravens pecked their eyes. The silent Soviet infantry trudged forward, accompanied by sleighs; guns lumbered up from the rear, and small-arms fire rattled through the woods.

Leningrad, the Soviet Union's second city, was a main German objective. Field Marshal Ritter von Leeb drove his Army Group North with such speed that on August 30, 1941, he cut the city's last rail connection with the rest of the Soviet Union, and a few days later his troops were in the suburbs and shelling the city, supported by Marshal Mannerheim's Finnish troops. But German expectations of taking Leningrad by storm faded as Marshal Zhukov took over the defense and turned the city into a maze of strong points. As the invaders settled down to a siege, Hitler told his commanders they were not to accept the surrender of the city. The city was to be razed to the ground by shelling and bombing, his directive said, and its people were to perish with it.

Because its last land link with the rest of the Soviet Union had been cut, Leningrad's plight was desperate: It had scarcely enough food to feed its three million people for little more than a month. A trickle of foodstuffs was flown in, but the defenders put their hopes on circumventing the German blockade by crossing broad Lake Ladoga to a point on the railroad east of where the Germans had cut it. But organizing the route took time, and for a multitude there was not enough time. They dropped of hunger and died even as they walked along the streets or worked at their factory jobs. They ate their dogs and cats; they swallowed hair oil and Vaseline; they made soup of dried glue from furniture joints and wallpaper. The "Ladoga Lifeline" across the frozen lake slowly began to catch up with food needs by January 1942, but the effects of the famine were felt for months afterward. It is believed, official figures notwithstanding, that close to a million may have died as a result of the siege. In January 1943, the Soviets at last opened a railroad link to the rest of the country, but not until January 1944 were the Germans routed and the siege and shelling of the city finally ended. In the middle of that dreadful 1941–42 winter, 3,500 to 4,000 people were dying of starvation every day. By official Soviet figures, 632,000 men, women, and children died during the blockade.

In the Ukraine, the Army Group South's offensive commanded by Rundstedt was speeding across the Dnieper and isolating huge Soviet formations. Stalin ordered the destruction of his enormous Dnieper dam and, with the same obstinacy so often shown by Hitler, commanded Budenny to hold Kiev. It was too late. German panzers forged a ring of steel around the Ukrainian capital. In a radio appeal, the Soviet dictator exhorted the besieged garrison to hold on. The defenders died in charred clusters around jumbled heaps of gutted tanks, guns, and trucks. When the Kiev area was finally quiet, the Germans claimed they had rounded up some six hundred thousand prisoners. Hitler replaced Rundstedt with Field Marshal Walther von Reichenau, and the latter swiftly overran all the Ukraine. In the Crimea, only Sevastopol

remained. After a nine-month siege, Sevastopol finally collapsed the following July, hammered to pieces by air attack, conventional artillery, and a giant siege gun that was called Dora.

Kharkov, the "Soviet Pittsburgh" on the Donets, was outflanked. Nikita Khrushchev, a Ukrainian commissar at the time, telephoned the Kremlin and protested that the endangered Soviet Army should be extricated. Stalin did not personally accept the call, but through Georgi Malenkov he passed on the abrupt message: "Let everything remain as it is." The Germans proceeded to smother the writhing pocket, and to the south they thrust into Rostov and the gateway to the Caucasus.

In January 1942 the Germans were able to re-establish a fighting line out of the chaos that resulted from Zhukov's victorious Moscow counteroffensive and the stalwart defense that prevented them from making Leningrad a winter base. Timoshenko recaptured Rostov in the south, and for the duration of the winter, an uneasy stalemate persisted on the lengthy front as both sides regrouped. By this time it was evident that Hitler would never again be able to muster an offensive along the entire fighting line. In fact, his generals thought he should stay on the defensive. Halder, his chief of the general staff, grumbled that Germany no longer had the power to mount a successful offensive and complained that Hitler's directives to attack "were the product of a violent nature following its momentary impulses, which recognized no limits to possibility and which made its wish-dreams the father of its acts." Once, Halder said, when a report was read to the Führer of Stalin's reserve strength, "Hitler flew at the man who was reading with clenched fists and

In the winter of 1941–42, the endless steppes, the never-ending snow, and the bitter cold made German soldiers more cautious, more confused. Who could tell if the barn ahead was empty or occupied by a T-34 tank, an antitank gun, or a squad of infantry (opposite)? Outside Leningrad, meanwhile, the women of the city had helped dig a massive antitank ditch and then went through a 900-day siege. Boris Ugarov's painting *A Leningrad Woman in the Year 1941* (above) depicts a woman hauling salvaged steel girders from shell-wrecked buildings while soldiers across the way head out for duty on the perimeter.

During the winter, the Russians were able to get food and supplies into Leningrad by constructing roads over frozen Lake Lagoda (above). The regular German bombardments destroyed the drainage system in Leningrad, so the citizens got their water from open mains in the streets (right). In a village outside Leningrad, civilians search for their dead at the site of a massacre (opposite), a familiar scene on the eastern front, where the Germans killed civilians on the slightest of pretexts, and often for no reason at all.

foam in the corners of his mouth and forbade him to read any more of such idiotic twaddle."

The *Wehrmacht* had lost an enormous number of fighting men—1.3 million casualties in twelve months. These were veteran troops, men who had been through Poland and France, the cream of the German Army. Even so, Hitler's plans for his 1942 summer offensive were ambitious enough: hold fast on the central front, capture Leningrad in the north, and make the main assault in the south, where Stalingrad would be captured or bombed into ruins, while other German forces would move on to seize the Caucasus, with

German tanks in the snow on the Lower Dnieper River (above) and an April 1942 cavalry charge somewhere on the steppes (opposite top; almost certainly a staged shot) give some sense of the vast distances. The endless expanses brought dismay to the Germans and salvation to the Soviets. German atrocities in the villages (opposite bottom) infuriated the Soviet troops, who liberated hamlets only to find that Germans had already killed the citizens. This one contained seventy-seven bodies; they had been tortured to death.

its rich oil fields. To flesh out its depleted forces, the Nazi high command went to its allies and associates and obtained fifty-two divisions: Hungarian, Romanian, Italian, Slovakian, and even one Spanish. The German offensive opened in early June, and at first it looked like the old story of blitzkrieg advances through bewildered Soviet defenders. But Hitler, with his vaulting ambition, now decided to capture both Stalingrad and the Caucasus at the same time, although his commanders warned him that the *Wehrmacht* did not have the strength for two such ambitious projects. Hitler was about to blunder the German Army into a catastrophe.

General Friedrich Paulus commanded the Sixth Army, objective Stalingrad. As the 1942 German offensive swept on, the Soviets could only fight desperate delaying battles. The German Sixth Army advanced rapidly toward Stalingrad during July and August 1942, while Soviet morale sank and the Soviet front threatened to collapse. On August 21, German troops set their flag on Mount Elbrus, highest peak of the Caucasus Mountains, while two days later Paulus's Sixth Army to the north reached the Volga not far above Stalingrad. Hitler's unenthusiastic Romanian, Hungarian, and Italian allies gave flank protection during the advance toward Stalingrad. But Hitler, playing the military expert again, bungled badly. When Stalingrad lay open for the taking in late July, he diverted to the south the panzer force that could have seized it. When he called the same force back two weeks later, the gates had closed. There would be a fight for Stalingrad.

The Luftwaffe began the Battle of Stalingrad with a bombardment from 600 planes that started vast fires and killed 40,000 civilians. Hitler ordered that the city be taken by August 25; but Soviet resistance had been stiffening, and Stalingrad did not fall. Yet in spite of instances of supreme heroism—soldiers, for instance, sometimes bound grenades to their bodies and

No matter how far the Germans advanced, it was never far enough for them. And no matter how many Red Army soldiers they killed or captured, there were always more. This remarkable photograph shows the Soviet infantry on the move near Stalingrad, unsupported, their lines stretching beyond the faraway horizon. These common soldiers of the Red Army were the men on whose performance the world hung in the balance, the forgotten heroes of the war. Without their sacrifices the Nazis would have won.

threw themselves under German tanks—German superiority in weapons gradually told, and the Soviet Sixty-second Army was pushed back into the city, surrounded on all sides but the Volga waterfront. (Stalingrad, a great industrial city, stretched for twenty-five miles along the Volga.) By mid-September the fighting had become a block-by-block, house-by-house affair and by the end of the month the Germans were in control of all the southern and most of the central parts of the city and were hammering at the industrial section in the north. Stalingrad was little more than rubble.

In September, Stalin again called upon Zhukov, his ace, and gave him command of the whole Stalingrad front. The city itself was confided to General Vasili Chuikov, commander of the Sixty-second Army, who had once advised Chiang Kai-shek and who was later to accept Berlin's surrender.

On September 13, a German division broke deep into Stalingrad and, progressing through the bomb-shattered city, almost reached Chuikov's command post. But Chuikov mined each building on the invader's path and set up zones of enfilading sniper nests. An unhappy German lieutenant wrote: "The street is no longer measured by meters but by corpses. . . . Stalingrad is no longer a town. By day it is an enormous cloud of burning, blinding smoke; it is a vast furnace lit by the reflection of the flames. And when night arrives, one of those scorching, howling, bleeding nights, the dogs plunge into the Volga and swim desperately to gain the other bank. The nights of Stalingrad are a terror for them. Animals flee this hell; the hardest stones cannot bear it for long; only men endure."

The fighting within Stalingrad was a fantastic kind of warfare, fought in cellars, in sewers, in blasted factories, behind the walls of blasted buildings. Every bit of the city was contested building by building, often in hand-to-hand fighting. Quarter was seldom asked or given, and in this savage battle it was common for surrounded units to fight on until annihilated. In spite of a heroic defense, the Soviets continued slowly to lose ground before the superior German weight of weapons, especially aircraft.

On October 14, the Germans attacked the tractor works (converted to making tanks) in the northern part of the city; it was an offensive of unbelievable ferocity, but though the defenders were pushed back they managed to hold. Fighting raged within the factory; tanks came off the assembly lines firing their cannon and machine guns at German soldiers. Soviet reinforcements and supplies had to come across the mile-wide Volga, under German bombing and shelling, and for a time the bridgehead became so small that only a single crossing remained, and it was under machine-gun fire. Soviet reinforcements were fed into the inferno as they became available, sometimes a division, sometimes a couple of dozen men—many of whom were killed before reaching the front. Not until the Red Army opened its great offensive on the entire Stalingrad front in late November was the imminent danger to the city removed, and not until the beginning of February did the last street fighting end.

While Chuikov held on, Zhukov brought up massive reinforcements and launched still another counterattack. On the morning of November 19, 1942, a tremendous Soviet offensive surprised and overwhelmed the Romanian Third Army, which held the Axis flank northwest of Stalingrad. The next day, south of the city, another massive assault sent German and Romanian armies on that flank reeling back. The two offensives, more than a hundred miles apart, drove ahead so irresistibly that they joined up west of Stalingrad in four days. General Paulus's Sixth Army was cut off and isolated in Stalingrad. The Nazi command urged Hitler to let Paulus break out while the Soviet cordon was still relatively weak, but the Führer refused. "I won't go back from the Volga," he shouted. He did create a special army corps to rescue the Sixth Army and put the exceptionally gifted Field Marshal von Manstein in command, but he refused to let Paulus fight his way to a junction with Manstein. The latter battled ahead through December blizzards for a week but was stopped thirty miles from Stalingrad.

Then began the real agony of the Sixth Army. The bitter Soviet winter set in with all its miseries. Medical supplies gave out, food ran short. As the Germans were forced into an ever-constricting area, their airstrip went, and it became impossible to send out wounded, who thereafter lay unattended. And all the while Hitler sent messages exhorting the doomed men to fight on

General Vasili Chuikov said of the Battle of Stalingrad, "It was like a boxer who has been called on to go from one ring to another without a break and fight opponents of varying weights; before the last fight there had not even been time enough to take a deep breath and wipe the sweat away." He was in almost continuous combat right to the end, when his army took Berlin.

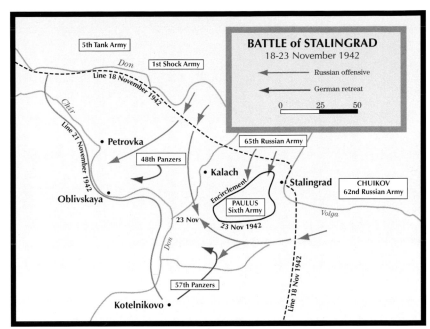

The early stages of the greatest battle ever fought—the Battle of Stalingrad—was also war at its absolute worst. The fighting went on day and night. During the day, the Germans would attack through the rubble, moving forward toward the Volga, advancing cellar by cellar. At night, the Red Army would counterattack, taking back the cellars. It went on for months. The strain on the combat infantry was unendurable, but it had to be endured.

to their death. Meanwhile, fighting went on as deadly as ever between Soviets and Germans among the ruins. Later, when Charles de Gaulle visited the devastated battlefield on his way to Moscow, he said quietly: "All the same, a formidable people, a very great people. I don't speak of the Soviets, I speak of the Germans . . . to have pushed this far."

On January 31, 1943, Paulus surrendered with ninety-one thousand emaciated, ragged survivors, all that were left of the three hundred thousand men of his Sixth Army who had first marched confidently into Stalingrad. Only about five thousand ever returned to Germany. The disaster, coming so unbelievably upon the heels of El Alamein, rocked the German people, and an overriding caution set in among their generals. Hitler had expected Paulus to commit suicide; instead he became the highest-ranking German officer of the war to turn traitor. After the war he made propaganda broadcasts for the Soviets and became the first commander of the East German Army.

In February 1943, following his unsuccessful attempt to rescue the Sixth Army, Manstein urged widespread withdrawal in the hope of enticing the Soviets into traps. But Hitler, fearing the political consequences in an Eastern Europe now crawling with guerrillas, spurned such strategy. He summoned his *Wehrmacht* to one final battle of annihilation. Choosing the Kursk salient, north of Kharkov, he built up a new force of five hundred thousand men, including seventeen panzer divisions equipped with the new Tiger tank. On July 4, 1943, this last initiative, what was to be the greatest of all tank battles, began.

Street fighting explodes in Stalingrad (below) in the opening weeks of the battle. The first rule of street fighting is: stay out of the streets. The best way to advance house to house is by blowing out the walls. By December, only skeletons of Stalinist high-rise apartments were left (opposite).

South of Stalingrad, the Germans had been successful in overrunning the Crimea. Here two Soviet soldiers try to surrender to advancing German troops, who appear to be hurrying on. They didn't go fast enough, however. By the time they got to the Kerch peninsula, shown here, the Soviets had reinforced their trans-Caucasus front. The oil in the Caucasus was the prize, but Hitler, obsessed by Stalingrad, stripped his forces in the south to send them to the meat-grinder along the Volga.

Stalingrad smolders on February 2, 1943, two days after the surrender. The battered city is in Soviet hands. Stalingrad lies 1,500 miles east of Berlin; it was the deepest penetration the Germans made into the Soviet Union. A city of 300,000 when the battle began now had no civilians left. There were about 91,000 German soldiers living, waiting to be marched to prison camp in Siberia (only 5,000 ever returned to Germany), and some 140,000 dead, most buried in the rubble. Russian losses were estimated at between 225,000 and 300,000 men.

The guileful Zhukov, forewarned by Soviet intelligence and familiarity with German strategy, had begun preparing for a Kursk battle as early as April. (Almost certainly there was a mole in the German High Command who was feeding information to the Red Army; in addition, the Soviets may have broken the Enigma code). Zhukov laid thick mine fields along stretches suitable to German tank advances and built up an immense artillery force of nearly twenty thousand guns and a thousand katyusha rockets. A Czech deserter tipped off the Soviets on the exact date of the German assault, and "Operation Citadel" was shattered by crunching barrages. Then, deliberately choosing his time, Zhukov attacked. He launched the Red Army's first massive summer offensive and put an end, once and for all, to the shibboleth that the Soviet soldier was good only when he was on the defensive.

The entire German front began to crumble. Orel, Kharkov, Smolensk, and Kiev were retaken before autumn ended. The first freeze caught the Nazis on the Ukrainian steppe, where infantry units, unable to dig trenches, made lean-tos of corpses roofed with canvas tenting to shelter themselves against the wind. A third Soviet winter settled in, grim and hopeless. Hitler, in his East Prussian "Wolf's Lair," cut himself off from his generals and henceforth heeded only the counsel of party fanatics, his physician, and his

Field Marshal Friedrich von Paulus shortly after the surrender. On January 22 he had radioed Hitler: "Rations exhausted. Over 12,000 unattended wounded. What orders should I give to troops who have no more ammunition and are subjected to mass attacks supported by heavy artillery?" Hitler replied: "Surrender is out of the question. The troops will defend themselves to the last." On January 28 Paulus stopped issuing rations to the wounded, to preserve the strength of the fighting troops. On January 31, he surrendered. Soon he was collaborating with the Soviets, urging German troops over the radio to surrender.

German artist Franz Eichorst's *German Soldiers Entrenched* captures the mood of the German Army during that terrible winter of 1943. These demoralized, ragged, wounded men are in great contrast to the spirited troops that raced east in the summer and early fall of 1941.

Soviet bombers strike at the Germans, summer 1942. Hitler believed that the Soviet system would collapse and the whole rotten structure come down at the first push. In fact, despite the loss of some of its largest and most valuable republics, the Soviet Union achieved miracles of production. In 1942 alone it built 25,000 aircraft, mostly fighters or two-engine bombers like these. The objective for the Soviet Air Force was to gain control of the sky over the front lines and provide direct support to the infantry.

astrologer. All illusions gone, the *Wehrmacht* began its creaking, tortured withdrawal.

The Red Army that now headed toward the Führer's Fortress Europe was a vastly different army from that which had fallen apart in 1941. It was a strange mixture: an army of quantity, slogging along with antiquated guns behind horse-drawn transport; and an army of quality, spearheaded by magnificent tanks. Huge amounts of material had been brought around the Arctic capes by British convoys and out of Iran by the American Persian Gulf Service Command. But useful as these tremendous numbers of trucks, planes, tanks, munitions, and shipments of food proved to be, they were nevertheless still fractional in importance. The U.S.S.R. itself had developed a huge ordnance industry, both around Moscow and in the Siberian reaches, where evacuated machinery was reassembled. From 1942 to 1944, Soviet factories manufactured 360,000 artillery pieces alone. The heavy Stalin-JS

tank replaced the old KV-2 and was supplemented by self-propelled guns and howitzers. Four aeronautic designers, Sergei Ilyushin, Alexander Yakovlev, Vladimir Petlyakov, and Semyon Lavochkin, were responsible for the production of improved series of fighters and bombers.

Although in the great encirclement of 1941 and 1942 the Red Army had lost 3,500,000 men in prisoners alone, by the time of the Kursk counteroffensive, Stalin had built a fresh force of 409 divisions. To direct this ponderous array Stalin created hundreds of generals and, ultimately, twenty-nine marshals. Promising officers like Konstantin Rokossovski, who had been purged in 1937 and was in a concentration camp when the invasion came, were forgiven trumped-up offenses and awarded high commands. Even the professionally minded Germans conceded the prowess of the Red Army soldier and the talent of his top commanders. They gave high marks to Konev, who first bloodied their noses at Yelnya, but they reserved their fullest admiration for the short, barrel-chested Zhukov, who came to symbolize Soviet military power, which had been held in contempt when World War II began and would be contesting global primacy when it ended.

In U. M. Neprintsev's *Rest after Battle*, the storyteller is a popular wartime fictional character, Vasili Tyorkin; he is a brave and shrewd soldier, cracking jokes as he works his way out of tough situations. Although a bit too romantic, the painting nicely catches the toughness of the Red Army by this stage of the war, its youthful vitality and strength, its ability to keep frontline troops well supplied, its self-confidence and its high morale.

Liberty

APRIL 18, 1942   10¢

WITH MacARTHUR — A THRILLING EYE WITNESS ACCOUNT

WARTIME BASEBALL: WHO'LL WIN? By Bill Cunningham

CHAPTER 9

THE POLITICS OF
WORLD WAR

The politics of World War II were as dazzling and confusing as a pin ball game. The West at first tended to equate the evil of Stalin's Communism with that of Nazism—and then after June 22, 1941, discerned in Communism previously unseen Jeffersonian qualities. Hitler insisted on the superiority of the Aryan race, but his closest allies were the Italians, and he accorded the Japanese the dubious accolade of "honorary" Aryans. Before Pearl Harbor the United States joined Britain in planning grand military strategy and fought the Germans at sea, all under the banner of neutrality. The Soviet Union was first Germany's partner and then its most deadly enemy. Italy changed sides. Roosevelt violated custom to win a third and fourth presidential term; Churchill, having led Britain through its toughest struggle, was voted out of office before its end.

Military requirements always took precedence over ideology. Washington successively coddled France's General Giraud and Admiral Darlan before begrudgingly accepting de Gaulle. London went to war to preserve Poland's integrity and then, when the conflict ended, grudgingly agreed to Soviet demands to change Poland's borders and to abandon the Poles to Communism. Communists around the world endorsed Hitler until he invaded the U.S.S.R.; then they played a major part in resistance to the Nazis. Until 1942, Stalin supported Tito's opponents in Yugoslavia; he consistently favored Chiang Kai-shek over Mao Tse-tung. Britain backed an émigré king for Greece and opposed an émigré king for Yugoslavia. Japan allied itself to Germany but told Berlin nothing about its plans for attacking Pearl Harbor and honored its nonaggression pact with Stalin even while fighting Hitler's other enemies.

The illustration opposite suggests the vigor with which the U.S. went into the war. Roosevelt and Churchill (in the cartoon above) were the leaders and the symbols of the greatest alliance ever formed. Despite many ups and downs, innumerable disagreements, and the terrific strain they were under, their friendship, like the alliance, held through the war. They enjoyed each other's company immensely; Roosevelt once told Churchill it was great fun being in the same century with him.

261

Allied generals squabbled with one another and yet joined in an unprecedented international command. Mussolini's and Hitler's generals squabbled less, but they quit the former and tried to murder the latter. The final showdown in Europe was run on one side from an East Prussian bunker by a madman listening to osteopaths and astrologers, and on the other side by a combined chiefs of staff whose strategy evolved from a series of conferences among heads of government and was based on facts.

"It is not so difficult to keep unity in time of war," Stalin acknowledged, "since there is a joint aim to defeat the common enemy, which is clear to everyone. The difficult time will come after the war when diverse interests tend to divide the Allies." But such interests, though always evident, were deliberately repressed. The principal arguments were about the time and place of a second front. The Soviets demanded it in 1942, in France. The Americans wanted to invade France in 1943. The British were not sure they wanted such an invasion at all, but certainly did not want it in 1943. Churchill wanted to go after the Nazi Empire's so-called "soft underbelly," meaning its operations in the Mediterranean and the Balkans. He had political motives, which were to get to Greece, Yugoslavia, and Czechoslovakia before the Red Army did, but the Americans and the Soviets felt that British cautiousness resulted from timidity. Having been kicked off the Continent in 1940, the British were reluctant to challenge the *Wehrmacht* in France again.

Churchill and Roosevelt could not have created and maintained the alliance on their own. Two of their principal advisers, Averell Harriman and Anthony Eden, are shown in London on September 15, 1941. Harriman, as Roosevelt's ambassador to Moscow, and Eden, Churchill's foreign minister, carried a heavy load from the beginning of the war to the end. Good personal relations were characteristic of the alliance, from top to bottom, from the politicians to the generals to the sailors to the troops in the field.

The Americans could see little point in going to North Africa to fight Frenchmen when the German enemy was but twenty miles away, across the Channel. But Churchill persuaded Roosevelt that something had to be done in 1942, and that it could not be done in France. Torch—the invasion of French North Africa—was the only alternative. The political repercussions of Torch were far more important than the military results. Torch cleared North Africa of the Germans but did nothing to hinder their efforts in the Soviet Union, or to threaten their defenses in France. And it caused bitter recriminations. Churchill tried to sell Stalin the idea that Torch opened a second front, but, as the Germans never had more than a handful of divisions in North Africa while the Red Army faced two hundred and more, Stalin wasn't buying.

Further, the British and Free French in the Mediterranean were fighting to retain their colonial empires. Roosevelt said he hoped to end them, but Stalin had his doubts. Still, Stalin could no more go it alone than could Churchill or Roosevelt, so, despite all the contradictions and underlying mistrust, the Grand Alliance held together.

The reason it cohered, General Lord Ismay, Churchill's military shadow, later observed, was perhaps partly because the Axis nations never coordinated their own actions. He wrote: "As we look back on that period we can never be sufficiently thankful that the three Axis powers had from the start pursued their own narrow, selfish ends, and that they had no integrated plan."

The Tripartite Pact never was much of an alliance and by the beginning of 1943 it was hardly more than words on paper. There was no coordination, no cooperation, just one Adolf Hitler, who busied himself as supreme commander of the *Wehrmacht* as well as absolute dictator of the Reich. Hitler had tried to get his old Fascist friend Francisco Franco to join the fight, telling him they would all be in the same boat should the Allies triumph. But Franco wisely decided to sit this one out. Hitler had also tried to get the Japanese to attack the Soviets, but he had no luck there either. About all he was left with were the Vichy Frenchman Pierre Laval and Mussolini. By then Mussolini was a sick man, living on a diet of milk and rice, whose political strength at home was growing more feeble by the day. In late 1942, he had tried to talk Hitler into making peace with the Soviets. It was their only chance to avoid disaster, he argued. The Führer would have none of it. About all Mussolini was good for now, it seemed, was strutting about in one of his snappy getups. But then, at least he still looked like he amounted to something.

The Allies, on the other hand, hammered out their overall strategy at dramatic meetings between Roosevelt and Churchill, Churchill and Stalin, the three together, and, on one occasion, Roosevelt, Churchill, and Chiang. They agreed that Germany must be defeated before Japan, and Stalin promised to help the Western powers in Asia within three months after Hitler's destruction.

Churchill, who was less naive than Roosevelt (the American president trusted "Uncle Joe," as Stalin was called in the States, almost to the end), showed much patience in dealing with Stalin. As he later wrote: "I tried my best to build up by frequent personal telegrams the same kind of happy

Germany and Vichy France had an entirely different relationship, one devoid of any hint of friendship or partnership. Here the leading Vichy collaborator, Pierre Laval, pledges his subservience to Hitler, in a railroad car in occupied France, November 18, 1940. Vichy supplied Germany with slave labor, food, raw materials, and the output of French factories.

relations which I had developed with President Roosevelt. In this long Moscow series I received many rebuffs and only rarely a kind word. In many cases the telegrams were left unanswered altogether or for many days. The Soviet government had the impression that they were conferring a great favour on us by fighting in their own country for their own lives. The more they fought, the heavier our debt became. This was not a balanced view."

Twice he flew to Moscow for private Kremlin talks, in August 1942 and again in October 1944. The first time he explained why an Allied landing in France was being delayed in favor of the North African invasion. He was rewarded with a series of insults, including a Stalin retort that the British were cowards. "When are you going to start fighting?" Stalin asked. "Are you going to let us do all the work?" The deal the Allies struck with collaborationist Darlan heightened Stalin's suspicions. It was beginning to look to him as if his capitalist allies had agreed to fight to the last Soviet. The second time, Churchill and Stalin divided the Balkans into spheres of influence—theoretically for the war period only. Churchill also acknowledged realities in Poland by persuading some leading Polish émigrés to accept the Curzon Line, which gave territory in eastern Poland to the Soviet Union. This deal was kept quiet until after the United States elections in November 1944 in order not to embarrass Roosevelt with Polish-American and other Catholic voters.

Roosevelt often deliberately played up to Stalin and sought to conciliate the Soviet dictator. At the Teheran Conference in 1943 and again at Yalta in 1945, the president strongly opposed the old-fashioned colonial system on

which the British Empire was founded, even once suggesting that Britain should abandon Hong Kong. Churchill was sometimes hurt and angered, but Stalin remained unmoved. He coldly pushed Soviet interests and ignored, both in the Soviet Union and in Eastern Europe, all promises of political liberty to which he had agreed.

The first effort to bring together Roosevelt, Churchill, and Stalin was made in early December 1942 when the time had come to discuss what moves should follow the conquest of North Africa. Roosevelt and Churchill invited Stalin to meet them at Casablanca, on Morocco's Atlantic coast, but the Soviet premier, although he professed to welcome the idea, said he could not leave the U.S.S.R. "even for a day, as it is just now that important military operations of our military campaign are developing." He also reminded the Western leaders of their promise to open a second front in Western Europe in the spring of 1943.

Nonetheless, Roosevelt and Churchill went to Casablanca along with their top military planners. The Americans reluctantly accepted British arguments that the 1943 cross-Channel assault, Roundup, was out of the question, and that therefore victory in Africa should be succeeded as quickly as possible by offensives in the Mediterranean. This action would drive Italy out of the war, which to Stalin meant that, instead of going after the most powerful enemy, the Anglo-Americans were going after the weakest partner of the Axis powers. Sicily was to be the target and July 1943 the date.

Although France as an immediate operational theater was relegated to the background at the Casablanca discussions, politically it was a central

The German-Italian alliance—the so-called Pact of Steel of the Axis powers—was based on a common ideology, fascism. But it was hardly an alliance between equals. Here, in the happier days before the war, Mussolini and Hitler appear to be as close as Churchill and Roosevelt, but as Mussolini discovered once the war began, such appearances were deceiving. Hitler dominated Mussolini as he did Laval and Vichy

The Big Three—Churchill, Roosevelt, and Stalin—were the leaders of the Grand Alliance. Sometimes called the Strange Alliance, it brought together the world's greatest colonial empire, its greatest capitalist nation, and its only Communist power. The alliance held for one simple reason: all three men realized that victory was scarcely possible if it did not. It took all three to defeat Hitler. Once he was gone, they inevitably split up.

and disagreeable theme. On January 22, General de Gaulle was flown to Morocco. His disgruntled mood did not improve when he found himself guarded by American soldiers on what he considered French soil. General Giraud was already at Casablanca. Roosevelt later insisted: "My job was to produce the bride in the person of General Giraud while Churchill was to bring in General de Gaulle to play the role of bridegroom in a shotgun wedding." Roosevelt heartily disliked de Gaulle, who, the president thought, saw himself as a new Joan of Arc, "with whom it is said one of his ancestors served as a faithful adherent." "Yes," Churchill is said to have replied, "but my bishops won't let me burn him!" Churchill admonished the general: "You claim to be France! I do not recognize you as France. . . ." "Then why," de Gaulle interrupted, "and with what rights are you dealing with me concerning her worldwide interests?"

De Gaulle wrote of this tense encounter: "I was starting from scratch. In France, no following and no reputation. Abroad, neither credit nor standing. But this very destitution showed me my line of conduct. It was by adopting without compromise the cause of the national recovery that I could acquire authority. At this moment, the worst in her history, it was for me to assume the burden of France."

At the close of the Casablanca meeting, Roosevelt and Churchill

Roosevelt and Churchill meet in Casablanca, January 1943. They met frequently, once before American entry into the war and four times after. Their military chiefs accompanied them—with considerable trepidation, as the generals and admirals feared what the politicians might conjure up. Left to right behind the heads of government are Admiral Ernest King, General George Marshall, Admiral Dudley Pound, and Generals Charles Portal and Alan Brooke.

This commemorative card, honoring the establishment of the Sixty-third Division, is one of the most valuable signature collections in existence. Roosevelt, Churchill, Lord Ismay, Admirals King and Mountbatten, Generals Brooke, Portal, and Arnold, among others, signed it during the Casablanca Conference, January 1943. This British division was committed to the North African campaign under the command of General Dwight Eisenhower. In the field, some U.S. units were meanwhile under the command of British generals. The relative ease with which this command arrangement was carried out speaks more eloquently than anything else to the uniqueness and solidarity of the Anglo-American alliance.

mischievously contrived to have de Gaulle and Giraud sit with them at a press conference at noon on Sunday, January 24. Churchill later confessed: "We forced them to shake hands in public before all the reporters and photographers. They did so, and the pictures of this event cannot be viewed even in the selling of these tragic times without a laugh." When pondering de Gaulle's subsequent actions, one wonders who laughed last.

After their handshake, which they repeated for the benefit of photographers, the two French generals retired while the president and the prime minister talked to the press. Roosevelt, discussing the conference, said: "Peace can come to the world only by the total elimination of German and Japanese war power. . . . The elimination of German, Japanese, and Italian war power means the unconditional surrender of Germany, Italy, and Japan. . . ." The British, particularly Churchill, disliked the phrase. Churchill said afterward: "I would not myself have used these words." He felt that the absolute and categorical expression could only stiffen enemy resolve. Many Americans came to agree with him. They felt that because the enemy had no incentive to surrender, the Germans and Japanese fought harder and longer than they otherwise would have—fought, indeed, until they could fight no more.

Roosevelt never explained the details of unconditional surrender. Presumably, it meant the Allies would fight until such time as the Axis governments put themselves into the hands of the Allies, but beyond that, what? What kind of governments would replace those of Mussolini, Tojo, and Hitler? Obviously there would be a period of military occupation, with control invested in an Allied military governor, but then what? A communist government? A democratic government? A monarchy? Roosevelt never said.

He did not because he did not know himself. Always a self-confident pragmatist, he was sure that he would handle situations as they arose. He made his decisions on the basis of military expedience. His goal was the destruction of Nazi Germany. That was a political goal of the first magnitude. Meanwhile, by refusing to discuss war aims beyond defeating Hitler, Roosevelt prevented bickering among himself, Churchill, and Stalin, each of whom had a different vision of postwar Europe.

In a sense, Roosevelt's unconditional surrender demand was a guarantee to Stalin. When the Darlan Deal was made, Stalin had to wonder if the Anglo-Americans might cut a similar deal with the German generals, perhaps even implementing a switch in sides—as Darlan had done with the French armed forces—that would bring on Stalin's worst nightmare, a German-American-British alliance directed against the Soviet Union. By announcing unconditional surrender, Roosevelt lessened Stalin's fears.

In late 1943 a second series of conferences was held. From November 22 to 26, Roosevelt and Churchill met with Chiang Kai-shek in Cairo. The talk centered on Far Eastern problems, and it was agreed to strip Japan of all her twentieth-century conquests, starting with Korea, Formosa, and Manchuria. The atmosphere was not happy. General Stilwell used the occasion to lobby savagely against Chiang. Chiang himself fought back, extracting concessions from Roosevelt, while his beautiful Wellesley-educated wife occupied herself with shopping tours and with casting poisonous conversational darts while attending the meeting's numerous social gatherings. But the serious negotiations were held with maximum secrecy, and little was made public.

Roosevelt first met Stalin at the subsequent Teheran meeting, the first Big Three conference or, as such gatherings would be called during the Cold War, the first summit conference. It lasted from November 28 to December 1, 1943. Roosevelt, who had looked forward to meeting the Communist boss, reported afterward to Congress that he "got along fine" with his host. Ismay rather less exuberantly recollected: "It is doubtful that many of those who listened to the discussion grasped the significance of Stalin's determination to keep Anglo-American forces as far as possible away from the Balkans. It was not until later that we realized that his ambitions were just as imperialistic as those of the czars, whose power and property he now enjoyed, but that he was capable of looking much further ahead than they had ever been."

Stalin was single-minded: When and where will the second front be opened? Roosevelt assured him it would come in the spring of 1944, in France, code-named Overlord. It would be supported by a landing from Italy on the south coast of France and a stepped-up Soviet offensive in the east. For his part, Stalin agreed that three months after Germany surrendered, the Soviet Union would enter the war against Japan. Further discussions centered on Eastern Europe. The three agreed henceforth to support Tito's Communist partisans and give parts of eastern Poland to the Soviet Union. Stalin opposed suggestions that Turkey be brought into the war and opposed Churchill's wish to invade the Balkans.

General Charles de Gaulle shakes hands with General Henri Giraud at Casablanca. De Gaulle, head of the Free French, insisted that France was still a great power and a member of the Grand Alliance. Roosevelt and Churchill found it convenient to pretend that this was so, even though de Gaulle gave Churchill some of his worst moments, while Roosevelt, deeply suspicious of de Gaulle, charged that he had confused himself with Joan of Arc. In the end, it was de Gaulle who outmaneuvered the other two.

Roosevelt appears with Churchill at the press conference held at the Hotel Anfa, outside Casablanca, January 23, 1943, where he announced the unconditional surrender policy. The U.S. president hoped that the announcement would boost morale at home (it did) and signal his intention to avoid the mistake Woodrow Wilson had made in 1918 in accepting an armistice while German troops were still in France. In a broader sense, Roosevelt wanted unconditional surrender to be a guarantee to Stalin that the Western powers were fully committed to the utter destruction of the Nazi government. Stalin worried because of the Darlan Deal, which seemed to indicate that the Anglo-Americans would be willing to deal with the German generals if and when they overthrew Hitler. Critics charged, with considerable truth, that the unconditional surrender policy only made the Germans fight harder.

The Big Three meet at Teheran, Iran, December 15, 1943. This classic photo catches the spirit of the Grand Alliance, a determination to see this thing through to the end. This was the first summit meeting and, of all the ones that followed, right through World War II and the Cold War, the most productive and friendly. At Teheran, the Big Three agreed on the strategy for the year 1944. Here it was that Roosevelt gave Stalin the pledge he had been demanding since June 1941—that the Anglo-Americans would open a second front in France in the spring of 1944. As this was Stalin's number one political objective in the war, he had cause to look satisfied.

Chiang Kai-shek poses with his wife and General Joseph Stilwell in Burma, April 19, 1942. Stilwell, Chiang's adviser and chief of staff, was commander of U.S. forces in China and chief administrator of Lend-Lease shipments to China. U.S. policy was to regard China as a great power and to support Chiang as China's leader. In fact, Stilwell could not abide Chiang, a feeling that was reciprocated, and China was so drained by the Japanese occupation of much of its eastern territory and by the continuing civil war between Chiang's Nationalists and Mao's Communists that China could make only a minor contribution to the war against Japan.

France featured at Teheran as a disagreeable footnote. On his way to the conference, Roosevelt told his Joint Chiefs of Staff that "France would certainly not again become a first-class power for at least twenty-five years," and that Britain was supporting the French in order to use their future strength. Roosevelt also adduced the strange theory that no Frenchman over forty should be allowed to hold office in postwar France. He agreed with Stalin that "the French must pay for their criminal collaboration with Germany."

At Teheran, Roosevelt raised the subject of France's most valuable Asian colony, Indochina. Pointing out that "the French have been there for one hundred years and the people are worse off for it," he suggested that Laos, Cambodia, and Vietnam be placed under a four-power trusteeship (the powers being the Big Three plus China) and placed on the road to independence. Stalin immediately endorsed the proposal. Only Churchill, fearful for the British Empire, objected to thus snatching away Indochina from France.

While the Great Power leaders were meeting in Casablanca, Cairo, and Teheran, a contest was taking place for influence in the enormously rich Middle Eastern petroleum fields. Stalin was not a prominent figure in the intra-Allied oil competition. He had made an unsuccessful effort to move into that area back in the days when he was courting Hitler. On November 26, 1940, he had virtually offered to join the Axis in exchange for dominance of the Persian Gulf region, but Hitler had by then resolved on Barbarossa. Less than a year later, on August 25, 1941, Soviet and British troops moved into Iran to end German intrigues with the shah. However, the southern oil fields fell within the British occupation zone. And at that time, the Soviets were preoccupied with German efforts to capture Soviet oil wells located around Grozny and the Apsheron Peninsula.

The British possessed extensive petroleum fields in the Arab provinces of the former Ottoman Empire, but in Saudi Arabia a potentially huge development had been started by a United States company, California Arabian Standard Oil Company (later Aramco), which had been granted a concession in 1933 by King Ibn Saud. Although Washington had opened diplomatic relations with Ibn Saud to insure adequate reserves for the U.S. armed forces, Aramco rejected a proposal by Interior Secretary Harold Ickes that the U.S. government become a shareholder in the operation. Nevertheless, rapid extension of American petroleum holdings for the first time engendered an active State Department involvement in the Middle East.

Oil was but one aspect of wartime economic competition. Hitler shaped his 1942 Soviet strategy around his petroleum needs, but his agents were also continually engaged in a search for other raw materials that were required for new weapons systems: hard metals needed for jet engines and missiles; rare minerals available only in neutral lands such as Sweden, Portugal, and Turkey. The income of those countries zoomed as Axis purchasers competed with Allied pre-emptive buying missions for chromium, wolfram, and cinnabar.

There was global competition, too, for public opinion. In this area, the Axis sacrificed their initial advantage through their occupation policies. As noted, millions of Soviets were ready to welcome the Germans as liberators from the Communists; in Asia, people were equally ready to welcome the Japanese as liberators from the European and American colonial occupiers. "Asia for the Asians" was the Japanese slogan, but the Chinese, Filipinos, Vietnamese, and others found that some Asians were going to be more equal than others, just as the Soviets discovered that the Nazis were at least as bad as the Communists.

Radio by this time had become a major weapon. Stalin, Roosevelt, Churchill, Hitler, and Mussolini—all were using it with powerful effect. The

Roosevelt is at his most persuasive on board the U.S. cruiser *Quincy*, in Great Bitter Lake, near Cairo, February 1945. Here he is at work on King Saud of Saudi Arabia, with Marine Colonel Eddy, the U.S. representative in Arabia, as translator. In 1939 the Standard Oil Company of California had received a concession from Saudi Arabia to explore for and extract oil from the desert kingdom. Although Saudi Arabia was a technical neutral until March 1, 1945, when the king declared war on Germany and Japan, throughout the conflict Saudi oil went only to the Anglo-Americans.

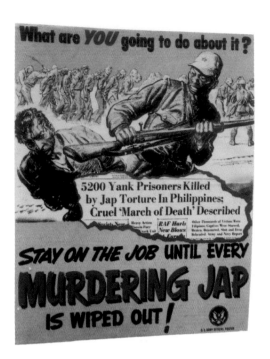

Wartime propaganda posters proliferated in every country. Most of them were simplistic, exaggerated, vicious, and sometimes, as the one below depicts, inadvertently amusing.

Axis found a pitiful chorus of traitors ready to echo its cause on the airwaves: "Axis Sally," "Lord Haw Haw," Jane Anderson, Fred Kaltenbach, and Otto Koischwitz. Broadcasts featured American and British popular music, which got the soldiers to listen to them. They were supplemented by leaflets, fired by artillery or dropped from bombers, that counseled soldiers to desert. The Soviets added a grim note by trussing up the corpses of frozen Germans and dropping them from aircraft behind the Nazi lines. Nazi brochures asked GIs in Italy: "Who is cashing in on the huge war profits at home while Americans shed their blood over here?" A constant theme of German propaganda directed at Americans was: "Why are you fighting for the communists?" "Tokyo Rose" broadcast to United States troops in the Pacific: "The girl back home is drinking with some 4-F who's rolling in easy money." The Americans distributed photographs of well-clad Axis prisoners eating enormous meals, captioned: "Better Free than a Prisoner of War: Better a Prisoner of War than Dead."

The British Political Warfare Executive (PWE) and the American Office of War Information (OWI) pooled their efforts to "reduce the cost of the physical battle" and undermine enemy morale. As the tide of conflict turned, the two organizations laid increasing stress on the terror that continued war would bring to Germany and Japan, and they dropped pictures of bomb-shattered cities on frontline troops. Code messages directed to guerrilla organizations and sabotage groups were mixed with skillfully camouflaged propaganda broadcasts that seemed to originate inside occupied territory. How effective this barrage of propaganda was must be doubted. In general, soldiers used enemy leaflets for toilet paper.

At the same time, the classical wartime use of spies and saboteurs was rendered far more effective by employing aircraft and submarines to deliver them. Both sides produced audacious special agents, trained in silent killing and equipped with gold coins, counterfeit notes, booby-trap devices, portable communications systems, and light weapons. Yugoslavia, Greece, Albania, north Italy, and most of France contained teams of Englishmen and Americans who fought beside local partisans and transmitted detailed information on enemy dispositions to air strike forces and commando assault groups abroad. The U.S. Office of Strategic Services (OSS, transformed after the war to the Central Intelligence Agency) had nearly 11,000 persons on its roster around the world by the time peace came. One OSS agent planted a microphone in the Luftwaffe's Paris headquarters. Allen Dulles, in charge of OSS operations from Switzerland and later head of the CIA, managed to penetrate the *Abwehr* (the German Intelligence Bureau) of Admiral Wilhelm Canaris, an anti-Hitler officer garroted after the 1944 attempt on the Führer's life.

On the German side, Nazi killers spread terror from Teheran to the Ardennes. And German spies were dropped in England (where every one of them was rounded up and forced to become a double agent), shipped by yacht to South Africa, landed by submarine in the United States. The FBI rounded up thirty-one Nazi agents on August 1, 1941. The following year, eight German saboteurs brought by U-boat to Long Island and the Florida coast were arrested and six of them were executed.

•

Victory in war usually goes to the side that is the best organized to use its assets most effectively. Only politicians can get a nation organized properly. In World War II, it was the Allies who produced the politicians who could get the human and material resources of their nations to pull together for the supreme effort. The United States took the lead.

President Franklin Roosevelt was the guiding genius of the war effort, even though little in his background had prepared him for running a war. He had never worn a uniform nor had he received any military education. True, he had served with much enthusiasm in the Navy Department during the first war, but his profession had always been strictly politics. It was a line of work few men were better at, and, perhaps because of that, he recognized from the first that victory would depend on American productivity and unity among the Allies. "The United Nations" was his phrase, and he used it often with great effect. But he also knew that real unity would take some tall doing: Stalin wanted a second front right away, Churchill did not, and there was strong feeling at home for punishing the Japanese first. Although Roosevelt decided for Torch, he simultaneously insisted that there was going to be no American straying from the beat-Germany-first strategy. Despite immense strain, that decision, reinforced by the unconditional surrender demand, held the Big Three together.

Roosevelt's other great contribution stemmed from his ability to judge men. Whatever he may have lacked for the job of commander in chief was more than made up for by the group of men he called on to help him. They

Looking like huge Fourth of July firecrackers, these containers filled with propaganda leaflets have just been released from U.S. Air Force planes over Merseburg, Germany. The containers were set to open at six thousand feet.

HEROES

Every army produced heroes, and every nation put its propaganda machine to work glorifying them. The genuine heroes, like Audie Murphy of the U.S. Army and Otto Skorzeny of the SS, became celebrities. More often than not, however, acts of heroism went unnoticed, and the hero got no award or publicity. Here are two examples.

Sergeant Wagger Thornton was a squad leader in D Company, the Oxfordshire and Buckinghamshire Light Infantry regiment, a gliderborne outfit in the British Sixth Airborne Division. He was in the initial D-Day attack, at 0015 hours, when his glider landed beside a bridge (later named Pegasus Bridge) over the Orne Canal. His company's mission was to seize and hold that bridge, which was vital to the landings that would be coming onto the Normandy Beach some five kilometers away, at first light. The operation, a surprise attack, went perfectly. The Germans never heard the gliders coming in; the British poured out of them and overwhelmed the hundred or so Germans guarding the bridge. Now came the hard part: holding the bridge until the seaborne invaders could reach them.

The Germans counterattacked at 0300. They came on with two old tanks. D Company had only one handheld antitank rocket. "It was a piece of junk, really," Thornton told Stephen Ambrose in an interview. "You couldn't hit a tank from twenty yards away and even if you did the charge wasn't powerful enough to do any real damage."

Heroes came in every shape and nationality. Here, British and Australian survivors are rescued by the USS *Sealion*, September 1944.

Thornton was crouched behind a house when he heard the lead tank clanking its way to the bridge. If he couldn't stop it, the Germans would re-take the bridge, with dire consequences for the invasion force. He stepped from behind the house, ran close to the tank, and fired his rocket at point-blank range. He went for the seam at the base of the turret and hit it. Sparks penetrated the tank and set off a shell in its magazine. Explosion followed explosion. The second tank backed away; the bridge was secure. Thornton had fired what might be called with only slight exaggeration the most important shot of the war.

When Ambrose met him, he was an old man, living in near-poverty in a tiny flat in London's East End:

"As I was packing up my tape recorder after our interview, Thornton said, 'Now, whatever you do in this book, don't go making me into a bloody hero.' I could only think to reply, 'Sergeant Thornton, I don't make heroes. I just write about them.'"

Gregory Orfalea tells the story of Private Ed Huempfner in *Messengers of the Lost Battalion*. At age twenty-six, Huempfner was the oldest enlisted man in his company, the U.S. Army's 551st Parachute Infantry Battalion. On December 22, 1944, in the Ardennes, Huempfner got separated from the others and found himself hiding in a toilet in a farmhouse being searched by Germans. He escaped through the back window and went to work. First, he gathered up some grenades and moved into the nearby village, where he managed to get on a tank and drop a grenade down the hatch, then did the same with a half-track. Next, he dashed into a barn, fig-uring there would be Germans inside—and shot a half dozen while the others ran out the back. Finally, he located a Ger-man machine-gun position and pumped eight rounds from his M-1 into it, putting it out of action. By nightfall the Germans pulled their infantry and tanks out of the village and billeted themselves in the woods. They thought an American company had driven them out of their positions. The company had been one man—Huempfner.

After the war Huempfner returned to his hometown, Green Bay, Wis-consin. There he managed to raise four children, making a living as a jani-tor, but he was one of those countless GIs who brought the war home with him. When his wife died of cancer at age forty-three he went to pieces. He drank heavily and lived in a single room above a shop. For nine years he was unemployed, living on a monthly pension of $21.60.

Whenever a World War II veteran died in Green Bay, Huempfner would show up at the funeral home and stand silently at attention all day. Some-times he was the only mourner. When he died, a thousand people came to a pauper's funeral.

Wounded U.S. Marines are helped onto an aid station by navy corpsmen in Iwo Jima, February 1945.

On April 25, 1945, U.S. Secretary of State Edward Stettinius addresses the delegates to the San Francisco conference that is creating the United Nations. Around the world, people hoped with all their hearts that the United Nations would be able to avoid the mistakes of the League of Nations and become a genuine world body powerful enough to prevent any future war. The photograph dramatically illustrates how difficult this would be: to Stettinius's left is Alger Hiss, a State Department official who served as secretary general at this meeting. Hiss was later accused of being a Communist spy who worked for the Soviet Union. To Hiss's left is Andrey Gromyko, Soviet ambassador to the United States and leader of the Soviet delegation at San Francisco, obviously skeptical and suspicious of everything Stettinius is saying.

were men cut from much the same cloth as the boss himself—male, white, Anglo-Saxon, members of what would later be called "the Establishment." Of the eight principal high-ranking government officials, all were from the eastern half of the country; four had attended FDR's own Harvard, and four were from his home state, New York. With few exceptions, they were Democrats from the worlds of finance, diplomacy, and the law. Lend-Lease executive, and later secretary of state, Edward Stettinius had been head of U.S. Steel; Secretary of State Cordell Hull had been a senator from Tennessee; Secretary of War Henry Stimson and Secretary of the Navy Frank Knox were prominent Republicans; Undersecretary of the Navy James Forrestal was a Wall Street financier. But while the overall pattern was predictable, the level of competence was unpredictably high. All of them, the military men included, were remarkably able. Some were among the best leaders the country ever produced: the quiet, patient Army Chief of Staff George Marshall was almost universally regarded as the best man in the country; Admiral Ernest J. King, although a difficult personality, was almost as respected. Through all the war, a cabinet shake-up was never necessary. Every man but three stuck to his job. (Undersecretary of State Sumner Welles resigned in September 1943 after a rift with Hull; Knox died in March 1944; and Hull resigned that same year because of illness.)

The Roosevelt lieutenant who did the most to give the war regime its zest and direction, and who stirred up more controversy than all the rest combined, was the son of an Iowa harness maker, Harry Hopkins, Roosevelt's brash, brilliant, sometimes devious, always resourceful troubleshooter, hatchet man, and alter ego. But more than anything else, he was the prime mover behind FDR's every maneuver to bring about a solid working relationship first with Churchill and then with the man the White House circle called "Uncle Joe."

Roosevelt's team did a superb job of guiding America through the war. Under its direction U.S. industry, operating at half capacity or less in 1939,

America's wartime leaders were an exceptionally able lot. Top left, Secretary of State Cordell Hull and Undersecretary Sumner Welles arrive for a lunch at the White House. Left, Secretary of War Henry Stimson, a leading Republican in Roosevelt's Cabinet, testifies before the House Foreign Affairs Committee on January 16, 1941. Stimson was advocating passage of Lend-Lease. Above, Admiral King and Generals Arnold and Marshall, the U.S. chiefs of staff, leave the White House on June 6, 1944, after briefing Roosevelt on the invasion of France.

Roosevelt, on his way home from Casablanca on January 30, 1943 (above), celebrates his sixty-first birthday with his principal personal adviser, Harry Hopkins, and his personal chief of staff, Admiral William Leahy (left). There is a haunting quality to this photograph; Roosevelt's boyish enthusiasm of spirit contrasts sharply with his deteriorating physical condition. Hopkins, too, was in ill health, and gave his life for his country; he died four months after the war ended.

Roosevelt gets a tour with General Eisenhower in Tunis, December 7, 1943 (right). Roosevelt was on his way home from the Cairo Conference. It was on this occasion that Roosevelt turned to the general and said, almost casually, "Well, Ike, you are going to command Overlord."

performed miracles of production. The U.S. government expanded enormously. So, of course, did the armed services. Together, the political and military leaders of the United States used the weapons and manpower produced by the nation to bring about victory, aided immeasurably by the cooperation between the Americans and the British. Although the president and the prime minister often disagreed, and their military chiefs disagreed among themselves even more, overall the Anglo-American alliance of World War II was the strongest ever seen. Together with the Soviet Union, they took on a government of criminals who were out to loot Europe and kill every Jew they could get their hands on.

In Germany an awful internal rot ran through the Nazi regime from top to bottom. Hitler and his minions wanted to annihilate Jews and other "undesirables," destroy Communism and democracy, make the Slavs into slaves, subordinate Western Europe to German domination, overrun England, and leave to the next generation the problem of conquering North America. These were contradictory and wildly unrealistic goals, far beyond Germany's capabilities without solid and trustworthy allies—something Hitler's personality and politics precluded. It was he who scorned the Japanese and Italians and made the United Kingdom, the United States, and the Union of Soviet Socialist Republics into enemies. Hitler believed that the Strange Alliance could never hold together, but it did, because of him, and it insured his defeat.

CHAPTER 10

THE SECRET WAR

The secret war captures the imagination: Spies, electronic intelligence, physicists in their labs, disinformation campaigns, new weapons, the beginning of the Space Age, and other aspects of science and technology played a central if unknown role in World War II. People were aware, at least in a general sense, about the development of new weapons; one popular saying had it that "this war is being fought on the drafting boards and in blueprints." Once a weapon was used, whether a guided missile or the T-34 tank or a jet airplane, its existence was immediately disclosed, if not yet fully understood. But there was a still more secret war, most of all in atomic development and electronics, which only a tiny number of experts knew of or understood.

The realm of secret weapons became the war's richest target for espionage. A combination of spy reports and expert interpretation of aerial photographs provided the Allies with important data about German V-weapons, missiles, and robot aircraft, and enabled them to bomb the experimental rocket center at Peenemünde. Allied and Axis scientists, who had shared a common fund of atomic knowledge before the war, kept watch on each other's subsequent efforts through intelligence reports rather than scientific journals.

In 1933, the year Hitler and Franklin Roosevelt came to power, the world's most famous physicist, Albert Einstein, left Germany to live in the United States. He was one of the first European Jewish scientists to flee the Nazis. Many followed, along with other physicists who could not abide the thought of living in a Europe occupied by Hitler and Mussolini. In January 1939, Otto Hahn and his German associates had achieved the first stage of nuclear fission, and French and American physicists were seeking to emu-

On September 10, 1945, J. Robert Oppenheimer, the leading physicist on the Manhattan Project, and U.S. Army General Leslie Groves, director, examine the base of the tower on which the first atomic bomb had hung when tested on July 16 at Alamogordo, New Mexico. The temperature at Ground Zero had been 100 million degrees Fahrenheit, three times hotter than the interior of the sun and ten thousand times the heat on its surface. All life, plant and animal, within a mile radius of Ground Zero simply vanished. Immediately after the explosion, Groves commented, "The war's over. One or two of these things and Japan will be finished."

Albert Einstein was a German-born physicist and a Nobel prize winner (1921) who in 1933 joined the faculty of the Institute for Advanced Study at Princeton. Although his letter to Roosevelt got the Manhattan Project started, he never worked on it. His politics were suspect: he was an outspoken pacifist and supporter of Zionism. Director Vannevar Bush of the Office of Scientific Research and Development (OSRD) explained, "I wish very much that I could place the whole thing before him but this is utterly impossible." So Einstein was frozen out of the project.

late his experiment as the war clouds gathered. The British were working on an atomic bomb, too, under the direction of a committee of physicists with the code name Tube Alloys.

Two years before Pearl Harbor, Einstein responded to a request from Italian physicist Enrico Fermi, who had fled Italy to continue his work in the United States, to light a fire under the U.S. government. On August 2, 1939, Einstein wrote to President Roosevelt to warn him: "A single bomb of this type, carried by boat and exploded in a port, might very well destroy the whole port, together with some of the surrounding territory." Roosevelt was sufficiently impressed to appoint the Advisory Committee on Uranium that October. The committee reported that the kind of bomb mentioned by Einstein was "a possibility."

Not quite a year later, on the day after Paris fell, Roosevelt made what would turn out to be one of the crucial decisions of the war. He set up a board of scientists that, working with the British and French, would investigate the possibility of making an atomic bomb. The team included military men and physicists from around the world. It was a unique development, the first active cooperation between governments in scientific and weapons research. The Axis powers had nothing remotely like it; German, Italian, and Japanese scientists worked on their own. But for the Allies, politics and physics had become irretrievably intertwined.

The German physicists, everywhere regarded as the best in the world, were working on a variety of scientific projects, including an atomic bomb. But Hitler was never willing to give his bomb program the kind of budget it required. When told by his physicists that they could build an atomic bomb and have it ready by 1945, he replied that would be too late. By then the war would have been won or lost. So he put them to work on other projects. Rockets were his special favorite. One of the ironies of the war was that Hitler's V-2 rocket weapons would come out of work done years before by the American rocketry pioneer, Robert Goddard, while the atomic bomb would come out of the original theories of a German, Einstein. Another irony: Had it not been for Hitler, it is possible that the world would never have seen an atomic bomb. It was an enormously expensive and terribly risky project. Tens of thousands of scientists and technicians worked on the atomic project (one reason Hitler got ahead of his enemies in rockets and other areas was that the Allies put so much of their scientific and technological effort into the atomic bomb); until the bomb was actually tested there were serious doubts that it would work. Had there not been the threat of Hitler getting an atomic bomb, it can be doubted that any country would have made such a huge investment on such a chancy undertaking.

Never were new weapons of such vital importance as during World War II. Had Hitler been able to wed a nuclear warhead to his missiles, he could have achieved at least a stalemate. Had the United States not possessed atomic bombs, hundreds of thousands of American lives might have been lost in the assault on Japan's home islands. The scientists on both sides knew that they probably held the key to success or failure, and this was particularly true of nuclear physicists.

The Nazi victories of 1940 disrupted Allied scientific endeavors. French physicists under Frédéric Joliot-Curie had been conducting atomic experiments with heavy water (a source of uranium 235 ((U-235)), or fissionable material) that was manufactured in quantity only at Rjukan, Norway. While the Battle of France was still being fought, Joliot-Curie sent one of his principal aides, Hans von Halban, to England with the French stock of heavy water. Anglo-French scientists at Cambridge then managed to achieve a chain reaction. Their work was later coordinated with that of American colleagues.

In May of 1941, Roosevelt created the Office of Scientific Research and Development (OSRD) under Vannevar Bush, and thirteen months later, he made the decision to attempt to manufacture an atomic bomb. Two months after that, an organization called the Manhattan Engineer District was established under U.S. General Leslie R. Groves. Groves managed to buy the entire existing stock of uranium ore from the Belgian Mining Union in the

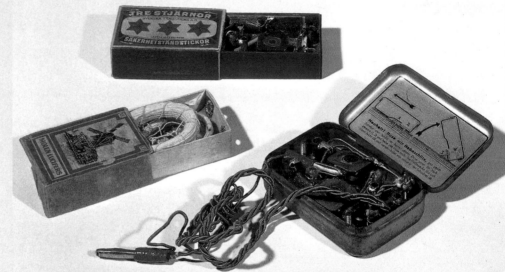

Tools of the espionage trade were many and ingenious. Clockwise from above: a hollowed out book from the Dutch resistance used to hide a revolver; a carboy with a hidden battery (most likely for radio transmission), used by the Danish resistance; three of the many containers used to conceal tiny, homemade radio receivers; a hollowed-out log used by the Norwegian resistance to smuggle newspapers or other printed material past the Germans; a shoe with a removable heel used by the Norwegian resistance to hide microfilm.

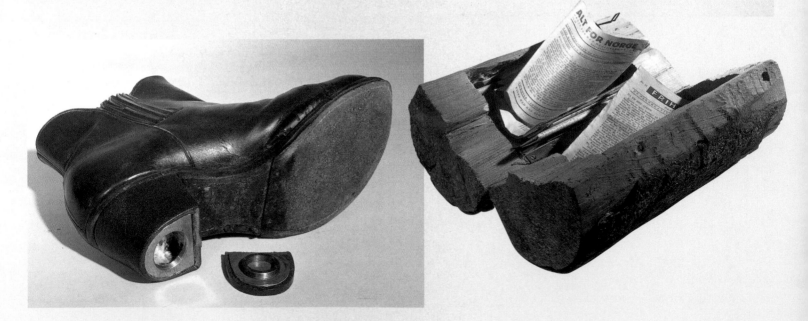

Left, Vannevar Bush, director of the Office of Scientific Research, is surrounded by A. N. Richards, J. C. Hunsaker, Harvey Bundy, and James B. Conant, president of Harvard University. Security at Los Alamos (below left) was tight during the summer of 1945. Three of the men who made the atomic bomb happen attend a conference in the spring of 1946 at Los Alamos. Below, from left to right: Ernest O. Lawrence, Enrico Fermi, and I. I. Rabi.

Right, the power plant at Rjukan under construction, and below, the interior of the power plant completed. The plant was almost impossible to attack, but British and Norwegian resistance groups did it anyway, regularly. They were effective enough to prevent the plant from ever achieving full production.

Congo, some 1,140 tons. On December 2, 1942, Enrico Fermi achieved a controlled chain reaction in an atomic pile at the University of Chicago that prompted the famous message from Nobel prize–winning physicist Arthur Compton to James B. Conant: "The Italian Navigator has just landed in the New World. The Natives are friendly."

What was needed for a bomb was the fissionable U-235, which had to be isolated from uranium. There were four possible methods: thermal diffusion, gaseous diffusion, separation by centrifuging, and electromagnetic processing. Groves, whose budget was literally unlimited, decided to try all four simultaneously. Industrial plants and research parks were set up in New Mexico, Tennessee, and Washington state. Groves selected physicist J. Robert Oppenheimer to be research director. Allied intelligence had, however, learned disquieting news. The Nazis, after occupying Norway, had ordered the factory at Rjukan to produce three thousand pounds of heavy water a year, and in 1942 this target was raised to ten thousand pounds. Norwegian underground agents reported that the heavy water was being

The secret Oak Ridge facility covered ninety-three square miles and was known as the Clinton Engineer Works until 1947. It was built to extract fissionable U-235 from U-238. Its workforce grew from zero at the beginning of 1943 to 82,000 two years later. It produced the uranium for the first atomic bomb.

shipped to the Kaiser Wilhelm Institute for nuclear research. For this reason, Rjukan was repeatedly attacked by Allied bombers, commandos, and saboteurs until its output came to a standstill. The Nazis decided to move the entire store of heavy water to Germany, but the ferry boat on which it was shipped was sunk by a Norwegian saboteur's time bomb. It was one of those awful decisions people had to make during the war; the ship had hundreds of Norwegian civilians aboard, all of whom perished.

Despite Hitler's indifference and the heavy water raids, German physicists, led by Werner Heisenberg, might have developed an atomic weapon had they had access to uranium, but General Groves had all the uranium then known to exist in the world. For the most part, therefore, the Germans concentrated on building what Hitler wanted, his V-weapon program. German scientists, led by the young and brilliant Wernher von Braun, were able to produce pilotless, jet-powered aircraft, which carried V-1 bombs to England, and the world's first intermediate-range ballistic missile, called the V-2 (the "V" stood for vengeance).

The Germans were years ahead of the rest of the world in rocketry; indeed the V-2 was so advanced that the Scud missiles used by Iraq in the Persian Gulf War of 1991 were basically V-2s. The liquid-fuel rockets were 46 feet long, weighed 13 tons, and carried a 1-ton warhead. They caused much damage to London and Antwerp in 1944 and 1945, killing some 2,500 in Britain and causing 30,000 casualties in Antwerp, but like the Scud they were so inaccurate they were more a terror weapon than an efficient military device. Some 8,000 V-2s were fired at England; less than one-fifth hit their target. Most of all, they lacked the totally destructive warhead that might have staved off German defeat.

The atomic bomb and the V-2s were only the most spectacular weapons developed by the scientific-technological teams during the war. The German secret weapons included the snorkel, a hollow retractable mast containing tubes for fresh-air intake and exhaust, which allowed the diesel engines on the U-boats to recharge their batteries without coming to the surface, thus reducing their vulnerability to radar and air spotters. Introduced in early 1945, it enabled the Germans to increase the tonnage of Allied cargo ships sunk during the first weeks of 1945.

Potentially, the first turbojet fighter aircraft could have been the decisive weapon of the war. In this field the Germans led the world. As early as July 1942, designer Willy Messerschmitt was ready to put the Me-262 into production. But when Hitler saw the model, he pronounced it too small. Messerschmitt told Hitler the Me-262 could defend Germany's skies from Allied bombers. Hitler replied that he didn't want to defend Germany; he wanted to bomb London, and ordered Messerschmitt to built a bigger jet, one that could carry bombs. But that was pushing the technology too hard and too fast. Not until early 1944 was serial production of the Me-262 begun; the first jet fighter unit was not formed until November 1944. By then fuel shortages plagued all German efforts, including the training of new pilots. Of the 1,433 Me-262s built, fewer than 250 were flown in combat. They were 100 miles per hour faster than any Allied fighter (575 miles per hour versus 475) and were armed with four 30-millimeter cannon and twenty-four 50-millimeter rockets. Had they been available on June 6, 1944, as they would have

At a hangar at Peenemünde, V-2s, painted in camouflage olive, stand ready for launching. The sign warns that smoking is prohibited. The village of Peenemünde, on an island off Germany's Baltic coast, was the center of German development of the V-1 and V-2 program. The Allies made a major effort to knock out the launch sites from the air, but never succeeded. Peenemünde was not put out of action until it was captured by Soviet troops in April 1945.

37
11/W 4156

Rauchen verboten.

11/W 4171

DETONATOR

EXPLOSIVE

COMPRESSED
NITROGEN

FUEL

LIQUID OXYGEN

COMBUSTION CHAMBER

FRED RIPPER D

FE-610

23

The science of jet rocketry took off during the war for the Germans. From top to bottom: the Me-262 was the world's first combat jet aircraft; the Heinkel Salamander was slated to be a mass-produced jet fighter (it never made it); this artist's rendition of a V-2 appeared in *Mechanix Illustrated Magazine* in January 1944, some nine months before any had been fired; a "Robot" bomb was found by members of the Ninth Airborne, June 1945.

German soldiers work on an Enigma machine in the field. It was light enough for one man to carry but required two or three to operate. The machine had a standard typewriter-style keyboard; it provided electromechanical encoding through nonrepeating ciphers. Five interchangeable rotors and numerous plug connectors provided up to 200 quintillion permutations. The rotor settings could be rapidly changed, up to several times per day.

been but for Hitler, the Germans, not the Allies, would have dominated the skies over Normandy. In March 1945, in one of the few coordinated attacks made by the Me-262s, six Luftwaffe pilots shot down fourteen B-17s in a matter of minutes. In dogfights with Allied fighters, the Me-262 was unbeatable. But thanks to Hitler's obsession with offense over defense, there were never enough of them to affect the outcome of the war.

Just as Hitler took a great risk in not giving priority to the atomic bomb, so did the Allies take a great risk in not giving priority to jet aircraft. The British and American airplane developers had been working on jets, but they were told to concentrate on propeller-driven fighters and bombers. The bet was that with more of these the Allies could win the war before jet fighters ruled the skies. They won the bet, barely. It was not until October 1945 that the British had a jet fighter (it was considerably better than the Me-262) and shortly after that before the Americans caught up.

The Germans also had a lead on the world in encoding machines. In an odd twist, that lead was a principal factor in Germany's defeat. The German machine was called Enigma. It involved a series of rotating drums that were so complex there were several million possibilities for each encoded message.

Listening to the message was simple; it was sent by radio. Breaking the message, however, required two things: an exact duplicate of the Enigma machine and the key to the settings. The Germans were certain the Allies had neither. But, in fact, the British had two Enigma machines, given to them by Polish intelligence agents in 1939, just as Poland was being overrun. And at Bletchley Park in England, the British built what has been called the first computer, which allowed them to break into the key and thus read the German messages. They called the system Ultra. They could not break every message and often could do so only a few days after the message had been picked up, too late to be of much use. But they got enough to give the Allies (the Americans were integrated into the system when the United States entered the war) a decisive edge in intelligence.

Ultra was the best-kept secret of the war. It was not revealed until three decades had passed. When people learned about it, some asked, "If we were reading German messages right through the war, how come we didn't win the war sooner?" The answer is: The Allies did win the war sooner, thanks to Ultra.

When the German paratroopers dropped into Crete in 1941, the British knew where and when they were coming, and inflicted unacceptable casualties on the enemy. In the Battle of the Atlantic, Ultra guided Allied destroyers and planes to German submarines. In the run-up to D-Day, Ultra gave the Allies an almost exact read on German forces in France. In the Battle of Mortain, August 1944, Ultra provided critical advance intelligence on the German counterattack. After the autumn of 1944, however, Ultra lost much of

The masterminds at Bletchley Park take a rest and watch a rounders match in the spring of 1940. Fifth from left, standing, is George McVittie, head of meteorological cryptanalysis. Standing at far right is A. G. Denniston, then head of Bletchley Park.

its usefulness, because once the Germans were back inside their own country they could use secure telephone lines rather than radio for communications. The lack of Ultra intelligence was one of the bigger factors in the German success in achieving surprise in the Battle of the Bulge.

Ultra was also critical to the success of many Allied deception operations, because it gave them a read on the German order of battle, which let them know if the Germans had bought into the deception or not. The best-known example is Operation Fortitude. Its aim was to convince the Germans that the D-Day attack would come at the Pas de Calais rather than Normandy. It had two major parts: the use of false radio traffic to indicate to the Germans a big buildup near Dover, at the place where the Channel was narrow and directly across from the Pas de Calais; and the use of captured and turned German spies to reinforce the deception. At Dover, the British and Americans set up radio teams who filled the air with messages, just as happened when a real army gathered, counting on the Germans to pick them up, break the code, and conclude that the big Allied buildup was around Dover, when in fact it was in the south of England, around Portsmouth, which kept radio silence. The turned spies, meanwhile, sent information via Morse code to their controllers in Hamburg that claimed vast numbers of troops were gathered near Dover. The Germans trusted these spies because the British, in a marvelous exercise of patience and taking great risks, had spent three years building confidence in the *Abwehr* in their British-based spies who sent over accurate information. The information always arrived too late to affect German operations, but it raised the *Abwehr*'s already high trust in the spies. Thus when the spies reported that the invasion was coming to the Pas de Calais, and after June 6 said that Normandy was just a feint designed to pull German forces south and west of the Seine River, the *Abwehr* bought into it. For a full month after the invasion, most German armor remained northeast of the Seine, waiting for an invasion that never came. And thanks to Ultra, the Allied high command knew that Fortitude was working.

In the Pacific, the Americans had their own Ultra, called Purple. The Japanese had the same conviction the Germans did, that their encoding machines were unbreakable. They, too, paid dearly for their complacency. Purple broke into the Japanese code and gave the Americans the winning edge during the critical first months. It was helpful in the Coral Sea battle and absolutely critical to the Battle of Midway. Thanks to Purple and some brilliant interpretive work, the Americans knew when and where and in what strength the Japanese were going to strike. Purple also provided the intelligence that made it possible to shoot down a plane carrying Admiral Yamamoto in 1943.

Radar (acronym for radio detection and ranging) was an intelligence-gathering device that used radio beams which reflected off airplanes, submarines, and ships at sea, or buildings and fortifications on the ground, bounced back to the sender, and revealed the object. All the combatants had some form of radar, but it was the British who used it most effectively. They taught the Americans; the official history of OSRD states that, when the British brought an early radar system to the United States in 1940, "they carried the most valuable cargo ever brought to our shores." German radar,

The American "Purple" decoding machine (above) was capable of reading Japanese code. That, however, was not enough; the intercepted messages had to be interpreted. The man who did it best was Commander Joseph Rochefort, chief cryptanalyst in Hawaii (below). He worked a twenty-hour day; he was the one who figured out in May 1942 that the Japanese fleet was headed toward Midway. It was this kind of intelligence that gave the Americans the decisive edge.

Frederick Cook painted a V-1 streaking over Tower Bridge, London. Londoners learned that as long as you could hear its roar, you were safe. When the fuel was cut off and the noise stopped, the V-1 began its free-fall descent, and you raced for shelter, not knowing where it might come down.

although in use by 1940, was not up to British standards. The Japanese were so far behind they were not even in the race.

Radar changed the world. From it sprang digital computers, cathode-ray displays, television, particle accelerators, microwave spectroscopy, microwave ovens and other modern devices. But it made its greatest contribution in saving the world from Hitler, because it was crucial to the victory in the Battle of Britain. Unquestionably, without radar Britain would have lost the battle. With radar, which gave the British exact intelligence on when and where and in what strength the German bombers were coming, the RAF prevailed.

The "wizard war" had many components. During the Blitz, the German bombers flying night missions located blacked-out London by flying along a radio beam until it crossed another beam coming from another part of the

French coast, which gave the pilots a triangulation over the target. British scientist R. V. Jones figured out how the system worked, persuaded Churchill that he was right, and began the "Battle of the Beams." By using the German frequency, the British sent up a cross beam that led the pilots to drop their bombs well short of London, in open countryside.

In the secret war, the British were the most inventive and risk taking. This was due to Churchill's enthusiasm for science and what it could do to win the war, and reflected a general British attitude: We are going to fight this war with brains, not brawn. Some of the multitude of ideas Churchill pushed for were silly. For example, he championed the idea of gathering together an enormous mass of seaweed and freezing it with a covering of dry ice to provide an unsinkable airfield that could be towed along the English Channel. But other ideas were spectacularly successful, and would never have been tried had it not been for Churchill. One was the artificial harbors used in Normandy following D-Day. Few thought it could be done, but the piers and breakwaters were put together in England and floated over to France immediately after the invasion. The system badly surprised the Germans, who had assumed the Allies would land near a major port and who had never suspected they would bring the ports along with them and make the harbors. In the event, these artificial harbors and the port facilities they contained made an invaluable contribution to the Allies.

Some weapons were so secret they could rarely be used. The Americans developed a proximity fuze, for example, that was a great step forward in anti-aircraft fire. Earlier preset mechanical fuzes could not predict the

Artifical harbors were set up on Normandy after the invasion. These synthetic "Mulberry" harbors—prefabricated in Britain and sent to the French coast—were designed to facilitate the landing of additional ground troops and the unloading of matériel.

DECEPTION

Before any offensive, an army will try to deceive the enemy into thinking the attack is coming here when actually it is coming there. The Germans did it successfully in December 1944; they got the Allies to worry about an offensive north of Aachen that instead came in south, in the Ardennes. The Soviets did it to the Germans on a number of occasions. But the war's most spectacular piece of deception was in support of Operation Overlord, the invasion of France.

The code name of the operation was Fortitude. Its objectives were to fool Hitler into thinking the attack would hit at the Pas de Calais rather than at Normandy and to believe, once the attack in Normandy did begin, that it was a feint. Fortitude had many features; the most important being Fortitude North, which set up Norway as a target, and Fortitude South, with Pas de Calais as the invasion site. To get the Germans to fear for Norway, the Allies first had to convince the enemy that they had enough resources for a diversion, a difficult hoax because of the acute shortage of Allied landing craft. They would have to create fictitious divisions and landing craft on a grand scale. They did.

The British Fourth Army, stationed in Scotland and scheduled to invade Norway in mid-July, existed only on the airwaves. Early in 1944, some two dozen over-aged British officers went to northernmost Scotland, where they spent the next months exchanging radio messages. They filled the air with an exact duplicate of the wireless traffic that accompanies the assembly of a real army, communicating in low-level, and thus easily broken, cipher. Altogether the messages created an impression of corps and division headquarters scattered all across Scotland. In addition, the British got their Double Cross System into the act. The British had "turned" every German spy in England who had proven their reliability to the German *Abwehr* (intelligence) over the previous two years by sending only authentic information along (although too late to do the Germans any good).

In the spring of 1944, the British sprang the trap. The spies sent messages to the *Abwehr* describing heavy train traffic in Scotland, new division patches on the streets of Edinburgh, and rumors among the troops about going to Norway. In addition, wooden twin-engine "bombers" began to appear on Scottish airfields. British commandos made raids on the coast of Norway, pinpointing radar sites, picking up soil samples, and in general trying to look like a pre-invasion force.

The payoff was spectacular. By late spring, Hitler had thirteen divisions in Norway. These were not high-quality troops, but they could have filled in the trenches along the Atlantic Wall in France. Rommel wanted them in Normandy and in late May persuaded Hitler to move five infantry divisions from Norway to France. The divisions had started to load up and move out when the *Abwehr* passed onto Hitler another set of "intercepted and decoded" messages about the threat to Norway. He canceled the movement order. To paraphrase Churchill, never in the history of warfare have so many been immobilized by so few.

Fortitude South was larger and more elaborate. It was based on the First U.S. Army Group (FUSAG) stationed in and around Dover and threatening the Pas de Calais. It included radio traffic, inadequately camouflaged dummy landing craft in the ports around Dover, fields full of papier-mâché and rubber tanks, and the full use of the Double Cross System. The spies reported intense activity around Dover. The capstone to the deception was Eisenhower's selection of George Patton to command FUSAG. The Germans thought Patton the best commander in the Allied camp and expected him to lead the assault. Patton heartily agreed, but Eisenhower did not; he wanted to save Patton for later in the campaign and meanwhile exploit his reputation with the Germans. FUSAG radio signals kept the Germans informed of Patton's comings and goings and confirmed that he had taken a firm grip on his new command.

FUSAG contained real as well as imaginary divisions. Patton's U.S. Third Army was a part of it, along with some elements of the Canadian First Army. Fortitude's success was measured by the German estimate of Allied strength. By the end of May, the Germans believed that the Allied forces included eighty-nine divisions, when in fact the number was forty-seven. The Germans thought the Allies had sufficient landing craft to bring twenty divisions ashore in the first wave, when they would be lucky to manage six. Partly because they credited the Allies with so much strength, partly because it made good military sense, the Germans believed that the real invasion would be preceded and followed by diversionary attacks and feints. So they stationed their tanks north of the Seine River, around the Pas de Calais. They kept them there through D-Day and beyond. On D-Day plus three, Rommel finally managed to convince Hitler that Normandy was the site of the real invasion. Hitler ordered the panzer divisions south, to hit the exposed British left flank in Normandy. But just as the tanks began to move out, one of the spies—code-named Garbo—sent a message to the *Abwehr:* Normandy is a feint designed to draw the German Army south of the Seine, he said, and he provided eyewitness accounts of how Patton's FUSAG was loading up in Dover to the cross-Channel attack on the Pas de Calais. Hitler ordered the panzers to stay where they were. The deception continued to influence German dispositions through June and well into July. Fortitude was critical to Allied success.

The proximity fuze was invaluable for anti-aircraft defense. It was first used against the V-1s, in both London and Antwerp, with good effect, and by artillery on the front lines during the Battle of the Bulge. It was the U.S. Navy's best defense against kamikaze attacks, fittingly enough, as it was the U.S. Navy that developed the fuze.

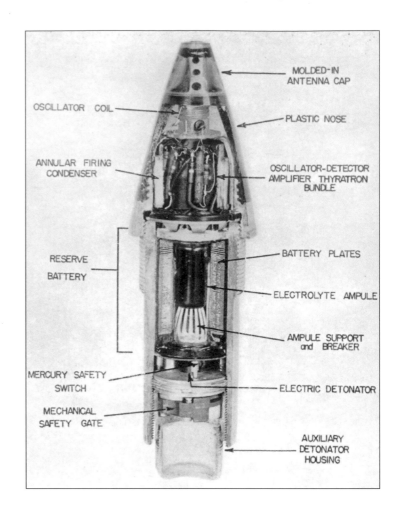

movements of attacking airplanes or calculate the exact point at which shells would have to go off in order to score fatal damage. Barrages of exploding projectiles had to be fired at attacking planes, with the hope that at least some of the aircraft would fly into the bursting shells. The newly developed proximity fuze incorporated a tiny transceiver that emitted radio waves after firing. When the projectile with a proximity fuze was close enough to its target to cause damage on exploding, the reflected beam from the aircraft would set it off. This dramatically raised the number of successful hits.

The fuze was adapted to artillery shells, which made it possible to explode them before they buried themselves in the ground (the reflection from the ground would set them off, scattering shrapnel over a wide area). But these shells were withheld during the autumn of 1944, for fear the Germans might capture one and figure out the system. During the crisis of the Battle of the Bulge, however, General Marshall ordered the shells put to use. They were, with great effect.

Secret weapons sometimes shaped strategy. In the 1930s, Carl Norden, a civilian consultant to the U.S. Navy, developed a precise optical device that incorporated a gyrostabilized automatic pilot to keep a bomber straight and level during a bombing run. The "Norden bombsight" was adopted by the Army Air Force. Its chief, General "Hap" Arnold, was convinced that with the bombsight the American B-17 "Flying Fortress" would be capable of precision bombing from high altitudes (as high as 20,000 feet). Americans boasted that they could "drop a bomb in a pickle barrel." They initiated a policy of strategic bombing that called for knocking out specific targets, such as factories or oil refineries. The British, who flew their bombing missions at night to escape German fighters, said it couldn't be done. The Americans tried anyway and discovered that the British were right. The Norden bombsight was great—when there were no clouds, no enemy flak, no enemy fighters harassing the bombers. When conditions were not ideal, the accuracy of U.S. pinpoint bombing was measured in miles from the target.

At the end of the war, the world had become a increasingly dangerous place, with the arrival of jet aircraft, atomic bombs, ballistic missiles, and so much more. Handheld rockets, for example (the German *panzerfaust* was the best, the American bazooka was second), quickly became cheap and abundant, making war between non-industrial nations far more deadly than they had been. The world was also changed by one of the war's chief legacies: the marriage of government and science. Before 1939, for the most part, scientists worked independently on projects that interested them and that would benefit mankind. After World War II, most scientists worked in government-sponsored laboratories (usually at a university) on projects designed to improve weapons of destruction.

It is a depressing thought, perhaps, but nonetheless true that the period 1939 to 1945 featured a greater leap forward in applied science than any other in history, all of it dedicated to more efficient killing and destruction; it is also a fact, however, that out of the work done during the war has come more spin-off progress in science and technology than from any other period.

The bombardier of a B-17 peers through his Norden bombsight. Development of the bombsight began in 1928 by Carl Norden, a Dutch-American. The bombsight was linked to the plane's autopilot. The bombardier entered data on air speed, wind, and bomb weight into the bombsight, which then calculated the trajectory of the bombs. Near the target, the bombardier took control of the plane as he aligned the bombsight's telescope on the target. When the bombsight reached the proper release point, it automatically released the bombs.

CHAPTER 11

COUNTERATTACK IN THE PACIFIC

In the summer of 1942 the eastern boundary of the Japanese Empire ran from the Aleutians in the North Pacific down past Wake Island in the central Pacific to the Gilberts on the equator; its western boundary ran from the Manchurian-Soviet border through eastern China and Burma to India; on the south it took in Sumatra, Java, Timor, half of New Guinea, and all of the Solomons. In square miles, the Japanese held the largest empire ever seen in the world (although mostly water).

But by the summer of 1942, Japan's time of swift and furious expansion was about over. The Japanese never felt strong enough to attack the Soviet Union; they could have pushed on into India without much trouble, but chose to hold off; and the Battle of Midway had already finished any hopes they had of destroying the U.S. Pacific Fleet and driving farther east. There was, however, one front left for them where the prospects for conquest still looked promising. If they could drive across the Owen Stanley Mountains on New Guinea and take Port Moresby on that island's southern coast, and if they could set up airfields on the southern Solomons, they would have bases almost on top of Australia and the supply lines from the United States.

Australia was the place where the Allies were organizing for a counterattack, and the buildup there under MacArthur was moving fast. Most Australian units in the Middle East had been called home. New units in Australia and New Zealand were being raised. And the United States Navy was moving planes, guns, and troops in impressive numbers across the Pacific. Germany may have been the priority target according to official U.S. strategy, but in the first half of 1942 about four times as many men and twice as many ships and supplies were being sent to the Pacific as to Europe.

So when it was discovered that the Japanese were constructing an air

The combat artist Kerr Eby catches the misery of the marines in Bougainville in the Solomon Islands, November 1943, in his painting *Ghost Trail*. Jungle fighting characterized the ground war with Japan. To most Americans, the jungle seemed another world, full of terror and hardship.

General A. A. Vandegrift, commander of the marines on Guadalcanal, with rifle and bayonet handy, uses the telephone to keep in touch with all units, October 11, 1942. Vandegrift led from makeshift quarters during his division's four months of action, "at the constant risk of his life," as his citation for the Medal of Honor reads.

base on Guadalcanal, one of the southernmost of the Solomon Islands, and that the lifeline to Australia might soon be cut by land-based bombers, an amphibious assault already agreed on in Washington was rushed into action. At dawn on the seventh of August, exactly eight months after Pearl Harbor, the first Allied invasion armada of the war appeared off the coast of Guadalcanal and its steaming little satellites, Tulagi, Florida Island, and Gavutu. After an intensive three-hour bombardment, combat groups of the First Marines went ashore. Although there was sharp fighting on the offshore islets, the initial Guadalcanal landing was unopposed. The marines, commanded by Major General Alexander A. Vandegrift, swiftly captured their main objective, the still unfinished airstrip, and renamed it Henderson Field.

Thus the road to Tokyo began on an island in the Pacific that few Americans had ever heard of and none of the military planners knew much about. To their surprise, the marines discovered great quantities of gasoline, ammunition, tents, and rice. The Japanese, it seemed, had fled in panic. But on the night of August 8–9, the United States Navy took one of its worst whippings ever near Savo Island, just off Guadalcanal, and withdrew, leaving the marines all alone. Then, to the astonishment of the beleaguered Allies, the enemy commander called off the attack and disappeared without touching a cluster of defenseless transports loaded down with reinforcements. But, within days, "the Tokyo Express," the name the marines gave the fast Japanese ships that came down "the Slot" between the Solomon Islands, began pouring in fresh troops and supplies. The fighting was fierce and kept up for six months. For a long while there was doubt as to just which way it would go.

Throughout August and September, the beachhead was built up until some seventeen thousand marines occupied a seven-by-four-mile strip, including Henderson Field. The Japanese decided that Guadalcanal had to be cleared and sent shiploads of reinforcements from Rabaul to the island. Japanese cruisers and destroyers hammered at the marines and at American and Australian convoys trying to supply them.

In mid-October, the Japanese moved a task force, which included four carriers, north of Guadalcanal. On the night of the twenty-sixth, the Battle of the Santa Cruz Islands began, when two U.S. carrier forces, led by the *Hornet* and the *Enterprise* and commanded by Admiral Thomas Kinkaid, went to meet them. The battle cost the Japanese two destroyers sunk and several heavier units damaged, including two carriers and two battleships. But it also cost the United States the *Hornet*, which was sunk by Japanese destroyers after it had been badly damaged by dive-bombers.

Finally, on the night of November 13, the Imperial Fleet staged a dramatic sortie. This, the most furious sea encounter of the Solomons, became known as the Naval Battle of Guadalcanal. Led by two battleships, a Japanese force came down the Slot to land more troops and delivered a heavy shelling attack on a much smaller U.S. task force. All night there was a tremendous mix-up, with the smaller, more maneuverable U.S. ships pressing the attack. Ships sometimes drew so close that they had trouble depressing their guns. The Americans lost two cruisers sunk (including the *Juneau,* which went to the bottom with seven hundred men, including five

In August of 1942, Allied forces took Henderson Field (above), the prize of Guadalcanal. Three months later, they were driving the Japanese back to the northern shores of New Guinea's Papua Peninsula; the photograph at right shows Australian soldiers taking a break on the Kokoda Trail over the Owen Stanley Mountains in New Guinea.

In a painting by Tom Lea, the U.S. carrier *Hornet* is under attack at the Battle of Santa Cruz, October 26, 1942. She was soon crippled, set ablaze, and abandoned. U.S. destroyers sank her the next morning. She had been in commission for only one year and six days but had earned four battle stars and launched the Doolittle raid.

brothers named Sullivan) and two cruisers damaged, which they could ill afford; but the Japanese lost a battleship. The following night, a second Japanese flotilla was located by planes from the *Enterprise* and was heavily punished. Bombers from Henderson Field took off in daylight and sank seven and damaged four of eleven Japanese transports ferrying reinforcements. On the night of November 14–15, the Japanese mustered their remaining naval strength, led by a battleship and four cruisers, in an effort to cut off the beachhead. At this moment a U.S. flotilla commanded by Admiral Willis A. Lee roared up "Ironbottom Sound," so named for the number of ships already rusting beneath its greasy surface. Lee sank another Imperial battleship and damaged two more cruisers, repelling Japanese efforts to build up their land forces. By dawn of the fifteenth, it was clear that the attempt had failed.

The land campaign, which lasted until February, was the first marine experience in that particular kind of jungle warfare with which they were to become so intimately acquainted during the next three years. They had to learn how to hack their way through tangles of roots, always on the lookout for snipers lashed to tree branches or hidden in the underbrush. They became familiar with malarial mosquitoes, scorpions, and snakes, as they learned to distinguish the cries of animals from those of enemy sentries. They fought their way forward through intense heat and the foul slime of decomposing vegetation.

Worst of all was the enemy. He came screaming out of the jungle at night in wild suicide charges. He fought according to no code an American could understand; he was tricky and deadly. He seemed to the marines to live in the jungle like an animal and he moved through it just as silently. The only way to beat him, the marines quickly decided, was to kill him as one did with a rabid animal. Progress at first was painfully slow and nerve-racking. However, once it was clear that the Imperial Fleet had been driven off and that the flow of enemy reinforcements was dammed, the jungle advance gathered momentum. The Army's Twenty-fourth Division had replaced the First Marine

A Marine Corps dive-bomber lies smoldering on Henderson Field, Guadalcanal, 1943. It had been smashed and left burning by a Japanese bomber that had a lucky hit. The plane had been wheeled into a coconut grove for concealment.

the five Sullivan brothers
"missing in action" off the Solomons

THEY DID THEIR PART

THE SULLIVAN BROTHERS

The first casualty in war is truth. Governments at war lie without compunction; in a total war, how could it be otherwise? The story of the U.S. Navy and the Sullivan brothers is one example.

There were five Sullivans living in Waterloo, Iowa, when Pearl Harbor was attacked: George, 28; Francis, 27; Joseph, 24; Madison, 23; and Albert, 20. When a friend, Bill Ball, was killed on the USS *Arizona*, they decided to enlist in the navy to avenge his death. They insisted on serving together, despite an official policy of separating brothers, and persisted until their request was finally approved. George summarized the brothers' philosophy: "If the worst comes to worst, why, we'll all have gone down together."

Eleven months later, on November 13, 1942, they were crew members on the USS *Juneau* when a Japanese submarine hit the cruiser amidships with a torpedo. The Juneau was sunk, taking all the Sullivan brothers with her. It was the biggest blow to any one American family in the war.

The U.S. Navy propaganda machine went into action. It portrayed the Sullivan brothers as heroes who went down with their ship. It sent the parents on a nationwide tour to speak at factories encouraging workers to greater output. Genevieve, the only sister, joined the navy as a WAVE. And the last son, Jimmy, enlisted in the navy on the day he turned seventeen. On April 4, 1943, in San Francisco, Mrs. Sullivan christened a destroyer named for the now-famous brothers, USS *The Sullivans*. The ship had a distinguished career in World War II and the Korean War before being decommissioned in January 1965. Another destroyer named the USS *The Sullivans* was commissioned in April 1997.

The problem is: the Sullivans did not go down with the ship. With some 140 other members of the crew, they managed to get into rubber life rafts, and they were adrift at sea for many days. Only ten of the crew survived; the others died of thirst and exposure. The U.S. Navy in the Pacific War had a primitive, almost nonexistent sea rescue service. They could never put enough planes and ships to work to conduct search and recover missions. Of course the officials would never admit this or let the public know in any way about the suffering of the Sullivans and the rest of the crew.

So the U.S. Navy exploited the Sullivans but failed to learn from the experience. Two and a half years later, on July 30, 1945, the cruiser *Indianapolis* was sunk by a Japanese submarine; it was the last major U.S. warship sunk in World War II. Not many people were told of the ship's sinking because it was not known to be at sea: It had just completed a top-secret mission, delivering the first atomic bomb to Tinian in the Marianas. For three full days, the members of the crew who managed to get away from the sinking ship floated adrift in life jackets and boats. It was a dreadful ordeal. On the morning of the fourth day a PBY Catalina flying on routine patrol spotted the survivors. There were only 318 of the original 1,199 men. Floating alongside the survivors were the remains of scores of men who had been attacked and torn apart by sharks on a three-day feeding frenzy.

A poster (opposite) uses the disappearance of the Sullivan brothers to encourage new recruits. Twentieth Century Fox cashed in on the brothers' fame by making a sentimental movie entitled *The Sullivans* (above).

Troops climb one of the many hills to the rear of the lines on Guadalcanal, January 1943 (right). The terrain and condition of the ground made it impossible to travel more than a mile in two hours. The weariness and fatigue that are evident on the faces of these GIs typified jungle fighting everywhere. Rest did come periodically, for instance at the Guadalcanal rest center, below. Here, under huge coconut trees, four men of the Third Marines stroll the main street of their division headquarters after a typical South Seas "shower."

The Japanese would not quit. Convinced the Americans would tire quickly of jungle war, they sent in some of their toughest, best-trained soldiers, including this artillery unit, which is using a 75-millimeter infantry gun.

Division. The GIs proved to be as good as the marines. Finally, in the first week of February, the Japanese managed to bring destroyers in at night and evacuate about twelve thousand troops at Cape Esperance, on the island's northwestern tip. By the ninth, not a single living enemy was left on Guadalcanal. The Japanese had suffered their first land defeat of the war, and the first American offensive was a success. By the time the last enemy sniper was silenced, there were 24,000 dead Japanese; the dead Americans totaled 1,752. Tokyo was still 3,000 miles away.

When MacArthur arrived in Australia from Bataan in March 1942, he found scant forces there for the defensive action needed if the Japanese were to be stopped in their surge southward. Even so, he decided that the best way to protect Australia was to throw as much strength as he could into New Guinea, in order to hold the Japanese on the far side of the Owen Stanley Mountains and secure the vital Australian base at Port Moresby. The first Japanese try at taking Port Moresby resulted in the inconclusive Battle of the Coral Sea in May 1942.

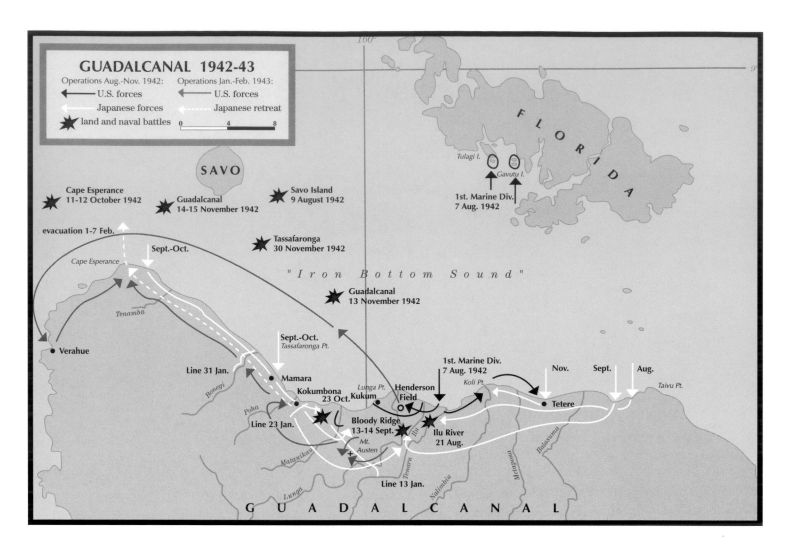

GUADALCANAL 1942-43

Operations Aug.-Nov. 1942:
← U.S. forces
→ Japanese forces
★ land and naval battles

Operations Jan.-Feb. 1943:
← U.S. forces
⇠ Japanese retreat

0   4   8

F L O R I D A

SAVO

Tulagi I.
Gavutu I.

1st. Marine Div.
7 Aug. 1942

Cape Esperance
11-12 October 1942

Guadalcanal
14-15 November 1942

Savo Island
9 August 1942

evacuation 1-7 Feb.

Sept.-Oct.

Cape Esperance

Tassafaronga
30 November 1942

"Iron Bottom Sound"

Guadalcanal
13 November 1942

Tenamba

Verahue

Line 31 Jan.

Mamara

Kokumbona
23 Oct.

Bonegi

Poha

Line 23 Jan.

Sept.-Oct.
Tassafaronga Pt.

Lunga Pt.
Kukum

Bloody Ridge
13-14 Sept.

Matanikau

Mt.
Austen

Lunga

Line 13 Jan.

Tenaru

Henderson
Field

Ilu River
21 Aug.

Ilu

1st. Marine Div.
7 Aug. 1942

Koli Pt.

Nov.   Sept.   Aug.

Tetere

Taivu Pt.

Nalimbiu

Metapona

Balasuma

G U A D A L C A N A L

Fierce sea battles were waged offshore Guadalcanal, as shown in this map. Both sides fought to stop the supply of their enemy's reinforcements, and both suffered heavy losses. At the end of 1942, bolstered by the U.S. Army and by air cover, the U.S. Marines went on the attack and soon cleared the island.

The distance across New Guinea's Papua Peninsula, from Port Moresby on the southern coast to Buna on the northern coast, is only 120 miles by air. But between the two coasts are the Owen Stanley Mountains, a jagged, jungle-covered range that rears up well over 10,000 feet. In the summer of 1942, the Australians were concentrated on the southern side of the mountains; the Japanese, after a series of amphibious landings on the northern shore, were pushing inland from Buna. The mountains, the Australians, and the Coral Sea were the last barriers between the oncoming Japanese and Australia. The Australians considered the mountains impassable. But the experienced Japanese jungle fighters, under General Horii, paid no attention to that; despite sickness and heavy casualties, they crossed the Owen Stanleys over the narrow Kokoda Trail and by mid-September were within thirty-two miles of Port Moresby.

Then the Australians counterattacked, along with American reinforcements, and drove the Japanese back over the mountains. The Japanese retreat turned into a rout. Japanese by the thousands died of starvation and disease; General Horii was drowned in a river crossing. By November, however, the Allies bogged down at Buna; they too were hollow-eyed with jungle fever and hunger, and casualties had been severe. MacArthur airlifted in some fifteen thousand fresh troops to help turn the tide. Then, in December, he sent in a new general, Robert L. Eichelberger, telling him to take Buna or not to come back alive. By the end of January 1943, Buna was in Allied hands.

The Buna campaign was an army show and did not get as much notice as Guadalcanal, but the fighting was every bit as savage, and the cost in dead and wounded was even higher. The long push up the northern coast of New Guinea began next. New Guinea is the world's second biggest island: the campaign would take two more years. The long drive up the northern coast of New Guinea was to be one side of a giant pincers movement that would eventually isolate Rabaul, Japan's Gibraltar of the South Pacific.

MacArthur had stopped the Japanese advance in New Guinea. The Japanese now tried to save their New Guinea forces by reinforcing the garrisons at Lae and Salamaua. On March 1, 1943, United States reconnaissance planes spotted a powerful Imperial convoy carrying seven thousand troops and trying, under cover of bad weather, to make from Rabaul through the Bismarck Sea to Lae, on New Guinea's northeastern coast. Two days later, on March 3, in the major action of the three-day Battle of the Bismarck Sea, Major General George C. Kenney's Fifth Air Force, operating from Papua, smashed the convoy and Japanese plans for holding New Guinea. The U.S. planes were equipped with slow-fused bombs that enabled them to roar in masthead high, "skip" their bombs into the enemy, and pull out before the explosion. The technique was astonishingly effective. By the time the Americans finished, they had sunk or damaged most of the ten warships and

During the Battle of the Bismarck Sea, in March 1943, a Japanese convoy bringing reinforcements to Lae, on New Guinea's northeastern coast, is hit by U.S. planes.

twelve transports in the formation, drowning all save a handful of the reinforcements. The Japanese lost 102 aircraft. This was the last time the Japanese would try a major seaborne troop movement. Kenney's B-17s and B-25s had given, as Churchill put it, "a striking testimony to the proper use of air power."

Thus, at last, Japan found its dynamism checked at its outermost fringes. Thrust back from Guadalcanal and New Guinea, it withdrew from the borders of India and the sea around Ceylon when those crucial areas lay open for the taking; and across the mainland Asian battlefront, Japan's energies continued to be drained in a brutal war with China that produced few, if any, definitive results.

By mid-summer of 1943, MacArthur had four U.S. divisions and six Australian divisions supported by Admiral William F. Halsey's South Pacific Fleet. Admiral Chester Nimitz, commander in chief in the central Pacific theater (MacArthur was head of the southwest Pacific theater) had nine U.S. Army and Marine divisions. Divided command came about because of the intense rivalry between the U.S. Army and Navy; the admirals were damned if they would serve under the egotistical MacArthur, while the generals felt the same about Nimitz. In the European theater of operations (ETO), there was one supreme commander; in the Pacific, there were two. Inevitably this arrangement, made for personnel rather than solid military reasons, led to a competition between the central Pacific and the southwest Pacific operations, for ships, planes, men, supplies, publicity. It led to a two-pronged counteroffensive against the Japanese, one led by MacArthur up the New Guinea coast to the Philippines, the other led by Nimitz across the central Pacific toward Japan.

One of the innovations developed by MacArthur and Nimitz came as a complete surprise to the Japanese, who had figured the Americans would have to take every island in their path at an enormous cost in time and expense and lives. The Americans, instead, took advantage of their growing fleet, which gave them air and sea superiority, to bypass the more strongly fortified islands, outflanking them, cutting the garrisons off from resupply or reinforcement, leaving them to wither on the vine.

The strategy was called island hopping. It enabled the Americans, with relatively small forces, to counterattack even as they bypassed the heavily fortified bases. They moved up the Solomons and New Guinea and inward

U.S. Marines make a frontal assault against a heavily reinforced pillbox in Tarawa, in the Gilbert Islands, on November 21, 1943. They had to get to the top and shoot down inside. If they bypassed such a position, the Japanese would rise behind them and shoot them in the backs.

across the little-known, savage Gilberts, Marshalls, and Marianas. Island after island, the story was nearly always the same: Japanese troops holed up in their elaborate bunkers, listening to distant radio broadcasts, dreaming of their girlfriends and wives, waiting for the inevitable storm of fire and death from offshore. Outside, the clear Pacific and the endless rhythm of the surf. And all the while, lumbering through swells, the gray ships filled with sweating GIs and marines; no smoking on the blacked-out decks; the dull thud of engines; the rattling of planes being readied by their mechanics; the creaking of davits and the hum of ammunition lifts in the quiet predawn. And then, the sudden and terrible explosion of light and sound, turning paradise to fury. When the last bomb and shell had fallen and the last machine-gun barrel cooled, swarms of Seabees (U.S. Navy construction battalions) came with their monstrous machinery to sweep away the mess and carve still another base for the inexorable advance.

The Seabees were in on every landing in the Pacific. On Tarawa, on Makin (taken at the time of Tarawa), on Kwajalein and Enewitok in the Marshall Islands, the Seabees turned acres of smoldering ruins and shell-pocked coral into what looked like tropical boomtowns, and they did it almost overnight. They moved in with bulldozers and earth movers, and plenty of the wonder bug-killer DDT; they built airstrips, harbor facilities, roads, bridges, hospitals, everything needed for a modern military base that was, as a sign on Tarawa pointed out, 9,137 miles from Connecticut.

All the time that MacArthur's forces were pressing along the northern coast of New Guinea, the marines and the army started up the Solomon Islands "ladder": the Russell Islands (February 1943), New Georgia (June), Vella Lavella (August), Choiseul and the Treasury Islands (October), and finally, Bougainville (in November), the biggest island of the chain. All the while, the Army Air Corps and carrier-based dive-bombers pounded away at Rabaul.

Within little more than a year, MacArthur's effective and economical strategy had reached far up the southwest Pacific archipelagoes and severed some one hundred thirty-five thousand Japanese from all prospect of rescue. Simultaneously, Nimitz guided Spruance's Fifth Fleet westward, encompassing the Gilberts, the Marshalls, the Carolines, and the Marianas, ravaging enemy ships and garrisons with the power of their carrier planes, and asserting a freedom of maneuver that seemed unimaginable less than two years after Pearl Harbor had temporarily crippled the U.S. Navy.

Makin and Tarawa in the Gilberts, where the central and southern Pacific commands met, were now assailed by Nimitz. On November 20, his carriers started a heavy bombardment of Makin. A few days later, the island was overwhelmed in a short, sharp series of amphibious assaults marked by a fanatical defense by a garrison well fortified with rice wine. Tarawa, an atoll of some two dozen islets linked by coral reefs, was a more difficult objective. Tokyo had boasted that it could not be taken by assault. The principal strong point at Betio, held by three thousand crack Imperial Marines, comprised hundreds of connected pillboxes made of concrete and coral work, reinforced with steel beams and coconut logs. These positions were intensely shelled and bombed by the Americans; nevertheless, when the marines waded ashore, they were met by withering fire.

The battle was one of the bloodiest fights of the whole Pacific campaign. U.S. ships maintained a steady artillery barrage as landing barges discharged troops and supplies and marines stormed each bastion with flamethrowers and grenades.

Hydrographic experts had warned Admiral Kelly Turner about the tricky tides around the Gilbert Islands. There was a chance the tides would be exceptionally low on November 20—D-Day for Tarawa—and the landing craft might run aground on coral ledges offshore: no one could say for sure. Admiral Turner decided to take the risk, and he lost. The first waves of marines went in on the amphibious tractors that marines called LVTs or amtracks, and they made it. But after that, the flat-bottomed landing craft ("Higgins Boats") began clanging onto the reefs, which were covered with only three feet of water. The marines had to wade in hundreds of yards, under murderous fire. Only about half of them made it.

No one had expected such resistance. The island had been pounded for hours from the sea, and it had been bombed for a full week. But what no one knew before Tarawa was just how well forty-five hundred Japanese, inside

The Seabees (U.S. Navy construction battalions) show their stuff in the Pacific (below). Their motto was "Can do." They could build airfields, roads, bridges, hospitals, harbor facilities, and whatever else was needed quicker than the wink of an eye. A Seabee bulldozer clears a path in New Guinea (right). The bulldozer was America's secret weapon. One Japanese officer commented, "The Americans don't fight in the jungle. They tear it down."

During an island assault, Seabees kept supplies coming in; the fighting over, they set up camp (above).

Island hopping was the the U.S. strategy to winning the Pacific. Opposite page, clockwise from top left: U.S. Marines move forward, cautiously, in the jungle of Bougainville, at the top of the Solomon chain, November 30, 1943; a U.S. soldier carefully examines a Japanese bunker made of logs and coral on the edge of Nunda airfield on New Georgia in the Solomon Islands in 1943 (the field had been bombed and shelled but this pillbox had not been damaged); U.S. carrier planes strike at Rabaul, on the northern tip of New Britain Island, as Japanese warships desperately maneuver out of the harbor for the relative safety of the open sea.

Casualties sprawl on the beach on Tarawa, November 22, 1943. The U.S. Marines had been hit by murderous fire; only about half made it inland unhurt. Such photos were not printed in the United States; only those of the wounded being treated, not the dead, got past the censors.

their sand-covered and reinforced bunkers, could hold out under bombardment. Nearly all the killing had to be done by marines. Colonel David Shoup, commander of the Second Marine Regiment, reported to the flagship standing offshore: "Our casualties heavy. Enemy casualties unknown. Situation: we are winning." Four days later, his optimism proved warranted: the Americans had won. But the cost was terrible: 991 U.S. Marines dead, 2,311 wounded. Of the more than 20,000 Japanese troops, only 17 came through alive.

Promptly the ingenious Seabees set to work constructing a base for an attack on the Marshalls to the north. There, the main target was the atoll Kwajalein, sixty-six miles long and eighteen miles wide. This time Nimitz took no chances before sending his men ashore; his ships and planes dropped fifteen thousand tons of explosives on Kwajalein before the first landing craft touched ground. The atoll was a mass of dust-covered rubble when the invasion began, but the Japanese, who were for the first time defending a piece of prewar Imperial territory, fought savagely from the debris.

Again the American advance was initially painstakingly slow as each fortification had to be reduced, blasted, or burned out. But by early 1944, Nimitz's task forces had succeeded in mastering all the Gilberts and Marshalls, and his carrier raids had so shattered the great Carolines air base of Truk to the west that its garrison of fifty thousand could be easily bypassed. For the rest of the war, Truk lay useless.

While the new technique of amphibious fighting was proceeding in the tropical Pacific, an odd, militarily unimportant but politically and emotionally vital campaign took place along the northeastern edge of the Japanese Empire, in the Aleutian sealing grounds. In 1942, when Yamamoto led his fleet to Midway, he simultaneously sent a small force to occupy the barren islands of Attu and Kiska. The move was, in fact, a strategic feint, but it was also a check to any designs the Allies might have for using the Aleutians as an invasion route to Tokyo. American public opinion saw it as just the opposite; Alaska and the Pacific Northwest were now, it seemed, seriously threatened. The American high command wished to choke off any such possibilities and to clear the way for Lend-Lease shipments to the Soviet Pacific port of Vladivostok. It was decided to eject the Japanese.

On May 11, 1943, U.S. Seventh Division troops began landings on mountainous, treeless Attu. They fought for eighteen days amid fog and rain, which hampered aerial and naval support and imprisoned armor in the cold,

The 165th Infantry attack Butaritari, on the Makin Atoll in the Gilbert Islands, November 20, 1943. The coral-bottom waters made for a difficult trek, and Japanese machine-gun fire from the right flank didn't help.

sucking mud. On May 29, the desperate Japanese defenders staged a suicide charge. Colonel Yasuyo Yamasaki led his surviving forces down from a ridge into the American lines, screaming: "Japanese drink blood like wine." Those who were not butchered along the slopes held hand grenades to their bellies and blew out their intestines. Among letters found in the pockets of the dead, one said: "I will become a deity with a smile in this heavy fog. I am only waiting for the day of death."

The liberation of Kiska three months later was a different story. A large force, including five thousand Canadians, nervously crept about the island for five days looking for the enemy, sometimes shooting at each other among exploding booby traps. At the end the astonishing discovery was made that, prior to the landings, shielded by the dank, boreal mist, the Japanese had quietly and quite brilliantly evacuated their entire garrison.

Though command arrangements for the war against Japan were often enormously complicated, the overall idea was simply that the United States had the responsibility for the entire "Pacific area," while Britain took charge of South Asia and the Middle East. But even so, China had to be accorded a special position, as it was regarded as a region of special U.S. interest. Chiang Kai-shek was recognized as supreme commander, but his chief of staff was an American general, Joseph Stilwell. Stilwell also commanded U.S. forces in what became the China-Burma-India theater (CBI) and thus had the dubious distinction of being simultaneously responsible to Washington, to Chiang, and to the British commander in India. Stilwell was not ideally suited to the task. He was brave and aggressive but almost totally without tact. He quarreled with the British and denounced Chiang for his "stupid, gutless command."

A marine moves forward loaded down with his machine gun and with his helmet on backward (right). The Japanese commander had boasted, "A million men cannot take Tarawa in a hundred years." The marines took it in three days. In a 1943 painting (opposite top) by Ogden Pleissner, *Sweating in the Mission*, U.S. bombers return to Adak, in the Aleutians, after a raid. Fog, mud, frost, and howling winds made the islands rough places from which to run an air war. A sign (opposite bottom) made by an English-speaking Japanese marked the grave of an American pilot downed over Kiska. It reads: "Sleeping here, a brave air-hero who lost youth and happiness for his mother land. July 25, Nippon Army."

Chiang on the other hand, thanks to circumstance, geography, and Roosevelt's personal prejudice, was accorded considerable influence and played his cards shrewdly. He gave more thought to his postwar problems and the inevitable power struggle with the Communists than to the war itself, confident that the Americans would eventually drive the Japanese out of his country. He banked on the traditional sympathy of the American people, whose commercial and missionary interests in China dated back for generations, on the American vision of a postwar China that could act as a balance to Japan, and on the fact of China's vast geography and population.

Washington was as adamant in its support of Chiang in Asia as in its opposition to de Gaulle in Europe; and oddly enough, although Mao Tse-tung's Communist armies, based around Yennan, were at times fighting Chiang as well as the Japanese, Stalin endorsed Roosevelt's backing of the generalissimo. Churchill, however, later on reported: "I had found the extraordinary significance of China in American minds, even at the top, strangely out of proportion. I was conscious of a standard of values which accorded China almost an equal fighting power with the British Empire, and rated the Chinese armies as a factor to be mentioned in the same breath as the armies of

Russia. I told the president how much I felt American opinion overestimated the contributions which China could make to the general war. He differed strongly. There were five hundred million people in China. What would happen if this enormous population developed in the same way as Japan had done in the last century and got ahold of modern weapons? I replied I was speaking of the present war, which was quite enough to go on with for the time being."

China's great potential was based not only on its population but on its position. It provided an overland way to get at the Japanese. Equip and train a Chinese army; put American officers in charge and strike across northern Burma into China's Yunnan Province; then head northeast across China, gathering strength from the Chinese people all the way. This, in essence, was one of two strategic ideas for CBI. The other idea was to use China as a base for air strikes against the Japanese Army in China and Burma, and against Japan itself. As it turned out, both ideas were tried; the result was some of the fiercest jungle fighting of the war, and some of the thorniest political infighting.

Stilwell was convinced that the best way back was by land. In October 1943 he launched an attack on Burma from near Ledo, India. As his two Chinese divisions pushed forward, he hacked out the Ledo Road, which

In Burma, General Joseph Stilwell and his party retreat to Imphal, Assam, starting on May 11, 1942, and ending on May 20. He told reporters, "We took a hell of a licking." But he would soon be back on the offensive.

A Chinese propaganda leaflet reads: "Happy New Year! This American pilot helped you to chase the Japanese out of the Chinese sky. Help him. The ancient, tired god of gates is sleeping now. The terror of Japanese devil entered millions of Chinese families. The ancient god cannot stop them anymore. This strong young soldier, this American fighting pilot, with the help of the courageous Chinese army, they together will protect the old and the young in your family. But he and his Chinese colleagues need your help when they are hurt, lost, or hungry. They need your comfort and friendship. Help them! They are fighting the war for you. Friends of the occupied territory, attention. Please do not let anyone see this leaflet. If the Japanese should see this, they will torture you."

would eventually cut through jungle and over mountains to link up with the Burma Road, the main supply route into China. At the same time, British and American guerrilla units (Wingate's Raiders and Merrill's Marauders) began a vicious campaign behind Japanese lines. But most of the fighting in Burma was carried on by the British Fourteenth Army, which suffered heavy losses before driving the enemy out of Mandalay and Rangoon in the spring of 1945.

By the time the Burma Road was reopened, the war was about over, and FDR had moved Stilwell out of his job at the request of Generalissimo Chiang Kai-shek. Stilwell had a low opinion of the Chinese dictator and made no effort to hide the fact. Chiang seemed reluctant to do much fighting; his government was seething with corruption, and, in the north, the Chinese

Workers clear the land at Laowingping Airfield, China, 1944. The Chinese had no bulldozers or other heavy earth-moving equipment, but they had labor in abundance. Such fields made it possible to bring in supplies and helped keep China in the war.

Communists had set up their own hostile regime. The result was often a three-way war in which the Japanese benefitted and Chiang called for more Lend-Lease while backing the other part of United States strategy—air power.

The man in command of the Allied air offensive over China was General Claire Chennault. Like Stilwell, Chennault was an old China hand and just as headstrong about beating the Japanese his way. Moreover, unlike Stilwell, he had Chiang on his side. Chennault had been an unofficial "adviser" to Chiang since 1937; in 1941, he had put together a group of volunteer American pilots, known as the "Flying Tigers," who were paid $600 a month for fighting for China, plus $500 a kill. Their kills were many. In the summer of 1942, Chennault's command became the U.S. Fourteenth Air Force and in-

A U.S. convoy ascends the famous twenty-one curves on the Burma Road at Annan, March 26, 1945. The road ran for 717 miles, from Lashio in Burma to Kunming in Yunnan. It was one lane built by hand by an army of 150,000 men, women, and children. With the Japanese in occupation of China's seacoasts, it was one of China's two links with the world.

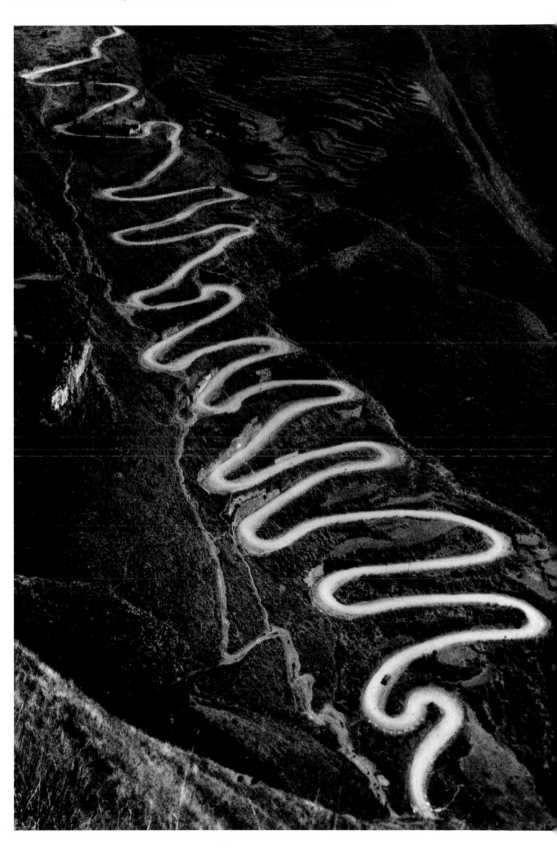

General Claire Lee Chennault, the head of the famed "Flying Tigers" (above) of the Sino-Japanese war, poses in front of his P-40 Tomahawk plane in his fighting garb (right). When the American Volunteer Group merged into the U.S. Fourteenth Air Force in July 1942, Chennault took command of the force.

cluded heavy bombers. But perhaps the greatest success of the whole theater was the convoy of C-47 transports that flew "the Hump," the 20,000-foot-high Himalayas, which separated China from Allied supply bases in India. The Air Transport Command was a costly business in every way (850 airmen would be killed before it was over), but it kept China alive and in the war.

Through the war, Chiang had Roosevelt's ear and attention, and Chiang insisted that Burma should be the scene of the initial mainland offensive against the Japanese. He opposed operations in the north, where his own divisions would have to provide needed manpower. Instead he argued: "Burma is the key to the whole campaign in Asia. After the enemy has been cleared out of Burma, his next stand would be in North China and, finally, in Manchuria." Churchill was unenthusiastic, agreeing with the American admirals King and Nimitz, who wished to force an ultimate decision by sea power. But by appealing for an extension of the supply route across Burma in order to sustain Chinese morale, Chiang gained Roosevelt's backing.

A Southeast Asia Command was created under the English king's cousin, Lord Louis Mountbatten, and was charged with conducting a war of which Mountbatten's own government did not heartily approve. The command depended upon a U.S. military system that sought different objectives and upon a Chinese government that was fighting almost a private war for purposes largely its own. The Casablanca Conference of January 1943 nevertheless agreed on a Burma campaign that, from its very genesis, was marked by quarrels and discord. Churchill complained to his chiefs of staff: "Going into the swampy jungles to fight the Japanese is like going into the water to fight a shark." Mountbatten viewed Burma as a subsidiary objective. Stilwell favored a Burmese drive but only in the north, where he wished Chiang would do some serious fighting. General Chennault agreed with Chiang that divisions were less important than aircraft but wanted the Japanese to be bombed out of Burma. No one was satisfied. Stilwell and Chennault carried their acrimonious debate right to the Trident Conference in Washington in May 1943. The irascible Stilwell shouted: "It's the ground soldier slogging through the mud and fighting in the trenches who will win the war." Chennault hollered back: "But God damn it, Stilwell, there aren't any men in the trenches."

The Allied planners managed to fashion an operation one of whose goals was to increase to ten thousand tons a month the capacity of the air transport supply system over the Burmese Hump to China. Their new plan assigned to Mountbatten and Stilwell the task of investing northern and central Burma. A specially trained American infantry combat team known as the Galahad Force, commanded by Brigadier General Frank D. Merrill, was ordered to join the Chinese Twenty-second and Thirty-ninth divisions coming down the Hukwang Valley.

Aware of Allied preparations, the Japanese initiated their own offensive during the 1943–44 winter. They attempted to capture the Indian province of Assam and to sever the link to China via the Hump and the Ledo Road. British and Indian airborne troops were able to check and finally reverse this short-lived invasion. Then, with the British driving along the Bay of Bengal in the south and the Chinese and Merrill advancing on Myitkyina in the north, the Japanese were forced gradually backward. Major General Orde

OVERLEAF: Unlike the war in Europe, where the lay of the land was familiar to most Americans, the war in the Pacific often seemed hard to follow. MacArthur's men fought at places with strange names that were a problem to find on the map. As this map shows, the scale of the Pacific war was enormous, the strategy essentially simple. Two great thrusts westward, one starting at Guadalcanal, the other at the Gilbert and Marshall Islands, would converge on the Philippines.

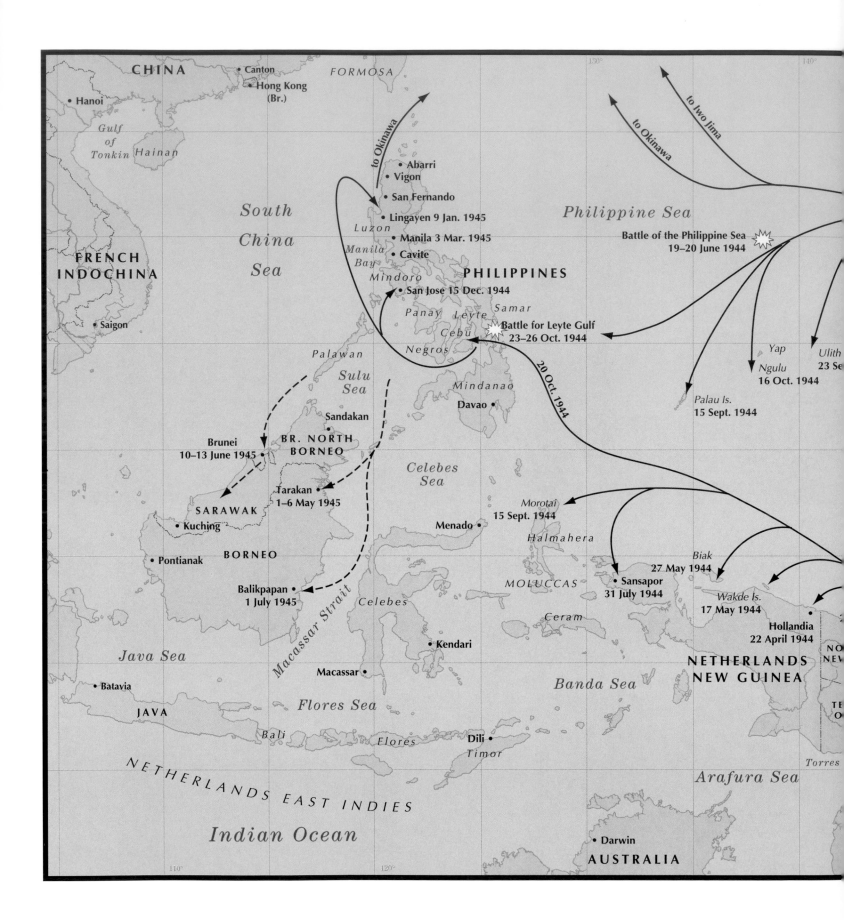

CHINA

• Canton

• Hong Kong
(Br.)

FORMOSA

• Hanoi

*Gulf
of
Tonkin* Hainan

*South
China
Sea*

to Okinawa

• Abarri
• Vigon

• San Fernando

Luzon

• Lingayen 9 Jan. 1945

• Manila 3 Mar. 1945

*Manila
Bay* • Cavite

Philippine Sea

to Okinawa   to Iwo Jima

Battle of the Philippine Sea
19–20 June 1944

FRENCH
INDOCHINA

• Saigon

Mindoro

• San Jose 15 Dec. 1944

PHILIPPINES

Samar

Panay Leyte

Cebu Battle for Leyte Gulf
23–26 Oct. 1944

Yap

Ngulu
16 Oct. 1944

Ulith
23 Se

Palawan

Negros

*Sulu
Sea*

20 Oct. 1944

Mindanao

• Davao

Palau Is.
15 Sept. 1944

• Sandakan

Brunei
10–13 June 1945

BR. NORTH
BORNEO

*Celebes
Sea*

Tarakan
1–6 May 1945

SARAWAK

• Kuching

• Menado

Morotai
15 Sept. 1944

Halmahera

Biak
27 May 1944

• Pontianak

BORNEO

MOLUCCAS

• Sansapor
31 July 1944

Ceram

Wakde Is.
17 May 1944

Balikpapan •
1 July 1945

Celebes

Hollandia
22 April 1944

NETHERLANDS
NEW GUINEA

NO
NEW

Java Sea

• Batavia

Macassar Strait

• Kendari

Macassar •

Banda Sea

JAVA

TE
O

Flores Sea

Bali

Flores

Dili •

Timor

Arafura Sea

Torres

NETHERLANDS EAST INDIES

Indian Ocean

• Darwin

AUSTRALIA

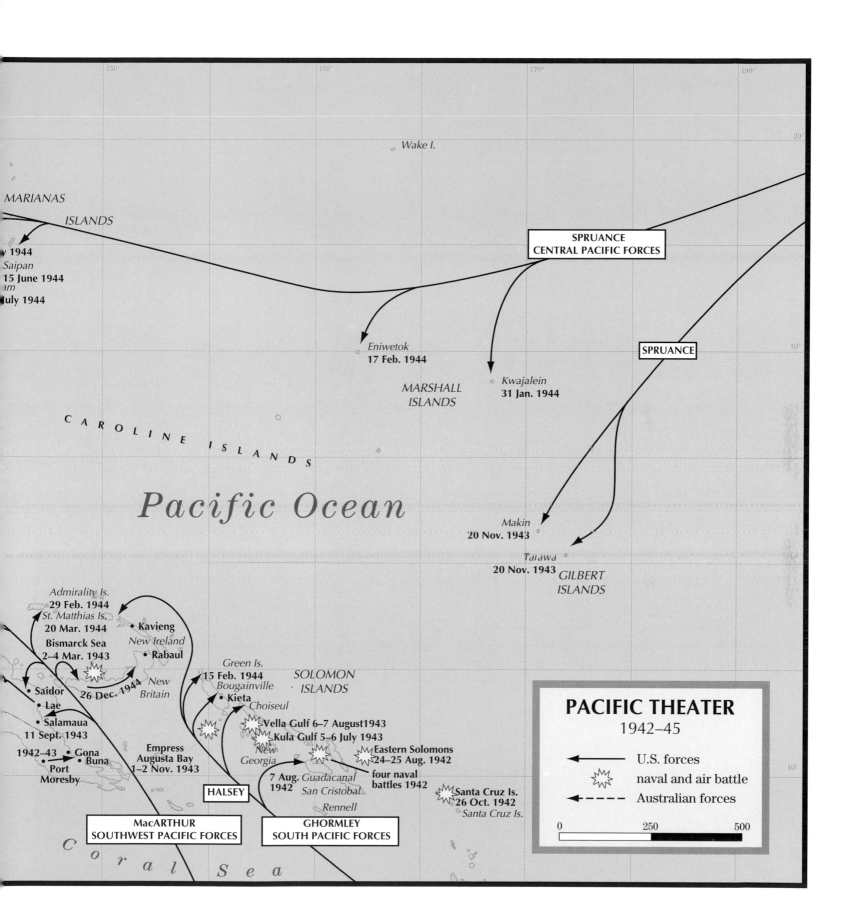

MARIANAS
ISLANDS

y 1944
Saipan
15 June 1944
am
uly 1944

Wake I.

**SPRUANCE
CENTRAL PACIFIC FORCES**

SPRUANCE

Eniwetok
17 Feb. 1944

Kwajalein
31 Jan. 1944

*MARSHALL
ISLANDS*

CAROLINE ISLANDS

Pacific Ocean

Makin
20 Nov. 1943

Tarawa
20 Nov. 1943 *GILBERT
ISLANDS*

Admirality Is.
29 Feb. 1944
St. Matthias Is.
**20 Mar. 1944
Bismarck Sea
2–4 Mar. 1943**

• **Kavieng**
New Ireland
• **Rabaul**

Green Is.
15 Feb. 1944
Bougainville
• **Kieta**
Choiseul

*SOLOMON
ISLANDS*

• **Saidor**
• **Lae**
• **Salamaua**
11 Sept. 1943

26 Dec. 1944 *New
Britain*

Vella Gulf 6–7 August 1943
Kula Gulf 5–6 July 1943

**Eastern Solomons
24–25 Aug. 1942**

1942–43 • **Gona**
• **Buna**
**Port
Moresby**

**Empress
Augusta Bay
1–2 Nov. 1943**

*New
Georgia*

7 Aug. *Guadacanal*
1942 *San Cristobal*

**four naval
battles 1942**

**Santa Cruz Is.
26 Oct. 1942**
Santa Cruz Is.

HALSEY

Rennell

**MacARTHUR
SOUTHWEST PACIFIC FORCES**

**GHORMLEY
SOUTH PACIFIC FORCES**

C o r a l   S e a

PACIFIC THEATER
1942–45

⟵ U.S. forces
✴ naval and air battle
⟵---- Australian forces

0   250   500

Wingate, the English disciplinarian who had already earned fame in Ethiopia, parachuted onto the Japanese rear with his long-range penetration groups.

Wingate's Chindits (a mispronunciation of *chinthe*, the Burmese word for "lion") and Merrill's Marauders fought remarkably well, outdoing the Japanese in a type of jungle combat the latter had originated. Throughout the end of 1943, when the Japanese tried again to move on India, Wingate's commandos kept the invaders off balance, severing their communications lines. The commandos were supplied exclusively from the air and managed to build a landing strip far behind enemy lines. Merrill, for his part, persuaded a tribe of dark, belligerent north Burmese, called Kachins, to join him in fighting the Japanese. American OSS representatives formed a Kachin unit called Detachment 101 and managed to kill 5,447 Japanese, with a loss of only 15 Americans and 70 Kachins. Despite divergent national political ambitions and despite rivalries and jealousies among strategists and commanders at the top, Allied field action in Burma was remarkably effective. Wingate, unfortunately, was killed on March 24, 1944, in a plane crash. Churchill called him "a man of genius who might well have become also a man of destiny." He was only forty-one.

The campaign against Japan covered flabbergasting distances; its scope was enormous, and Allied interests were so disparate and contradictory that it was difficult to coordinate strategic plans. The critically important Soviet-Manchurian frontier remained quiescent until weeks after the Nazi surrender in Europe, as it was in the interests of both the Soviet Union and Japan to honor their nonaggression pact. Native nationalism in colonial Indochina, Malaya, Indonesia, Burma, and India initially favored the Japanese. Subsequently, however, the invaders' barbarity turned these populations against

This photograph of Mount Fuji in Japan was taken in 1943 through a U.S. submarine periscope a few minutes after firing its torpedoes, which were running "hot, true and normal." Never in their worst nightmares had the Japanese expected the Americans to get this close to the home islands.

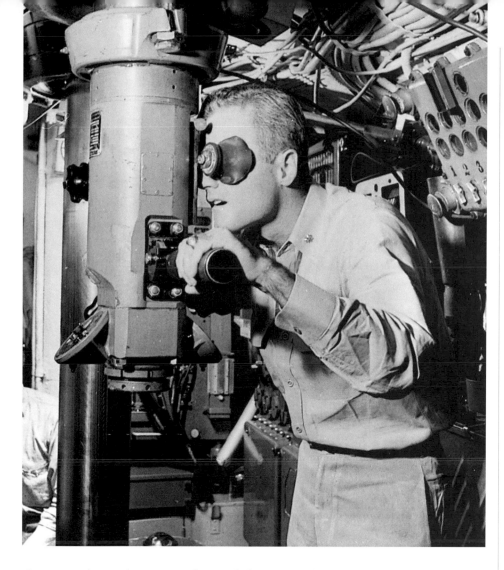

An American officer looks through a periscope on the USS *Marlin*. The "silent service" took only volunteers. One out of seven of them lost his life. But in return, the submarines sent much of the Japanese merchant fleet to the bottom.

them, much as Ukrainians changed their attitude toward the Germans once they got acquainted with the facts of life under the Nazis. China's principal contribution to the Allies was as an enormous bog that sucked up Japanese armies. The real road to Tokyo would be by sea, and at the close of 1943 there was still plenty of road to travel.

From Midway until the Japanese surrender, the navy fought another kind of war in the Pacific, about which the people back home heard very little. The United States, which had entered World War I because of the German unrestricted U-boat campaign that sank U.S. merchant vessels, developed over the course of the war the world's second largest (Germany was first) and by far most effective submarine fleet. These "subs" were the U.S. Navy's secret weapon; although only 2 percent of the navy's ships and men, they sank more Japanese ships, both merchant and armed, than the rest of the navy—air and sea—put together.

In the early part of the war, U.S. torpedoes were faulty, kills few. But by the fall of 1943 the problem had been licked, and the year's tally would be 22 enemy warships sent under and 296 merchant ships. Japanese defenses against underwater attack were scanty. The Japanese High Command, aggressive and offensive-minded, had given a defensive war at sea little thought. About one U.S. sub out of four never came back, but by the spring of 1945, the Japanese lifeline had been cut.

CHAPTER 12

ITALY

The Italian campaign that began in July 1943 and lasted until May 1945 ended with Allied armies in complete control of Italy, but the victory was gained at such a cost that this campaign has been the most criticized of the war. The first and most basic criticism is strategic: Italy led nowhere. Once it was conquered, the Alps still stood between the Allied armies and Germany. Further, Italy represented a poor investment of assets because it tied down more Allied troops than it did German. Finally, on the tactical level, Italy was unsuitable for offensive operations because of its narrowness and rugged terrain.

Italy did yield its benefits. It provided airfields that allowed the Allies to bomb oil refineries and other targets in Austria, Poland, and the Balkans. It gave the Allies badly needed experience in amphibious operations. And it boosted morale by showing that Britain and the United States were on the offensive on the Continent, and that liberation had actually begun. At bottom, however, the Italian campaign can be best characterized by the words of a World War I song: "We're here because we're here because we're here." The invasions of Sicily in July 1943 and of the Italian mainland in September were foreordained on the day the Allies made the decision to proceed with Operation Torch. The commitment of massive armed forces to North Africa dictated that Italy be invaded. Transporting the men and equipment back to England after Torch cleared the Germans from North Africa made no sense, especially when the invasion of France would not be mounted before 1944. Had the Allies not gone into Sicily and Italy, they would have spent the second half of 1943 and the first half of 1944 doing nothing against the Germans beyond bombing German factories and cities.

The basic decision to attack at Sicily was reached at the Casablanca Con-

The crowd cheers as the American flag is displayed in front of Palazzo Venezia in Rome on June 5, 1944 (opposite). The celebration lasted through the next day, as word arrived of the invasion of France.

339

American forces board a Landing Craft Vehicle Personnel (LCVP), popularly known as a Higgins Boat, Sicily, July 8, 1943. They had been mislanded near Gela and had to reboard for transportation to the right sector of the beachhead.

ference in January 1943. That same month, General Mark Clark activated the U.S. Fifth Army in northern Morocco and set to the planning for the invasion of the mainland. Meanwhile generals Montgomery and Patton went to work on plans for invading Sicily. The code name for the operation was "Husky." On July 5, the U.S. Seventh Army under Patton embarked from Oran, Algiers, and Bizerte for Sicily, in an armada commanded by Vice Admiral H. Kent Hewitt. Simultaneously, Montgomery's British Eighth Army sailed from Tripoli, Benghazi, Alexandria, Port Said, and distant Haifa and Beirut. There were nearly 3,000 landing craft and warships, 160,000 troops, 14,000 vehicles, 600 tanks, and 1,800 artillery pieces. Britain undertook to supply 80 percent of the naval cover and 45 percent of the air cover required; the rest was assumed by the United States. This was by far the largest amphibious operation ever to that date.

Enemy defenses had been softened by continued bombing on Sicily, south Italy, Sardinia, and the little cluster of offshore islands that included strongly fortified Pantelleria. Eisenhower had decided to invade Pantelleria as a first step, but on June 11 the Italian garrison surrendered without a fight after heavy aerial bombardment. The only Allied casualty was a private bitten by a mule. Sicily itself was a far tougher nut: barren, mountainous, and held by three hundred thousand Italian and German soldiers under Field Marshal Alfred Kesselring. Kesselring thought that if Sicily were Eisenhower's next target the landing must come on the southwest coast, opposite Tunisia, or on the north coast, close to Messina, the escape route to the mainland. Instead, Patton and Montgomery were landing on the south coast, with Monty on the right, Patton on the left.

On the afternoon of July 9 the invasion armada for Husky converged south of Malta, in the midst of heavy seas and thirty-five-mile-an-hour winds. The gale kept blowing as night fell, and the landing faced disaster. But by dawn of the tenth, both gusts and waves subsided. The landing craft pitched through the breakers and began discharging men and machines, including an ingenious new amphibious load-carrier known as DUKW, on Sicily's south coast. Despite the fact that a large number of British airborne troops were drowned when their gliders were prematurely released and fell into the sea, and that the anti-aircraft gunners on the U.S. destroyers mistook planes carrying the Eighty-second Airborne paratroopers into the battle and shot down a number of them, Eisenhower was able to report before noon: "The success of the landings is already assured." Thanks in part to the foul weather on July 9, the initial lodgment had come as a tactical surprise.

The Germans recovered quickly. They sent panzers to the coast to fire into the beachhead. The U.S. destroyers got into a shoot-out with the tanks; the destroyers won. Meanwhile the great majority of Italian defenders offered only token resistance. They surrendered in droves or, wearing civilian

A Luftwaffe officer, Field Marshal Albert Kesselring (above) took command in Italy in September 1943. He was one of Germany's more successful generals, waging a skillful campaign in Sicily and Italy. He was opposed in Sicily by Montogomery and General George S. Patton Jr., shown here wading ashore in Sicily, July 8, 1943, with a photographer handy to record the moment (left).

clothes, vanished into the hills. The Sicilians themselves greeted the invaders joyfully, handing out fruit, flowers, and wine. There was scarcely a squad in the U.S. Army that did not contain at least one private of Italian heritage who spoke the language fluently; many of them were busy looking up Sicilian relatives.

Montgomery's Eighth Army slashed up the east coast, swiftly taking ancient Syracuse, and entered the malaria-infested Catanian plain. There, meeting stiff German resistance, the British commander cautiously halted to bring up his main strength—a decision that inspired American complaints. Patton's Seventh Army landed at Gela and Licata in the south and proceeded, according to Patton's theory of war, to "go like hell." Within two weeks he would drive all the way to Palermo on the northern coast of Sicily, slicing the island in half and becoming the liberator of the first city in Europe. That got him headlines, but he had been attacking in the wrong direction against the wrong enemy. Patton's plunge to the north against Italian "opposition" freed the Germans to prepare fortifications in the mountainous country between Palermo and Messina. At the eastern tip of Sicily, Messina was the strategic objective.

On July 20, Eisenhower ordered Patton to head for Messina. The Germans withdrew slowly toward the northeast, fighting a dogged defense. This was the final and toughest phase of Operation Husky. Pursuing the elite German troops from crag to crag, U.S. forces pushed toward Messina. Allied engineers performed miracles, throwing trestles over deep gaps after the retreating enemy had destroyed bridges. Masses of heavy equipment had to be moved over narrow, primitive roads. At Troina, more than a dozen desperate German counterattacks were thrown back. But Patton was so frustrated by the slow progress that he was in a furious state of mind when he visited a field hospital and saw a soldier who had nothing apparently wrong with him, except that he was shaking and crying. Patton accused the GI of cowardice and slapped him, twice, hard. As it turned out, the soldier had malaria and a fever of 104 degrees; Patton was in trouble.

For a month, however, the slapping incident was covered up, and Patton had the satisfaction of beating Montgomery to Messina. He drove into the city on August 17. More headlines, which hid the fact that the Allies had squeezed the Germans out of the toothpaste tube rather than blocking their escape route: some sixty thousand German troops escaped via the Strait of Messina and took up positions in Italy, ready to fight another day. Allied casualties in Sicily came to a total of 31,158.

The Allies, whose intelligence from Italy was both accurate and extensive, had prepared the political and psychological machinery to benefit from the collapse of Sicily. On July 17, United States and British aircraft had begun dropping leaflets over Rome and other cities. Signed by Roosevelt and Churchill, the leaflets read: "Mussolini carried you into this war as the satellite of a brutal destroyer of peoples and liberties. Mussolini plunged you into a war which he thought Hitler had already won. In spite of Italy's great vulnerability to attack by air and sea, your Fascist leaders sent your sons, your ships, your air forces, to distant battlefields to aid Germany in her attempt to conquer England, Russia, and the world. . . . The time has now come for you, the Italian people, to consult your own self-respect and your own inter-

Authorized at Casablanca, the Allied invasion of Sicily in July was to be a campaign of limited objectives, aimed at freeing Mediterranean shipping from Axis harassment, diverting German strength from the Soviet front, and increasing the pressure on Italy to desert Hitler.

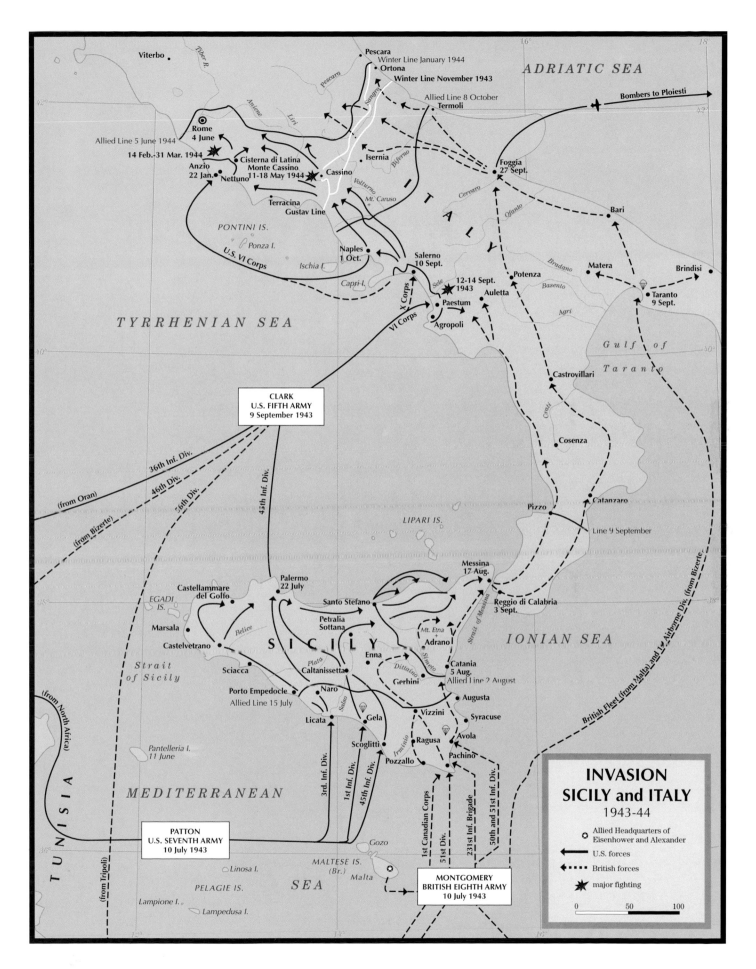

Viterbo

ADRIATIC SEA

Pescara
Winter Line January 1944
Ortona
Winter Line November 1943
Allied Line 8 October
Termoli

Bombers to Ploiesti →

Rome
4 June

Allied Line 5 June 1944
14 Feb.-31 Mar. 1944

Cisterna di Latina
Monte Cassino
11-18 May 1944

Anzio
22 Jan.
Nettuno

Cassino

Isernia

Foggia
27 Sept.

I T A L Y

Bari

Terracina
Gustav Line

Mt. Caruso

Matera

Brindisi

PONTINI IS.

Ponza I.

U.S. VI CORPS

Ischia I.

Naples
1 Oct.

Salerno
10 Sept.

12-14 Sept.
1943

Potenza

Auletta

Taranto
9 Sept.

Capri I.

X Corps

Paestum

Basento

VI Corps

Agropoli

Agri

Gulf of
Taranto

TYRRHENIAN SEA

Castrovillari

CLARK
U.S. FIFTH ARMY
9 September 1943

Cosenza

36th Inf. Div.

(from Oran)

46th Div.

56th Div.

45th Inf. Div.

Pizzo

Catanzaro

Line 9 September

LIPARI IS.

(from Bizerte)

Messina
17 Aug.

Palermo
22 July

Reggio di Calabria
3 Sept.

Castellammare
del Golfo

Santo Stefano

EGADI
IS.

Marsala

Relice

Petralia
Sottana

Mt. Etna
Adrano

IONIAN SEA

Castelvetrano

S I C I L Y

Enna

Catania
5 Aug.
Allied Line 2 August

Sciacca

Plata

Caltanissetta

Dittaino

Gerbini

Porto Empedocle
Allied Line 15 July

Naro

Salso

Gela

Augusta

Vizzini

Syracuse

British Fleet (from Malta) and 1st Airborne Div. (from Bizerte)

Licata

Scoglitti

Ragusa

Avola

Pachino

MEDITERRANEAN

Pozzallo

PATTON
U.S. SEVENTH ARMY
10 July 1943

Gozo

3rd. Inf. Div.

1st Inf. Div.

45th Inf. Div.

1st Canadian Corps

51st Div.

231st Inf. Brigade

50th and 51st Inf. Div.

(from Tripoli)

Linosa I.

MALTESE IS.
(Br.)

Malta

MONTGOMERY
BRITISH EIGHTH ARMY
10 July 1943

**INVASION
SICILY and ITALY**
1943-44

✪ Allied Headquarters of
Eisenhower and Alexander

→ U.S. forces

▸▸▸ British forces

✹ major fighting

PELAGIE IS.

(from North Africa)

Pantelleria I.
11 June

Strait
of Sicily

SEA

Lampione I.

Lampedusa I.

T U N I S I A

0   50   100

ITALY   343

American troops enter Palermo, Sicily, on July 23, 1943. This was the first European city to be liberated. Critics charged that by making Palermo his objective, Patton was after headlines; the strategic objective of the campaign was at Messina, on the other (eastern) end of Sicily.

Italy's king, Victor Emmanuel, formally stripped Mussolini of power on July 25, 1943.

ests and your own desire for a restoration of national dignity, security, and peace. The time has come for you to decide whether Italians shall die for Mussolini and Hitler—or live for Italy, and for civilization."

Mussolini's control had started to crumble long before the Sicilian landing. As Allied air power had smashed Italian cities and communications, national morale faded; the food situation worsened; strikes and riots broke out in industrial centers. Mussolini's secret police advised him that many ardent Fascists were now conspiring against him, including Count Dino Grandi; Marshal Pietro Badoglio, the conqueror of Ethiopia; and General Vittorio Ambrosio, chief of the General Staff.

On July 19, as the British and Americans were fighting in Sicily, Mussolini conferred with Hitler at a villa near Rimini. The Führer counseled: "Sicily must be made into a Stalingrad. . . . We must hold out until winter, when new secret weapons will be ready for use against England." But he offered no further reinforcements for the collapsing Italian Army, and the dialogue was punctuated by the bleak news that seven hundred Allied aircraft had bombed Rome. The Allies had previously avoided Rome, for fear of damage to the Vatican, but Eisenhower insisted on hitting the railroad marshaling yards in the city. As they were more than two miles from the Vatican, the risk was run. The result was the complete collapse of Mussolini's support. Under intense pressure, the Duce summoned the Fascist Grand Council to the Palazzo Venezia for its first meeting since 1939. In a passionate two-hour speech, he sought to fire up his black-shirted collaborators as he used to do in the good old days. But this time he utterly failed. Grandi had the audacity to introduce a resolution demanding that Mussolini relinquish to King Victor Emmanuel the command of the armed forces. Nineteen of the Fascist Grand Council supported this motion, seven opposed, and two abstained. Mussolini strode out of the room aware that his game was up.

The council ended in the early morning hours of Sunday, July 25. Later that day, the angry Duce called on Victor Emmanuel, who informed him that he was no longer head of the government. "The soldiers don't want to fight anymore," said the king. "At this moment you are the most hated man in Italy." When he left the palace, Mussolini was arrested by *carabinièri,* shoved into an ambulance, and smuggled off to internment on the island of Ponza. The king took command of his dissolving military forces and instructed Badoglio to form a new cabinet. The Italian people danced for joy.

Even before the invasion of Sicily, Badoglio had sent secret agents to Eisenhower's headquarters in Algiers to propose an Italian double cross. When Allied troops under General Clark landed at Salerno, he offered, Italy would surrender and immediately declare war on Germany. Eisenhower was for it, but Churchill and Roosevelt were taken aback by the proposal because they had demanded Italy's unconditional surrender and because dealing with Badoglio—until recently an enthusiastic Fascist—was like dealing with Admiral Darlan. As a result of their political opposition, the Allied negotiators proved inept and slow moving at this critical moment. For five weeks they bickered over surrender negotiations, most basically over the words "unconditional surrender." Then, on August 19, General Giuseppe Castellano met American and British military representatives in Lisbon. They agreed that Italy would surrender "unconditionally," but immediately be allowed to become a co-belligerent and keep the government and monarchy intact. This would be announced by Badoglio over the radio on September 8, to coincide with the Allied landing that same night on the mainland at Salerno.

Eisenhower drafted an emergency plan for a daring parachute landing of the Eighty-second Airborne, based in Sicily, on Rome's airfield. On September 7, he sent General Maxwell Taylor on a secret visit to the Italian capital to estimate German military strength and how much support the Allies might expect from the Italians, to look over the proposed landing site, and to otherwise prepare for the imminent paratroop drop. But he found Badoglio demoralized and helpless; the Germans, who had their own sources of information, had caught on to the double cross and were pouring troops over the Brenner Pass and down to Rome. Badoglio said he could do nothing, that there was no Italian Army left. By this time, on the evening of September 8, the Eighty-second's transport planes were circling over Sicily, preparing to go to Rome. Taylor had to send a message canceling the opera-

Field Marshal Pietro Badoglio (center) talks to General Maxwell Taylor (left) after his announcement of unconditional surrender on September 8, an hour and a half after Eisenhower had broadcast the same news to the troops aboard ships bound for Salerno.

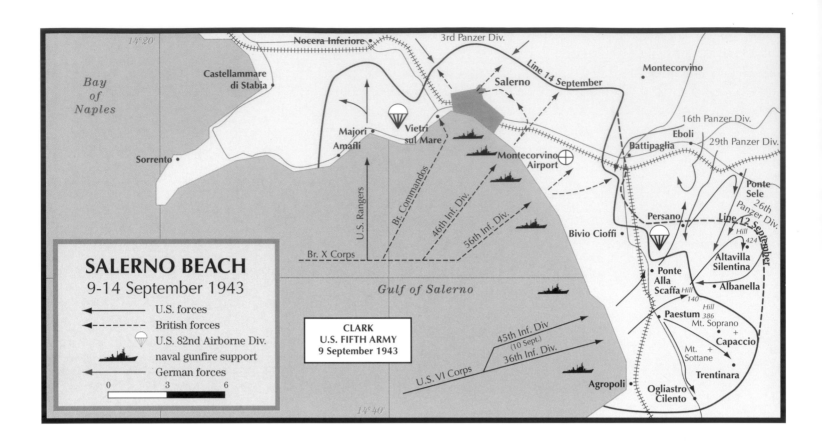

SALERNO BEACH
9-14 September 1943

→ U.S. forces
⇢ British forces
U.S. 82nd Airborne Div.
naval gunfire support
→ German forces

0   3   6

CLARK
U.S. FIFTH ARMY
9 September 1943

The Salerno invasion began at 3:30 A.M. on September 9, 1943 (above). With incredible courage, the Fifth Army fought its way up the beaches, around or over mines, barbed wire, machine-gun emplacements, tanks, and fallen bodies. Of all the invasions of the war, Salerno came the closest to failure. For a number of days it was touch and go. General Mark Clark came close to withdrawing. Below, Allied troops try to advance on the Salerno beachhead, September 9.

tion; the Germans had taken control of the airfield. Meanwhile Badoglio announced on the radio that the nation was giving up its fight.

The first lodgment on the Italian peninsula had been made by Montgomery's Eighth Army, which on September 3 had crossed the Strait of Messina under heavy artillery and air cover and moved slowly northward through Calabria. Montgomery had a relatively easy time. As his veteran troops fanned northward and eastward, they were joined by six thousand men of the British First Airborne Division, which seized the naval base of Taranto on September 9 and then swept up to the Adriatic port of Bari.

Clark's forces at Salerno, however, ran into difficulty from the start. The Italians had quit, but the Germans had not. Kesselring had anticipated a landing at Salerno and was prepared for it. The Americans were landed by night without benefit of preliminary shelling, in the hope of achieving surprise. It was believed that by entering Italy as far north as Salerno they could quickly take nearby Naples. But the German coastal defenses were inviolate. Furthermore, the GIs, having just heard the announcement of Italy's surrender, expected an easy landing. Instead they were met by heavy artillery and tank fire. They found themselves compressed into a small beachhead that extended less than five miles inland. Many assault boats were unable to reach their designated targets. Paratroopers sent to back them up suffered heavy losses en route. German loudspeakers meanwhile kept roaring in English: "Come on in and give up. You're covered." The invasion fleet suffered from confused communications and had trouble discharging heavy weapons.

A Sicilian offers wine to GIs in 1943 (above). There were many Sicilian-born soldiers in the U.S. Army. Fraternization began immediately and lasted throughout the campaign. After the alien terrain of North Africa, American troops moved into Italy and made themselves at home. On September 22, 1943, Headquarters Company, 480th Field Artillery Battalion, are hard at work in their "office" between the Doric columns of an ancient Greek temple of Neptune in Paestum, Italy, built about 700 B.C. (opposite).

Four days after the landings, Kesselring staged a massive counterattack that almost split the Fifth Army in two. Clark contemplated withdrawal from the beachhead, and Berlin radio began hailing the prospect of "another Dunkirk."

At this crucial point, from bases in Sicily and North Africa, the U.S. Strategic Air Force began bombing the hills surrounding Salerno, while British and U.S. destroyers and cruisers provided line of sight artillery support. Eisenhower ordered Montgomery to speed up his advance in order to relieve the pressure on Salerno. Clark organized everyone into fighting units: truck drivers, mechanics, and even a regimental band, which defended a hill thenceforth called Piccolo Peak.

Under the pressure of air and sea bombardment, the Germans began to waver and finally, on September 15, to withdraw to Naples. Clark seized the initiative. Within a month he had unloaded 135,000 troops, 30,000 vehicles, and 100,000 tons of supplies to nourish a northward drive. At the same time, French Forces of the Interior, aided by local guerrillas, captured Corsica, and the Germans abandoned Sardinia. The bulk of the Italian fleet sailed into Malta for internment.

Italy had by now become a battleground in which the Italians themselves figured only as doleful victims. Rural Italians found it difficult to comprehend why young Germans should be fighting young Britons and Americans in Italy. Badoglio's and the king's scheme to switch sides and thus

avoid disaster had backfired. In 1940, Mussolini had said: "If the Germans ever get here they will never go home." He was right. Hitler left Kesselring to fight the campaign in the south, sent Rommel to organize northern Italian defenses, and took ruthlessly effective control of all the area not already in Allied hands.

Badoglio and the royal family had fled Rome in a panic on September 9 and had reconstituted the semblance of a government in Brindisi, far to the south. A week later, Badoglio summoned his countrymen "to fight the Germans in every way, everywhere, and all the time." According to Eisenhower, calling on the Italians to rise up against the Germans was like beating a dead horse. There was no fury left in the war-weary Italians. On October 13, Victor Emmanuel formally declared war on Germany, and Italy was recognized by the Allies as a co-belligerent. Italy was promised that the country's punishment would be lessened according to the amount of help Italy gave the Allies.

The German answer to Italy's betrayal was formidable. *Wehrmacht* headquarters ordered immediate disarming of all Italian troops. Within an hour of Badoglio's announcement of an armistice, German patrols took over from Salerno to Nice and the Brenner Pass. Italy's Fourth Army on the French border was disbanded. Rommel seized Trieste and the routes to Yugoslavia, thus completing the isolation of thirty-two Italian divisions. Most of these capitulated. It has been estimated that Germany took 640,000 Italian prisoners on the peninsula and in the Balkans; the majority were shipped to slave labor camps in Germany, where some 30,000 died. On September 11, Kesselring proclaimed all Italy a war theater under German control. The Nazis seized Italy's gold reserves and began immediate persecution of those Jews who had managed to survive Mussolini's half-hearted strictions.

Mussolini himself had one more great adventure in store. From Ponza

Mussolini poses with German paratroopers at Gran Sasso resort, in northern Italy, on September 18, 1943. He had been overthrown and arrested by King Victor Emmanuel and his provisional grovernment, then freed in a daring rescue led by the famous German Waffen SS officer Otto Skorzeny.

he was removed to a small mountain resort in the Abruzzi, from which Hitler swore to save him. In mid-September 1943, Otto Skorzeny, the remarkable Nazi commando leader, overran the resort with glider troops and kidnapped the Duce in a light airplane. He was thenceforth set up as the puppet head of a Fascist Republic in the north, proclaiming: "I, Mussolini, resume supreme direction of Fascism in Italy." No one paid any attention; Mussolini was now in the ash can of history.

Meanwhile, General Clark's Fifth Army had successfully passed its test at Salerno and now drove on the port city of Naples, the most important single prize in south Italy. The Germans, fighting a skilled defense, did not bother to defend the city but, taking vengeance for Italy's defection, smashed it and withdrew northward. When the Americans and British entered Naples early on the morning of October 1, they found that the port and everything within three hundred yards of it had been destroyed. The population was half starved, frightened by looters, and bullied by criminals released from prison by the departing Germans. The grand old university had been deliberately wrecked; hospitals had been looted; and a number of hostages had been taken. The citizens of Naples gave their Allied conquerors a wild welcome. American engineers set to work on the wreckage and soon had the harbor and neighboring airfields in operation.

To the northeast, Montgomery's Eighth Army had succeeded, against relatively slight opposition, in achieving its initial objectives. The extensive network of airfields at Foggia began furnishing fighter cover to advancing Allied

Two Landing Ship Tanks (LSTs) discharge men and equipment at Anzio, January 1944 (left). The LST was a sea-going vessel that brought goods all the way from the States. The invaders were pinned down in the beachhead for almost four months. General Lucian Truscott (above, with Eisenhower) who in February replaced the commander of the VI Corps, General John Lucas, was an aggressive officer who was finally able to break out of the beachhead in May.

troops as well as dispatching bombers over Austria and the Balkans. But Kesselring, with his fine eye for terrain, established a new position to frustrate Clark on the north bank of the Volturno River, where Garibaldi had won a significant victory in 1860. There began the slow hacking campaign in which, pushing between rock ridges and along muddy valleys through Italy's worst winter in decades, the Allies inched toward Rome and Tuscany.

To pursue this strategy, the Allies installed another team of commanders. Eisenhower had been recalled to England to prepare for the Normandy invasion. With him he took his most renowned generals: Montgomery, Bradley, and Patton (by this time reporters had printed accounts of the Patton slapping incident and Eisenhower had been forced to remove him from command, but he brought Patton with him to England, explaining to the press that he had to have Patton at his side for the assault on France). Sir Harold Alexander, who had with minimal fanfare supervised Montgomery's operations from the Nile to Tunisia, was left behind as commander in Italy. Under him were Clark and the calm, little-known Sir Oliver Leese, who headed the British Eighth Army on the Adriatic. General Ira Eaker, a tough, poker-faced American, took over the Allied Mediterranean air forces. General Sir Henry "Jumbo" Wilson replaced Eisenhower at the top in the Mediterranean theater. Hitler likewise reordered his command. He sent Rommel to France and left Italy to Kesselring, ordering him to hold "at all costs for the sake of the political consequences which would follow a completely successful defense. The Führer expects the bitterest struggle for every yard."

Kesselring did what he was told. Clark was slowed up on the Volturno and at successive hilltop villages, but the Allies hoped to outflank the Germans by amphibious tactics. On January 22, 1944, they swept by sea around the right flank of the German Gustav Line and landed two divisions thirty-three miles south of Rome, at the pleasant resort towns of Anzio and Nettuno.

Anzio came close to being a disaster. The initial landing went well, but it was not exploited, and the surprised Germans had ample time to mass troops and artillery on the high ground surrounding the beachhead's perimeter. Their eventual counterattacks almost succeeded in wiping out the beachhead. The purpose of the landing—to relieve pressure from the main drive along the road to Rome—failed. Churchill, who had endorsed the project, admitted: "The story of Anzio was a story of high opportunity and shattered hopes, of skillful inception on our part and swift recovery by the enemy, of valor shared by both." But, he noted ruefully, "I had hoped that we were hurling a wildcat onto the shore, but all we got was a stranded whale." For almost four months the invaders were trapped in the beachhead, every inch of which was covered by German artillery. Foxholes filled with rainwater; the only protection came from surface shelters built of sandbags and the few buildings that had not been smashed to complete rubble. All told, the Americans suffered 59,000 casualties, many of them victims of shell shock.

The failure at Anzio threw the main weight of the campaign back on the positions around the town of Cassino, hinge of Kesselring's Gustav Line. Apart from its magnificent position along the Liri and Rapido rivers, giving it domination of the narrow valley leading up toward Rome, Cassino was marked by a monastery built on the massif above it by St. Benedict in the sixth century. The historic Abbey of Monte Cassino had been successively

The area surrounding Monte Cassino Abbey (below), near the Rapido River in central Italy, was still occupied by German paratroops after heavy Allied air and artillery attack in February 1944. The abbey had been built by Saint Benedict in 529 A.D. The bombing of Cassino was one of the most controversial of the war. The abbot of Monte Cassino (seen at left with German soldiers) and a few priests remained in a subterranean chapel throughout the bombing.

Cassino burns after a bombing raid. The Germans claimed they did not occupy the abbey; the Allies were certain they were using it for an observation post. It was finally taken by Polish troops on May 18.

ravaged by conquerors and an earthquake in the Middle Ages. It was now to be destroyed again.

From the heights around the abbey, German 88s were picking off Allied armor, while mortars and *nebelwerfers,* dubbed "screaming meemies" by the Americans, were plastering the advancing infantry. The Allied command concluded that the advantages posed by the monastery could no longer be ignored. There was a suspicion that German outposts actually had been established within the abbey—although this was later disproved. At any rate, a conclave of generals resolved that the fortress sanctuary must be destroyed. Leaflets were dropped over enemy lines saying: "Against our will we are now obliged to direct our weapons against the Monastery itself. We warn you so that you may now save yourselves. Leave the Monastery at once." And on February 15 the vast abbey was bombed by 254 planes. Only the cell and tomb of St. Benedict escaped damage.

The attack on this holy shrine achieved nothing but a worldwide wave of protest, which was carefully fanned by Nazi propaganda. The German defenders moved into the ruins and set up impregnable positions amid the shattered masonry. The town of Cassino itself was hit again and again by Allied guns and aircraft. One raid involved more aircraft than had yet been used on any operation; the entire town was obliterated in a cloud of flame, smoke, and shattered stone. Yet despite the attacks, when Allied patrols sought to enter Cassino, they were promptly driven back by the expert German First Parachute Division, its men emerging from the cellars to fight.

Between Anzio and the Gustav Line, General Kesselring held off the Allies through the hard winter of 1943–44. From well-fortified positions in the mountains, the Germans poured their fire down on the attackers day after day. For all the modern weapons used by both sides, it was a strange, old-fashioned kind of war: trucks and tanks were rendered virtually useless by mud, snow, and mountains; supplies were moved by mules, and men lived not unlike they did in World War I. For both sides, it was a bloody, nerve-racking, and seemingly endless business. It was a winter of deep discontent for Alexander's armies, which included Americans, British, Canadians, French, New Zealanders, South Africans, Poles, Indians, Brazilians, Greeks, Moroccans, Algerians, Senegalese, a brigade of Palestinian Jews, and a handful of royalist Italians. The mud was like glue at midday and like iron in the freezing nights. Cold winds and snow swept the jagged crags. Dead GIs lay in the cratered valley they called Purple Heart, their throats eaten out by scavenger dogs. Trench foot and frostbite were common. A force of Nepalese Gurkha was cut off for days on an outpost below the abbey. Each day, in this battle in a bowl, American fighter-bombers dropped gaily-colored parachutes with canisters of ammunition, food, and water to the isolated hillmen, who scrambled to secure them amid withering machine-gun fire. Among the most disheartening sights of all was Vesuvius, far to the south of the battle line. The volcano exploded in a sudden eruption that cast an ashen cloud far exceeding anything the Allies, with all their aircraft and artillery, could produce at Cassino.

But with the approach of spring, the Allies moved to break the stalemate. In April, the Strategic Air Forces flew 21,000 sorties against bridges,

This is what the GIs who fought in Italy recall about the campaign—jeeps stuck in the mud. The jeep was a marvelous vehicle that could go almost everywhere—but not through mud, at least not without assistance.

ARTILLERY AND HANDHELD WEAPONS

In many artillery and handheld weapons the Germans had the lead. It was the opinion of every GI who fought in North Africa, Italy, or northwest Europe, that the German 88-millimeter cannon was without doubt the best artillery piece of the war. It was a high-velocity, fast-firing, flat-trajectory weapon that could fire armor-piercing shells at tanks and high-explosive airburst shells against enemy bombers. The shell traveled faster than the speed of sound.

The Germans had more and heavier mortars than the Americans, but they were not so accurate. The German MG42 machine guns fired 1,200 rounds a minute, the American light machine gun less than half that. But the American .50-caliber machine gun, mounted on tanks, half-tracks, and jeeps had no equal in penetrating power. The American M-1 Garand was the best all-purpose military rifle in the world, renowned above all for its reliability.

In weapons, design differences lead to losses as well as gains, obviously so with tanks but also in so simple a thing as a hand grenade. The German "potato masher" could be thrown farther in part because of its design, but also because it was lighter; it had less than half the explosive power of the U.S. grenade. The GIs said it made more noise than damage.

The Germans also had the *nebelwerfer*, a six-barreled rocket launcher whose bombs produced a wail that was terrifying when they flew through the air. The GIs called them "screaming meemies." They could fire a salvo of six rounds every ninety seconds. There was no American counterpart.

Then there was the *panzerfaust*, the German handheld antitank weapon, which was far superior to the U.S. bazooka. It did not have the range of a bazooka, but it was operated by a single soldier and was so simple no special training was required. It was a one-use, disposable weapon; cheap to produce, it was effective and easy to transport. The bazooka, by contrast, required a

A PT marksman draws a bead with a .50-caliber machine gun (above) on a boat off New Guinea, July 1943. The reliability of the U.S. M-1 Garand rifle (opposite top) was unsurpassed. The German potato masher (opposite bottom) had a handle that made it easier to throw it farther than the American grenade.

trained two-man team. The *panzerfaust* launched a bomb that was bigger and better designed than the bazooka's bomb, and had greater penetrating power.

The British counterpart was the PIAT (personal infantry antitank). Spring-loaded and often jamming, it was inaccurate and had no penetrating power. "The PIAT actually is a load of rubbish, really," Sergeant Wagger Thornton of the British Sixth Airborne Division explained. "The range is about fifty yards and you're a dead loss if you try to go farther. Even fifty yards is stretching it. Another thing is that you must never, never miss. If you do you've had it because by the time you reload the thing and cock it, which is a bloody chore, you're done for."

Men of the 141st Infantry Regiment fire an 81-millimeter mortar during the crossing of the Rapido River on May 12, 1944 (right). In January, an attempt to cross the Rapido had been repulsed with heavy losses; this time it worked and the German Gustav Line began to crumble. Bill Mauldin, the GIs' favorite cartoonist, depicts life on the front lines in Italy (below).

Italians greet General Mark Clark as he tours Rome, June 10, 1944, the day after the country's liberation (opposite). The Italian people, who had never wanted war, were delighted to have it over.

"Didn't we meet at Cassino?"

railroads, and other German supply lines. The British Eighth Army relieved parts of the American Fifth Army at positions along the Gustav Line, so that the Americans could move up the Tyrrhenian coast toward Anzio. The big offensive started on May 11; the next day the Allies crossed the Garigliano and Rapido rivers. The crossing of the Rapido was routine; an earlier attempt in January had been terribly costly both in American lives and to General Clark's reputation. The German Gustav Line began to crumble. Then, on May 18, came word that Cassino had fallen. The Polish troops of General Anders, reassembled from prisoner-of-war camps in the Soviet Union and allowed to join the British in the Middle East, led the way into the abbey. Their role is still marked by a cemetery filled with Polish names.

Once again the Germans began a difficult but orderly withdrawal. The Fifth Army thrust out from its separated Cassino and Anzio positions, entering Rome at last on June 4, 1944, and marching through the Piazza Venezia. Clark, who rode into Rome with the vanguard on June 5, recalled: "There were gay crowds in the streets, many of them waving flags, as our infantry marched through the capital. Flowers were stuck in the muzzles of the soldiers' rifles and of guns on the tanks. Many Romans seemed to be on the verge of hysteria in their enthusiasm for the American troops. . . . It was on this day that a doughboy made the classic remark of the Italian campaign, when he took a long look at the ruins of the Colosseum, whistled softly, and said, 'Gee, I didn't know our bombers had done that much damage in Rome.'"

The fall of Rome marked the beginning of the last phase of the European war. Two days later, Eisenhower's forces landed in Normandy and burst through the front door of the Führer's Fortress Europe.

CHAPTER 13

OVER THERE

T he figures are staggering: In 1939 the U.S. Army and Army Air Corps (after 1942 the Army Air Force) numbered 190,000 men and women. By 1945 it had grown by a factor of forty-four, to 8,300,000. The U.S. Navy jumped from 125,000 to 3,380,000, and the U.S. Marines from 19,000 to 475,000. These stark figures speak to a point then Colonel Dwight Eisenhower made the day the war began with the German invasion of Poland: "Hitler should beware the fury of an aroused democracy." In addition to the staggering scope of American industrial mobilization for the war, the United States managed to put into the field more active military personnel than any other country. At peak strength the United States had 12,364,000 men and women in uniform. The figures for the other major combatants were: the Soviet Union 12,300,000; Germany 10,000,000; Japan 6,095,000; France 5,000,000; Britain 4,680,000; China 3,800,000.

The American armed forces had not only numbers, but also quality. Their men in uniform were highly selective in age and physical health; of the eighteen million men examined for induction, 36 percent (6,500,000) were rejected for service as physically or mentally unfit, a sad commentary on how poorly Americans ate and maintained their health during the Depression. For those men who were inducted, World War II was the most important experience of their lives. To begin with, boot camp added inches to their chests and leg and arm muscles. "You never had it so good" was the standard reply of the drill sergeant to the complaining recruit. "You get three square meals a day and boots on your feet."

In the armed services, Americans from all parts of the country came together: the lumberjack from Oregon found himself in a squad with a tailor from New York, a fisherman from Louisiana, an iron worker from Pennsylvania, a

On June 15, 1943, U.S. troops on their way to Oran for the invasion of Sicily relax on a transport somewhere in the North Atlantic, (opposite). Literally millions of young American men, and thousands of women, made their first trip ever out of the United States in such circumstances. Wartime stamps and postcards (above) were specially printed for the voluminous overseas correspondence. In many cases families were separated for the first time, and telephone connections were nearly impossible to make.

"Boot," was what a U.S. Navy photographer entitled this portrait of a recruit (above). It contrasts nicely with the shot below of Admiral Mark Mitscher aboard the USS *Lexington* off Saipan, June 19, 1944. The fresh-faced kid and the grizzled veteran illustrate the face of America at war—professionals in charge, amateurs in the ranks. Together, eventually, they made a great team.

dairy farmer from Wisconsin. This heterogeneity had a tremendously broadening effect on the young recruits. So did their experiences in traveling to the training camps; most of them had never been out of their home states, many never out of their own counties.

Almost 75 percent of the recruits served overseas, with an average of sixteen months abroad. They did not necessarily go to the country or even the continent of their choice, but what they saw and experienced made them far more knowledgeable about the world than they had been. Very few GIs came home as isolationists; they had learned that the United States could not duck her international responsibilities.

Few GIs wanted to be over there. Given a choice, they would have preferred throwing softballs rather than hand grenades, shooting .22s at rabbits rather than M1s at men. But an evil force was loose in the world and it fell to ordinary American soldiers to destroy it. They accepted the responsibility—they had little choice—and fell to work.

When American troops went into action in North Africa and Italy, their abilities were assayed with considerable curiosity by their more experienced allies and enemies. Britain's Chief of Staff, Sir Alan Brooke, decided: "The Americans had a lot to learn. . . . But in the art of war . . . when they once got down to it they were determined to make a success of it." Field Marshal Rommel reflected afterward: "What was really amazing was the speed with which the Americans adapted themselves to modern warfare. They were assisted in this by their tremendous practical and material sense and by their lack of all understanding for tradition and useless theories." He concluded: "Starting from scratch an army has been created in the very minimum of time, which, in equipment, armament, and organization of all arms, surpasses anything the world has yet seen."

Coming into the service, the average American soldier of World War II was taller and heavier than his father who had fought in World War I. When he went off to serve his country, he had had some high school education; the American armed forces were the best educated in the world, by far, a consequence of the most extensive public education system in existence. The GI also had skills learned outside the classroom; for example, he knew how to drive a car and how to repair it, which gave the U.S. Army more mobility than any other (Red Army soldiers driving American-supplied trucks had hundreds of accidents; when a spark plug failed, they just walked away from the truck). A major asset for the GIs was their language ability. This was thanks to the great wave of immigration into the States in the first two decades of the century. Because of it, there was scarcely a company in the army that didn't contain at least one man who could speak Polish, French, Russian, Italian, or another European language, along with dozens who could speak German.

The U.S. armed forces were built, to use Rommel's phrase, "in a minimum of time," out of whatever the draft boards were able to send along. Training camps sprang up like mushrooms after a rain, all across the nation, enough to provide facilities for making millions of young men into soldiers. Once inducted into the army, the raw recruit was given a remarkably fast haircut at no charge, then punctured with inoculations, garbed in a floppy olive-drab outfit called "fatigues," and put under the tutelage of a hard-

American recruits had a lot to learn about making war. The trainee (left) thrusting his bayonet into a sketch of Hitler is learning to be aggressive, but in combat he would have faced almost certain death if he had exposed himself in this manner. Bill Mauldin's cartoon is far more realistic (below); men soon learned to fire only when necessary.

"Stop shootin' at him, ya idiot! Wanna give away our position?"

cussing buck sergeant who barked out commands and soon had him throwing out his chest and talking in a jargon that he would remember for the rest of his life.

As the immense machinery for turning civilians into soldiers picked up speed and units became ready to head for the Pacific, Africa, and England, the War and Navy Departments thoughtfully issued them pocket guidebooks with tips on how to get along overseas. Those who were bound for England were advised: "The British don't know how to make a good cup of coffee. You don't know how to make a good cup of tea—It's an even swap"; and a special glossary explained that dust bin means ash can, lift is elevator, first floor is second floor, flicks are movies, and a dickey is a rumble seat. Soldiers embarking for North Africa were cautioned that Arabs are not "heathens," and that when indulging in a local meal, "it is advisable not to drink much liquid after eating kuskus as the grain is only partly cooked and bloating will result." They were also admonished: "If you enter a bakery, leave your shoes at the door. . . . Never try to remove the veil [from a Moslem woman]. This is most important. Serious injury if not death at the hands of Moslem men may result. . . ."

Once overseas, the GI was kept in touch with relatives and friends at home by V-mail—little letters that could reach even the most outlandish des-

To save space, V-mail from soldiers overseas (above) was put on microfilm, sent home, then enlarged to four-by-five-inch prints to be put into the conventional postal delivery system. The logo encompassed the Morse code for V . . . —. Below, Mauldin always got it right. In this case, he captures the critical importance of mail from home to the boys overseas.

"I wuz just kiddin', Joe—you got three letters."

tination in about ten days—and by miniature overseas editions of magazines and books. The armed forces also distributed hundreds of thousands of free "pocket books," paperbacks that put reading material in an inexpensive, easily transportable, disposable form. These were produced for the first time during WWII and started a revolution in publishing. Titles ranged from Homer to Shakespeare to Hemingway (German troops got copies of *Mein Kampf)*. Red Cross volunteers went over there, where they helped nurses in the hospitals, set up "clubmobiles" that served coffee and doughnuts, and in a variety of other ways contributed to the well-being of the troops. The USO put on dances and stage shows and sent such Hollywood celebrities as Joe E. Brown, Bing Crosby, Bob Hope, Jo Stafford, and Frances Langford to far-flung desert and jungle sites and to the Aleutian Islands. They gave the lonely GI a laugh or the rare chance to let fly with a wolf call. Bob Hope endeared himself to hundreds of wounded men by coming up to their beds and saying: "Hi. Did you see my show tonight or were you already sick?"

To keep the American soldier fit and fighting, an array of new drugs and preventive medicines was developed. Special clothing—jackets, boots, headgear—were devised to protect him against extremes of temperature and terrain. To keep him out of trouble, especially when he went on leave, a police force was set up; its white belts, gloves, leggings, helmet liners, and "MP" armbands became well-known symbols around the world. And to advise "the folks back home" on his latest doings, a force of some seven hundred correspondents was mustered by American newspapers, magazines, and radio stations. During 1944, they sent back some 200 million words from the battlefronts. (The Normandy landings alone were reported by some four hundred fifty correspondents.) Traveling by landing craft, tank, truck, jeep, mule, and on foot through Italy, France, Germany, and, island by island, across the Pacific, the correspondents wrote about the men who were making the decisions that affected the GI's life—Eisenhower, Bradley, Patton, Arnold, and Spaatz in Europe; MacArthur, Nimitz, Halsey, Smith, Vandegrift in the Pacific. For millions of mothers and fathers, wives and sweethearts, knowing just who these commanders were was vitally important.

But the man about whom the most was written was, inevitably, the man who was himself commanded, who did the bulk of the fighting even in an age of mechanized war: the nearly always uncomfortable, unromantic, anonymous infantryman. Correspondents described the terror of war, its filth, fear, and loneliness, its comradeship, heroism, and humor; the hours and hours of boredom, and the moments of indescribable exhilaration. There was John Hersey on Guadalcanal, Joe Liebling in North Africa; there were John Dos Passos, Ernest Hemingway, John Steinbeck, Ed Murrow, and others less famous. Some were killed. Of these, perhaps the best, and certainly the GIs' own personal favorite, was a middle-aged newspaperman named Ernie Pyle, who wrote with compassion and distinction and who followed the "mud-rain-frost-and-wind-boys," as he called them, right up until the day that he was shot and killed by a sniper's bullet on the Pacific island of Ie Shima.

Pyle wrote: "I believe that I have a new patience with humanity that I've never had before. . . . I don't see how any survivor of war can ever be cruel to anything, ever again." When he was buried, the following inscription was

The GIs loved Rome and its gelato (opposite), but they loved a reminder of home even more. The Red Cross doughnut stand below is near the Vatican, but no site could compete with American girls. This little touch of home drew the GIs like a magnet.

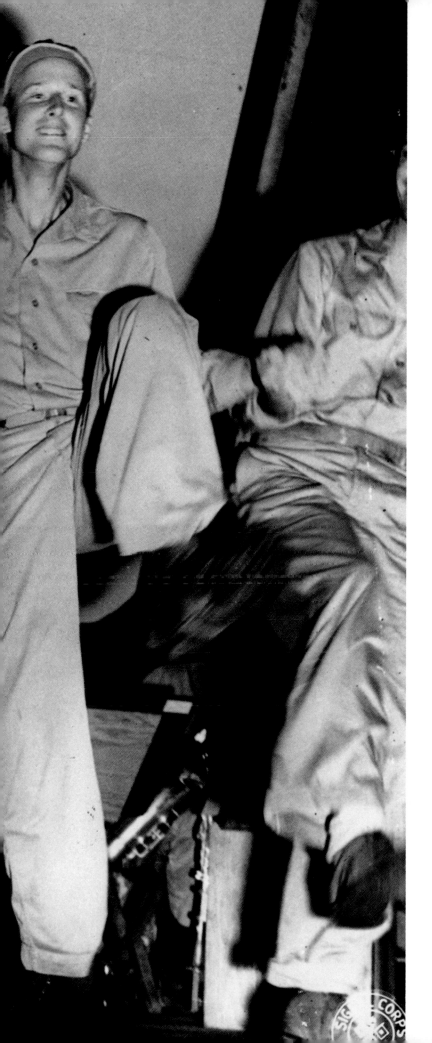

Peggy Alexander of the United Service Organization has GIs join her onstage somewhere in the Southwest Pacific theater in October 1944. The USO provided "home away from home" entertainment for homesick troops. Bob Hope and Marlene Dietrich may have been the most famous of the USO entertainers, but there were hundreds of others. As the poster below shows, the USO also helped raise money to send the comforts of home to troops all over the world.

You help someone you know...when you give to the **USO**

"Now that ya mention it, it does sound like th' patter of rain on a tin roof."

"Maybe Joe needs a rest. He's talkin' in his sleep."

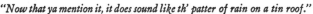

For most GIs, most of the time, life in Europe didn't include sightseeing in Rome, Paris, or wherever, or being entertained by movie stars. It was mud and rain and exhaustion, punctuated by moments of pure terror and days, weeks, months of misery. No one ever caught this better than Mauldin.

put on his grave marker: "At This Spot the 77th Infantry Division Lost a Buddy. Ernie Pyle. 18 April 1945."

Among the hardiest of those who sought to describe the war were the photographers, many of whom were in the heart of the action, and who, often as not, remained anonymous. Perhaps the best of them was Hungarian-born Robert Capa—who survived the war, despite the risks he took, only to be killed in Indochina in 1954. Capa was determined to immortalize "the little man whose future was at stake in a world he could not change."

The man who did the most to immortalize the American infantryman was Bill Mauldin, a boyish-looking GI who drew cartoons for the army newspaper, *Stars and Stripes*. Mauldin was only twenty when he went overseas, and he rapidly became the best-known American war cartoonist. He captured the grim wit of the foxhole in a way loved by the enlisted men themselves, detested by some of their officers. The secret of his humor and of its impact among the men was that it was caste-conscious; it said to the enlisted man, "I'm with you, and only we together know what it's all about." His two cartoon characters, Willie and Joe, became the heartbreaking and hilariously funny heroes of an army that was fighting as hard as it could, with little fanfare and a lot of griping, to get the job over with and get home, *alive*.

After the war Mauldin wrote a book, *Up Front*, which included the pick of his cartoons and his own comments on the war. What he had to say, like his drawings, put the "glories" of life at the front on their proper level. For

"You gents relax. We got three inches of armor."

"Th' socks ain't dry yet, but we kin take in th' cigarettes."

example: "It's a little better when you can lie down, even in the mud. Rocks are better than mud because you can curl yourself around the big rocks, even if you wake up with sore bruises where the little rocks dug into you. When you wake up in the mud your cigarettes are all wet and you have an ache in your joints and a rattle in your chest."

There were only three punctuations to the dreary life of a frontline infantryman: relief, wounds, or death. A marine's grave marker on Guadalcanal summarized the period in between:

And when he gets to Heaven,
To Saint Peter he will tell:
One more marine reporting, sir—
I've served my time in Hell.

Combat was indeed hell. In their foxholes, around the world, the GIs lived in the ground, with no sense of past or future. Only the present counted. Fatalism ruled among the veterans. Paul Fussell, a company commander in Europe, described the stages of rationalization combat soldiers went through: going into battle for the first time, the GI felt "it can't happen to me" because "I'm too young, too good-looking, too well-trained, too loved," followed by a realization that "it can happen to me" unless "I'm more careful, dig my foxhole deeper, don't expose myself," followed in turn by a stage of "accurate perception: it is going to happen to me, and only my not being

There is a bittersweet quality to the lieutenant's remark to the infantry riding on his tank (above left): the Sherman tank's armor was not thick enough to turn back a German 88 shell, and this was one of the most bitter complaints of the U.S. tankers. Above right, Willie and Joe take advantage of a break in the weather.

SHELLING

Combat is one of the worst of human experiences, because it is so dangerous and inhuman. Combat infantry live in the ground, where they try to kill men they have never known, and strangers, in turn, try to kill them. They are deprived of food, sleep, and shelter, not for just a few hours but for weeks on end. All around them they see destruction and death.

Perhaps the most terrible combat experience is undergoing a shelling. Private Arnold "Ben" Parish of the Second U.S. Infantry Division recalled being in a foxhole in the Ardennes during the Bulge when shelling began: "It was raining shells and they were exploding all around our hole. The air was full of shrapnel and spent pieces were hitting us as we laid on our backs with our helmets over our faces. The noise was unbearable and the ground was shaking and we were shaking from fright and cold. We didn't dare raise our heads. It would have been impossible to survive outside of the hole."

Parish remembered there were cries of "Medic!" Tree limbs hurling through the air. The smell of powder. Screams and bangs and flashes and

A medic, Private Harvey White, gives blood plasma to Private Roy Humphrey after he was wounded by shrapnel, Sicily, August 9, 1943.

booms. The only movement he could make was to press ever closer to the ground. Those who endured the cataclysm were forever scarred by it, even if untouched by shrapnel.

"We were helpless and all alone and there was nothing we could do, so I prayed to God. . . . The time went by very slow. I thought about my mother and hoped she didn't know where I was or what I was doing. . . . Maybe this is the end of the world, I thought."

Feelings of helplessness were universal. Corporal Stanley Kalberer, in the U.S. Eighty-fourth Division, also got caught in a shelling during the Bulge: "I never felt so alone, frightened, forgotten, abused, and degraded." In his first shelling, Sergeant Bruce Egger of the U.S. Twenty-sixth Division recalled: "The concussions for the explosions shook the ground so violently that I felt like I was bouncing and in danger of sliding off the face of the earth. . . . After each explosion I was amazed to find myself unscathed and gritted my teeth as each new screaming artillery or whispering mortar shell approached. I was continually showered by mud from the exploding shells and the shrapnel, which tore up the ground around me." The whine of the artillery sounded "like the scream of a madwoman." Egger reflected that "neither words nor film can fully describe war. You have to be there. . . . There was no way the Army could have prepared me for this day."

The damage shrapnel did was horrible. Dr. Joseph Gosman was

American infantry take shelter behind a tank to wait out a shelling, Geich, Germany, December 11, 1944.

an orthopedic surgeon with the 109th Evacuation Hospital. He had a patient who had a Swiss Army knife in his pants pocket that got hit by a piece of shrapnel. Bits of knife and shell entered his thigh together. The "X-ray picture looked like a table setting with knife, fork, and spoon and other stuff." The shell came faster than the speed of sound, on a flat trajectory, and blew hell out of whatever it hit, worst of all overhanging tree limbs, whose innumerable splinters were almost as dangerous as shrapnel. For the Germans, the P-47 fighter-bombers were the worst. They called them "Jabos." They brought down rockets, 500-pound bombs, and .50-caliber machine-gun fire on any German who dared to move during the day. Corporal Helmut Hesse said, "The Jabos were a burden on our souls."

Shells came in all sizes, from grenades thrown by hand to 205-millimeter cannon, from light and heavy mortars to 88s and 75s, from rockets to bazookas and *panzerfaust* (handheld antitank rockets). If the Germans had the best artillery pieces—the 88s—the Americans had the most.

Straw caskets were used for the dead aboard a Navy hospital ship, January 8, 1943. This photo illustrates a coming-home every American family who had a boy overseas feared.

there [on the front lines] is going to prevent it." For the marines in the Pacific and the GIs in Italy and northwest Europe, that was almost always true; divisions in combat for more than three months took 200 percent casualties.

Until the last months of the war, censors kept photographs of dead Americans out of the newspapers, but as the first shiploads of coffins began coming back to the United States, they brought home to America the hard truth of war as nothing else could—not even those letters and telegrams being delivered to so many front doors: "We regret to inform you. . . ." As the death toll steadily mounted, little-known villages that were tucked away in obscure corners of the country suddenly felt as if they had suffered from some biblical plague. Salinas, California, with a population of 11,586, and Harrodsburg, Kentucky, with 4,673, respectively contributed 150 and 76 men to the tragedy of Bataan. Bradford, Virginia, lost 14 young men in the first five minutes of Omaha Beach.

There was a determined effort by the U.S. command and its Graves Registration Service to keep track of all those who died, even when their remains were unidentifiable. Nevertheless, there were places in Europe and on islands in the Pacific where trenches were dug, the bodies dumped in after

identification had been removed, a row of crosses put up, and a dog tag hung on each cross. And the sailor's grave, as always in war, was the sea. Before it was all over, 292,131 Americans were killed, more than the battle dead of the Union and Confederate armies in the Civil War.

Those who lived stumbled back from the edge of the canyon, psychologically neither dead nor alive. Ernie Pyle wrote: "In their eyes as they pass is not hatred, not excitement, not despair, not the tonic of their victory. There is just the simple expression of being there as if they had been doing that forever, and nothing else." Pyle also said: "A soldier who has been a long time in the line does have a 'look' in his eyes that anyone who knows about it can discern . . . it is a look that is a display room for what lies behind it—exhaustion, lack of sleep, tension for too long, weariness that is too great, fear beyond fear, misery to the point of numbness, a look of surpassing indifference to anything anybody can do." (It was a "look" that the GIs called "combat fatigue" or "nervous in the service" and that, by 1945, had translated itself into mental collapse for some five hundred thousand men.)

The incredible psychological pressures of war produced a strange form of spiritual bends in a good many men, who, when granted a momentary

Marines on Eniwetok in the Marshall Islands get a coffee break, February 17, 1944. Combat is one of the most extreme of human experiences. Only those who have been there can fully understand the toll it takes on the human body and soul. And these faces tell us more about what it was like than any combat action photograph can.

"We've just landed. Do you know any good war stories?"

By the summer of 1944, there was a steady flow of replacements to the Italian and northwest European fronts. By the fall of 1944, most combat divisions contained more replacements than veterans. By the winter, a large majority of the GIs were replacements. Most of them had been in high school in 1943; some of them were 1944 high school graduates. They arrived as innocent kids; after a day or two of combat, if they survived, they became veterans.

In a Quonset hut at the air base on Adak, in the Aleutians, men kill time gambling, a universal passion. The Quonset hut (so named because it was made at Quonset Point, Rhode Island) was produced in the tens of thousands and provided shelter for millions of GIs around the world. A half-cylindrical design made of corrugated metal, it was modeled on the earlier British Nissen hut.

release from duty, sought to express their very joy in survival, sometimes in the age-old ways of the soldier, other times in fashions that seemed almost inexplicable. With millions of young men overseas, far from the restraining influence of their parents, church, and society, living in a situation in which death might come at any moment, the vices that accompany any army were ever present—gambling, womanizing, and, most of all, drinking. The GIs indulged in wild ecstasies of gambling, often playing for stakes they never would have believed possible in their civilian days. After all, what was three or four thousand dollars, when they were used to putting up their lives? As Glen Gray, a counterintelligence officer in Italy and northwest Europe, put it: "In campaigns of extreme hazard soldiers learn more often than civilians ever do that everything external is replaceable, while life is not."

In England and, after their liberation started, in Italy and France, the juxtaposition of GIs and old, hitherto stable societies produced jealousies and conflict, heightened by emotional strains and contrasting economic levels. Quarrels over women erupted as normal peacetime sexual morality lapsed into confusion, and as different army pay scales gave the Americans an advantage in entertaining that they were quick to use. One sour complaint among Britons was: "The trouble with you Yanks is that you're overpaid, oversexed, and over here." The GIs quipped back: "You're sore because you're underpaid, undersexed, and under Eisenhower."

Few of these children of the Depression had much experience with any form of alcohol other than beer. In North Africa they bought huge quantities of a terrible home brew from Arab traders. In Europe they helped them-

The GIs in Europe fought through rain, mud, snow, and ice. As a consequence they suffered badly from all sorts of maladies, beginning with every lung disease known and including dysentery and trenchfoot (which put almost as many men out of action as wounds or death). One thing about fighting in Europe, as opposed to the Pacific, however, was that every village had its wine shop.

"She must be very purty. Th' whole column is wheezin' at her."

"Them rats! Them dirty, cold-blooded, soreheaded, stinkin' Huns. Them atrocity commitin' skunks . . ."

Private Elmer Sittion is kissed by an overjoyed Italian woman (left) on June 5, 1944, the day Americans entered Rome. Around the world, when the Americans came they were greeted as the liberators they were. Everywhere they went, they drew a sketch of a mythical character named Kilroy (below), and proclaimed that he had been there first. Kilroy provided a symbol of the American presence from the Aleutians to Zanzibar; the United States was now a worldwide power.

KILROY WAS HERE

selves to the wine available in almost every cellar and certainly in every village. They drank champagne, when they could get it, like soda pop—and paid a price in the morning. Out in the Pacific, marines and sailors improvised every imaginable means of producing a potation with a kick to it. One technique was to filter hair tonic through bread and then mix it with grape juice. Like virtually every other drink devised in the Pacific, it was known as "Jungle Juice."

Although the Americans are known to have committed some atrocities against enemy military personnel and civilians, their record of violence comes nowhere close to that of the Germans or Japanese. No other army of such numbers or power ever behaved better or, for that matter, was so well received, even among conquered enemies. The GI came not to conquer but to free people, whether in Europe or in the Pacific. He took home new notions about the earth, about people who were not American, not rich, not powerful, who represented a different race or faith. He left behind some of his own ideas and a great many dead comrades. He also left behind a curious marking that was chalked on rocks, on city walls, on lavatories: "Kilroy was here." No one ever found out for sure who Kilroy was, where he came from, or why anyone would care enough about him to scrawl his name across half the globe. But that Kilroy was there was absolutely certain; and if he had not made the world safe for democracy, he had at least helped to rid it of an inhuman despotism.

CHAPTER 14

THE AIR WAR

One of the worst legacies of World War II was the acceptance of civilians as targets—not as individuals nor in small groups but in massive numbers in the great cities of Europe and Asia. It happened because of airpower. Airplanes had grown in size and extended their range through the 1920s and 1930s. By 1944 they were so improved that four-engine bombers, numbering a thousand or more, could penetrate hundreds of miles beyond the front lines, carrying loads of bombs with an explosive power measured in the kilotons to devastate enemy cities.

This development was not wholly unexpected. After World War I, military theorists sought some way to avoid the senseless slaughter in the trenches. They were led by the Italian airpower theorist Guilio Douhet, whose 1921 book, *Command of the Air*, explained his vision of "victory through airpower." Douhet argued that land armies were a thing of the past; in the next war, victory would come to the side with the biggest bombers, with planes that could not be stopped by fighters or anti-aircraft fire. The bombers would pulverize the enemy cities and induce panic in the civilian population. The civilians would then demand that their governments make peace.

The British Royal Air Force (RAF), the first independent air force (formed in 1918) adopted Douhet's theory and built a fleet of bombers designed to attack targets far behind the front lines. The U.S. Army Air Corps (after 1942 the Army Air Force [AAF]; after 1947 the U.S. Air Force) also followed Douhet's ideas, putting its major effort into building the B-17, a four-engine bomber that could carry up to eight tons of bombs. It was called the "Flying Fortress," and its proponents said it would always get through because its thirteen .50-caliber machine guns—mounted on the top, on the bottom, in the nose, in the tail—could drive off any enemy fighters that came in

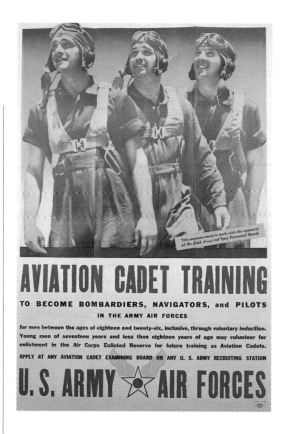

The idealized airmen in these recruiting posters are obvious exaggerations, but they do bear a resemblance to reality. The Army Air Force chose men in peak physical condition and with high IQs and the best education. Of course the romance of flying, better living conditions, and the chance to learn a skill that could be transferred to a civilian job helped attract the best and the brightest.

Below is a B-17G Flying Fortress, as painted by Dennis Knight. The "G" meant that it was the seventh modification of the original. The U.S. went into the war with the B-17D, which had no tail or nose guns and no ball turret below. The B-17G carried thirteen .50-caliber machine guns. It could carry a maximum bomb load of 17,600 pounds for a short distance; for a raid deep inside Germany, it carried a 4,000 to 5,000-pound bomb load. Top speed was 300 miles per hour; cruising speed about 160.

This Spitfire Mk Vb (opposite) from the 222nd Squadron of the RAF is being rearmed and refueled, May 1942. The Spitfire has a reputation that is almost legendary: It was the only RAF fighter able to take on the Messerschmitt 109 on equal terms. Both had top speeds of around 400 miles per hour, and while the Me-109 could outclimb and outdive the Spitfire, the latter was much more maneuverable.

range. In both Britain and the United States, the air force generals envisioned a single, separate role for their service: a strategic bombing campaign aimed at enemy morale and enemy factories.

The Luftwaffe had a different doctrine. The German generals in charge of the *Wehrmacht* assigned the Luftwaffe a ground support role to concentrate on fighters and fighter-bombers rather than four-engine bombers. (In Japan, where the navy was the dominant service, the main effort went into building fighters and fighter-bombers for aircraft carriers). But after rejecting Douhet's advice to build four-engine bombers, the Germans embraced his idea of terror bombing cities and began the process in the attacks on Warsaw in September 1939 and on Rotterdam in May 1940.

In the Battle of Britain, each contestant found it had concentrated too many resources on the wrong kinds of airplanes. The German two-engine medium bombers were not designed to carry a bomb load big enough for a genuine city-destroying attack, while the RAF Fighter Command was seriously short of Spitfires at a time when RAF Bomber Command had a sufficiency of bombers.

Once Germany began making targets of cities, the British followed the precedent. When the Germans invaded the Soviet Union, they used the Luftwaffe to smash Soviet cities. President Roosevelt protested, forcefully, against this descent into barbarism, and called on all nations to foreswear attacks on cities. But once the United States entered the war, Roosevelt became the leading proponent of strategic bombing, and of course the war ended with the Americans using atomic bombs against enemy cities—a logical outcome of a war in which for the first time in history more civilians than soldiers were killed.

The long-term consequence of this new form of war was that for the half century of the Cold War following World War II, civilians everywhere were targets of nuclear weapons that could be carried halfway around the world in supersonic rockets. Civilians in American, European, and Asian cities became hostages to the destructive power of the new weapons.

In World War II, rockets gave a whole new dimension to the air war. The Germans had them first; their V-2, operational in the fall of 1944, was the world's first intermediate range ballistic missile. Another revolution in the air, the jet airplane, came during the last year of the war. Again, Germany was first.

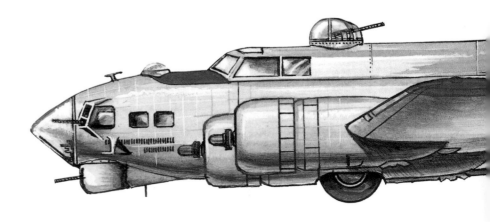

The German artist Fritz Junghaus painted this German Focke-Wulf 190 breaking off a successful attack on a British Stirling. The first four-engine bomber to join RAF Bomber Command, the Stirling flew its first raid in February 1941 against oil storage tanks in Rotterdam. It had a top speed of 270 miles per hour and could cruise 2,010 miles with a 3,500-pound bomb load. By 1943 it was no longer used as a bomber; its tasks were laying mines, towing gliders, and serving as transport aircraft.

Airpower was decisive in most World War II campaigns, on sea as well as on land. This was not so much because of strategic bombing—where the results of the enormous effort made by the AAF and RAF remain controversial—but rather as a consequence of gaining and maintaining air superiority. The side that controlled the air could gather excellent intelligence on its enemy's order of battle, thanks to its reconnaissance aircraft and improved cameras. Even more telling, it could use fighters and fighter-bombers to shoot up enemy columns on the road, making it virtually impossible for the enemy to move tanks, trucks, and men by day. Of all the weapons in the Anglo-American arsenal, the one the German soldiers feared most was the "Jabo," a generic term for such single-engine fighters as the P-47 Thunderbolt and the P-51 Mustang. These fighters carried .50-caliber machine guns, rockets, and two 500-pound bombs. Sweeping down on a German column, unhindered by German fighters, they struck terror into the hearts of the Germans on the ground.

But it took the Allies until 1944 to win control of the air. In the initial campaigns of the war, it was the Luftwaffe that ruled the sky with the Junkers Ju-87 Stuka terrorizing enemy troops from Poland to France to the Soviet Union. When it dove, the Stuka screamed like a siren. It became a symbol of German air superiority.

By 1942 things began to change. The Stuka was too slow to match Allied fighters, and Germany was overextended. The Luftwaffe found itself engaged in a four-front aerial war: over England, over North Africa, over the Soviet Union, and over the Reich itself. In 1939, Göring had pompously boasted: "If bombs drop on Germany, my name is Meyer." Within a year, sardonic Germans were calling him by that Jewish name, "Herr Meyer."

In August 1940 a small number of British bombers attacked Berlin; rather like the Doolittle raid against Japan in 1942, the attack was more a morale booster than a militarily significant move. On November 13, 1940, another small raid had an even bigger effect. On that night, Soviet Foreign Minister Molotov had been bargaining with Ribbentrop for spheres of influence in Central and Eastern Europe. The two ministers and their staffs were forced to take shelter, where Ribbentrop assured his guest that Britain was finished. Molotov shrewdly inquired: "If that is so, why are we in this shelter, and whose are these bombs which fall?" Those were the last significant Nazi-Soviet talks. They failed. Churchill remarked with relish: "We had heard about the conference beforehand and, though not invited to join in the discussion, did not wish to be entirely left out of the proceedings."

As the British and, later, the Americans intruded ever more deeply and persistently, Göring moved his fighter squadrons into occupied nations facing Britain and established an early warning system. When the Allied bombers headed east for German targets, they were hit first by these "outer" squadrons and then met by successive fighter wings.

The RAF's harassing raids increased in 1941 as the Luftwaffe was drawn into the Soviet Union, and by 1942 enough British planes had been prepared for broadscale strategic bombing. On May 30, 1942, came the first of the war's vast saturation raids: a thousand English planes attacked Cologne and left the Rhineland city blazing. Soon afterward came a succession of raids

When it went into action in 1942, the P-47 (top) was the heaviest fighter in the world, but despite its weight the 2,000-horsepower engine gave it a 412-miles-per-hour top speed. The P-51 (bottom), which came into full service in 1944, was faster (487 miles per hour) and could fly higher (42,000 feet versus 31,350) and farther. The P-51's range allowed it to provide fighter escort for bombers all the way to Berlin.

Bryan de Grineau sketched the scene above in the winter of 1941–42, when the Allied air assaults on Europe were just beginning. It shows an RAF Handley Page Halifax bomber being loaded late in the afternoon in preparation for a night raid over Germany. The Halifax carried a crew of seven and up to 13,000 pounds of bombs. It had a top speed of 265 miles per hour and a range of 1,860 miles.

The Luftwaffe heads out to attack British tanks in the Western Desert of North Africa, November 23, 1941 (opposite). These are Junkers Ju-87 fighter-bombers, the famous Stukas that struck terror into the heart of Europe. When the Stuka was diving on its target, it screeched in an ungodly way. But although it was a tremendous success as a ground support airplane when there was no opposition, it was slow and not very maneuverable. Hence, it was vulnerable to the RAF's fighters.

against Berlin, Hamburg, Dortmund, Leipzig, Essen. The RAF's Sir Arthur Harris reported that his planes were destroying, on average, two and a half German cities a month and warned the Germans that they had but two alternatives—annihilation or surrender. The nation suffered thousands upon thousands of killed and wounded, but German morale and Nazi discipline held firm. Douhet's prediction that civilians living in cities—whether in Germany, Britain, or Japan—subjected to bombing raids would rise up against their governments if those governments did not make peace proved wrong.

Still the Luftwaffe was extensively overcommitted by 1942, and the size and scope of Allied raids, smashing railway yards, factories, and cities from Cologne to Berlin, brought the war home to the German nation, making a mockery of all the Nazi regime's grandiose promises of security. There were public calls for retaliatory strikes on Britain, just as the British had demanded similar strikes on Germany during their arduous year 1940–41, but the Luftwaffe no longer had enough planes and pilots to satisfy any such craving for revenge. In October 1942, Göring was forced to confess in a speech broadcast from Munich: "There are those who ask why we do not go in for reprisals. The answer is simple: it is because most of our bombers are needed more urgently at Stalingrad and in the Caucasus."

In 1943, Bomber Command of the Royal Air Force and the U.S. Eighth Air Force were committed to long-range, strategic bombing, but on different principles, based on the conflicting visions of Bomber Command's Sir Arthur ("Bomber") Harris and Eighth Air Force commander General Carl ("Tooey") Spaatz, who led the American bomber force based in Britain. Harris believed that if German cities were pulverized, German morale

would crack. Furthermore, he argued, it would be foolish to accomplish the job by day bombing, which cost too heavily in planes and trained crews. Spaatz, on the other hand, refused to limit himself to the night-bombing methods of Harris or to broad metropolitan targets. He claimed it was unrealistic to assume that the Germans would knuckle under once their cities were smashed, just as it had been unrealistic for the Germans to assume that Britain would quit when it was being hammered by the Luftwaffe. He insisted on pinpoint bombing in long-range day raids that would knock out vital industrial and transportation centers.

When it entered World War II, the United States was determined to concentrate on destroying Germany before Japan. But eight months after going to war with Germany, nowhere were U.S. ground forces in contact with German forces. Only the U.S. Army Air Corps could strike out at the Germans. Its first effective unit in Europe was the Eighth Air Force, organized on January 28, 1942, and in May placed under the command of Spaatz, who established a series of bases in Britain with headquarters at Bushy Park, near London. Initially, Spaatz had crews and a staff, but no planes. The first U.S. action against the Germans took place on July 4, 1942, when American crews flying British planes bombed German submarine pens in France.

By the fall of 1942 the planes coming off the assembly lines in the States in record numbers began to arrive in Britain. From the start, the Americans were given wholehearted cooperation by the battle-tested RAF, but there was no letup to the British argument against daytime raids. They had seen the Luftwaffe defeated over Britain in 1940 when it had employed such tactics, and they themselves had suffered heavy losses from daytime raids on Germany. But Spaatz was eager to use his four-engine planes for so-called pinpoint bombing. The B-17 was equipped with the supposedly precise Norden bombsight, which, its admirers claimed, could "drop a bomb in a pickle barrel."

On September 8, 1942, the Washington and London high commands agreed to go ahead with a program of "around the clock bombing" called the Combined Bomber Offensive. When the sun went down over Hitler's *Festung Europa*, RAF Stirlings and Lancasters rumbled through the Rhineland mists and on to Saxony and Brandenburg. And when, through the swirling smoke, the sun arose in the east again, U.S. Liberators and Flying Fortresses came roaring down the aerial avenues. A complicated timetable was devised to avoid congestion of the narrow airspace above the British Isles.

By 1943, the Eighth Air Force was growing into a mighty force. Spaatz and his superior, AAF Chief of Staff Henry Arnold, were committed to the idea of precision bombing. They were convinced that if they could find the right target and destroy it, they could force a surrender by making it impossible for Germany to continue the war. But which target? What was the key? They decided it was ball bearings. Nothing mechanical moved without ball bearings. Destroy the factories making ball bearings and German tanks, trucks, self-propelled artillery, and all other vehicles could not be made. Eureka!

On August 17, three hundred seventy-six Eighth Air Force bombers attacked Regensburg and Schweinfurt, where German fighters and the ball bearings for their engines were manufactured. Casualties were very heavy,

RAF Bomber Command flew its first night raid against Mannheim, on the Rhine, on December 16–17, 1940. The purpose was to terrorize civilians. As this German photograph (opposite) vividly demonstrates, it succeeded. Whether terror shortened the war or not is another question.

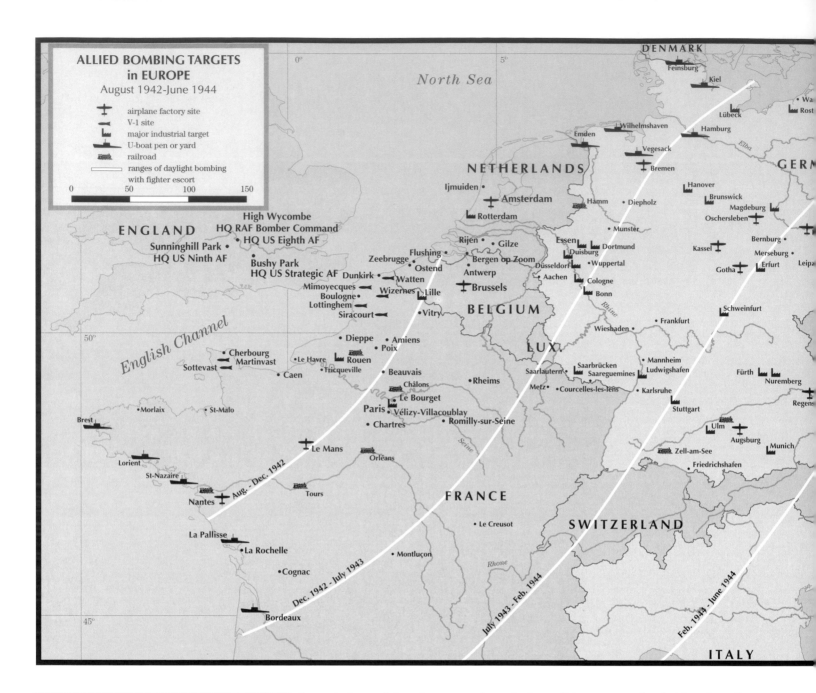

ALLIED BOMBING TARGETS in EUROPE
August 1942–June 1944

- airplane factory site
- V-1 site
- major industrial target
- U-boat pen or yard
- railroad
- ranges of daylight bombing with fighter escort

0   50   100   150

North Sea

DENMARK
Feinsburg
Kiel
Lübeck
Hamburg
Wilhelmshaven
Emden
Vegesack
Bremen
Hanover
Brunswick
Magdeburg
Oschersleben
Bernburg
Merseburg
Kassel
Gotha
Erfurt
Leip...
Wa...
Rost...
Elba
GERM...

NETHERLANDS
Ijmuiden
Amsterdam
Hamm
Diepholz
Munster
Rotterdam
Rijen
Gilze
Essen
Dortmund
Duisburg
Düsseldorf
Wuppertal
Cologne
Aachen
Bonn
Rhine
Schweinfurt
Frankfurt
Wiesbaden

ENGLAND
High Wycombe
HQ RAF Bomber Command
Sunninghill Park
HQ US Eighth AF
HQ US Ninth AF
Bushy Park
HQ US Strategic AF
Dunkirk
Zeebrugge
Flushing
Ostend
Watten
Mimoyecques
Wizernes
Boulogne
Lille
Lottinghem
Siracourt
Vitry
Antwerp
Brussels
BELGIUM
LUX.
Saarlautern
Saarbrücken
Saareguemines
Metz
Courcelles-les-lens
Karlsruhe
Mannheim
Ludwigshafen
Fürth
Nuremberg
Stuttgart

English Channel
Cherbourg
Martinvast
Sottevast
Caen
Le Havre
Tricqueville
Dieppe
Amiens
Poix
Beauvais
Rheims
Châlons
Le Bourget
Paris
Vélizy-Villacoublay
Chartres
Romilly-sur-Seine
Morlaix
St-Malo
Seine
Le Mans
Orléans
Tours
Augsburg
Munich
Zell-am-See
Ulm
Friedrichshafen
Regens...

Brest
Lorient
St-Nazaire
Nantes
Aug. – Dec. 1942
FRANCE
Le Creusot
SWITZERLAND
La Pallisse
La Rochelle
Montluçon
Rhone
Cognac
Dec. 1942 – July 1943
July 1943 – Feb. 1944
Feb. 1944 – June 1944
Bordeaux
ITALY

50°

45°

0°   5°

In the spring of 1944, the major operations were designed to isolate Normandy. Allies concentrated on bridges and railway targets in France, and by June 6 had knocked out every bridge over the Seine River. After D-Day, the big bombers went deep into Germany; three times more bombs were dropped on Germany after D-Day than before.

and sixty of the planes on the missions did not come back. But the pilots reported Schweinfurt destroyed, so the Allies sat back to await the German surrender.

Nothing happened. Production of new planes, tanks, and trucks went on unimpeded. It turned out that at the factories building the vehicles there were sufficient ball bearings in storage for two weeks of production. Furthermore, there were ball bearings in the pipeline, in crates on trains and trucks headed toward the factories, enough for another two weeks of production. Then there was a prewar stockpile in warehouses the Germans could draw upon. And before the month was up, the damaged factories were repaired, and manufacturing facilities for ball bearings were back at work.

The search for the single target that would lead to victory continued. In 1944 the bombers went after hydroelectric plants, oil storage depots, oil refineries, and other key targets. They never forced a surrender, although they

Sir Arthur Tedder, Commander in Chief of the Mediterranean Air Command, offers a light to General Carl Spaatz, commanding the American air contingent in North Africa, 1943 (above right). Tedder went on to become Eisenhower's Deputy Supreme Commander at SHAEF; Spaatz later commanded the U.S. Eighth Air Force in England.

A B-26 Marauder, somewhere over France in 1943, is in flames after being hit by anti-aircraft fire (right). The twin-engine bomber was used for low-level raids. It was accurate but vulnerable.

A B-17 heads for home, leaving Schweinfurt, Germany, apparently in ruins on October 14, 1943. In fact, the Germans won this battle. Sixty B-17s were shot down and the ball bearing plants that were the target were back in production in less than a month. After Schweinfurt, long-range raids into central and eastern Germany were abandoned, until the P-51 came along to provide fighter escort all the way to the target.

did disrupt German productivity at every level. One reason they did not accomplish more was the sheer number of potential targets, which meant they were constantly being sent to new targets before finishing the job on the old ones. Another was weather: the bombers were heavily dependent on good weather and in northern Europe in the fall and winter, the weather is seldom good.

German defenses were much more formidable than Spaatz and Arnold had anticipated. Between anti-aircraft weapons (primarily 88-millimeter cannon—very fast shooting, highly accurate, devastating when they scored a hit) and German fighter planes, the daylight U.S. raids were taking heavy casualties, in some cases as high as 10 percent on a single mission. Another problem was inaccurate bombing. Flying from 10,000 feet to as high as 25,000 feet, they couldn't come close to dropping a bomb in a pickle barrel. In fact, those free-falling bombs coming down from such altitudes scattered in a radius of as much as five miles.

Typical of the combined Anglo-American air strategies were the attacks on Hamburg, Germany's principal seaport, which housed some of the Reich's biggest oil refineries, and on Ploiesti, the Romanian oil-producing center on which Hitler drew heavily for fuel. Hamburg was easily identifi-

Allied bombs hit key targets in Germany: a Focke-Wulf aircraft factory in Bremen, December 20, 1943 (above); marshaling yards in Hamm, April 22, 1944 (above right); and an oil plant in Merseburg (right). With oil, the Allies finally found the right target for strategic bombing, the genuine key to rendering the *Wehrmacht* immobile and thus helpless.

"OPERATION SOAPSUDS"
PLOIESTI OIL FIELDS, RUMANIA.
AUGUST 1, 1943
NINTH & FIFTEENTH AIR FORCES

The Germans recognized their greatest strategic vulnerability, so they greatly increased the anti-aircraft defenses around oil refineries and storage depots. At Ploiesti, Romania, on August 1, 1943, they shot down scores of bombers. Nixon Galloway's painting *Operation Soapsuds* portrays a B-24 Liberator over the oil complex.

able to bombers coming in across the North Sea's open water or groping up the Elbe. During daylight hours, U.S. bombers battered its refineries and U-boat pens; at night its docks, refineries, and dwellings were hit by British heavy bombers flying in close formation and employing for the first time a very simple but highly effective method of fouling the enemy's radar. The planes dumped huge batches of tinfoil of the right length and width to float slowly down over the target as a shield against radar waves. German fighter defenses and flak directed by radar were thus knocked totally out of whack. The RAF alone, in four raids between July 24 and August 3, 1943, killed an estimated forty-three thousand people in the grand old Hanseatic city. This terrible event became known to Germans as *Die Katastrophe*. Countless lives were snuffed out by lack of oxygen in the firestorm produced in Hamburg. After *Die Katastrophe*, one Hamburg woman watched rescue workers stack corpses in trucks, then shivered and said: "If there were a God, He would have shown some mercy to them." An elderly man replied: "Leave God out of this. Men make war, not God."

Ploiesti was an obvious target; without fuel the German Army would surely grind to a halt. But its importance was as obvious to the Germans as to the Allies, and it was heavily defended. Nevertheless, an initial attack was launched on August 1, 1943, by a force of 178 U.S. B-24 bombers taking off from Libya. They made a 1,500-mile flight across the Mediterranean and the German-occupied Balkans and met successive fighter attacks long before they approached their target. They fought their way through, and soon the refineries and oil tanks were covered with brilliant orange flame and billowing black smoke. The damage wreaked was substantial, but losses were a catastrophe. Four hundred forty-six of the 1,733 men on the mission were killed, and only 33 of the original 178 planes came through fit to fly again. Many planes were shot down over Romania (where 108 men were imprisoned) and Bulgaria, while others gradually collapsed into the Aegean as they struggled to make their way back toward Africa. The damage to the refineries turned out to be repairable; the Americans had lost the battle of Ploiesti.

By the end of 1943, the "bomber barons"—as Spaatz, Arnold, Harris, and other advocates of strategic bombing were called—were close to despair. An enormous effort—the building of the bomber fleets, the training of their crews, the lives lost over Germany—had apparently failed. British night bombing had not destroyed German morale. U.S. daylight bombing had not destroyed German productivity (which rose in 1943 and again in 1944; Germany produced more in March 1945 than in June 1941), and the Flying Fortress had proved to be incapable of defending itself against German fighters. In the fall of 1943 one out of three bombers sent over Germany suffered battle damage on each raid. The Eighth Air Force discontinued raids beyond fighter-escort range.

Hope returned to the bomber barons in 1944 with the development of a fuel container known as the "drop tank," which extended the range of U.S. fighters. Thereafter, Thunderbolts and especially Mustangs could accompany the lumbering B-17s and B-24s to their targets deep inside Germany. The speedy P-51 Mustang, World War II's longest-range fighter, became known to bomber crews as "little friend." Historians later said it was one of the weapons that won the war.

Insignias of the squadrons that participated in the Ploiesti raid: top, the 67th Bombardment Squadron; middle, the 409th; bottom, the 329th.

An airman's life was exhausting and tension-filled, not nearly as dashing and romantic as public perception had it. Clockwise, from top left: A carrier crew checks *Dauntless* dive-bombers after a strike; firemen douse a Corsair after it crashed against the tower of the carrier *Prince William*; Colonel James Stewart, much admired by his fellow pilots, receives a medal for his combat missions over Germany; a Hellcat fighter crashes on the *Lexington*'s flight deck; a crewman of the B-17 "Grin' n Bare It" wears his plane's insignia and a tally of her thirty-six missions on his jacket; Jesse D. Franks, Jr. is the first man to die in the ill-fated Ploiesti raid. (He jumped from his burning B-24 at treetop level and his chute did not open. "One never knows what tomorrow may bring," he had written his father the night before.)

The pilots on Allied bombing raids were as remarkable as their planes. Here a pilot of a B-17 with one wing on fire manages to stick to the formation, flying his plane low and steady, then dropping its bombs on its target of Berlin, March 22, 1944.

The British likewise improved the deadliness of their nocturnal armadas. They developed the Beaufighter, which could accompany night bombers for six hours without refueling and whose sophisticated radar equipment could spot German planes in the foggy dark. Thereafter, without cease, the two air forces roared over Germany. During "Big Week," February 19–25, 1944, the RAF put 2,300 bombers over Germany at night, and the U.S. Air Force, 3,800 during daytime. Desperately seeking to fend off this particular series of assaults, the Luftwaffe lost 450 planes—a rate it could not long sustain. By the end of May, Göring's air fleet had been badly damaged and forced to withdraw to Germany for air defense. Thus the Allies had won control of the air over France, perhaps the single greatest contribution to the final victory made by the bombers. Eisenhower was able to reassure his D-Day troops in early June: "If you see fighting aircraft over you, they will be ours." During the fighting in France that followed D-Day, the saying in the German Army was, "If the plane is blue it is British, if it is silver it is American, and if it is invisible it is ours."

It was one of the ironies of the war that the big bombers, built for long-range strategic bombing in Germany, made a critical contribution through tactical bombing in France. Eisenhower wanted the bombers to go after the French railway system in order to isolate Normandy, so that the Germans could not use trains to supply and reinforce the troops fighting at the front. Harris and Spaatz protested; they wanted to continue the strategic campaign. Eisenhower's threat to resign his post unless he could implement the so-called Transportation Plan carried the day. For three months before D-Day, whenever the weather was suitable, the bombers went after French marshaling yards, railroad turntables and bridges, and rolling stock. The result was spectacular. Virtually every bridge over the Seine River and in Normandy was knocked down; rolling stock was badly shot up; repair facilities and turntables were destroyed. Eisenhower said that his insistence on the Transportation Plan was his great contribution to the D-Day victory.

German scientists sought to recapture the upper hand by ingenuity. They developed and produced impressive numbers of the Messerschmitt 262 jet, which could easily kill normal propeller-driven fighters, thanks to its astounding speed—540 miles an hour. But the severe fuel shortage was a

The Messerschmitt Me-262 was the world's first operational fighter jet. The Germans were well ahead of the Allies in jet propulsion, but Hitler wanted jet bombers, not Me-262s, so they never got the benefit of their innovations.

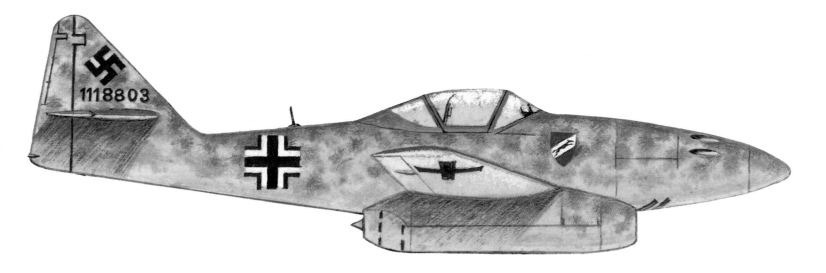

A V-1 pilotless aircraft, called a "buzz bomb," is about to fall into East London. The V-1 was a terror weapon, Hitler's answer to the bombing of German cities.

major problem; among other things, it meant fresh German pilots got almost no training time in the air.

Further, production was hampered by Hitler's insistence on giving priority to the manufacture of bombers and *Vergeltungswaffen,* or revenge weapons—the V-1 and V-2, with which he wanted above all to punish Britain's civilian population. The Führer became obsessed with this idea. When Luftwaffe generals and Göring explained the immense value of the Me-262 in staving off Allied attacks, Hitler became furious. "I want bombers, bombers, bombers," he shouted. "Your fighters are no damned good!" He wasn't interested in defending Germany; he wanted to bomb London. He refused for almost half a year even to look at a test flight; then he promptly commanded that the new jet be converted into a bomber, for which it had neither the range nor the load capacity. Thus the Me-262, which was ready for serial production in late 1942, was not produced until mid-1944. It could

have been the decisive weapon of the war, but thanks to Hitler it is not much more than an interesting footnote. Not until Korea in the 1950s did jet fighters rule the skies.

Hitler's view of the V-1 and V-2 was equally illogical. At first he remained convinced that the war could be won without bothering to give priority to experimental weapons. When the first doubts of victory finally began to bother him, he ordered sudden mass production of the V-2. Walter Dornberger, a scientist involved in the project, complained that he himself had not envisioned the rocket as an annihilation weapon. Hitler replied: "No, I realize that you didn't think of it! But I did."

Both V-1 and V-2 originated at the experimental center of Peenemünde, on the Baltic. The V-1, dubbed "buzz bomb" by the British, was a pilotless plane loaded with explosives, of which more than 8,000 were aimed at London in Hitler's frenzy for vengeance. However, many went astray (one even

Bystanders gaze curiously at a V-2 rocket in the streets of Rheims, France, 1944. The first ballistic missile, the V-2 was liquid-fueled, 46 feet long, and weighed 13 tons. It carried a one-ton warhead and could attain a height of 60 miles. The main targets were London (2,500 casualties) and, after the Canadians captured the port, Antwerp (30,000 casualties). At the end of the war, Hitler had a plan to tow containerized V-2s to the United States with U-boats and fire them at New York City and Washington.

hit Hitler's bunker) or were shot down, and only 2,420 reached their target. These did extensive but far from crippling damage.

The V-2 was more frightening. It carried a tank of liquid oxygen that allowed it to fly above the earth's atmosphere, and it was aimed from fixed positions, like long-range artillery. Fortunately Hitler, by according priority of materials and labor to conventional arms, deferred assembly-line production of this terrible instrument until it was too late for it to have a material effect on the war's outcome. By then, Allied reconnaissance and espionage had learned of the Peenemünde experiments and located many rocket sites under construction. As a result, bomber raids concentrated on these targets in 1943 and 1944, killing many leading scientists and reducing the power of the V-weapon's counteroffensive. Only about eleven hundred V-2s were successfully exploded in England. They destroyed hundreds of buildings, caused thousands of casualties, but did not alter the war's course.

Meanwhile the RAF and AAF bombers ranged over Germany, bringing death and destruction. The city that suffered most was Dresden. It was a medieval city, world famous for its beauty, a trading center rather than a manufacturing site. Refugees from other cities had come to Dresden believing that it would not be bombed. But it was, on February 13–14, 1945. First a British raid, then an American, then one more British attack—1,200 bombers in all—devastated Dresden. Some 100,000 civilians are estimated to have lost their lives. This was a larger death toll than Hiroshima. The Dresden bombing is frequently cited as the supreme example of aerial overkill.

Kurt Vonnegut was there; he later wrote *Slaughterhouse Five* about the experience. On the fiftieth anniversary of the event, he commented that "the bombing of Dresden did not shorten the war by one second. Only one person ever got any benefit from Dresden, and he is me."

Dresden was but a prelude to what happened to Japan.

Preparations for American involvement in the Asian air war were going on before the United States actually became a belligerent. A retired air corps officer named Claire L. Chennault had formed a flying foreign legion for Chiang Kai-shek in his struggle against Japan. This formation was soon destroyed, but with Washington's permission, Chennault recruited U.S. Army Air Corps pilots for an organization with the cover name of Central Aircraft Manufacturing Company (CAMCO). Washington loaned Chiang the money to buy one hundred Curtiss P-40 Tomahawks and to hire pilots. This force, called the American Volunteer Group (AVG), was shipped in small batches to Burma, under assumed identities, and began training in September 1941. The pilots had scarcely completed their course when Pearl Harbor happened, and they went into action as the Flying Tigers, so called for their winged tiger insignia devised by the Walt Disney Studios. These Flying Tigers became romantic heroes, and they were an important morale factor back home. It was somehow comforting to know in December 1941 that a group of American fliers were shooting down Japanese Zeros. The AVG subsequently became the U.S. Fourteenth Air Force. It was the first Pacific air formation to employ rockets, and it also introduced an internationally integrated unit, the Chinese-American Combat Wing.

Durable and easy to fly, the Curtiss P-40 (below) performed poorly at high altitude and thus was vulnerable to enemy fighters, but it was successful in bombing attacks and strafing runs. It was best known, with a shark's mouth painted under its nose, as the plane used by the Flying Tigers. The Mitsubishi Zero (bottom) was a low-wing fighter designed primarily for agility rather than protection or endurance. It was the standard Japanese fighter for ground or naval forces throughout the war. In the first year and a half, the Zero was a superior dogfighting plane to anything the Americans had, but by 1944 the situation was reversed.

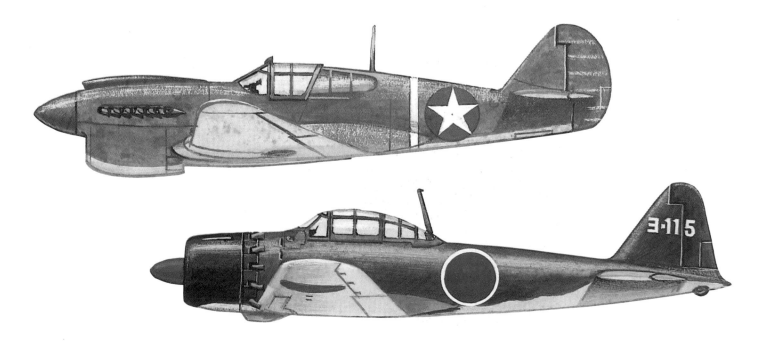

THE BOMBING OF DRESDEN

The most famous bombing raid of World War II, against Dresden on February 13–14, 1945, has been called the most barbaric, senseless act of the war. During the night, RAF Bomber Command carried out a raid with 873 bombers, dropping thousands of incendiaries and high-explosive bombs of up to four tons. This set the city on fire and started a firestorm as the rising column of intense heat sucked up oxygen and burned it, creating hurricane-like winds and temperatures up to a thousand degrees Fahrenheit or higher. At noon, 311 B-17s from the Eighth Air Force released 771 tons of bombs on the flaming city, with the aim of catching firemen and rescue workers when they were out on the streets. The following day 210 B-17s dropped another 461 tons. The fire-storm raged for four days and could be seen for 200 miles. People in air-raid shelters suffocated or were baked alive.

But although Dresden is generally considered to be the most destructive raid in the European war, it was not. Just before Dresden, the Allied bombers had hit Berlin (a 1,000-bomber raid) and Leipzig even harder. Those bombings were feebly protested, if at all. What made Dresden special was its apparent absence of military or industrial targets. People were outraged at the destruction of the heart of a relatively undamaged city known throughout the world for its beauty. Further, the death toll at Dresden was initially wildly inflated, to as high as 250,000. The Germans later revised the figure to 135,000. Recent disclosures have put the figure at 35,000. No one knows for certain, as Dresden had many refugees in the city.

The protest came first from Nazi propaganda, but as soon as the widespread damage in Dresden became known as fact there was an outcry in the Allied world. British critics of area bombing in general raised numerous questions about the necessity for the raid. Even Churchill, who had helped set the Dresden raid in motion by asking RAF Bomber Command to find more means of "harrying the German retreat," backed away. On March 28 he warned his chiefs of staff of the folly of any "bombing of German cities simply for the sake of increasing the terror" and as a result coming into possession "of an utterly ruined land."

Why would the Allies want to bomb a commercial city devoid of genuine targets? There are many answers. The one that makes the most sense is that the Allies had just plain run out of targets. The cities along the Rhine-Ruhr in western Germany had been demolished and/or occupied by mid-February. Berlin,

B-17s and B-24s drop hundreds of tons of incendiaries on their bombing run over Dresden, February 14, 1945.

Leipzig, and other central German cities were rubble. Dresden was one of the few relatively intact cities left (it is not true that Dresden attracted refugees because it had never been bombed; it had been, twice, although in much smaller raids). When questioned by Secretary of War Henry Stimson about the need for the raid, General Marshall indicated that the Soviets had asked the Allies to disrupt German communications (there was a significant railroad marshaling yard in Dresden), seeming to put the blame on them. But the Soviets said they had made no such request. By this time—mid-1945—the Soviets were already creating what would become Communist East Germany and thus had a political motivation to pretend that they were the great friends of the common German people, while the capitalists were destroying their homes and families.

The British, unjustifiably, got most of the blame. Dresden became something of a mark of shame to the British establishment, as it became the symbol of terror bombing. Their sense of disgrace was so great that General Arthur Harris, commander of RAF Bomber Command, was the sole major British wartime leader not honored with knighthood.

The Americans involved in the raid have justified it to this day. Lieutenant Dave Nagel said in an interview, "If you saw London, like I saw it, you wouldn't have any remorse. I don't know anyone who was nervous, uptight. . . . As time went on, for me a dead German was the best German. To this day, I won't buy German goods, if I can help it. I am prejudiced."

Lieutenant John Morris declared, "I'm hardly ashamed of having gone to Dresden that day. It was sound strategy to prevent the *Wehrmacht* from falling back to regroup and be lethal again. So we bombed the hell out of the railroad marshaling yards and road hubs along the *Wehrmacht*'s line of retreat, up and down Germany's eastern border. I don't rejoice at the 35,000 Germans killed there. I doubt there were many Jews in that number. The good burghers of Dresden had shipped them all off to Auschwitz." Morris went on to put the raid in perspective: "It is true that the RAF purposely started a firestorm, causing many of the casualties. It was a tactic they frequently tried. But they, and we, killed more people in other cities, on other days. So did the Russians. So did the Japanese. So did the Germans. Dresden was not unique."

The Eighth Air Force, which prided itself on its pinpoint bombing, all but denied its role in the Dresden bombing. But from a German point of view, in the last few months of the war one could hardly tell if those were British or American planes dropping bombs on their cities. Captain Dan Villani of the 398th Bomb Group was a B-17 pilot who was part of the massive raid on Berlin in mid-February. Decades later, he recalled that "most of the formation spread out to avoid the flak and in so doing ruined the accuracy of the drop. I'm sure many of the pilots didn't give a damn. They just wanted out of a target area as fast as possible. . . . The aiming point was the center of Berlin, and I don't think this was bombing a military target. But I personally felt no remorse. They brought Hitler to power and supported him and sealed their fate."

Dresden, known for its architectural beauty, was all but destroyed by the Allied raid on the city.

A Douglas A-20 twin-engine bomber goes down after being hit by Japanese anti-aircraft fire in New Guinea, 1943 (above). The most numerous model, the A-20G, of which 2,850 were built, was powered by two 1,600-horsepower engines, had a top speed of 339 miles per hour, and carried 2,600 pounds of bombs.

The air war in Asia was from the start a paramount factor both over sea and over land. Its importance can be summed up simply by two terminal events: Pearl Harbor and Hiroshima-Nagasaki. They signify the enormous change that occurred so rapidly in control of the skies.

When the Pacific conflict started in 1941, Japan held a perceptible lead in numbers of planes and crews who were veterans of the China campaign. The Japanese Army and Navy together had some three thousand operational aircraft and twice that number of pilots with at least five hundred hours flying experience. (These original pilots were far more skilled than the Americans had imagined; but the quality of their replacements declined.) Japan was already producing 425 planes and 225 pilots each month. The United States possessed fewer than nine hundred planes in the Pacific area. A heavy proportion of these were destroyed in Honolulu and the Philippines during Japan's initial surprise attacks. Furthermore, although the early U.S. fighters were sturdier and more heavily armored, none of them could rival the maneuverability of the famous Japanese Zero.

Nevertheless, as the immense United States production facilities began turning out ever greater numbers and ever better plane types, the balance began immutably to shift. Japanese aircraft strength attained an approximate top level of four thousand, but by the end of 1944, the United States had about ten thousand war planes plus eight thousand transports at its disposal in the Pacific. These included the fastest propeller fighter ever built, the Mustang, and, in the end, the B-29 Superfortress. From a steadily constricting circle of land bases on the Pacific islands, from China, from India, and eventually from Burma, the U.S. Army Air Corps moved in ever more menacingly, while Admiral Nimitz's immense carrier task forces sailed closer and closer to Tokyo itself.

The B-29 was the ultimate air weapon of World War II. It developed from General Arnold's insistence on a superbomber that could fly farther and with a bigger load than any other aircraft. It was blueprinted in 1940, before the United States was in the war. By the time it was in production, it had become a sixty-ton machine, capable of flying sixteen hours nonstop when loaded. The first of these monsters was sent to India in April 1944, and enormous airfields were built for them both in eastern India and in western China. The first actual Superfortress raid was on June 5, 1944, from India to the railroad marshaling yards of Bangkok. Ten days later, another raid took off from the Chinese base network against Yawata, the Japanese steel center on Kyushu Island. But it was only after Major General Curtis E. LeMay,

The B-29 (below) was the biggest plane of the war, with a wingspan of 141 feet, a length of 99 feet, and a weight of 100,000 pounds (including ten tons of bombs), and with ten .50-caliber machine guns in remote-controlled turrets and a 20-millimeter cannon in the tail. Its top speed was 365 miles per hour; it cruised at 220 and had an incredible range of 4,200 miles. It was truly a flying fortress: in the last year of the war the Japanese shot down 147 B-29s, while the B-29s shot down 1,128 enemy fighters.

B-29s fly past Mount Fuji in central Honshu, on their way to Tokyo, sixty miles distant. In all, B-29s flew 34,790 sorties and dropped 170,000 tons of bombs on Japanese cities. By the summer of 1945 there was little opposition; General Arnold planned to level every Japanese city, and he would have if the Japanese had not surrendered.

thirty-eight years old, took over the XX Bomber Command and began to use it for close-formation daylight raids, a tactic he had mastered while serving with the Eighth Air Force in England—that the B-29s began to do their most terrible and insistent damage.

The planes were shifted from the China-Burma-India theater to the XXI Bomber Command in Saipan, Tinian, and Guam as soon as aviation engineers, hard on the heels of the conquering marines and U.S. Army soldiers, had managed to carve sufficiently large airdromes out of the jungles and atolls of the Marianas. At last, by November 24, they began their final campaign in earnest with a raid on the aircraft plants outside Tokyo. From then on, relentlessly, they were employed with increasing force against the plane factories and harbors of Japan's home islands, hammering the main cities one by one. The objective, never directly stated, was to burn out the cities and to burn to death Japanese civilians.

In 1945, tons of explosives made of jellied gasoline and magnesium (napalm) began to whistle down on Tokyo, Kobe, Nagoya. On March 9, 334 B-29s took off from the Marianas, roared over Tokyo, and rained down napalm containers on the city. The devastation was appalling. A quarter of all buildings were consumed by fire, 84,000 people killed. On August 2, 855

Superfortresses wiped out six Japanese cities in a single day. LeMay and Arnold were prepared to level every city in Japan, and there was nothing the Japanese could do to stop them. In early August 1945 there were 6,000 B-29 sorties over Japan. Only 136 bombers were lost. It was thus entirely plain before the first nuclear bomb was dropped that the so-called conventional plane using the so-called conventional explosive was, all by itself, a weapon of staggering destructive capacity. The bomber, so long considered the ultimate in strategic might, had reached its moment of total and awful triumph.

A B-29 firebomb raid devastates Toyama, Japan, on August 1, 1945. Toyama was an aluminum production center; all but four tenths of a percent of the city was destroyed.

Hasten the Homecoming

BUY VICTORY BONDS

CHAPTER 15

THE HOME FRONTS

For millions of people, World War II was a catastrophe. Those who suffered most were the Jews, Soviets, Germans, Japanese, Poles, Yugoslavs, Filipinos, and Chinese. For other millions, World War II was a boon. Those who benefited most were the Americans.

For the United States, the cost of victory was relatively low, since fewer than 300,000 Americans were killed in combat out of an armed force of some 16 million. Compared with that of most other combatants, this death rate was extremely low. Although there was some destruction of U.S. property in Hawaii and a great deal in the Philippines, there was none in the forty-eight states. These two facts—a low casualty rate and almost no property damage—meant that the American experience of war was as different from that of the other combatants as it could have been.

Around the world, fear was the most common emotion in the period 1939 to 1945; hunger, the most common feeling. In the United States, fear and hunger were almost totally absent. During the six-year war, no elections were held in Europe, Asia, Africa, or the Middle East; even in Great Britain elections were suspended for the duration. But the United States during those six years saw two presidential, three congressional, and hundreds of state elections, all hotly contested.

So insulated were Americans from the direct effects of war that the biggest difference between America in the 1930s and the first half of the 1940s was that everyone had a job. Unemployment fell from 25 percent and higher to 1 percent, and that 1 percent consisted of people moving from one job to another. Many good things flowed from this employment boom. Between 1939 and 1945 per capita income doubled, rising from $1,231 to $2,390. Thanks to effective wage and price controls, inflation was moderate,

Norman Rockwell's 1945 painting (opposite), originally a *Saturday Evening Post* cover, depicts what America was working hard for—a homecoming. The government flooded the country with patriotic buttons (above), which presumably helped morale.

Students in New York collect tinfoil from chewing gum and cigarette packages for the defense effort (right). There were similar programs for collecting tin cans, grease, milkweed (for life jackets)—and even altering clothes to save material (below). These government-run programs were designed to give everyone a sense of being part of the war effort, and to some measure they succeeded.

USE IT UP – WEAR IT OUT –
MAKE IT DO!

OUR LABOR AND OUR GOODS ARE FIGHTING

so that most of the increase was real gain. Since there were no new cars, new homes, washing machines, or other durable consumer goods for sale, most of the income went into savings, which went up from personal savings of $2.6 billion in 1939 to $29.6 billion five years later, a tenfold increase.

A steady job and money in the bank meant financial security, something most Americans under thirty-five years of age had never before experienced. Another new experience was travel. Most Americans in 1940 had never been out of their home state, many of them never out of their home county. Only a tiny percentage had ever been overseas. But between 1941 and 1945, some 12 million young Americans went overseas into a different culture and part of the world. Within the United States, more than 15 million civilians moved during the war, over half of them to new states. With 17 percent of the population on the move within a four-year period, this was a mass migration that dwarfed the westward movement of the nineteenth century.

Nearly all those who left home were in their late teens, twenties, or thirties, which meant that nearly everyone in those age groups moved at least once. This had an enlightening effect on U.S. politics and culture. The internal migration helped break down regional prejudices and provincialism. Yankees and Westerners who moved south, where most of the army bases were located, or southerners who moved west or north, where most of the war industries were located, learned to tolerate or understand, if not actually to like, the different mores they encountered.

Today, we remember the America of the war years with a certain nostalgia. City dwellers went to shop "downtown" in solid masonry buildings of two or three stories. There were no shopping centers, no malls, few drive-ins or suburbs, almost no air-conditioning. Americans had more cars in 1940 than anyone else in the world, but the rule was the same for bathrooms: one to a family. There were almost no four-lane roads. Nearly everyone had a radio—again, one to a family (in 1945 there were 34 million households, of which 33 million had a radio, more than had indoor plumbing).

Store shelves went empty, as goods ranging from facial tissues and hairpins to cameras and alarm clocks disappeared. Cigarettes were scarce, and many people learned to roll their own. The ration stamp was a necessity of life, for among the items on the rationed list were meats, butter, sugar, coffee, almost all canned and frozen foods, gasoline, and shoes. Men's trousers went cuffless to save cloth, and an old toothpaste tube had to be turned in when buying a new one. There were tin can collections, wastepaper collections, and aluminum drives; housewives even salvaged grease from cooking. Manufacturers with nothing to sell advertised their contributions to the war effort: automakers boasted of their tanks, a typewriter manufacturer bragged about its armor-piercing shells.

Broadway at Times Square suddenly empties out in a before-and-after look at the famous New York City intersection during an air-raid drill, December 15, 1941. Although there was not the slightest possibility of New York being bombed, at this time or later, Americans everywhere were seized by fear and by a desire to do something—anything—to get prepared for the war that had already started.

For entertainment other than the radio, people went to the movies. In 1945 some 85 million people went to the movies each week. Almost everyone saw the popular movies, such as *Casablanca, Thirty Seconds Over Tokyo, Bambi,* or *Guadalcanal Diary*. Patriotism was profitable for Hollywood, and the movie industry cashed in on the war in its typical shameless fashion. Some good war movies were made and one or two classics, along with hundreds of clunkers.

Wartime movies ranged from the sentimental to the silly to the truly wonderful. Clockwise from top left: Tyrone Power and Betty Grable find each other in *A Yank in the R.A.F.* (1941); Bob Hope enjoys harem life in *Road to Morocco* (1942); British commandos attack Nazis in Norway in *The Commandoes Strike at Dawn* (1942); Arthur Kennedy, Ronald Reagan, and Errol Flynn play three American pilots downed over Germany in *Desperate Journey* (1942); Monty Woolley goes against Otto Preminger as Woolley helps a group of children escape from the Nazis in *The Pied Piper* (1942); Judy Garland stars in a musical about one family's experiences in 1903 in *Meet Me in St. Louis* (1944); Humphrey Bogart and Ingrid Bergman play old flames in the classic *Casablanca* (1942).

For young women, the war brought great change. For one thing, unless they lived near an army or navy base, there were few to no young men around. This circumstance had many repercussions, the first of which was that the young women spent much more time with each other—providing support, entertainment, working together—than their mothers had or their daughters would. The housing shortage, especially around the bases or the industrial plants, forced the young women to share living space, not infrequently five or more to one home, with one bathroom and one kitchen. Gasoline was rationed—three gallons per week—not to save gas, which was abundant, but to save rubber, which was impossible to get after the Japanese overran Southeast Asia. With a national speed limit of thirty-five miles per hour (also to save rubber tires), a limited gas supply hardly mattered, as

"THE GIRL HE LEFT BEHIND"
IS STILL BEHIND HIM
She's a WOW
WOMAN ORDNANCE WORKER

In a photograph (opposite) as in a poster (left), Rosie the Riveter is hard at work. If the poster by Adolph Treidler is an idealization, the photograph shows the truth: women worked in factories in record numbers, taking over highly skilled jobs. The utilization of the full potential of the female labor force was far superior in the democracies and the Soviet Union; in the Axis states, women were supposed to spend the war years producing baby boys.

it took too long to get from one place to another. The women learned to carpool.

Women entered the workforce in record numbers, a fact so well known that one only need say the words "Rosie the Riveter" to make the point. In hundreds of thousands of cases, young mothers managed to balance night shifts with child care. They were helped by the women's magazines, which were full of exhortations. "Now is the time to prove to your husband and to yourself that you have the stuff in you that our pioneer ancestors had," one writer remarked. "You'll be on your mettle to prove that you are every bit as good a manager as you are a sweetheart."

Many of these young wives and mothers were teenagers. Quickie marriages were the norm; there were a million more marriages during the war than would have been expected at prewar rates. Teenagers got married because the boy was going off to war and in the moral atmosphere of the day,

While the United States excelled in including women in the war effort, it allowed racism to prevail over the needs of war. Black Americans remained segregated and seldom had any opportunity to excel or make their full contribution. Above, Private Sarah Parker of the Women's Army Corps does semiskilled work in a machine shop; right, Jim Crow prevails in Lumberton, North Carolina. Opposite, Second Lieutenant Edward Robinson is commissioned as a U.S. Army officer at Fort Benning. Even officers like Robinson remained in support positions for most of the war.

if the couple wanted to have a sexual experience before he left, they had to stand in front of a preacher first. Scholars worried that hasty marriages followed by long separations would never work; although 1946 was the peak year for divorces, many marriages did work. The girls became women. They traveled alone, or with their infants, to distant places on hot and stuffy or cold and overcrowded trains, became proficient cooks and housekeepers, managed the finances, learned to fix the car, and wrote consistently upbeat letters to their soldier husbands. "I write his dad everything our baby does," one young mother explained, "only in the letters I make it sound cute."

It is one of the ironies of U.S. history that while the nation fought its greatest war against the world's worst racist, it maintained a segregated army abroad and a total system of discrimination at home. In the capital of the nation leading the worldwide struggle for democracy and freedom, African-Americans got their water from separate drinking fountains, used segregated toilet facilities, could not eat in "white" restaurants, sat in the balcony in their own section in movie theaters, sat in the back of the bus, and otherwise were degraded in public in every way possible. The extent of the racism that prevailed in wartime America cannot be exaggerated or excused, but only marveled at. As the propaganda extolling democracy swelled, the subjugation of blacks increased. Throughout the South, and in much of the North, blacks could not vote. They were drafted, they fought, they died, they paid taxes, they provided essential labor, but they could not vote.

Despite everything, however, many African-Americans did improve their financial situation, most of them by moving out of the rural South to the urban North and West and taking jobs in war industries. It was the beginning of a mass migration that would sweep the nation in the decades after the war. And in the army, senior officers concluded that maintaining segregated units was inefficient, so the process of integration of the armed services got its first halting start during the war.

For Japanese-Americans, the war had no redeeming features. There were 127,000 people of Japanese ancestry in the United States in 1941, some 80,000 of them native-born American citizens, or Nisei. Most of the Nisei were simple truck farmers in California. This tiny group caused the greatest panic. They were suspected of sabotage, of sending signals by bonfires or automobile headlights to Japanese submarines, and of espionage. A demand arose, fed by the politicians, including California Governor Earl Warren, to evacuate them to camps in the interior. That most of them were American citizens was irrelevant; as one official put it, "A Jap is a Jap"; that not one single act of sabotage had been charged also made no difference.

In February 1942, President Roosevelt ordered the War Department to move the Nisei out of California. General John DeWitt, who oversaw the evacuation, defended the policy with a curious logic: "The very fact that no sabotage has taken place to date is a disturbing and confirming indication that such action will be taken." The Japanese-Americans were rounded up, forced to sell their property at outrageously low prices, and shipped off to camps in the Western desert, where they were put to work harvesting crops by day, living in camps surrounded by barbed wire at night. Two years later the Supreme Court ruled the evacuation constitutional. Forty years later

JIM CROW

Throughout the States, especially in the South, Jim Crow was there during the war years. "Colored Only" and "White Only" signs were on public accommodations of every kind, from drinking fountains to bus and train depot waiting rooms to the seats on the bus (the back for the blacks) to movie theaters (blacks in the balcony) to city parks and swimming pools to schools, and more. *Plessy* v. *Ferguson*, separate but equal, was the law of the land, and wherever there were African-Americans (which was mainly in the South) the first part was rigidly enforced, while the second part—equal accommodations—was never enforced. Blacks could be drafted, but overwhelmingly they could not vote. Along with the treatment of Japanese-Americans, Jim Crow is a permanent stain on the American record in World War II, and on a far greater scale.

The war brought great changes because of its demands, not because of the will of the American people. With labor scarce and high wages available in the factories, Southern blacks began the greatest mass migration in U.S. history, moving from Mississippi to Chicago or Georgia to New York. Even with jobs available, blacks were the last hired and first fired and, along with women, received lower pay than white men.

In the U.S. Army, they got equal pay but nothing else. The great majority of African-American soldiers were put in Services of Supply, where they drove trucks or unloaded things. The official attitude was that blacks could not fight. It was almost impossible for a black soldier to get a commission, and white officers commanded the black troops. For blacks, there was no reward for doing well, yet ample punishment for doing poorly.

In April 1944, Corporal Rapiered Trimmingham wrote to *Yank* magazine and recounted an experience he had while traveling through the South from one post to another. He and the other five black soldiers with him could not get a cup of coffee. Finally a lunchroom manager at a Texas railroad depot said they could go around back for a sandwich and coffee. As they did, "about two dozen German prisoners of war, with two American guards, came to the station. They entered the lunchroom, sat at the tables, had their meals served, talked and smoked, in fact had quite a swell time. I stood on the outside looking on, and I could not help but ask myself why they are treated better than we are?"

On the battlefield, as in the factory, the demands of the war got Jim Crow on the run. During the Battle of the Bulge, Eisenhower was forced to give

Despite the blatant racism of the day, African-Americans wanted to fight. At Mitchell Field, Long Island, on March 24, 1941, the Army Air Corps opened enlistments for black Americans (above). The first all-black division to be formed was the Ninety-third Infantry Division, shown on an exercise (opposite top). Its officers were overwhelmingly white. The requirements of war did demand some integration. In the mess hall at the Naval Operating Base on Adak in the Aleutian Islands (opposite bottom), everyone dressed up and ate together because President Roosevelt was present on an inspection tour.

African-American troops an opportunity to serve in the frontline units on a non-segregated basis. Thousands volunteered, including sergeants who had to give up their stripes for the privilege of fighting for their country. Overall they did remarkably well and thus started the U.S. Army on the task of re-evaluating its use of black soldiers.

There were other hopeful signs of progress. When *Yank* printed Trimmingham's letter, it got thousands of letters from GIs, "almost all of whom were outraged by the treatment given the corporal." Trimmingham reported that he had received 287 letters, 183 from white men in the armed service, most of them from the Deep South. "They are all proud that they are from the South but ashamed to learn that there are so many of their own people who are playing Hitler's game."

Based on the experience of World War II, by the end of 1945 the ground had been prepared for Jim Crow's grave. Chief Historian Walter Wright of the U.S. Army concluded his wartime report on the employment of black troops with these words: "My ultimate hope is that in the long run it will be possible to assign individual Negro soldiers and officers to any unit in the Army where they are qualified as individuals to serve efficiently." That was done, under the command and leadership of the colonels, majors, captains, and lieutenants of the Battle of the Bulge, who had seen with their own eyes what excellent soldiers black men could be when given the opportunity. Within a decade, the military had changed from being one of the most tightly segregated organizations in the country to being the most successfully integrated.

Fifty years after the war ended, African-American soldiers finally received long overdue recognition for their service in World War II. On January 13, 1997, seven veterans were awarded the Medal of Honor that was originally denied them because they were black.

Elderly Nisei are shown being "evacuated" to Santa Anita. Then it was off to "relocation" camps in the desert. In its treatment of the Nisei, the United States came closest to becoming like its enemies. The government, simultaneously leading and bowing to public hysteria, labeled these American citizens "enemies of the state" and had them deported to places that were not death factories—the Nisei were adequately fed and provided with shelter, reasonable work hours, and opportunity for education and leisure activities—but they were still internment camps.

Congress condemned the relocation policy as a product of "war hysteria, racial prejudice, and failure of political leadership," and compensated internees with a payment of $20,000 each. It was too little, too late.

But if the United States made many mistakes during the war, it did even more things right. And what it did best was to take other people's ideas and research and improve the designs, then develop techniques for mass production. The atomic bomb is but one example. The key to America's success was engineering skill plus mass production. A nation that had been stuck in the doldrums of the Great Depression for ten years, unable to figure out how to put people to work or to utilize its industrial plant at even half capacity, responded to the stimulus of the war with an industrial mobilization that was staggering in scope and stunningly successful.

President Roosevelt set the priorities and established the goals in his famous January 1942 address to Congress. He promised that by 1943 the United States would produce an annual 125,000 airplanes, 75,000 tanks, and 8,000,000 deadweight tons of shipping. People thought he was crazy. But soon locomotives, planes, trucks, steel landing mats, telephones, aluminum sheets, radar, and above all guns and ammunition poured out in previously unimaginable quantities. In 1944, U.S. factories produced 96,318 aircraft; the total number of planes produced in the war was over 250,000. There were roughly similar figures in trucks, jeeps, and tanks, all of which came off the assembly lines in a never-ending stream. Shipyards built aircraft carriers faster than the Japanese or Germans could build patrol boats, even as the shipyards simultaneously turned out thousands of landing craft and Liberty Ships. In 1945, half of all the ships afloat in the world had been built in the United States.

The U.S. Army, at 175,000 men, hardly existed in 1939. It was virtually without equipment. Five years later, at more than 8 million strong, it was far

An officer inspects luggage at the Santa Anita reception center, spring 1942. In Hawaii, where Japanese-Americans made up a quarter of the population, and where at least a few had engaged in espionage, there was no demand to remove them, because to have done so would have disrupted the economy and thus the war effort. But in California fear ran very high.

Aircraft production in the United States increased tenfold during the war. On June 6, 1944, D-Day in Normandy, workers at factories around the United States paused when the news came over the loud-speaker and prayed that they had done the job right. The Germans used slave labor in their factories. In three decades of interviewing veterans on both sides of the war, Stephen Ambrose has heard dozens of stories from GIs about duds landing beside them. He has never heard such a story from a German veteran. Clearly, the slave laborers sometimes found ways to make a shell inoperative but still pass inspection.

and away the best-equipped army in the world, especially in tanks, artillery, and other heavy weapons, as well as trucks and jeeps. In 1945, U.S. industry built half of all the weapons produced in the world in that year.

On October 27, 1944, Roosevelt proudly told his fellow citizens: "The production which has flowed from this country to all the battlefronts of the world has been due to the efforts of American business, American labor, and American farmers, working together as a patriotic team." It was a fine statement, even if not entirely accurate, as, inevitably, there had been friction along the way among labor and management and government. (At the start of the war, the AFL and the CIO had agreed to a no-strike pledge, and union officials, if not all unions, lived up to it. One exception was John L. Lewis, who took his coal miners out on strike four times during the course of the war.)

For the majority of Americans, the theme of the war was teamwork. "We are all in this together" was a phrase heard daily. During the Depression, people had felt isolated, alone, fearful. During the war, people felt a sense of belonging. Obviously in the armed services, but also on the home front, there was a commitment to the notion that society's needs came before individual desires. The war created a "we" generation, as opposed to later "me" generations.

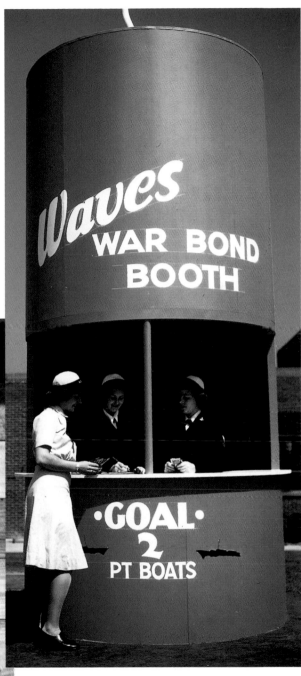

Government propaganda was everywhere, such as on a poster promoting the air force, above left. People responded with their own exhortations: WAVES (Women Accepted for Volunteer Emergency Service) sell war bonds at a booth shaped like a firecracker (above); a man waters a "Victory Garden" window box in Roosevelt Field, New York, 1943 (left).

Another feature of the war experience was deferred gratification. The theme of almost all advertising and much government propaganda was the rewards that were coming after victory was attained. The message to those sharing a kitchen and bathroom with three other families, to mothers and children living in a single room, to soldiers shivering in a foxhole outside Bastogne was that all the hardships of today would disappear once the job was done. Tomorrow was worth saving for and delicious to dream about.

All over the world, people dreamed of tomorrow, of that day when the war would end. Nowhere did it come soon enough. Everywhere outside the United States, the people of the home front suffered, some right from the beginning, some only toward the end. For Germany, the first years were good ones. Adolf Hitler's early successes on the battlefields of Europe and the Soviet Union made most Germans, even many opponents of the regime, proud. As Hitler set about remaking Europe for Germany's benefit, life on the German home front improved. With the help of loot from conquered areas, redirected Continental factory and farm output, the planning of an efficient and highly centralized Berlin government, and the use of enslaved laborers from subject territories, the Führer's Third Reich flourished. The Gestapo brooked no opposition to the regime or whatever it was up to, including its most heinous offenses against human decency: extirpation of Jews, enserfment of foreign civilians, mockery of a free press, and a growing intolerance of religion. Although a small German underground existed inside the Reich and was in touch with such distinguished émigrés as Ernst Reuter, future mayor of West Berlin, and although this underground included certain brave and renowned individuals, such as Carl Goerdeler, ex-mayor of Leipzig, and Pastor Dietrich Bonhoeffer, it was ineffectual. The terror mounted. Indeed, in 1944, one out of every twelve hundred German adults was arrested for political or religious "offenses"—the latter being equivalent to the former.

The morale of the Germans withstood the ardors of Allied air raids, although by the time Berlin was becoming a shambles, its citizens were caustically reminding each other of the Führer's architectural forecast: "Give me ten years and you will not recognize Germany."

In his desperate effort to regain the initiative after the tide began to turn, Hitler filled Germany with forced labor to replace drafted workers. By early autumn 1944, some 7.5 million foreigners had been rounded up in occupied Europe and shipped to the Reich in boxcars, to a brutal existence of endless toil, semistarvation, illness, and, in the end, often death. To these were added about 2 million prisoners of war, many of whom, in violation of the Hague and Geneva conventions, were made to work in ordnance plants.

And so the Reich's formidable war machine rolled on. During the first four years of war, ammunition production multiplied 2.6 times, artillery 4.8 times, armor 8.7 times, and aircraft 2.7 times. Albert Speer, youthful Reichminister of Armaments and Production, saw to it that whatever happened in the totalitarian state, ordnance production increased. The postwar U.S. Strategic Bombing Survey found that despite intensification of Allied bombing and huge *Wehrmacht* losses, "the German Army [as distinct from the Luftwaffe] was better equipped with weapons at the beginning of 1944 than at the start of the Russian War." The only serious shortages were in steel, oil, and certain metals.

While Germany's cities lay in ruins, the countryside was untouched until April 1945, when enemy armies closed in on the Elbe River. In the east, the Red Army raped, pillaged, burned, and otherwise got revenge for what the German Army had done to their villages and women. In the west, the American GIs were astonished at how well the Germans outside the cities were living in the last month of a six-year total war—much, much better than the Belgians or the French or the Italians. They had ample food stocks, telephones, electricity, plumbing (including soft white toilet paper), and intact buildings. The British and American troops acted correctly, for the most part. Many American soldiers found they got on better with the Germans than with the French. Here was laid the foundation for the NATO alliance.

Like Germany, Japan prospered at first. When Japan entered the war, its masses, reared in a heritage that emphasized their superior qualities, were easily subject to propaganda. After their initial startling successes, there seemed to be little anxiety about the nation's future. The first shocking awareness of potential trouble came on April 18, 1942, when Doolittle's bombers suddenly pecked at Tokyo. One capital resident later said: "We finally began to realize that all we were told was not true—that the Government had lied when it said we were invulnerable. We then started to doubt that we were also invincible."

After Midway, after Guadalcanal, after successive German setbacks in the West, these doubts grew, but it was only on June 15, 1944, when sixty-eight Superfortresses struck Kyushu, that the Japanese people saw what lay in store. Tokyo was forced to tell them that "since the outbreak of the East Asian War everyone has recognized the difficulty of avoiding air attacks." The press began to talk of "a front behind the lines" and to exhort each civilian to remember he was "a warrior defending his country." Air-raid drills were frequent, even at night. Women were made to practice running uphill, bearing buckets of water; sandbags and pails were placed outside homes; enormous instruments resembling fly swatters were distributed to beat out flames.

Life was more austere by 1943. The rice reserve disappeared. Food became perilously scarce; the hungry were everywhere. Rations of electricity and gas became more strict. Women were asked to do without their colorful kimonos, and civilian consumption of cloth fell 95 percent. Black market profiteering spread.

Until 1944, Tojo's officer-dominated dictatorship remained politically secure. Backed by the powerful Imperial Rule Assistance Association, it had gained 80 percent of the seats in the Diet early in the war and later had persuaded Japan's skeptical industrial barons, the zaibatsu, that the economic program for subduing East Asia was bound to succeed. The Japanese stock market continued to boom. By 1944, when Japanese industry had achieved maximum efficiency, Allied successes were amputating Japan's access to raw materials. The air offensive against the home islands had cut output by 60 percent before the war ended.

In 1945, life on the Japanese home front was an unmitigated hell: food shortages, no electricity, and no heat. People gathering pine cones from which an oil could be extracted to power an internal combustion engine. Women and children being trained with bamboo stakes to oppose the U.S.

The price of war was felt throughout Japan and its occupied territories: Right, a U.S. Marine on patrol in Saipan finds a Japanese family hiding in a hillside cave, June 21, 1944. The mother, her four children, and their dog sought shelter from the fierce fighting in the area. Below, citizens of Okinawa await their fate after the Japanese surrender.

Women dig an antitank ditch in the Donbars region of the Soviet Union, 1941. There are no whips, no guards, not even a foreman to be seen. The Soviets were united and threw themselves into the war effort without hesitation or question. Everyone was underfed and overworked, and very few thought about Communism. The people were united in the defense of Mother Russia.

Marines when they landed. Half the buildings in Tokyo and every other major city, gone. A military dictatorship that remained determined to never surrender, no matter how severe the suffering of the people.

On the Allied side, morale in the Soviet Union was at first severely shaken during the war's early months, although it remained constantly high in Britain and never faltered in the United States. The war in the Soviet Union came after Stalin had spent seven years repressing his subjects, murdering millions, sending millions to prison camps, and spreading fear through a muted nation.

However, any initial hopes there may have been for a better life under the Nazis were short-lived, and Stalin focused his propaganda on national rather than ideological themes. The monolithic Soviet state harnessed everyone to the war effort. Women were mobilized to run tractors on collective farms. Those not fit for military service, the wounded, and the very old were conscripted into the labor force and were called upon to fight in emergencies like the battles for Leningrad and Moscow. Most Soviet citizens, even those who bitterly resented Stalin, dug in with grim determination, living on the edge of starvation, often cut off from news of soldier relatives.

The Soviet home front was resolute, bitter, and marked by a wild hatred of the Germans that exceeded anything in Britain or in the United States. And as the Red Army regathered and surged forward on the attack, a new aura of confidence started to spread through the ravaged, suffering nation. At night, batteries around the Kremlin began to boom salutes to victories, and the country's war songs assumed a note of savage joy.

The Soviet people suffered, survived, triumphed. Their diet was inadequate, as was their clothing and shelter. But they worked, on their farms, digging antitank ditches, at the factories, everywhere for ten to twelve hours a day, usually seven days a week.

The British worked long hours, too, though not so long as the Soviets. The British likewise suffered from bombing and from shortages. They adopted a system of tightly rationing food, shoes, and household goods. Gasoline and textiles were rigidly restricted; newspapers and magazines, thin. The BBC assumed an immense new importance as the essential organ for both informing and entertaining the English people and their restless allies in occupied Europe.

The British survived two aerial ordeals—the Blitz and the V-1, V-2 terror—with courage and endurance. Good-naturedly they went into shelters or helped local police forces as air-raid wardens and fire-fighting patrols. Somehow they managed to get to work despite scrambled transportation systems. Beside the ruins of their dwellings, they cheered Churchill as he visited his home front, cigar between clenched teeth, giving his victory signal.

These boys and girls, who lived on a collective farm in Belorussia, had been slave laborers for the German occupiers a year earlier. Their growth had been stunted by their living conditions. One of them told the photographer he was fifteen years old; he looked to be nine or ten.

As early as 1940, life had become appallingly thin and threadbare, and it was to remain so until long after the war ended. Shipping on which the island depended was almost wholly devoted to essential cargoes, and the treasury was bare. Housing was strained as buildings in cities were destroyed by bombing, families were evacuated to the country to be billeted with others, and the United Kingdom filled with troops mustered by the Americans, Canadians, Poles, and Free French for the final invasion.

Women played a far greater role than ever before, taking jobs as chauffeurs, laborers, ferry pilots, wardens, and farmers, and asserted a new, energetic independence of their own. Most important, the old social structures and traditions of personal diffidence were broken down as rich and poor rubbed shoulders in air-raid shelters. The atmosphere of the English pub, with all its cozy intimacy, managed somehow to grip the nation in its time of most arduous difficulty. "Roll Out the Barrel" and "Kiss Me Goodnight,

Bombed-out Londoners arrange for emergency food and new ration books in a converted music hall in Grace Golden's *The Emergency Food Office.* **Long lines and waiting were an integral part of the experience of war for the British.**

A Londoner buys bread at the height of the Blitz, September 1940. In Britain, weekly rations were stretched with unlimited bread, cereal, potatoes, and whatever vegetables—usually brussels sprouts—were available. The food was bland, dull, and unvarying, but the diet was balanced, and overall the British ate better during the war than they had during the Depression.

Sergeant Major" were sung in dire moments with as much fervor as "God Save the King" when theater curtains rolled down early to allow the audience time to get home before the Luftwaffe arrived.

The spirit of England in the spring of 1944, as the Allied invasion force built, was soaring. "London to me was a magic carpet," Private Gordon Carson of the U.S. Airborne wrote. "Walk down any of its streets and every uniform of the Free World was to be seen. Their youth and vigor vibrated in every park and pub. The uniforms of the Canadians, South Africans, Australians, New Zealanders, Free French, Polish, Belgium, Holland, and of course the English and Americans were everywhere. Those days were not lost on me because even at twenty years of age, I knew I was seeing and being a part of something that was never to be again. Wartime London was its own world."

In 1944, of all the great cities of Europe and Asia, only London was full of life, hope, anticipation, good spirits. Everywhere else, except the United States, life on the home fronts during World War II went from bad to worse to worst.

CHAPTER 16

THE HOLOCAUST AND OTHER ATROCITIES

B etween 1939 and 1945, uncountable millions of wholly innocent civilians who posed no threat to anyone were killed in the most bestial manner imaginable. No description of the horrors can approach the reality of what was done by some human beings to other human beings. From the shooting of individual POWs to the mass executions of prisoners to the systematic slaughter of villages and climaxing with factories of death for an entire race, the scope and scale of savagery in World War II are unsurpassed.

Atrocities came in every form, beginning with casual violence, such as the killing of an unarmed soldier holding his hands high above his head, or the rape or shooting of civilians, something done on every front by every army. Atrocities are an inevitable part of war. When nations send their young men to foreign places, far from church or parental influence, arm them with automatic weapons, teach them to kill, and urge them to hate, many bad things are sure to happen.

Killing in the heat of combat or immediately after is one thing; the execution of groups of unarmed prisoners under guard is another. This last was done regularly, by the Japanese Army, the Red Army, the German army, by the Croats and Serbs fighting each other in Yugoslavia, by the Nationalist Chinese and the Communist Chinese, and by others. Even by the U.S. and British armies, it happened—not often, but it happened.

Lieutenant Paul Fussell was a platoon leader in a rifle company in the U.S. Army in Europe. In his memoir of the war, he recalled that in the November 1944 fighting, his platoon came on a deep crater in a forest where a squad or two of German soldiers, some fifteen to twenty men, were gathered. "Their visible wish to surrender—most were in tears of terror and

A detail of Leslie Cole's painting *Who Are These Soldiers?* (opposite) catches the moment of liberation of the women's compound at Bergen-Belsen. British troops have just entered. The inmates have come out of their barracks to see strangely uniformed soldiers. Did it mean that others had come to torment them? The full horror of the concentration camps is captured better here than in photographs.

The identity card of Cyrla Rosenzweig (above) was issued in Kraków, May 5, 1941. She survived, one of the *Schindlerjuden*, or Schindler Jews, made famous by the movie *Schindler's List*.

despair—was ignored by our men lining the rim," Fussell wrote. As the Germans held their hands high, Fussell's men, "laughing and howling, hoo-ha-ing and cowboy and good-old-boy yelling, exultantly shot into the crater until every single man down there was dead. If a body twitched or moved at all, it was shot again. The result was deep satisfaction, and the event was transformed into amusing narrative, told and retold over campfires all that winter."

Murder for political or ideological reasons was common. The Japanese did it to the Filipinos and Chinese; the Communists and Nationalists in China did it to each other and to the Japanese; the Germans did it to the Soviets and the Soviets did it to the Germans. In December 1937, the Japanese captured Nanking, on the Yangtze River, capital of Nationalist China. The atrocities Japanese troops committed are called "the rape of Nanking." Almost 200,000 civilians were massacred. In the spring of 1940, Stalin, who wanted to destroy Polish nationalism, ordered the execution of some 15,000 Polish officers who were POWs in the custody of the Red Army. The young

Some of the mass graves of the 15,000 Polish officers slaughtered by the Soviet NKVD in the spring of 1940, on Stalin's direct orders, are discovered in Katyn Forest, Poland, February 8, 1952. Stalin wanted to wipe out the Polish intelligentsia. When the Germans discovered one of the graves in April 1943, and broadcast the news to the world, the Soviets denied everything. Not until 1989 did former Soviet officials admit the truth.

officers, the cream of Polish nationhood, had their hands tied behind their backs and were then shot in the head. The shootings took place in Katyn Forest, near Smolensk.

Hypocrisy, like atrocity, goes hand in hand with war: in this case, the British and U.S. governments joined Stalin in the cover-up, as they felt that the need to maintain the alliance with the Soviet Union was greater than the need for truth. Thus they chose not to challenge Stalin when he asserted that Hitler had been responsible for Katyn, even though they knew better.

Many POWs who were not shot almost came to wish they had been. Throughout history, POWs have fared badly, but in World War II the mistreatment of prisoners reached unprecedented heights. To be a German soldier in Soviet hands, or a Red Army soldier in German hands, was in most cases the equivalent of a death sentence. Both sides worked their prisoners hard, fed them inadequately or worse, provided insufficient shelter, and watched as they died—by the millions. Americans and British in Japanese hands fared little better. For comparison's sake, between 34 and 38 percent of Americans held as prisoners by the Japanese died. Some 69 percent of Soviet prisoners held in Germany died. The proportion of Germans captured on the eastern front who died in Soviet captivity has been estimated as high as 80 percent. By contrast, in their treatment of French, British, and American prisoners, the Germans made an attempt to live by the rules of the Geneva Convention regarding prisoners of war. As a result, only .7 percent of the Americans held as POWs by the Germans died.

Standish Backus's *Recent Guests of Japan* expresses the near-hopeless condition of American POWs held by the Japanese. Men like these, subjected to brutality on an unprecedented scale, were overworked and so inadequately fed that they were on the verge of death by starvation. Only liberation could save them.

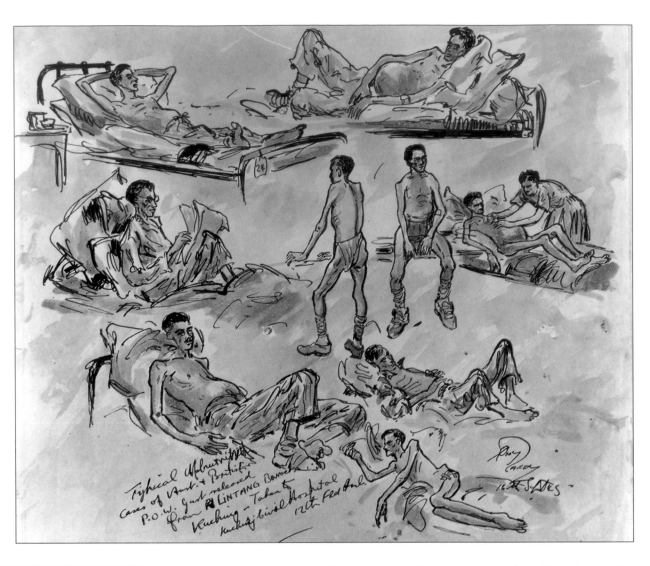

Typical Malnutrition
Cases of Aust. + British
P.O.W. just released
from LINTANG Barrack
Kuching – Taken to
Kuching Civil Hospital
+ 12th Fld. Amb.

Tony Rafty's sketches depict liberated British and Australian prisoners in Borneo. Captured early in the war, not liberated until the very end, they endured years of boredom, brutality, ill health, backbreaking labor, and starvation rations.

The Americans brought German prisoners captured in Tunisia in May 1943 to the United States, where they were put to work as migrant agriculture labor. That was the best place of all to be in the winter of 1944–45 for a German male born between 1910 and 1927. There the German soldiers had security, shelter, and ample sustenance, along with humane guards and a decent camp administration.

A terrible place for anyone to be during the war was in a Soviet, Japanese, or German concentration camp. These were places worse than hell. They contained political prisoners, religious prisoners, common criminals, and certain classes of people such as Gypsy bands and physically handicapped or developmentally retarded people. In these camps, no inmate had any right whatsoever. The power of the commander and his guards was absolute, and the guards, brutal to begin with, were encouraged to beat, rape, torture, and degrade the prisoners. These generalizations are true of Stalin's gulag in Siberia, where hundreds of thousands of Soviet citizens suffered and died; of the Japanese camps holding Filipinos, Chinese, American, British, and Dutch civilians; and of the Nazi camps. Comparisons are odious, especially when one is comparing the odious, but it would be difficult to say of Stalin, Hitler, and the Japanese warlords which one brought more misery and suffering and death to the largest number of people.

But for sheer bestiality, the Nazis stand out. The Holocaust is exactly what Churchill called it: "the greatest and most horrible crime ever committed in the whole history of the world." Its aim was to make Germany, Europe, the world *Judenfrie* (free of Jews). An ancient race of people was to be exterminated. The world had to coin a new word to describe the phenomenon: genocide. The victims were totally innocent people who had done Germany no harm, had threatened Germany in no way, and whose skills and abilities could have done Germany much good.

The first German concentration camp was set up at Dachau, outside Munich, in the spring of 1933, a few weeks after Hitler came to power. Other camps quickly followed. The legend over the camp gates read: *Arbeit macht frei*—"work makes you free." Inside, the inmates were slave labor for various German arms manufacturers, including some of the great German corporations. They were overworked and underfed, deprived of rest, entertainment, medicines and sleep, degraded in every way imaginable. They died in such numbers that Himmler was forced to tell his SS doctors that they had to lower the death rate "at all costs" and increase productivity.

Inmates line up as officials take roll call at Buchenwald, Germany, November 1938. Buchenwald was one of the first concentration camps, set up outside Weimar, capital of the democracy the Nazis destroyed. The prisoners at this time were enemies of the state and the party, violators of racial-purity laws, homosexuals, Gypsies, prostitutes, conscientious objectors, Jehovah's Witnesses, and others.

Heinrich Himmler, chief of the SS, was the architect of horror and terror on a scale never before imagined. This chicken farmer turned Nazi came to control the entire concentration camp system until the very end of the war. He was responsible for the massacre of the Warsaw Ghetto, he ordered the killing of Jews and others at Auschwitz and other death camps, and more. He was responsible for more deaths than any other man who ever lived, save only Hitler and Stalin.

Everywhere the Germans conquered, they exploited the civilians and resources. They also created ghettos to isolate the Jews. Here a child slave-laborer works at his machine in a factory in the Kovno Ghetto, Lithuania.

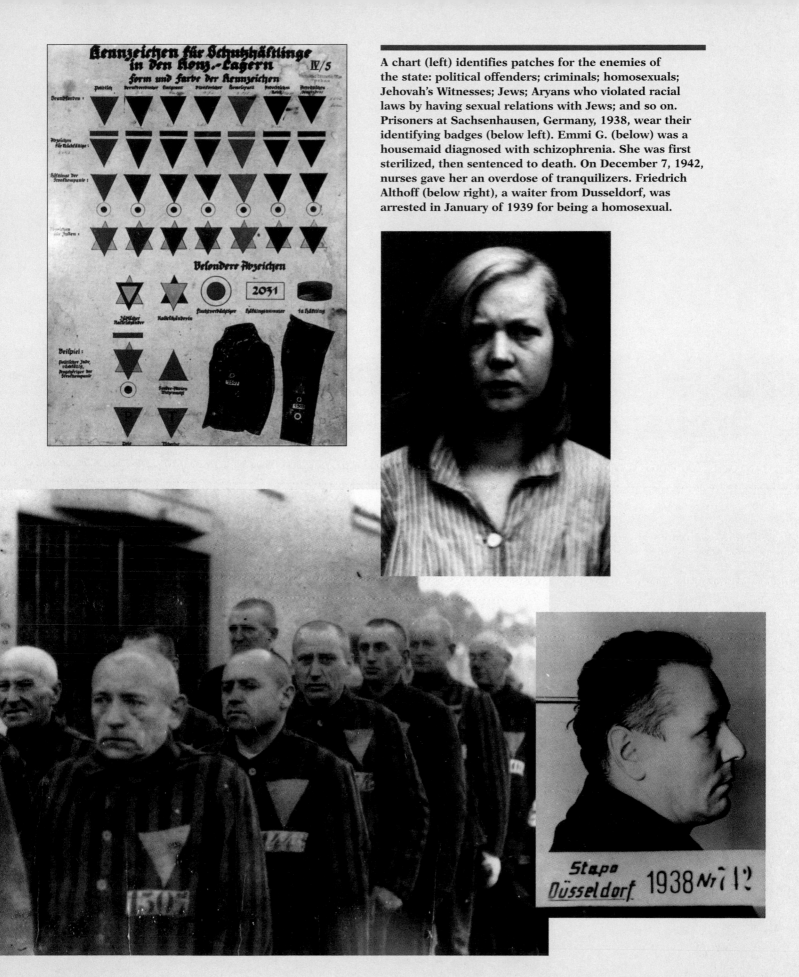

A chart (left) identifies patches for the enemies of the state: political offenders; criminals; homosexuals; Jehovah's Witnesses; Jews; Aryans who violated racial laws by having sexual relations with Jews; and so on. Prisoners at Sachsenhausen, Germany, 1938, wear their identifying badges (below left). Emmi G. (below) was a housemaid diagnosed with schizophrenia. She was first sterilized, then sentenced to death. On December 7, 1942, nurses gave her an overdose of tranquilizers. Friedrich Althoff (below right), a waiter from Dusseldorf, was arrested in January of 1939 for being a homosexual.

The Holocaust began with the German invasion of Poland. By that time—September 1939—two-thirds of the Jews of Germany and Austria had been persecuted and driven into exile. But when the *Wehrmacht* got into Poland, the Nazis suddenly had in their grasp millions of Jews (in 1939 there were 3.3 million Jews in Poland, 2.1 million in western Soviet Union, and 1.5 million in Czechoslovakia, Hungary, and Romania). In Poland, special SS units roamed behind the lines, rounding up Jews in the villages and cities, herding them to the outskirts of town, forcing them to dig mass graves, and then executing them by machine-gun fire—old men, women, children, by the hundreds, sometimes by the thousands. It was a slaughter such as the world had never seen.

It was exceeded in the summer of 1941, when four SS units of 3,000 men each went to work in the Soviet Union. These action groups were called *Einsatzgruppen*, and although "Bolshevik leaders" were supposedly their major target, most of their victims were Jews. Other victims were "Asiatic inferiors," Gypsies, and "useless eaters" such as the mentally ill or terminally ill people. One *Einsatzgruppen* unit reported killing 6,400 Polish mental patients. According to the Nuremberg International Military Tribunal on War Crimes, altogether in the Soviet Union the SS killed 2 million men, women, and children. Most were shot. Himmler, who had witnessed an execution, was upset at the sight of women and children being killed in this way, so he ordered another method: they were put in "gas vans so constructed that at the start of the motor the exhaust gas was conducted into the van, causing death in ten to fifteen minutes."

That kind of killing was inefficent, and mass graves left evidence—not that the Nazis cared very much—and could breed disease that might spread among German troops. On July 31, 1941, Himmler ordered his deputy, Reinhard Heydrich, "to submit to me as soon as possible a general plan showing the measures for organization and for action necessary to carry out the desired final solution [*Endlosung*] of the Jewish question."

Above, young partisans are hanged by the Germans in Minsk. They were charged with helping Red Army officers escape from a nearby prison camp. Left, naked Soviet officers stand at attention in the POW camp at Mauthausen, Austria. Only a small percentage of Soviet prisoners survived.

PRISONERS OF WAR

Even for the relatively well-treated British and American POWs in German camps, the stalags were hell. POWs were always inadequately fed, clothed, and housed. Medical care was almost nonexistent. POWs lived in constant fear of getting sick or suffering an injury. They were often brutalized by their guards, most commonly by being forced to stand at attention on the parade ground, in rain or snow, for hours on end. They slept on wooden bunks, usually without cover but always with lice, in inadequately heated barracks. Men generally lost a third or more of their body weight.

Some tried to escape; a very few made it. The rest endured, as best they could. Rank counted; officers did not have to work and received somewhat better rations. Rumors swept through the stalags: there is going to be a parachute drop and we're going to be liberated tomorrow; there is going to be an exchange of prisoners this afternoon; the Germans are going to distribute the Red Cross parcels this morning. Sometimes solid information came from hidden radios that could pick up BBC broadcasts. Everyone worried about what would happen when Allied troops did finally arrive. Would the Germans move them farther east? Would they machine-gun the POWs?

Thus the happiest moment ever experienced by any Allied POW was his first sight of a British or American soldier at the gates. Captain Pat Reid of the British Army provided a written description of that moment as he experienced it.

Reid was in Colditz, a special stalag in a rural part of eastern Germany. A supposedly escape-proof castle, it held more than a thousand British, French, Polish, Czech, American, and other Allied POW officers. The prisoners were "bad boys" who had escaped from regular stalags and had been re-captured. Incorrigible, they kept escaping, even from Colditz (what was perhaps the world's first successful hang glider carried one escapee out of the castle; he jumped from the roof in his hand-made contraption). But the Germans mounted extensive search missions and generally caught the escapee before he got to Switzerland.

Reid, in his 1953 book, *Escape from Colditz*, described the sudden entrance into the prison courtyard on April 15 of a single GI, his belt and straps festooned with ammunition clips and grenades, submachine gun in hand. Everyone froze. What was this? An Allied officer standing near the

The U.S. Army distributes food to German POWs from the Afrika Korps in Algiers, May 1943. The total tally of prisoners, including Italians, was nearly a quarter million men. As this photo suggests, the U.S. Army was in no way prepared to handle such numbers.

gate approached the soldier, who grinned at him, extended his hand, and said cheerfully, "Any doughboys here?" That broke the spell:

Suddenly, a mob was rushing toward him, shouting and cheering and struggling madly to reach him, to make sure that he was alive, to touch him, and from the touch to know again the miracle of living, to be men in their own right, freed from bondage, outcast no more, liberated, their faith in God's mercy justified, their patience rewarded, the nobility of mankind vindicated, justice at last accomplished and tyranny once more overcome.

Men wept, unable to restrain themselves. It was not enough that the body was free once more to roam the earth. Feelings, pent up and dammed behind the mounting walls of five successive torturing, introverted years, had to erupt.

They welled up like surging springs, they overflowed, they burst their banks, they tumbled unhindered and uncontrolled. Frenchmen with tears streaming down their faces kissed each other on both cheeks. They kissed the GI, they kissed everyone within range.

U.S. Marines unload a Japanese POW from a submarine returned from war patrol, May 1945 (below). American POWs celebrate the Fourth of July in the Japanese prison camp of Casisange in the Philippines (bottom). Had they been discovered, the Japanese would have put them to death. They celebrated anyway.

The Auschwitz-Birkenau concentration camp (above) in Poland was the largest and most efficient of the death camps masterminded by Reinhard Heydrich (opposite left) and Adolf Eichmann (opposite right). Heydrich was Himmler's number two as chief of the Reich Central Security Office. He called the Wannsee Conference that set up the "final solution of the European Jewish question." Eichmann was chief of the Jewish Office of the Gestapo, responsible for deporting close to 3 million Jews, principally from Austria and Hungary. Together, they were the personification of evil.

Heydrich, assisted by Adolf Eichmann, created an organization for assembly-line killing. On January 20, 1942, at the Wannsee Conference, Heydrich gathered all agency heads involved in the deportation or killing of Jews and told them—in somewhat veiled but still chilling language—what their roles would be in carrying out the "final solution." Eichmann was, in practice, the administrator of the whole genocide operation. Existing concentration camps were expanded into death camps, including Sobibor, Treblinka, and, the most notorious, Auschwitz.

Auschwitz, in Poland west of Kraków, was on the main rail line from Kraków to Vienna. Built in 1941, it was originally a POW camp. Of some 12,000 Red Army POWs sent there in December 1941 only 150 survived the winter. But that was just a start. Within weeks of the Wannsee Conference, Auschwitz had expanded from a capacity of 30,000 slave-labor prisoners to 200,000. I. G. Farben, Krupp, and other armament industries set up factories there. Eichmann, meanwhile, set up the killing machine.

It worked like this: Trainloads of Jews in sealed boxcars, packed so tightly for so long without food or water—often for days—that the dead could not fall down, arrived regularly at the Auschwitz siding. Guards threw open the doors and began shouting at the Jews to get out and line up. They were marched to an SS doctor who made a visual scan and pointed either to the gas chamber or to the labor camps. Infants, young children, old people, pregnant women, the disabled, and the sick were sent to their immediate death; between 20 and 40 percent were sent to the labor camps where they remained until, too weak to work any longer, they too were sent to the chambers.

A Jewish prisoner in Jasenovac, Yugoslavia, takes off his ring before execution (right). An incredible amount of gold was taken from the victims, a vast fortune in gold teeth yanked from the mouths of the dead alone. The Nazis later found more efficient ways to kill. Cyanide pellets await shipment to Auschwitz and the other death camps (below).

A group of Hungarian Jews have just arrived at Auschwitz in May of 1944 (opposite top). They had been locked in their boxcars for two and a half days and were badly confused as they were let out. An immediate selection was made; healthy younger Jews were sent to the factory complex, while the old, infirm, and children went straight to the gas chambers. A fortunate group of Jews are saved at the last minute from deportation, November, 1944 (opposite bottom). They have been given "safe passes" from Raoul Wallenberg and are returning to the ghetto.

Outside the chambers, the Jews were ordered to strip and told they were going to take showers, for delousing purposes. First they were shaved, and their hair saved for stuffing for mattresses and the like. Then they were herded into the chamber, which looked like a shower room in a high school gym. Once they were packed in, the door was sealed shut and cyanide gas was pumped into the room through the shower heads. After a minute or two of screaming that no one except the other victims heard, there was silence. After clearing the gas from the room, inmates—often Poles, sometimes Jews, always under extreme duress—entered and pulled gold teeth, and tore up anuses and vaginas of the cadavers to prob for hidden jewelry. That task completed, the bodies were taken by handcart to the crematory furnaces. The ashes of the dead went to farmers to enrich their soil.

In March 1944, when Hungary tried to drop out of the war, Hitler ordered the country occupied by the German Army. Up to that point, the Hungarian government had protected Hungarian Jews. Now they fell into Eichmann's grasp. He tried to barter Jewish lives for money and material for Germany, at one point offering 350,000 Jews for 2,000 trucks. The Allies refused. Eichmann then began deporting Hungary's Jews to Auschwitz, all 350,000 of them. Within two months, 250,000 had been gassed.

At Auschwitz, in 1944, 10,000 Jews a day were exterminated. Between 2 million and 4 million Jews and another 2 million non-Jews had been gassed by the time the Red Army arrived at the gates to the camp in late 1944. Total figures are guesswork because by then the SS had evacuated the camp and destroyed the gas chambers and crematoria and burned all records.

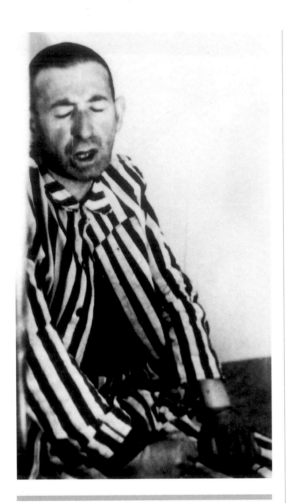

The Germans carried out medical experiments on camp inmates on a regular basis. A prisoner in a special air chamber responds to changing air pressure during high-altitude experiments carried out for the Luftwaffe.

Another horrifying practice in Auschwitz and other camps was the use of prisoners for so-called medical experiments—something the Japanese also engaged in. These were highly unscientific—in fact, murderous—experiments conducted by incompetent and sadistic doctors from the SS. They were unspeakable.

What did the world know about the Holocaust? What did it do about it? For most ordinary people, in England and in the United States, next to nothing was known, so that after the war there was a great shock wave as the existence and purpose of the camps was exposed. But Allied leaders knew what was going on at Auschwitz and elsewhere, at least in general terms. Ultra intercepts in 1941 revealed what the *Einsatzgruppen* were doing in the Soviet Union. People escaped from the camps, resistance leaders gathered information, the word went out to various Jewish organizations in Palestine, London, New York, and Washington. These groups tried to get some attention paid to the Nazi crimes, but were unsuccessful. Hollywood, with many Jewish-owned studios, would not touch the subject. Newspapers owned by Jews, including *The New York Times*, would not print stories about the Holocaust. Jewish congressmen refused to speak out. This cover-up, a conspiracy of silence, had many causes. Even when confronted by hard evidence, many found it difficult to believe that the Germans would kill off highly skilled laborers in the middle of a total war. And there were fears that if the facts about the Holocaust were made public, there would be an irresistible demand to do something to stop it.

Why wasn't something done to stop it? Because there was precious little the Allies could do. Proposals to bomb the train facilities at Auschwitz were put before Roosevelt and Churchill, but they would not order the bombing, for three main reasons: Poland was out of range for most bombers based in Britain; bombing Auschwitz would have led to the deaths of many Jewish prisoners there; and it would have been a diversion of the war effort.

The last point was the main one. Roosevelt and Churchill and their advisers agreed that the best thing they could do for the Jews of Europe was to win the war sooner. So long as the war went on, the Germans would be killing Jews, and the slaughter wouldn't stop until the Germans surrendered unconditionally. Bombing Auschwitz was not going to shorten the war; using the same planes to bomb oil storage facilities would.

So the Allies concentrated single-mindedly on winning the war. By the beginning of 1945, the Red Army and the Allied armies were racing across eastern and western Germany. As these armies of liberation approached the camps, the inmates had one more hell to go through. The guards rounded them up and marched them away. The prisoners incapable of walking were shot. The paths taken by these "death marches" were lined with corpses with bullet holes in the nape of the neck. The liberating troops discovered heaps of naked cadavers. Those still alive were in the extremes of debility. In Bergen-Belsen, liberated by the British on April 13, some 10,000 corpses lay on the ground, and of the 38,500 remaining, alive but inert, barely one third could be saved. Thus on V-E Day, although the killing stopped, the dying went on.

As the Nazi crimes were unique, so unique action was required to seek justice. In June 1945 a conference began in London of jurists from Britain, the United States, the Soviet Union, and France. Six weeks later the jurists agreed on a statute creating the International Military Tribunal at Nuremberg. In November, a four-judge court began to hear evidence in the trial of twenty-two top Nazis. The charges were grouped into four main headings: count one, conspiracy to commit crimes; count two, crimes against the peace (planning, preparing, starting, or waging aggressive war); count three, war crimes in occupied countries (murder of civilians, deportations for slave labor, killing of POWs and hostages); count four, crimes against humanity (murder, extermination, enslavement, deportation, persecution on political, racial, and religious grounds).

The evidence presented at Nuremberg included moving pictures of the camps, still photographs, documents, and eyewitness accounts from survivors. Thus there was an almost immediate and relatively systematic exposure before the eyes of the world of the appalling culpability of the Nazi regime. This must be considered a good thing, insofar as one of the purposes of Nuremberg was to let future tyrants know that world is watching and retribution is, if not certain, at least possible.

Yet much about Nuremberg was subject to legitimate criticism. The trials applied a code of law retroactively. They adopted an Anglo-American form of procedure unfamiliar to the German people. The accusers were also the judges. And the defendants included foreign ministers, generals and admirals, industrialists, and others who had no direct involvement in the Holo-

The world was astonished when the concentration camps were uncovered in the spring of 1945. A 1938 publication distributed by Candid Pictures, Inc. (below left), tried to warn Americans of the persecution of Jews in Germany, but even the authors never guessed how far Hitler had gone with the final solution. Still, government officials were aware of the Holocaust. In January 1944, Treasury Secretary Henry Morgenthau Jr. (below), the highest ranking Jew in Roosevelt's administration, protested against "the acquiescence of this government in the murder of Jews." Roosevelt's response was to spur efforts to win the war sooner in order to stop the killing.

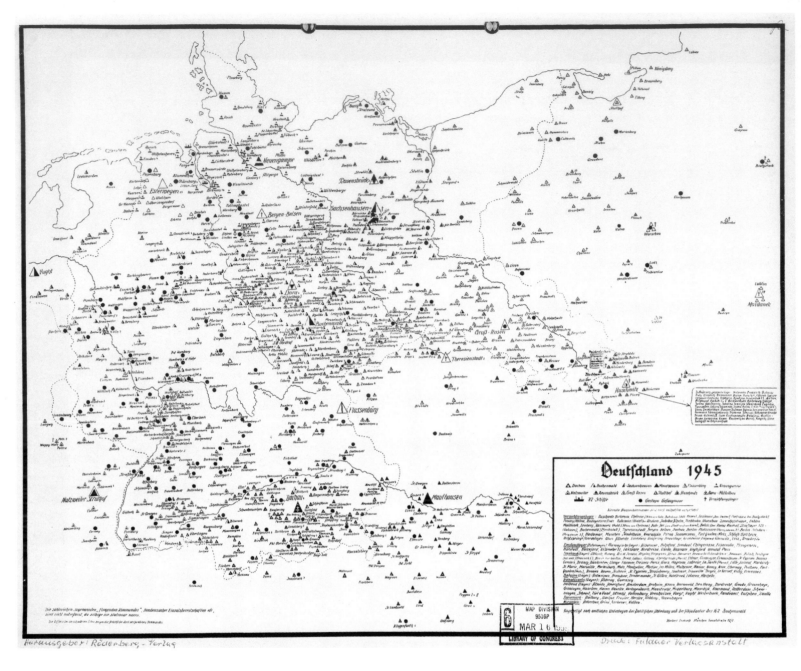

Deutschland 1945

A map of German concentration camps (above) reveals how many there were of them. The photograph of a death march from Dachau, on the way to the gas chambers (opposite top), was secretly taken by a German civilian. Survivors (opposite bottom) cheer as American troops arrive at Dachau on April 30, 1945. The SS had disappeared a couple of days earlier. This was the greatest moment of all—liberation.

caust, and who could claim with some truth that they had only followed orders in their service to Germany.

Perhaps most embarrassing was the presence of a Soviet judge sitting in judgment of Germans. One of the specifics in the crimes against humanity charge was that the Nazis had carried out a program to exterminate the Polish intellectual elite. It was true: in May 1940, the SS had massacred students at the universities of Kraków and Lublin. But it was also true that the Katyn Forest massacre of some fifteen thousand Polish officers, ordered by Stalin and carried out by the Red Army, took place on almost the same day.

But it would have been impossible to hold war crimes trials without the Soviets, and it would have been criminal to not hold the trials. Otherwise, real monsters would have gone free, and the evidence that convicted them would not have been collected or made public. Eleven of the defendants were condemned to death, including Göring who cheated the hangman by

British troops force former SS guards at Bergen-Belsen to load corpses onto trucks for transport to mass graves on April 21, 1945. Located near Hanover, Germany, Bergen-Belsen had been opened in July 1943 as a POW camp. It was here that Anne Frank died in March 1945. The British found 10,000 unburied corpses and hundreds of others in mass graves. Some 14,000 people who were liberated nevertheless died within a few days.

War Crimes Commission officials examine a mobile killing van in which Jews were believed to have been gassed while being transported to the crematoria at Chelmno, Poland.

swallowing a cyanide capsule; Himmler had escaped the trial by committing suicide shortly after his capture in May. Seven were condemned to imprisonment. Three were acquitted.

Twelve additional trials were held at Nuremberg, beginning in November 1945 and stretching out to 1948. These were based on the finding of the original court that certain Nazi organizations—SS, *Einsatzgruppen*, Gestapo—were criminal groups. In 1948, the Germans took charge of the prosecution of war criminals. Trials went on for decades. One, conducted by West Germany in Frankfurt am Main, involved twenty-one former SS officers at Auschwitz. It ran from December 1963 to August 1965. Nineteen were convicted and sentenced to prison terms ranging from three years to life.

As for the two principal participants after Himmler—Heydrich and Eichmann—there was a retribution, one coming early, the other late. On May 27, 1942, two Czech agents, trained in England and parachuted into Czechoslovakia, ambushed Reinhard Heydrich's car on the streets of Prague, fired into it, and rolled a bomb under it; Heydrich died soon thereafter. The Nazis indulged in an orgy of bloody reprisals, including destroying the village of Lidice and killing thousands of Czechs.

Eichmann expected to be tried as a war criminal and boasted to an associate that he would "leap laughing into the grave because the feeling that he had five million people on his conscience would be for him a source of

German POWs in the U.S. Army's Halloran General Hospital are made to watch army films of the atrocities committed in the camps (above). Every effort was made, from General Eisenhower on down, to publicize what had been discovered, and to force the Germans to recognize what they had done. The major criminals of the Holocaust were tried in 1945; twelve additional trials took place in Nuremberg beginning in October 1946 and lasting until 1948. At right is the Nuremberg dock on December 3, 1947.

At Buchenwald, April 26, 1945, a survivor demonstrates SS methods of torture and execution to American soldiers (above). Field Marshal Hermann Göring (below), sentenced to death at Nuremberg, cheated the hangman by swallowing a poison capsule the night before he was to be executed, October 14, 1945. He had told his judges, "I am determined to go down in German history as a great man."

The Israeli government put Adolf Eichmann on trial in 1961 (above) after finding him in Argentina. He had escaped at the end of the war by donning a corporal's uniform and lived a quiet, unpretentious life in Argentina for fifteen years.

extraordinary satisfaction." But he escaped and got to Argentina, where he lived peacefully until May 1960, when Israeli agents found him, kidnapped him, and flew him to Israel. In a trial that lasted from April to August 1961, Eichmann asked, "Why me? Everybody killed the Jews." He said he only followed orders and asserted that he was not anti-Semitic. The court nevertheless found him guilty and sentenced him to death. He was hanged on May 31, 1962.

In Tokyo, an International Military Tribunal for the Far East tried twenty-five Japanese military officers and government officials charged with crimes against peace, crimes against humanity, murder, and other atrocities. Unlike Nuremberg, these trials were largely ignored by the American public. The only celebrated defendant was Hideki Tojo, Japan's wartime prime minister. In a trial that dragged on until November 1948, Tojo and six others were sentenced to death; sixteen additional Japanese were sentenced to life imprisonment.

Tomoyuki Yamashita testifies before the International Military Tribunal, November, 1945. He was charged with committing atrocities in the Philippines, where he was in command until the final surrender. He was found guilty and was hanged on February 23, 1946.

CHAPTER 17

ASSAULT ON FORTRESS EUROPE

very invasion of the war had its "D-day." (The "D" had no significance, beyond indicating the day the operation started.) But Operation Overlord, June 6, 1944, the invasion of France, is everywhere recalled as the D-Day because it was the biggest amphibious operation ever undertaken and because it was the climactic battle of the war.

It had been a long time coming. From June 1942 onward, Stalin had been demanding that the Allies open a second front in France. He suspected that the West was secretly delaying a cross-Channel invasion in the hope that Germany and the Soviet Union would batter each other to death. (Where, the British had a right to ask, was the second front in 1940?) In the spring of 1942, Britain and the United States were working on various plans for an assault on France, but it became increasingly evident that neither the troops nor the technical equipment yet existed for any operation sufficiently large to stand a chance of success. Churchill had no intention of sacrificing another generation of young Englishmen like those of World War I, and Roosevelt soon discovered that the United States, heavily engaged in the Pacific, was short on warships and landing craft.

Therefore, although Allied planners continued to contemplate a future landing in France, in the end they settled on a large commando sortie against Dieppe, on the coast of France, in August 1942. A raiding force of five thousand men, primarily Canadian, attacked Dieppe, and more than half were killed, wounded, or captured.

That France should be the target of a later and larger assault was agreed on by both Washington and London. Planning was started on what would be known as Operation Overlord. In late 1943, at Cairo, Roosevelt selected Eisenhower to command the operation. A few days earlier, at Teheran, he

Albert Richards painted an event, *The Drop— Paratroopers*, in which he had participated. In Normandy, between midnight and dawn on June 6, 1944, the Allies dropped three divisions—the U.S. 82nd (All-America) and 101st (Screaming Eagles) and the British 6th Airborne (Pegasus)—behind the German coastal defenses. Assembly in the dark was difficult, especially as most of the drops were not so tight as this one, but the units managed to get together and seize their objectives.

Montgomery and Eisenhower query a GI during an inspection in March of 1944. They got to see the troops and study maneuvers. Their determination and dedication to making D-Day work is obvious. "This operation is being planned as a success," Eisenhower declared. "We cannot afford to fail." It was a special trait of Eisenhower's that he always looked the man he was talking to straight in the eyes. Monty had that trait, too, but not to the same degree.

had promised Stalin that the cross-Channel invasion would take place in the spring of 1944.

Fresh from victories in Africa and Italy, Eisenhower set up headquarters in England in January. His orders from the Combined Chiefs of Staff read: "You will enter the continent of Europe and, in conjunction with the other United Nations, undertake operations aimed at the heart of Germany and the destruction of her armed forces." His title was supreme commander. His office was called Supreme Headquarters, Allied Expeditionary Force—SHAEF.

Eisenhower picked the time and place of the assault. Early June would be the time, when the good campaigning weather came to northwest Europe. Normandy would be the place. There, surprise could be achieved, as the Germans assumed the Allies would attack on the direct line London–Dover–Pas de Calais–Rhine–Berlin.

Surprise was critical because the Germans had fifty-five divisions, eleven of them armored, while Eisenhower could put only eight divisions ashore in France on D-Day. If the Germans knew where the attack was coming, they could surely hurl it back into the sea. So Eisenhower chose Normandy, which made no sense as there were no ports along the Calvados coast and landing in Normandy put the Seine and Somme rivers between the Allies and their objectives. Because it made no sense, defenses in Normandy were nowhere near as formidable as at the Pas de Calais—so it made perfect sense to Eisenhower.

The training was intense. The planning was detailed to an extraordinary degree. It had to be, since the operation had 175,000 fighting men scheduled to go ashore on D-Day, carried by nearly 1,000 transport airplanes or on ships—5,000 ships of all types—with some 6,000 fighters and bombers over-head. The scope of Overlord defies imagination; one comparison is that Overlord was the equivalent of moving the Wisconsin cities of Green Bay, Racine, and Kenosha—every man, woman, and child, with every vehicle—across Lake Michigan in one night.

Allied intelligence, based on thousands of reconnaissance flights over the coast and on the French resistance, a prime source of information, was so good it was able to locate most machine-gun nests or artillery bunkers along the Calvados coast. Allied counterintelligence mounted an elaborate deception scheme, one that drew on the talents of Hollywood and the British film industry, to produce cardboard tanks, landing craft, and airplanes, to convince the Germans that the invasion force was gathering at Dover for an attack on the Pas de Calais. Called Operation Fortitude, and starring General Patton as the commander of the "army" gathered in Dover, it was a smash-

The lines on this map of the Allied invasion routes to Normandy indicate lanes that had been covered by minesweepers. This was an extraordinarily complex operation, involving thousands of ships and planes and 175,000 troops, coming out of eleven ports, headed for five targets. What is amazing today is how few mishaps there were, even though it was all done without a computer.

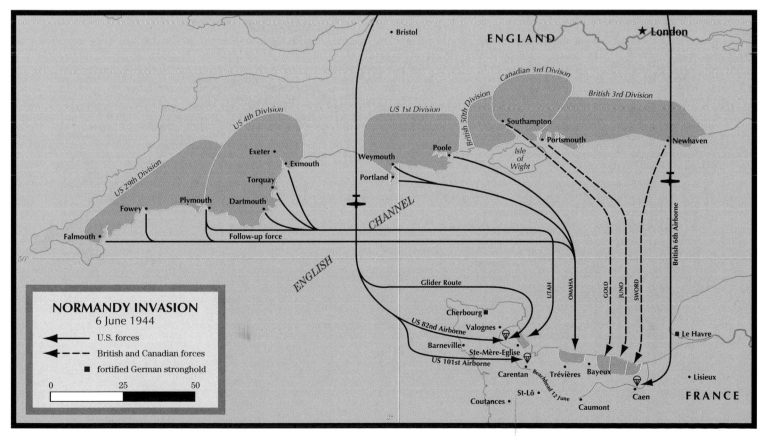

NORMANDY INVASION
6 June 1944

◄──── U.S. forces
◄- - - - British and Canadian forces
■ fortified German stronghold

0   25   50

The supply buildup for Overlord was gigantic. Here is a supply depot somewhere in England, May 8, 1944. There were miles of jeeps, trucks, tanks, typewriters, medicine, canned rations, gliders, and airplanes lined up on runways; in the harbors there were thousands of landing craft, hundreds of warships.

ing success. It led Rommel to keep nine of his eleven armored divisions in the Calais region, northeast of the Seine, far from Normandy.

The buildup of men and equipment in the United Kingdom the first months of 1944 was so great that people joked that the barrage balloons (scattered across the country to prevent German fighters from coming down and strafing the city streets) were necessary to keep Britain afloat. Tens of thousands of tanks, trucks, jeeps, landing craft of all types, artillery pieces, and other weapons were piled up alongside the roads, waiting to go to the Continent.

Allied ingenuity seemed limitless. There were the awkward DUKW amphibious personnel carriers. There were swimming tanks, each having an inflatable rubber skirt and a propeller attached to the drive shaft that enabled it to land side by side with the infantry. Flail tanks to beat out mines with whirling chains were developed by inventive technicians, as well as a trans-Channel fuel pipeline called PLUTO (Pipe-Line Under the Ocean). Meanwhile the British put a tremendous effort (more than twenty thousand workers) into building two prefabricated, concrete harbors, known as "Mulberries," that would be floated across the Channel on D-Day Plus One and set up on the invasion beaches. Winston Churchill rightly called Overlord "the most difficult and complicated operation ever to take place."

Southern England gradually became one huge military encampment. Ports filled up with transport ships; airfields became packed with fighters and bombers; the pleasant English countryside was cluttered with parked tanks, trucks, jeeps; and urban areas were jammed with billeted troops. By early June, nearly 3 million Allied soldiers, sailors, and airmen were ready for the assault. Eisenhower recalled: "The mighty host was tense as a coiled spring, and indeed that is exactly what it was—a great human spring, coiled for the moment when its energy should be released and it would vault the English Channel in the greatest amphibious assault ever attempted."

On the far shore, meanwhile, Hitler had called Field Marshal Gerd von Rundstedt out of retirement to command the German forces in the West. Rundstedt had no use for Hitler's Atlantic Wall of concrete fortifications as an effective way to stop the Allies. His idea was to hold his strength well back

Landing Ship Tanks (LSTs) in Brixham, England, are loaded for the invasion, May 27, 1944. The Germans believed the Allies could not make a major invasion over an open beach, because they could not supply their troops. But the LST gave Eisenhower and his people confidence that it could be done.

Rommel and his staff stand before a fortification in the Atlantic Wall, February 1944. It is low tide; the obstacles in the surf were designed to tear the bottoms out of landing craft, thus forcing the Allies to land at low tide, when the killing zone would be at its greatest. Rommel ordered hundreds of thousands of them put in place, along with land mines, barbed wire, and antitank ditches—creating a gauntlet of fire the attacking troops would have to cross before they even got to the Atlantic Wall.

from the beaches and to fight decisive battles at places of his own choosing. But Rommel, in immediate command in France, believed Germany's only hope was to stop the invasion on the beaches. So as Eisenhower prepared through the winter and spring for the attack, Rommel worked frantically to improve the Atlantic Wall. For six months, half a million men labored, constructing giant pillboxes and murderous hazards of every variety. Rommel planned to use the static defense to check the momentum of the initial attack, then to counterattack with tanks to drive the Allies back into the sea. He erected advance barriers at beaches where he thought a debarkation likely. He booby-trapped and flooded rear areas where airborne landings might come. "The war will be won or lost on the beaches," he told his aide. "The first twenty-four hours of the invasion will be decisive." It would be, he said, "the longest day."

Eisenhower had chosen June 5 as D-Day. The tide was right—low at dawn. But on Sunday, June 4, a gale blew up. The weather forced him to postpone. His forecaster predicted fair weather Tuesday morning, to be followed by more bad weather. Faced with the choice between a possible critical delay of two weeks, when the next low tide at dawn would come, or a gamble with the elements, he gave his order: "OK, let's go!"

With that order the largest amphibious force ever seen began to cross the Channel. Eisenhower's issued an order of the day: "The tide has turned. The free men of the world are marching together to victory. The hopes and prayers of liberty-loving people everywhere march with you. . . . Good luck!

And let us all beseech the blessing of Almighty God upon this great and noble undertaking."

As the invasion armada headed toward France on the evening of June 5, American and British paratroopers and glider units landed behind the German lines. They were scattered throughout Normandy. But despite the mix-ups and confusion, before daylight on the sixth the paratroopers had secured their main objectives—bridges, crossroads, and exits from the beaches.

At 0530, the landing craft began their runs onto Utah and Omaha beaches, carrying the U.S. First, Fourth, and Twenty-ninth divisions, and onto Sword, Juno, and Gold beaches, carrying British and Canadian troops. The first assault wave hit the Normandy beaches by 0630 on June 6. Planning had been as complete as possible, and the men had been thoroughly briefed;

Many of these obstacles (above) had Teller mines placed on them. Some had wires attached so that a German in his bunker could set off a mine when a landing craft or advancing troops got close to it.

German troops are briefed on an exercise, June 1 or 2, 1944 (left), practicing what they will do when the Allies come. Their plan was to counterattack the first day, throwing everything they had into the battle. Everything included hundreds of formidable 88s, like the one looming in the background, mounted on awesome panzers. But this exercise was being held in the Pas de Calais, where the Germans had placed most of their armor, not in Normandy.

Eisenhower's Order of the Day for June 5, 1944, perfectly captures the momentous event about to take place. Eisenhower spoke for liberty-loving people everywhere. The order was immediately recognized as a classic. GIs and Tommies folded it up and put it in their wallets; when they got home after the war, they had it framed and hung it in their homes.

Opposite: General Alfred Jodl's personal situation map for June 6, 1944, shows how much the Germans had been misled by the deception operation, Fortitude. It shows the main strength of the Allies in and around Dover, pointing like a sword at the Pas de Calais. It misses most of the buildup in Portsmouth, Southampton, and the southern ports. By contrast, thanks to Ultra, Eisenhower's read on the German order of battle in France was almost as good as Rommel's.

SUPREME HEADQUARTERS
ALLIED EXPEDITIONARY FORCE

Soldiers, Sailors and Airmen of the Allied Expeditionary Force!

You are about to embark upon the Great Crusade, toward which we have striven these many months. The eyes of the world are upon you. The hopes and prayers of liberty-loving people everywhere march with you. In company with our brave Allies and brothers-in-arms on other Fronts, you will bring about the destruction of the German war machine, the elimination of Nazi tyranny over the oppressed peoples of Europe, and security for ourselves in a free world.

Your task will not be an easy one. Your enemy is well trained, well equipped and battle-hardened. He will fight savagely.

But this is the year 1944 ! Much has happened since the Nazi triumphs of 1940-41. The United Nations have inflicted upon the Germans great defeats, in open battle, man-to-man. Our air offensive has seriously reduced their strength in the air and their capacity to wage war on the ground. Our Home Fronts have given us an overwhelming superiority in weapons and munitions of war, and placed at our disposal great reserves of trained fighting men. The tide has turned ! The free men of the world are marching together to Victory !

I have full confidence in your courage, devotion to duty and skill in battle. We will accept nothing less than full Victory !

Good Luck ! And let us all beseech the blessing of Almighty God upon this great and noble undertaking.

Dwight D. Eisenhower

but in the vast confusion of invasion under enemy fire, the best-laid plans often came unglued. No one had expected that so many men would become seasick in the choppy Channel. Men died uselessly when they left their landing craft too soon and stepped into water over their heads; others fell into underwater shell craters and drowned. Many tanks equipped with the flotation devices that had worked so well in practice foundered as they tried to come in through the rough surf. The Allied air bombing that was to have knocked out German beach defense guns at Omaha Beach had not been accurate; the bombs had been laid down too far inland to do much good. As

Übersichtskarte 1:1000000

Lage West
Stand: 6.6.44
OKH-Gen St d H
Op.Abt.IIIb Prüf Nr.

"OK, LET'S GO!"

By the first day of June, SHAEF had prepared for everything, except the weather, which could not be predicted for more than a day or two in advance and now became an obsession. The scheduled date for the invasion was June 5, but on the fourth, even as the men were loading up in their transports for the trip across the Channel, a low-pressure system from the northwest

brought stormy weather to the Channel. Eisenhower postponed the invasion for a day, hoping for better weather.

On the evening of June 4, Eisenhower met at his headquarters with his principal subordinates. The wind and rain shook the windowpanes in the French doors of the mess hall at Southwick House in a sharp staccato beat. At 2130 hours Group Captain Stagg, a twenty-eight-year-old Scot and chief weatherman at SHAEF, gave his latest prediction: he anticipated a break in the storm. The rain would stop before daybreak, June 5. There would be thirty-six hours of more or less clear weather. Winds would moderate. Or so, at least, Stagg hoped, but he was careful to point out that other weathermen disagreed with him and thought the storm would continue for one or two more days.

Eisenhower began pacing the room, head down, chin on his chest, hands clasped behind his back. Suddenly he shot out his chin at his chief of staff,

The Supreme Headquarters of the Allied Expeditionary Force meet in England 1944 (above). These were Eisenhower's closest advisers. Knowing there was no turning back, Ike encourages the 101st Airborne, June 5, 1944 (right).

General Walter B. Smith. "What do you think?" he demanded. "It's a helluva gamble but it's the best possible gamble," Smith replied.

Eisenhower nodded, paced some more, stopped, looked at his deputy, Air Marshal Arthur Tedder, and asked his opinion. Tedder thought it "chancy" and wanted to postpone again. Eisenhower nodded, paced, stopped, turned to General Montgomery and asked, "Do you see any reason for not going tomorrow?" Montgomery looked Eisenhower in the eye and replied, "I would say . . . Go!"

Eisenhower asked all fourteen men in the room for their view; they split down the middle on going on the sixth or postponing again. Only Eisenhower could decide. Smith was struck by the "loneliness and isolation of a commander at a time when such a momentous decision was to be taken by him, with full knowledge that failure or success rests on his individual decision." Eisenhower paced, chin tucked on his chest. He stopped and remarked, "The question is just how long can you hang this operation on the end of a limb and let it hang there?"

No one spoke up to answer that question. Eisenhower resumed pacing. The only sounds in the room were the rattling of the French doors in the wind. It hardly seemed possible that an amphibious attack could be launched in such weather. At 2145 hours, Eisenhower gave his decision: "OK. Let's go."

Mitchell Jamieson captures in his painting *Rubber Boat and Men Cleaning Rifles* the mood on an LST, loaded and ready to go, on June 5. The men couldn't be allowed off their landing craft because they might get the order to move at any moment and because they had now been briefed on where they were going and were thus a security risk. They killed time—the longest wait any of them ever went through.

Members of the British Sixth Airborne Division travel over the Channel en route to Normandy, June 5–6, 1944. They landed between the Orne and Dives rivers; their mission was to seal off the Allied left flank, to prevent the Germans from bringing down their panzers from the Pas de Calais. They got the job done, but at great cost.

British commandos cross the Channel on their way to Normandy, June 6, 1944. Although Britain had been at war with Germany for almost four years, this was to be the first combat experience for the majority of British troops—as was also true of the Americans. On these young men hung the fate of the world. Could they stand up to the mighty *Wehrmacht*?

Sometime around 0700 hours on June 6, 1944, Higgins Boats with U.S. Coast Guard crews head for the shores of Omaha Beach, in the face of heavy German fire—far heavier than had been anticipated. But these little craft shuttled back and forth through the day, picking up reinforcements from the troop transports and bringing them ashore.

a result, the gunfire that met American troops at Omaha was more murderous than anything they had been prepared for. Initial losses at Omaha were ghastly; in some assault companies the casualties were at 90 percent within minutes of landing. By midday, however, magnificent navy gunfire gradually put many of the German guns out of action.

The Americans kept coming, and by afternoon the beaches were swarming with men, tanks, and amphibious supply carriers. Tanks flailed through mine fields, and infantry scrambled over underwater and shore obstacles to burst through to the high ground inland from the beaches. At Utah Beach the defenders, as had been predicted, were second-rate troops who soon surrendered; but behind Omaha, a German infantry division was stationed. It had been moved into the defenses weeks before, without having been detected by Allied intelligence. On the other hand, the beaten Luftwaffe put

On the morning of June 6, 1944, a column of Landing Craft Infantry (LCIs) heads across the Channel toward Normandy (right). A platoon of American infantry wade ashore to Omaha Beach, about 0730, June 6, 1944 (below). The tide is out; these men have a long slog ahead of them before they can find any cover. In the first wave the casualties were enormous, but the GIs kept coming.

LSTs unload at Omaha Beach, June 7, 1944. The amount of equipment and numbers of men coming ashore were staggering. An American pilot who saw all this action from his P-47 thought, Hitler must have been mad to declare war on the United States.

As soon as they hit the beach, Allied troops engaged in fierce combat. Clockwise, from right: British troops from the Fiftieth Division struggle ashore Utah Beach, many with bicycles (which are quickly discarded); a smoke screen is laid and troops advance across a field; a U.S. Coast Guard rescue vessel saves a drowning soldier; German troops surrender at Utah Beach; hundreds of men lie wounded while still in the water at Sword Beach.

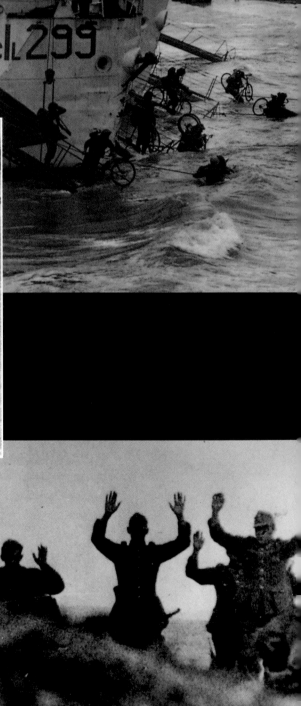

As the day wears on, there are the badly wounded, the dead, and the captured. Clockwise from above: exhausted GIs huddle at the base of the bluff at Omaha; a wrecked U.S. glider looms behind a row of dead soldiers near Sainte Mere Eglise; an unknown GI has a temporary burial site on Utah Beach; survivors from a destroyed Higgins Boat are helped onshore; German troops, many of them boys, surrender.

A member of the Twenty-ninth Infantry Division crouches in a foxhole by a protecting hedgerow and fires at the enemy. The hedgerows of Normandy were ideal for defense, and the Germans took every advantage of the piled-up earth, the jumble of trees and hedges, and the sunken roads. For the GIs, it was about the worst place imaginable to begin the offensive to liberate Europe.

in even less of an appearance than intelligence had predicted. Thousands of Allied planes ruled the sky, providing constant air cover and bombing bridges, roads, and railways to prevent enemy reinforcements from being brought up from the interior.

That evening, over coast-to-coast radio, President Roosevelt led the American people in prayer: "Almighty God: Our sons, pride of our Nation, this day have set out upon a mighty endeavor, a struggle to preserve our Republic, our religion, and our civilization and to set free a suffering humanity. . . ."

The invasion had achieved complete surprise, and within a few days it was evident that the Allies were in France to stay. Lieutenant General Hans Speidel, Rommel's chief of staff, subsequently acknowledged: "The first phase of the invasion ended with an obvious military, political, and psychological success for the Allies. . . . From June 9 on, the initiative lay with the Allies." When Rommel and Rundstedt warned Hitler that the position was critical, the Führer shut them up. He repeated his familiar instruction: hold at all costs.

Fighting in the hedgerow country, where almost impenetrable hedges enclosed small fields to make almost perfect defensive positions, the Germans were able to check the Allied advance. Through June, there was a virtual stalemate in Normandy. It extended into July.

As his army held in Normandy, Hitler began to put his secret weapons into play. His scientists and engineers had made astonishing progress in weapons development. At Peenemünde, a number of rockets and jet-propelled flying bombs were on the drawing boards or in advanced stages of construction. By the spring of 1944, two were operational, and Hitler ordered them used as his *Vergeltungswaffen* (vengeance weapons) shortly after it became clear that the Allies had indeed landed in force in Normandy. Typically, the Führer decided to use these new weapons against England's civilian population rather than Allied troops or supply concentrations, and on the night of June 13–14, 1944, the first V-1 came down on London. During that summer, two thousand V-1s, launched from Belgium and northern France, killed some six thousand Londoners and wounded some forty thousand others. The flight of the buzzbomb, at about four hundred miles per hour, was perfectly visible as well as audible, and the Royal Air Force became adept at intercepting and destroying them before they reached their

Painter Leslie Cole depicted a V-1 that had been targeted at London but was shot down over the English countryside. Because it flew on a predetermined course, it could not dodge, so it was vulnerable to anti-aircraft fire and fighters. Still, enough got through to cause considerable damage to lives, to buildings, and most of all to morale.

Smoke fills the sky after a V-1 attack in Vincent Square, London, June 18, 1944. Some 2,300 of the 8,000 V-1s launched against London fell near or in the city. They carried a one-ton bomb and could be devastating. For almost the first time since 1941, the British had to take shelter when they heard a plane overhead.

targets. Much more menacing, because there was no defense against it, was the giant V-2. Coming down from a parabola whose peak was sixty miles up, it struck at a speed over four times that of sound. Hundreds hit London late in the summer and on into the fall; even more hit Antwerp; only the capture of the launching sites by Allied armies finally put an end to them. The Germans were also first into the skies with jet-propelled military aircraft, a few of which would get into action against the Allies before V-E Day.

A few days after the first V-1 hit England, an event took place inside Germany that, had it succeeded, might have ended the war in Europe that year. The rather disorganized anti-Nazi conspirators who had been intermittently plotting against Hitler recruited a resolute professional army officer, Lieutenant Colonel Count Klaus von Stauffenberg, a brave soldier who had lost an eye, a hand, and two additional fingers fighting for his fatherland, and who loathed the Führer. Together with General Friedrich Olbricht, deputy commander of the German Home Army, Stauffenberg planned a coup d'etat. He personally would undertake to murder Hitler, and once word of his deed had been flashed by the code word "Valkyrie," Olbricht and other commanders in the conspiracy would quickly seize control of the Reich.

On July 20, when Stauffenberg was summoned to a meeting at Hitler's East Prussian headquarters, he took a briefcase containing a time bomb. He intended to leave this inside the concrete bunker where such conferences were normally held, and then to leave. Although the place of the meeting was changed to a wooden guest house, Stauffenberg followed his plan, placed his briefcase underneath the oaken conference table, just six feet from Hitler's legs, then left the room.

At 12:37 P.M., July 20, there was a tremendous explosion. Four men were killed, twenty wounded. That there were no more casualties was due to someone's accidentally having shifted the briefcase away from Hitler. Although he was partly protected by the table leg as a result, Hitler was temporarily paralyzed in one arm, and also burned and deafened. Stauffenberg had confidently flown back to Berlin, but Olbricht received a telephone message telling him the Führer was still alive. As the conspirators issued and countermanded confused orders, loyal Nazi units moved to round them up. Some, including Olbricht and Stauffenberg, were immediately shot; others committed suicide. Rommel, who was suspected of being directly involved in the plot (which he was not), was offered the chance to take poison and thus save his family from retribution. It was announced that he had died of wounds suffered when his staff car was shot at, and he was given a hero's funeral. A huge Gestapo roundup took place; almost fifteen thousand suspects were arrested, and perhaps as many as five thousand were put to death.

The failure of the July 20 plot is one of the great what-ifs of the war. Had Hitler been killed, no one knows what would have happened, but it seems safe to say that the war would have come to an end six months or more be-

An aristocrat and one of the best young officers in the German Army, Count Klaus von Stauffenberg (above) lost his right hand and forearm, the third and fourth fingers of his left hand and his left eye in North Africa. He remained on active duty and became the driving force behind the conspiracy to assassinate Hitler. On July 20, 1944, he planted the bomb that almost did the deed. It was in a briefcase; the case got knocked over after Stauffenberg left the conference room and was placed on the far side of the table leg from Hitler. The damage (left) was extensive, but had the bomb been on the correct side of the table leg, Hitler would have died. After the failure of the plot, Stauffenberg was executed, along with nearly five thousand others.

A badly shaken Hitler is surrounded by happy officers on his staff—happy because he survived. He lost his hearing in one ear and his right arm trembled uncontrollably, but he remained in charge—and continued to command for ten more months.

fore it did. In those months there was more death and destruction than in any comparable period in the war.

In Normandy, meanwhile, Eisenhower moved as rapidly as his logistical difficulties permitted into the second phase of his plan. This phase had two objectives: the capture of Cherbourg, and the buildup of sufficient forces and material to break out toward Germany. By June 27, when General "Lightning Joe" Collins's U.S. VII Corps took Cherbourg, there were a million Allied troops in Normandy. Ordering Montgomery's British and Canadian forces to hold a "hinge" at Caen, in the first week of August, Eisenhower brought Patton and his Third Army to France. Patton plunged ahead, swinging southward, eastward, and around to envelop the main German Army. As his command car moved through fields of burning rubble and blackened German corpses, Patton shouted above the roar of his artillery: "Compared to war, all other forms of human endeavor shrink to insignificance. God, how I love it." He wrote to his wife: "Peace is going to be hell on me."

Then, before dawn on August 7, the Germans counterattacked from the town of Mortain, striking toward Avranches on the sea. Thanks to Ultra, the Allies knew they were coming. A combined infantry-artillery-airplane team combined to stop the German tanks cold. With Patton completing his end run and Montgomery ready to push inland from Caen, it seemed that the Germans were about to be caught in a mammoth envelopment. But Montgomery was slow to close the German escape corridor in the Falaise gap. He was sharply criticized for this caution. Americans charged that he had let far too many enemy troops escape. Bradley wrote in his memoirs: "If Monty's tactics mystified me, they dismayed Eisenhower even more." The arrogant

Patton was aching to get into the battle, but through June and most of July his mission was to continue Fortitude by making the Germans think the real invasion would come at Pas de Calais, while Normandy was a feint. Here Patton makes a show of driving around Kent, just across the Channel from the Pas de Calais.

Dwight Eisenhower (left) and General Omar Bradley (right) talk with General Louis Craig (center). Bradley, commanding officer of the U.S. First Army in Normandy, was as unlike Patton in personality as it was possible to be: calm, dignified, deliberate, and modest. But he shared with Patton the highest degree of professional competency and total dedication to the job.

Patton proposed to Bradley: "Let me go on to Falaise and we'll drive the British back into the sea for another Dunkirk."

But despite the American complaints, a great victory had been won. Eight German infantry and two panzer divisions were obliterated. Those who escaped left their equipment behind. The battle for Normandy was over. The Germans were in full retreat.

On August 15, a second Allied landing, code-named Dragoon, came in southern France. Churchill, who had argued against this invasion, considered it at least well named, "because I was dragooned into it." A fleet of more than fifteen hundred ships, including nine aircraft carriers, arrived off the Riviera between Toulon and Cannes. The landing took place with minimal resistance. Helped by French resistance agents, the U.S. Seventh Army, under Lieutenant General Alexander Patch, and General Jean de Lattre de Tassigny's French First Army rolled up the Rhône Valley and, within a month, joined Patton's forces north of Switzerland at Épinal, giving the Allies a continuous line from Switzerland to the North Sea.

As the Americans approached Paris, the greatest excitement prevailed in the city. On August 19, the Paris police went on strike, and three thousand armed gendarmes seized the prefecture. The following day, Hitler sent an order to destroy Paris. He followed with a message demanding, "Is Paris burning?" But the German commander in the city, General Dietrich von Choltitz, refused to go down in history as the man who burned Paris. He negotiated a surrender that permitted him to withdraw the occupying garrison while leaving the city intact. On August 25, General Jacques Leclerc, commanding the French Second Armored Division (equipped with American-built Sher-

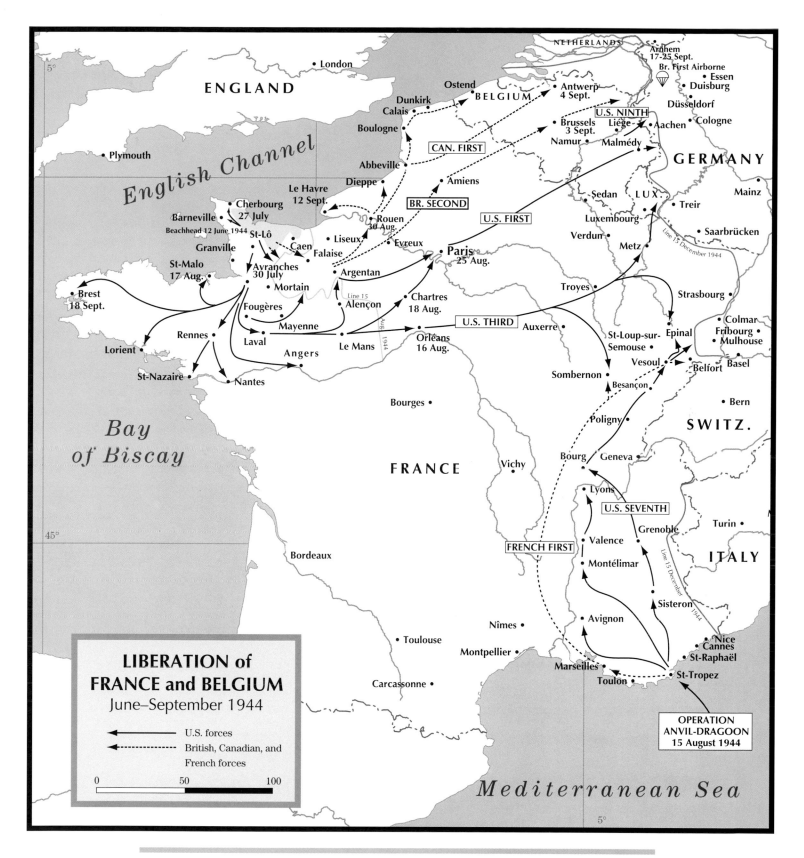

LIBERATION of FRANCE and BELGIUM
June–September 1944

→————— U.S. forces

→- - - - - - British, Canadian, and French forces

0   50   100

OPERATION ANVIL-DRAGOON 15 August 1944

England

London •   Plymouth •

ENGLAND

English Channel

NETHERLANDS

Arnhem 17–25 Sept.
Br. First Airborne

Essen •   Duisburg •

Ostend   BELGIUM   Antwerp 4 Sept.

Dunkirk   Düsseldorf •

Calais •

Boulogne •

Brussels 3 Sept.   Liège •   Aachen •

U.S. NINTH

Cologne •

Abbeville •

CAN. FIRST

Dieppe •

Namur •   Malmédy •

GERMANY

Le Havre 12 Sept.

Amiens •

Mainz •

Cherbourg 27 July

Barneville •

Beachhead 12 June 1944

Rouen 30 Aug.

BR. SECOND

U.S. FIRST

Sedan •   LUX.

Treir •

St-Lô

Caen •

Liseux •

Evreux •

Paris 25 Aug.

Luxembourg •

Saarbrücken •

Granville •

Falaise •

Verdun •

Line 15 December 1944

Avranches 30 July

St-Malo 17 Aug.

Mortain •

Argentan •

Metz •

Strasbourg •

Brest 18 Sept.

Fougères •

Line 15

Alençon •

Chartres 18 Aug.

Troyes •

Colmar •   Fribourg •   Mulhouse •

Mayenne •

Laval •

Le Mans •

U.S. THIRD

Auxerre •

Epinal •

Rennes •

Lorient •

Angers •

Orléans 16 Aug.

Aug. 1944

St-Loup-sur-Semouse •

Vesoul •

Basel •

Belfort

St-Nazaire •

Nantes •

Bourges •

Sombernon •

Besançon •

Bern •

SWITZ.

Bay of Biscay

FRANCE

Vichy •

Poligny •

Bourg •   Geneva •

FRENCH FIRST

Lyons •

45°

Bordeaux •

U.S. SEVENTH

Valence •

Grenoble •

Turin •

ITALY

Nîmes •

Montélimar •

Toulouse •

Montpellier •

Avignon •

Sisteron •

Line 15 December 1944

Carcassonne •

Marseilles •

Toulon •

St-Tropez

Nice •
Cannes •
St-Raphaël •

Mediterranean Sea

After almost two months of fighting in the hedgerows, the Americans finally broke through the German left flank in late July. Patton activated his Third Army and began a sweep across France, as the British were able finally to take Caen and attack to the northeast. The majority of German forces in Normandy were caught in the Falaise pocket; after the Norman front crumbled, the Germans could offer no more serious resistance in France.

In mid-August, the skies above the French Riviera blossomed with Allied parachutes, part of the Seventh Army's amphibious assault from the Mediterranean. Less than a month later, these troops met Patton's near the Swiss border, putting most of France in Allied hands.

The liberation of Paris, when it came, was relatively peaceful. Hitler ordered the German commander of Paris, General Dietrich von Choltitz (right), to destroy the city; von Choltitz refused to be the man responsible for burning Paris and declared it an open city. Parisians reacting to the news retaliated against those who had collaborated with the Germans. Opposite, two Parisian women are forced to walk the streets of Paris—barefooted, with shaved heads, and with swastikas painted on their faces. Below, a French collaborator is shot by a firing squad, November 1944.

man tanks), drove into Paris. He was followed by the U.S. Fourth Infantry Division, which marched down the Champs Élysées on its way to battle east of the city.

Liberation of Paris involved many troops and much fuel, and it undoubtedly delayed the rush toward Hitler's Rhine defenses. But the momentum of the offensive was slowing in any event, because as the tanks and trucks got closer to Germany they were farther from the beaches of Normandy, where their supplies came ashore. An acute gasoline shortage began in the first week of September. It got worse throughout the month.

Men of the U.S. Twenty-eighth Infantry Division parade down the Champs Élysées, August 29, 1944. They were dressed for combat and in fact saw action east of Paris that afternoon. De Gaulle had asked Eisenhower to march them right through Paris as a show of strength for the Communist-dominated resistance in the city.

Still, as summer ended, German territory was being terribly constricted. The Soviets drove in hard from the east, and Tito's Yugoslav partisans were carving up *Wehrmacht* units in the Balkans. The Fifth and Eighth armies in Italy, although weakened by Dragoon, nibbled through Tuscany toward the Po. And Eisenhower's steadily growing forces pushed into Belgium and, from Switzerland northwestward, established themselves near the Rhine.

For the Allies in France, however, there was insufficient gasoline to fuel a further advance along the front. Montgomery said to Eisenhower: Stop Patton outside Metz, give me his daily fuel allotment and the use of the Al-

General Patton adds a new pistol to his arsenal, somewhere in France, August 22, 1944. His army was racing east from Paris; the sun was shining; he had ample cause to be happy.

Opposite: General de Gaulle marches down the Champs Élysées on his way to mass at Notre Dame, August 26, 1944. This was one of the great scenes of the war; everywhere men and women cried and called out, "Vive la France! Vive de Gaulle!" He said, "These are moments which surpass every one of our poor lives."

lied Airborne Corps, and I'll cross the Rhine north of the Ardennes and get to Berlin before winter. This was the so-called single thrust. Patton said to Eisenhower: Stop Monty in Brussels, give me his daily fuel allotment and the use of the Allied Airborne Corps, and I'll cross the Rhine south of the Ardennes and get to Berlin before winter.

There was a third option. The British had taken the town and docks of Antwerp, Europe's largest port. With Antwerp at work, the supply problem would end. But the Scheldt River leading to the port, nearly a hundred kilometers long, was in German hands, so no ships could get to Antwerp. Eisenhower could have stopped both Montgomery and Patton and put the major

Among the many other blunders of Operation Market-Garden was, as portrayed in the Canadian artist Alex Colville's *Infantry, Near Nijmegen, Holland*, the British decision to attack through the low country, where raised roads were the only way to proceed—easy prey for German 88s.

offensive effort into opening Antwerp. But he felt there was a chance to end the war before winter, and that Montgomery in the north had the better prospects. In early September, Eisenhower told Montgomery to go ahead with Operation Market-Garden.

It was a complex, daring, and dangerous but potentially decisive operation, designed to get Allied forces over the Lower Rhine River in Holland. The plan called for the Guards Armored Division to lead the way for the British Second Army across the Rhine on a line Eindhoven-Son-Veghel-Nijmegen-Arnhem. The British tanks would move north along a single road, following a carpet laid down by British and American paratroopers, who would seize and hold the many bridges between the start line in Brussels and Arnhem.

Market-Garden got off to a good start, but it began to sputter on the second day, when bad weather in England prevented the transport aircraft from bringing more men and supplies to Holland. The Germans fought fiercely. In Arnhem, although a British battalion managed to get the east end of the bridge, the remainder of the British First Airborne Division was cut off and cut up. An operation that had come close to achieving its objective ended up being a dismal failure. The British First Airborne Division went into Arnhem ten thousand strong. Fewer than two thousand came out.

In October, the Americans captured their first German city, Aachen, ancient citadel of Charlemagne. They moved into the Hurtgen Forest, where they battled through snow-covered mine fields, taking heavy losses. Patton, meanwhile, was battering his way into Metz, taking heavy casualties for little gain. These bloody offensives were reminiscent of General Grant's Wilderness Campaign of 1864.

Colville also made a sketch of Nijmegen Bridge. One of the biggest in Europe, it was the last bridge between the ground forces and the British paratroopers in Arnhem. The Eighty-second Airborne seized the bridge on the third afternoon of Market-Garden, but British tanks never got to Arnhem.

A V-2 rocket has just exploded in Antwerp, November 27, 1944. Hitler made Antwerp the primary target of the V-2s after the Allies took the city and began using its docks to bring in men and equipment.

Even as the German Army beat off American attacks against the Siegfried Line, Hitler was planning a counteroffensive. Military logic said he should fall back slowly to the Rhine, then defend that line, but Hitler hated being on the defensive. He lusted to strike out at his enemies, and he rightly felt that only through a brilliant stroke could he bring about a German victory. In 1940 he had broken the French-British defenses by going through the Ardennes. In late 1944 he had more and bigger tanks than in 1940, and a larger army. He began to shift troops from the eastern to the western front in preparation for his last and greatest offensive, its objective to break through the thinly held American line in the Ardennes, then drive onto Antwerp, severing Eisenhower's supply lines and splitting the British on the north from the Americans on the south. Another Dunkirk! Then he could shift his armies east, to fight the Soviets on a single front.

Everything depended on secrecy and bad weather. Hitler could count on surprise, because no one in the Allied camp thought there was the remotest possibility of a German attack. The SHAEF intelligence summary on December 16, 1944, stated: "The enemy is at present fighting a defensive campaign on all fronts; his situation is such that he cannot stage major offensive operations." But the Germans managed to build two army groups opposite the Ardennes, well equipped with new Tiger tanks, without the Allies discovering it. ("Where in hell has this son-of-a-bitch gotten all his strength?" an incredulous Bradley asked. The answer was teenagers; a large number of the German troops Hitler put into the battle were fifteen or sixteen years old). Bad weather was sure to come to northern Europe sometime in the late fall; when it did it would cancel out the Allies' greatest single advantage over

American infantrymen move into Arnhem, September 19, 1944, hoping to relieve Colonel John Frost's battalion, which was holding— barely—the east end of the bridge into the city.

The Battle of the Bulge took its name from the nature of the German penetration of American lines.

BATTLE of the BULGE
16 Dec. 1944–16 Jan. 1945

U.S. forces
- - - - British forces
German forces

0   10   20

the *Wehrmacht*, the command of the air. On December 11 and 12, at his headquarters near Frankfurt, the Führer received the division commanders who would be involved in the crucial operation. So secret had he kept his plan, this was the first the division commanders heard of it.

There were twenty-four divisions altogether, many of them elite panzer, or Waffen SS, units. On December 15 they moved to the take-off line under cover of heavy forest and a continuing fog. On the morning of December 16, eight panzer divisions broke through weak Allied defenses on a seventy-mile front.

The attack was a total surprise and at first achieved astonishing success. One U.S. division in the Ardennes was overrun and destroyed, others nearly so. German tanks pressed westward. There was something akin to panic in the air, as everyone recalled the way the Germans had come through the Ardennes in 1940. But in the field, individuals and small groups of GIs began to fight back, hampering the Germans and disrupting their tight timetable. Conditions were miserable: deep snow, below zero temperatures at night.

At SHAEF, meanwhile, Eisenhower announced that the German offensive was to be regarded as an opportunity rather than as a threat. The Germans had come out of their fortifications and thus made themselves vulnerable. He began moving troops from north and south of the Ardennes into the battle. The 101st Airborne Division got into Bastogne on December 19; the next day it was surrounded. After four days of repelling attacks by as many as six divisions (two of them armored), the 101st still held out. Brigadier General Anthony McAuliffe answered a German surrender demand with the now famous laconic reply: "Nuts."

At Saint Vith, north of Bastogne, the Eighty-second Airborne blocked the German advance toward Antwerp. Eisenhower had Patton change the direction of his attack, from east to north, to relieve the 101st in Bastogne. On Christmas Eve, the skies cleared. The Allies put 10,000 planes in the air; they pounded the Germans. By January 3, 1945, it was the Allies on the offensive. By the end of the month they had driven the Germans back to the original position. Hitler's great gamble had failed.

Germany paid a terrible price—30,000 killed, 40,000 wounded, 40,000 prisoners of war, thousands of tanks destroyed. On the U.S. side, of the 600,000 troops engaged (this was the biggest battle the U.S. Army ever fought), 20,000 were killed, 40,000 wounded, 20,000 made prisoners of war.

Although the Battle of the Bulge ended close to where it started, it was a great victory for the Americans. Hitler had bet too much, and he had lost heavily in men and matériel at a time when he could ill afford to lose any-

Some eighty-six American POWs were slaughtered in a massacre at Malmedy, Belgium, December 17, 1944. News spread along the line with amazing speed: "Germans are shooting POWs."

Men of the 209th Regiment stand out against the snow, Belgium, January 4, 1945. The Germans wore white sheets for camouflage, but the Americans had none. In addition, their winter clothing was inadequate and their boots inferior. As a consequence, the weather caused almost as many casualties as did the Germans.

thing. And now, on the eastern front, the Red avalanche was moving fast. "Those bottom-of-the-barrel reserves that might have slowed the Russian onslaught," wrote Bradley, "had been squandered instead against us in the Ardennes." At the same time, the Allies in the west had been shaken out of all complacency by the viciousness with which the Nazi could strike in his death struggle. Clearly there were still months of savage fighting ahead, but the last hundred days of the "thousand-year" Third Reich had begun.

By January 22, 1945, the Americans, supplied by an endless stream of trucks, were well launched in their counteroffensive to reduce the Bulge. The 101st Airborne had held Bastogne, Belgium, the crossroads town so vital to Hitler; now the Americans were using it to their advantage.

CLOSING IN ON JAPAN

I n the war in the Pacific, quarter was neither asked nor given. The hatred of Japanese for Americans and of Americans for Japanese was very great, possibly exceeding, certainly equaling, that of Germans for Soviets and vice versa.

As the Americans retook the island of Guam in July 1944, for example, Japanese fanaticism was almost unbelievable. Sergeant Alvin Josephy, a U.S. Marine combat correspondent, described a wild, drunken Japanese suicide charge:

Action around two heavy machine guns was typical of what was occurring. A Jap grenade hit one gun, temporarily putting it out of action. . . . The other gun was also silenced. Riflemen in foxholes nearby heard a sudden unearthly screaming from the gun position. By the wavering light of flares, they saw one of the crew members trying to pull a Japanese bayonet out of another Marine's body. The same instant a wave of Japs appeared from nowhere and swept over both men. . . . A Marine automatic rifleman blasted them with his BAR. . . . Two of them fell over the bodies of the Marine crew. The third pulled out a grenade and, holding it to his head, blew himself up. . . . From the darkness a lone, drunken Jap raced headlong at [the Marines], tripped several feet away over a body, and flew through the air. There was a blinding flash as he literally blew apart. He had been a human bomb, carrying a land mine and a blast charge on his waist. . . . A last wave of Japs charged over the top of the hill. It was the wildest, most drunken group of all, bunched together, howling, stumbling and waving swords, bayonets, and long poles. Some were

WARNING

Anybody who damages or attempts to damage in any way the telephone and telegraph wires, power cables, railway equipments, water pipes, roads, bridges and other military installations used by the Japanese Army and Navy shall be shot to death on the spot. November 21, 1944

THE COMMANDER OF
THE IMPERIAL JAPANESE FORCES
IN THE PHILIPPINES .

A month after the invasion of Leyte, the Japanese posted this general warning to the Philippine people (above). The Filipinos had lived under Japanese rule since early 1942 and knew that the Japanese meant what they said; nevertheless, MacArthur's invading army got plenty of help from Filipino guerrillas.

U.S. Army troops (opposite) prepare to go ashore on Hollandia, New Guinea, April 22, 1944. They are on a Higgins Boat, a Landing Craft Vehicle and Personnel (LCVP), with a coast guard crew. The Higgins Boat became one of the symbols of U.S. military might around the world; the boats carried men from ship to shore in every invasion of the war, covering three continents.

already wounded and were swathed in gory bandages. The Marines yelled back at them and chopped them down in their mad rush. In a moment it was over. The last wave of the three-hour attack died to man.

From the Battle of Midway on, the Japanese had no chance of winning, but there were similar scenes in every island battle in the Pacific. Japanese military dictators were prepared to carry on until the entire nation had gone under, rather than accept the humiliation of surrender.

By the end of 1943, the Japanese Empire, which in 1942 covered more square miles than any in history, was shrinking considerably. All the outer island bastions had been reconquered, from the Solomons to the Aleutians. The Allies were pushing slowly forward in the Burmese jungles. Japan's large land army was still bogged down in China. Of all these widespread fronts, by far the most important was that on the ocean itself. In the two years since Pearl Harbor, much to Japan's astonishment, United States industrial energy had produced an incomparable new fleet and new air forces, and the U.S. High Command had developed a technique of island-hopping amphibious advances, moving westward over the Pacific. The Third, Fifth, and Seventh fleets, reorganized in March 1943 by Admiral Ernest J. King, chief of Naval Operations, were assigned special carrier task forces bearing Grumman F6F Hellcat planes that were at last able to outfight the Japanese Zeros. There were also new torpedo planes and dive-bombers. A generation of air-minded commanders had assumed direction of this new kind of naval war: admirals Halsey and Spruance; vice admirals Marc A. Mitscher and John H. Towers; rear admirals Arthur W. Radford, Frederick C. Sherman, Alfred Montgomery, and Charles Pownall. They had devised the famous leapfrog method of circumventing enemy strongholds, harrying them with bombing attacks and landing far behind them on islands that could provide airfields and ports from which to stage further advances. By 1944, thousands of square miles of contested waters had been reconquered. U.S. naval strength had become paramount on the world's seas: some 4,700 vessels, including 613 warships, and more than 18,000 aircraft. By late summer of 1944, almost a hundred U.S. fleet and escort carriers were roaming the Pacific.

From the start, as they planned their offensive, the Joint Chiefs of Staff foresaw that Japan itself would have to be bombed mercilessly prior to any climactic invasion in order to wear down the defending army and disrupt its communications and the ability to move reserves against a landing. At first it was hoped that such an aerial assault could be mounted from eastern China, and blueprints were drawn up for the eventual capture of a South Chinese port to supply such an operation. In 1943, the high command had hoped to work toward this by occupying Luzon, in the Philippines, and Formosa. And though Admiral King originally had wished to save time by bypassing the Philippines, it was decided in March 1944 to take those islands where the United States had suffered such a humiliating defeat.

General MacArthur's long, tough leapfrogging campaign along the northern coast of New Guinea had only one purpose: to bring him closer to the Philippines. As mid-1944 neared, the pace of the campaign quickened. On May 27 landings were made on Biak, a Japanese base off the New Guinea coast, an island honeycombed with caves from which the defenders had to be blasted. On July 30 the final landing began on Vogelkop Peninsula, the western tip of New Guinea. As soon as the enemy was cleared from each site, airfield construction commenced to support the advance toward the Philippines. Plans called for MacArthur to take the island of Morotai to the northwest in mid-September, while Admiral Nimitz, coming through the central Pacific, was seizing the Palaus. Then, using those islands as advance bases, the next move would be against the Philippines.

MacArthur was ordered to prepare a Luzon invasion for February 1945, while Nimitz would simultaneously attack Formosa. Having two, rather than one, major objectives was less a military decision than a political one caused by a divided command. MacArthur insisted that the offensive have its center of gravity in his southwest Pacific theater, while Nimitz pushed for his central Pacific theater. Eventually, to Nimitz's displeasure, the Formosan project was dropped and the date for the Philippine invasion advanced. But first it was necessary to secure more advanced bases in the western Pacific from which to counter Japanese air and naval attacks.

Therefore, on June 15, 1944, just as Eisenhower was consolidating his

GIs from the 163rd Infantry Regiment, 31st Division, hit the beach at Wakde Island, New Guinea, May 17, 1944. Resistance was spotty; by May 20 the island was secure. There were more U.S. Army divisions in the Pacific theater than there were U.S. Marines, but the Marine Corps got most of the publicity, so that few now remember the strength of the army's commitment. Yet the army made more amphibious assaults than did the marines.

B-25s attack a Japanese airfield on Dagua, New Guinea, February 3, 1944. Airfields were unsinkable aircraft carriers, but they were vulnerable to bombers nonetheless. Those the Americans did not overrun, they destroyed.

In November 1942, Vice Admiral Jisaburo Ozawa (above) relieved Admiral Nagumo (below) of his command of the Third Fleet, which contained most of the Japanese carriers. Ozawa commanded the carriers in the Battle of the Philippine Sea and the Battle for Leyte Gulf; he lost three carriers and 350 out of 385 fighters.

U.S. carriers, led by the *Essex*, steam ahead in the South Pacific, November 1944 (opposite). These carriers enabled the Americans to dominate the Pacific waters and became the symbol of U.S. naval power.

Normandy beachhead, Nimitz's forces hit Saipan in the Marianas, some thirteen hundred miles east of the Philippines and more than three thousand miles west of Hawaii. Saipan was defended by 32,000 Japanese under the elderly Lieutenant General Yoshitsugu Saito. An armada of 535 ships, commanded by Admiral Spruance, carried 127,000 men, of whom two thirds were marines.

Four days after the landing, the Japanese fleet streamed into the area, and in a hot, cloudless sky with optimum visibility, the most intensive carrier battle of the war took place. The Japanese fleet had assembled planes and had trained pilots (though poorly, by U.S. standards) to replace its disastrous losses in the fighting around Rabaul. The competent Vice Admiral Jisaburo Ozawa was given the assignment of bringing to battle and destroying the U.S. Pacific Fleet. He headed for Saipan. Although outnumbered fifteen to nine in carriers and in every other type of ship except heavy cruisers, Ozawa's planes outranged the American fleet, and he would have the help of some hundred land-based planes on Guam. The Japanese fleet was the first to locate its foe and began sending out air strikes the morning of June 19. But a U.S. submarine had sighted the Japanese fleet leaving the Philippines heading in the direction of the Marianas and signaled the U.S. fleet, which picked up the Japanese task force on radar (which the Japanese did not have on their ships) when it was still hundreds of miles away. When the Japanese launched their planes against what they thought were unsuspecting Americans, the Americans launched their interceptors and caught the Japanese totally by surprise. Neither fleet ever saw the other.

The battle that resulted was so one sided that it has been dubbed "the Great Marianas Turkey Shoot." In a few hours, Ozawa lost 350 planes, while only 30 U.S. aircraft were downed. Damage to U.S. ships was negligible—one battleship was hit by a single bomb—but while the Turkey Shoot was going on, U.S. submarines sank two Japanese carriers. The fleeing enemy fleet was struck again the next afternoon, at a cost to Ozawa of another carrier, two oilers, and almost all his remaining planes. When American fliers returned in the darkness, almost out of gas, Vice Admiral Marc Mitscher, on board his flagship, the *Lexington,* ordered all ships to turn on their lights despite the danger of Japanese submarines. Eighty planes, out of gas, ditched in the water, but almost all the pilots were rescued. Meanwhile, Ozawa returned to base with only thirty-five planes left. This, the Battle of the Philippine Sea, had been the greatest carrier battle of the war. Never again would Japanese carrier forces be a threat.

The fighting on Saipan itself was ferocious. The Japanese staged successive banzai attacks, particularly against the U.S. Twenty-seventh Division. But the defenders fought with more ardor than skill and in three weeks' time were overwhelmed. Saito himself had no wish to outlive his troops. On July 7, as the end neared, he knelt on the floor of his cave command post and, shouting "Hurrah for the Emperor," stabbed himself with his ceremonial sword. His principal officers followed suit. Admiral Nagumo, who had commanded the carrier strikes at Pearl Harbor and at Midway and was at this time in command of a small-craft fleet at Saipan, shot himself.

The American forces started mopping up isolated pockets of resistance, and when they had finished they counted 23,811 Japanese dead. Among the

A fleet aircraft carrier was a huge and complex creation, an intricately organized floating community of almost three thousand men who were all needed to keep it functioning. Everything about it was in superlatives, from its huge engines to the dial telephone system that connected all rooms. And these ships existed for one single purpose: to get planes into the air and down again. The photographs on these two pages, all made on the second *Lexington,* catch glimpses of life on and around the flight deck. As often as not, that life consisted of waiting and killing time. Clockwise, from upper left: A wounded pilot is taken to sick bay; plane handlers relax, waiting the return of a strike; mechanics overhaul a dive-bomber; an F6F Hellcat gets the signal to take off; all hands take setting-up exercises on the flight deck; a fighter ace indicates six kills.

casualties were hundreds of Japanese civilians who had taken refuge along the pitted line of escarpments on Saipan's northern shore. When they saw that all was lost, they disregarded the surrender appeals of the Americans and set about the ghastly business of mass suicide. In one of the war's most dreadful episodes, they hurled babies down from cliffs and jumped after them, or blew themselves up with grenades. United States losses on Saipan were also heavy: more than 16,000 casualties, including 3,426 deaths.

On July 23, Marine Lieutenant General Holland M. ("Howling Mad") Smith continued the Marianas offensive by seizing Tinian. He had only 195 deaths against almost thirty times that number of Japanese. On August 10, Rear Admiral W. L. Ainsworth reoccupied Guam, the last of the Marianas, after almost three weeks of combat.

Here again there was a tough, swirling struggle. Even cooks and clerks were at times thrown into action when Japanese counterattacks pierced the American lines. Bulldozers sealed hundreds of snipers in caves, while ferocious night banzai charges were cut down by marine riflemen and machine-gunners. When the marines finally entered Agana, the capital of Guam, a combat correspondent reported that they "found nothing there." But there was more than a little joy among the victors when they discovered that Guam had been Japan's main liquor dump for the central Pacific and was rich in Scotch, rye, bourbon, beer, and sake.

Thus by August the Marianas as well as the Gilberts and strategic airfields along the northern coast of New Guinea were in American possession. The British general Orde Wingate's famous raiding forces had chopped deep into northern Burma. Merrill's Marauders, the comparable U.S. force, were working with Chinese troops to safeguard the new Ledo Road, designed to connect South China and Allied bases in India.

But although the Japanese were being slowly driven westward and northward in the waters of the Pacific, on the Asian mainland their strength was largely intact. These mainland forces blocked further advances in Burma. And, fearing the long-range B-29s that the air corps was just bringing into action from India and China, the Japanese overran seven Chinese airfields where Chennault's Fourteenth Air Force had been established to support Chiang Kai-shek. This China offensive was, in fact, the most serious Tokyo managed to launch during the final two years of the war. Driving southward from Hunan Province and westward from Canton, battle-hardened divisions expelled Chiang from much strategically valuable territory and delayed the opening of overland communications between China and Calcutta, India.

One result of Japan's 1944 land campaign in Burma (now also known as Myanmar) and China was a change in the Allied command structure for Southeast Asia. When it was agreed that an American would command the invasion of Europe, the British, who had hoped for Sir Alan Brooke, were somewhat disappointed. As a result, they were given the consolation prize of Southeast Asia, and Lord Louis Mountbatten was placed in charge of that difficult theater. He established headquarters first at Delhi and subsequently at Kandy in Ceylon (now Sri Lanka) and resolved to be as diplomatic as possible with his independent-minded American subordinates, above all the headstrong Stilwell.

MEDICINE IN THE U.S. ARMY

It wasn't any different getting killed in World War II from how it had been in the Civil War or World War I, but if the shrapnel, bullet, or tree limb wounded a GI without killing him, his experience as a casualty was infinitely better than Johnny Reb's or Billy Yank's or a doughboy's, beginning with his survival chances. In 1864, 50 percent or more of men admitted to hospitals died; in 1918, it was 8 percent; in 1944, 4 percent.

Wonder drugs, especially sulfa and penicillin, and advanced surgical techniques helped make the improvements possible, but the first reason for such success was the speed with which wounded men were treated. It began with the medics. In training camps they had been mildly despised because most of them were conscientious objectors, and often ridiculed, called "Pill Pushers" or worse. But in combat they were loved and admired without stint. "Overseas," medic Buddy Gianelloni recalled, "it became different. They called you medic and before you knew it, it was Doc. I was 19 at the time."

The medic's job was to get the wounded away from the front line. That often entailed running out of his foxhole during shelling or into no-man's-land to help a fallen soldier. Once with the wounded man, the medic would do the briefest examination, apply a tourniquet if necessary, inject a vial of morphine, clean up the wound as best he could and sprinkle sulpha powder on it, slap on a bandage, and drag or carry the patient to the rear. This was often done under enemy fire, although generally the Germans respected the Red Cross armband.

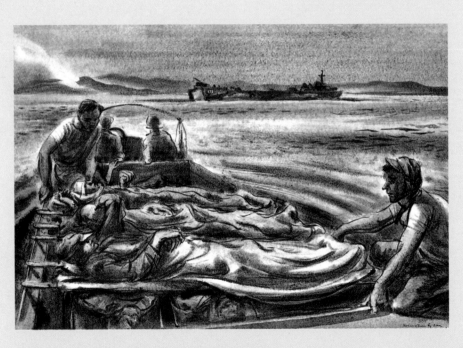

Mitchell Jamieson's *Evacuation by Sea* shows a DUKW taking stretchers of wounded from the beach at Okinawa out to an LST waiting offshore.

It was the universal opinion of the frontline infantry that the medics were the bravest of all. Captain John Colby of the Ninetieth Division commented, "We had so much faith in our medics' ability that we firmly believed we would not die if they got to us in time."

Once the medic got the patient behind the lines, he put him onto a litter or jeep, to be taken back to an aid station, anywhere from a couple of hundred meters to a kilometer or more to the rear. That usually took about fifteen minutes. In early August 1944, Lieutenant Charles Stockell of the Second Infantry Division was hit badly in the leg. A medic treated him, then helped him to the rear and onto a jeep. "I am laid across the hood," Stockell wrote in his diary, "like a slaughtered deer." At the aid station he was stabilized, given plasma, and sent onto an evacuation hospital. His condition was critical, so rather than being admitted after triage, he was marked for evacuation. He traveled by train and ship and after being unconscious for twenty hours woke up in a hospital in England. There he recovered, as did more than 99 percent of the men evacuated from northwest Europe.

Corporal Walter Gordon of the 101st Airborne was hit outside Bastogne on Christmas Eve. The bullet went in the left shoulder and out the right. It had brushed Gordon's spinal column; he was paralyzed from the neck down. A medic gave him morphine and plasma and got him on a jeep. Within minutes he was at the aid station. An hour after he was wounded, he was in an ambulance headed toward an evacuation hospital, where he was immediately marked for air evacuation to England. Once there, the doctors kept him immobile for six weeks. His recovery was not rapid but it was nearly complete. Gordon went on to live a full and successful life thanks to the speed of his treatment.

The less severely wounded were treated in the evacuation hospitals where assembly-line medicine was practiced. During the Normandy battle, ambulances coming from the aid station to the hospital had to line up, three abreast, in lines reaching up to two hundred meters. The doctors worked as rapidly as possible but were only just able to keep up with the litter bearers. The tents had space for a hundred litters and were nearly always filled, with litters bearing wounded on the ground outside. Along the sides of the tent sat the walking wounded. A tag showed whether and how much morphine the casualty had received from the medic. The doctors went from patient to patient, asking questions, scanning each record, lifting the dressing to check each wound.

One nurse, Lieutenant Aileen Hogan, recalled, "I have never worked so hard in my life. The boys get in, get emergency treatment, penicillin and sulfa, and are out again. It is beyond words."

In a letter home, nurse Ruth Hess described setting up an evacuation hospital in the wake of the American sweep through France. "We arrived late in the evening and spent all night getting ready to receive patients, setting up the tents and equipment. Then went to work, for nine days we never stopped. Eight hundred eighty patients operated; small debridement of gunshot and shrapnel wounds, numerous amputations, fractures galore, perforated guts, livers, spleens, kidneys, lungs, everything imaginable. We cared for almost 1,500 patients in those nine days." Then the hospital packed and moved forward, closer to the front.

Medics help a wounded soldier in France, 1944. If a casualty was still alive when the medics got to him, he had an excellent chance of survival. They could do the necessary in a matter of seconds: stop the bleeding, lessen the pain, apply a bandage, and head toward an aid station.

Because the hospitals were in the combat zones, they kept black-out conditions. Lieutenant Aileen Hogan described how that affected her nursing duties:

At 1900 hours all the penicillin needed for the first round is mixed and two technicians and one nurse make the rounds of the hospital, giving penicillin to the patients. One loads the syringes and changes needles, the other two give the hypos. It is an art to find your way around at night, not a glimmer of light anywhere, no flashlights of course, the tents just a vague silhouette against the darkness, ropes and tent pins a constant menace, syringes, and precious medications balanced precariously on one arm.

Behind the evacuation hospitals were field hospitals, where most of the wounded were brought for treatment and recovery. The doctors were magnificent. Their patients were often mangled beyond imagination. Their minds went numb. "Legs off, arms off, faces shot away, eviscerations, chests ripped open, and so on," one doctor commented. "I've never seen such horrible wounds. We worked at top speed, hour after hour, until we were too tired to stand up—and then we still kept going." Because the doctors and nurses kept working even when their tents were under enemy fire, tens of thousands of wounded GIs survived.

A U.S. Navy chaplain reads a service for three dead Japanese on a Saipan beach, June 24, 1944. His altar is laid on the front of a knocked-out Japanese tank. On Saipan, 29,000 of the 32,000 Japanese defenders died, many of them in suicidal charges fueled by sake and fanaticism.

This was no easy undertaking. Stilwell's own diaries confirmed, posthumously, that he felt scant loyalty either to the dashing royal admiral, whom he somewhat scornfully called "Loooie," or to Mountbatten's plans. Nor, for that matter, did Stilwell's successor, Major General Albert C. Wedemeyer, improve relations much, despite his more agreeable manners. Stilwell was recalled in late 1944, and to improve operational control after the Japanese drive, his former command was divided between Wedemeyer, in charge of the China theater under Chiang, and Lieutenant General Daniel I. Sultan, another American, in charge of the Burma-India theater.

Despite their resurgence in China and their relative success in holding the Burma front, the Japanese saw quite plainly that their fate hung upon the outcome of the Pacific Ocean campaign. Following the loss of Saipan and the obvious harbinger of disaster in the first B-29 raids on Japan, the Tojo government fell. It was replaced by a cabinet, under the venerable General Kuniaki Koiso, that was clearly lacking in confidence of final victory.

At this juncture the United States amphibious giant leapt forward once again, ignoring the isolated Japanese strongholds of Truk and Rabaul far to the east and striking the Palau Islands in the direction of the Philippines. This offensive opened at Peleliu in mid-September 1944. Some forty-five thousand marines and soldiers hit the tiny island and were immediately faced with stiff resistance. The brutal, difficult battle lasted a month. It is not much remembered today, except by the marines, who said later that Peleliu was the toughest fight they had in the island campaigns, even including Iwo

Jima and Okinawa. A particularly effective defense was put up by the island garrison along a cave-pocked massif dubbed "Bloody Nose Ridge" by the Americans, who suffered almost eighteen hundred dead and another eight thousand wounded. More than eleven thousand Japanese were killed.

Slowly the gateway to the Philippines was opening. That sprawling cluster of islands held the strategic key to Southeast Asia, the South China coast, and Japanese Formosa. In an effort to gain Filipino cooperation, Tokyo had established a puppet government in October 1943 under Jose Laurel, a rich, nationalistic, and anti-American politician. However, his regime failed to gain any substantial popularity. With the assistance of American agents, armed resistance movements sprang up in the mountains, in hinterland villages, and, underground, in some cities. As early as March 1944, Imperial General Headquarters acknowledged that "even after their independence, there remains among all classes in the Philippines a strong undercurrent of pro-American sentiment . . . something steadfast, which cannot be destroyed. . . . Guerrilla activities are gradually increasing."

Defense of the archipelago was in the hands of Field Marshal Hisaichi Terauchi, whose main combat strength was the Fourteenth Army under General Tomoyuki Yamashita, Japan's most celebrated general. Yamashita, who had conquered Singapore, bragged that he would issue to MacArthur the same ultimatum he had presented to British General Percival: "All I want to know from you is yes or no." The Japanese had established numerous strongpoints, airfields, and naval bases throughout the islands, but their primary concern was to hold Luzon at all costs.

Tokyo very properly assumed that MacArthur had meant what he said in 1942 when he had promised to return to the Philippines. Imperial Headquarters had drawn up the plan—called *Sho-Go* ("Victory Operation")—for a "general decisive battle" that was to smash any U.S. assault along the vast island chain starting at the Philippines in the south and ending at the Kuril Islands in the north. The operation was to start just as soon as the intentions of the Allies became clear.

On October 6, 1944, the Japanese ambassador in Moscow learned from the Soviet foreign office that the U.S. Fourteenth and Twentieth Air Forces were about to start heavy bombing offensives designed to cut off the Philippines. After studying U.S. fleet movements and spotting a large assemblage of transports near Hollandia (now Djajapura) and Wakde, off the north coast of New Guinea, Imperial Headquarters calculated that the invasion would aim at Leyte and would begin during the final ten days of October.

Tokyo was right. However, for fear of committing his main fleet too soon, before being certain of MacArthur's precise target, Admiral Toyoda, the cautious Japanese naval commander, did not begin to move his forces until U.S. warships were discerned approaching Leyte Gulf, north of Mindanao. It took four days before the Imperial Fleet was in position to make its final challenge against the U.S. Third and Seventh fleets.

American preparation for the landing had been careful and extensive. The offensive brought together the two Pacific offensives—MacArthur up from New Guinea and Nimitz through the central Pacific—for the first time. All through mid-October, air strikes hammered up and down the Philippines. Admiral Mitscher's Task Force 38 attacked Japanese airfields as far to

OVERLEAF: Three U.S. Marine divisions and one U.S. Army division fought on Peleliu, during September 1944, in what was one of the toughest and bloodiest battles in Marine Corps history. The Japanese made excellent use of the hundreds of caves that provided natural bunkers within the jungle. Night brought banzai charges as the Japanese poured from their caves. During the day, they would pop up from their caves and bunkers to fire, then disappear. It took napalm and flamethrowers to drive them out or suffocate them.

the north as Formosa, destroying or crippling an estimated 3,000 Japanese aircraft. But only after the first large elements of MacArthur's liberating army had landed on Leyte did the Imperial Navy begin its desperate riposte. In the last days of October, some 70 Japanese warships and 716 planes, split into three separate commands, opposed 166 U.S. warships and 1,280 planes in one of the greatest naval battles of all time, the Battle for Leyte Gulf.

The landings were not difficult, but they brought out the Japanese Navy in its last big bid for victory. The action, lasting from October 23 to 27, 1944, was complex, but basic Japanese strategy was to lure the U.S. Third Fleet away with a northern force made up largely of empty carriers; meanwhile, Vice Admiral Takeo Kurita, whose Singapore fleet then constituted 60 percent of Tokyo's major naval units, was to take his central force through San Bernardino Strait between Luzon and Samar and come down into Leyte Gulf from the north. At the same time, a smaller southern force under Vice Admiral Shoji Nishimura was to come through Surigao Strait and enter Leyte Gulf from the south. The beachhead with its unloading ships, caught between the two of them, would be wiped out, and so would Kinkaid's Seventh Fleet. Then when Halsey returned, they would fall on him and destroy him.

The central force had two cruisers sunk and a third damaged by U.S. submarines on October 23. The next day, planes of Halsey's Third Fleet attacked the central force, sinking a battleship and sending a damaged cruiser home, while Japanese land-based planes mortally wounded the light carrier *Princeton*. But now Halsey discovered the decoy northern force and set off in full cry, forgetting all else. At the same time, Admiral Kinkaid of the U.S. Seventh Fleet, guessing correctly that another enemy force would approach from the south, steamed to Surigao Strait, where his battleships and cruisers blew the southern force to bits as it came in range.

On October 25, the central force entered Leyte Gulf. It had suffered damage but was still very strong, and the two U.S. fleets that could have protected the invasion beaches were far away. But the Japanese had charged almost into the middle of a force of escort aircraft carriers. The battle should have been completely one-sided, but the Americans, though badly hurt—a carrier and three destroyers sunk—were able to sink three enemy cruisers and so confused the Japanese that they withdrew without shelling the invasion beaches. Meanwhile, Halsey was chasing the decoy force far to the north. His planes sank four carriers, a cruiser, and two destroyers, but he finally had to answer urgent pleas for help from the escort carriers. He arrived too late either to help or to intercept any ships of the retiring central force.

The next day, Admiral Kurita brought his central force, still powerful and consisting of four battleships, six cruisers, and numerous destroyers, through San Bernardino Strait and found himself near a force of sixteen escort carriers with their destroyer escorts. The carriers were divided into three tactical units; one, called Taffy Three and commanded by Rear Admiral Clifton Sprague, almost immediately came under fire from the guns of the Japanese force. After a heroic battle, in which the planes of all sixteen carriers as well as the destroyers of Taffy Three took part, Kurita finally broke off the action. One U.S. carrier and three destroyers had been sunk and other ships badly hurt, but three enemy cruisers had also gone down.

Kurita could have gone in and shelled the defenseless beaches, but instead he turned and retired west. Later he explained that intercepted messages had led him to believe a large American force was on its way to cut him off.

Halsey to the north meanwhile had discovered Ozawa's decoy force and exacted swift revenge. He sank four carriers, a cruiser, and two destroyers. Thus, in the entire series of battles off Leyte, Japan suffered immense naval losses, which it could ill afford. Unfortunately, despite the magnitude of this great victory, it soon became a matter of acid argument among the admirals. Just the way Bradley and Patton blamed Montgomery for allowing the encircled Germans in Normandy to flee through the Falaise gap, Kinkaid blamed Halsey for falling for the Japanese trick and not blocking the San Bernardino Strait. Through that strait the badly mauled Kurita was able to escape with four capital ships, about all Tokyo had left. Halsey in turn resented that he could not finish off Ozawa's force but had to return urgently southward to help out Kinkaid. In any case, the strategic results of the combined victory were enormous. The naval power that Japan had first established in 1905 by sinking a mighty Soviet fleet was finally and irreparably crushed.

The Battle for Leyte Gulf marked the first appearance of kamikaze, or suicide, planes. On October 19, Vice Admiral Takijiro Ohnishi had met with senior commanders at Mabalacat fighter base in the Philippines and announced: "With so few planes we can assure success only through suicide attack. Each fighter must be armed with a 550-pound bomb and crash-land on a carrier deck." This was the origin of the technique of kamikaze, which is Japanese for "divine wind." The word refers to a typhoon that blew away a Mongol fleet which had sailed to invade Japan in the Middle Ages.

Even while Admiral Clifton Sprague's carriers of Taffy Three were fighting with Kurita's force, the escort carrier *Santee* of Rear Admiral Thomas Sprague's Taffy One, a few miles away, was hit by a suicide plane. It thus became the first ship to be crashed by a kamikaze. The time was 7:40 A.M. Soon after, another kamikaze hit the *Suwannee* in the same force. Then, just before eleven o'clock, when Kurita had turned away and Taffy Three was counting her wounds, she came under attack. Five kamikazes either did minor damage to carriers or were shot down, but a sixth crashed through the flight deck of the *St. Lo*, set off bomb and torpedo explosions, and sent her to the bottom. Thus Japan first tested what was to become one of her most terrible weapons.

The kamikaze pilots pressed home their attack with great persistence and resolve. From that moment until the war was actually ending, it was considered a great privilege among some young Japanese airmen to volunteer for these one-way missions. (There is considerable evidence that by no means were all kamikaze pilots volunteers, but many did their duty and obeyed the orders to fly into the U.S. ships.) Farewell letters written by these pilots to their families have since been collected. One said: "Think kindly of me and consider it my good fortune to have done something praiseworthy." Another sadly reflected: "Every man is doomed to go his own way in time." Still another pilot concluded the last page of his diary: "Like cherry blossoms/In the spring/Let us fall/Clean and radiant." All were in their early twenties.

Together, Admiral William "Bull" Halsey (above) and Admiral Thomas Kinkaid (below) won the Battle of Leyte Gulf.

The USS *Kalinen Bay* is under attack by the Japanese fleet off Leyte Gulf, October 25, 1944 (above). Near misses shower the deck with water, as smoke from the stacks help in screening the escort carrier from the enemy. Vice Admiral Takijiro Ohnishi (opposite top) had conceived of the idea of using kamikaze attacks at the Battle of Leyte Gulf. Japanese artist Usaburo Ihara painted this scene (opposite bottom) of a Japanese Special Attack Unit—kamikaze, or "divine wind"—taking off to attack the American fleet in the Philippines. Not all the pilots were volunteers, not all the enthusiasm was as spontaneous as it appears in this idealized version. Still, the kamikazes did terrible damage.

Although they could not turn the tide of war and although they were shot down in droves by the protecting U.S. aircraft and by concerted anti-aircraft fire of the vessels that they attacked, the kamikazes did great damage, above all later on at Okinawa. Before the conflict ended the following August, the kamikaze special attack corps had sunk or damaged more than three hundred U.S. ships and had exacted some fifteen thousand casualties. On the eve of the final surrender, when he committed hara-kiri, Ohnishi, who had first conceived of the idea of a flying suicide corps, wrote: "They fought well and died valiantly with faith in our ultimate victory. In death I wish to atone for my part in the failure to achieve that victory. I apologize to the souls of those dead fliers and to their bereaved families."

The liberation of the Philippines was now well begun. Carrying out the pledge he had made at Corregidor, MacArthur had returned and planted the Stars and Stripes on Filipino soil, nine hundred forty-eight days after he had been ordered to leave by President Roosevelt. On October 20, the charismatic old general waded ashore on the Leyte beach of Palo, and shortly afterward, in a sudden monsoon rain, he stood by a truck-mounted microphone and broadcast: "This is the Voice of Freedom, General MacArthur speaking. People of the Philippines: I have returned! . . . At my side is your president, Sergio Osmena, worthy successor of that great patriot Manuel Quezon, with members of his cabinet. The seat of your government is now, therefore, firmly re-established on Philippine soil."

Yamashita managed to reinforce his garrison, and the last grim phase of the Asian campaign started. On October 21, MacArthur occupied Tacloban airport. By early November, he had expelled his enemies from the island's southern and northeastern sectors. By now the guerrilla movement was producing aid on Leyte and becoming increasingly active on the other islands. The Japanese sought desperately to contain and reverse MacArthur's surge and, despite their loss of control over the sea passages, attempted to bring up reinforcements. However, on the night of December 6–7, almost exactly three years after their first raids on the Philippines, they lost six warships crammed with soldiers and supplies. The following week, an additional three transports were sunk, and Yamashita's position became hopeless.

General MacArthur lives up to his pledge—"I shall return"—at Leyte, in the Phillippines, October 20, 1944. He waded ashore twice, to make certain Army Signal Corps photographers got the picture.

After Leyte, the next big move was into Luzon, Manila's island. But first, as a stepping-stone, to provide airfields to protect the long, exposed route to the invasion area, landings were made on Mindoro on December 15. The Luzon landings began January 9, 1945, in Lingayen Gulf. Opposition was light, but the voyage there had been a nightmare because kamikaze suicide planes appeared. On February 3, American troops reached the suburbs of Manila and freed some 5,000 Allied prisoners, but it took until March 4 to clear the city, for the 20,000 Japanese fought almost to the last man. In the house-to-house struggle, Manila was almost destroyed. Corregidor fell on February 26, after holding out ten days against paratroops who dropped on the island while destroyers just offshore blew up pillboxes and fired directly into caves full of Japanese. After that, it was a matter of flushing out scattered Japanese from mountain and jungle, a task that was still going on in the Philippines when the Japanese signed the instrument of surrender of September 2. The Japanese lost over 300,000 men in the Philippines, but tens of thousands of Japanese troops fled to the jungles and U.S. forces were still fighting there against these holdouts when the war ended.

By the time the Leyte struggle ended, the Japanese had lost 56,263 men against only 2,888 Americans, an impressively disproportionate victory. Only 389 Japanese had, however, surrendered. Marshal Terauchi, lacking the necessary naval support to move his troops from one island pocket to another and hammered by constant aerial attacks, withdrew to the Asian mainland and established headquarters in Saigon.

An unknown GI in Manila rescues a wounded Filipino girl, February 1945. Manila saw some of the worst street fighting of the war. The Japanese utilized both the city's old Spanish buildings and its modern ones built by the Japanese; MacArthur forbade the use of air bombardment against the city, hoping to spare it, but Japanese resistance forced the Americans to bring in the heavy artillery. Virtually the entire city was destroyed; some 100,000 Filipino civilians lost their lives.

In his report on the war, General George Marshall recalled that at the end of the Leyte battle, men of the U.S. Thirty-second Division found a letter written by an unknown Japanese soldier. It read:

> I am exhausted. We have no food. The enemy are now within 500 meters of us. Mother, my dear wife and son, I am writing this letter to you by dim candle light. Our end is near. What will be the future of Japan if this island should fall into enemy hands? Our air force has not arrived. . . . Hundreds of pale soldiers of Japan are awaiting our glorious end and nothing else. This is a repetition of what occurred in the Solomons, New Georgia and other islands. How well are the people of Japan prepared to fight the decisive battle with the will to win. . . ?

By the time the fighting in Leyte Gulf and on Leyte Island was over not only did the Philippines lie open but Japan itself was naked, unprotected by its customary shield of naval power, exposed to assault from almost anywhere. The answer to the Japanese soldier's question would come soon—and terribly.

General MacArthur and entourage ride on a PT boat off the Philippines, 1945. He had escaped in 1942 via a PT boat; he returned the same way. His detractors liked to say, "MacArthur got back to the Philippines with the help of the Navy and a few Marines."

No rows of white crosses mark the graves of men who pay the price of victory—and defeat—at sea. Those who die on the deep lie in the deep. Wrapped in their canvas shrouds, the bodies of coastguardsmen from the crew of the troop transport *Callaway* await commitment to the ocean. They were some of the hundreds of navy men killed by kamikaze attacks during the invasion at Luzon's Lingayen Gulf.

CHAPTER 19

SMASHING THE THIRD REICH

Following the Allied victory in the Battle of the Bulge, the Nazi position was hopeless. Germany was going to be overrun, occupied, forced to accept an unconditional surrender. Far better to surrender and save what could be saved than to drag the whole nation down in a *Götterdämmerung*. But Hitler would never surrender, and so strong was the grip of the Nazi Party on the German nation and its army that they fought on with such determination that the last months of the European war were the worst in terms of lives lost and property destroyed.

On January 3, Eisenhower's armies went over to the offensive in the last stages of the Bulge. On January 6, 1945, Churchill asked Stalin in a special message to renew the Red Army offensive and thus relieve pressure on the western front. In SHAEF's view it was a most unfortunate message, as it gave the impression that the Western Allies needed to be saved by the Soviets.

Worse followed: when Stalin promised a new thrust along the Vistula, Churchill wired: "May all good fortune rest upon your noble venture." It would have been a much nobler venture had it come four months earlier, when an uprising of the Polish underground Home Army, first encouraged by Moscow, was denied desperately needed Soviet aid. Stalin wanted all home-grown patriotic Polish leaders eliminated and was quite pleased that the Nazis were doing it for him. So as intense battles raged inside Warsaw, Stalin held his armies on the east bank of the Vistula, dismissing the Polish uprising as an "adventuristic affair." The Red Army made no attempt to cross the Vistula and enter the capital until the Nazis had crushed the rebellion early in October. As many as 250,000 Poles died. The Germans leveled more

Above, painter Edward Ardizzone who was with British units in north Germany captured a typical village scene (detail). At the end of the war SS or Nazi Youth would sometimes put up resistance; when they did, the Allies destroyed their villages. So most civilians tried to surrender before a fight could get started. Opposite, *Wehrmacht* POWs march west to prison camps while American forces roll eastward on the Autobahn, somewhere in central Germany, April 1945. Such scenes were commonplace.

533

than 85 percent of the city, then sent 600,000 residents, virtually the entire surviving population, to concentration camps. One desperate Polish patriot wrote:

> We are waiting for thee, red pest,
> To deliver us from black death.

On January 12, the Soviet drive began on a huge front between the Danube and the Baltic. The most famous Soviet commanders were engaged: Zhukov, Rokossovski, Vassilevski, Konev. The target was Berlin. As described in the official Soviet history, the Soviets had now mustered an overwhelming superiority over the Germans: "5.5 times more men, . . . 7.8 times more guns, 5.7 times more tanks, and 17.6 times more planes." They ground on across Poland and into the Prussian province of Brandenburg.

Hungary, which since 1943 had sought intermittently to sign an armistice with the West in secret negotiations at Istanbul, surrendered to Moscow on January 20, 1945. Nazi units, however, held on in Budapest until February 13, ruining that splendid city in the process. The Yugoslav partisans and a few regiments of Bulgarians, who had now turned against Hitler, joined the Red Army as it smashed up into Austria. Subservient governments were established by Soviet henchmen in Sofia, Bucharest, Budapest. Coalitions clearly dominated by Communists took over in Poland, Yugoslavia, and the Slovakian portion of Czechoslovakia.

By early 1945, the military situation required the principal Allied leaders to meet for the purpose of making basic decisions on the shape of the postwar world. Roosevelt had put off such decision making as long as possible—a brilliant piece of international statecraft on his part, because inevitably when the three leaders of the Grand Alliance sat down to divide the spoils of victory they were going to have major disagreements. Churchill wanted to preserve the British Empire. Roosevelt wanted to end European colonialism. But the two Western leaders agreed on their desire for a free, self-governing Poland and the establishment of democracies throughout Europe. Stalin wanted just the opposite: to impose Communist dictatorships, responsible to him, in the ancient capitals of central, southern, and eastern Europe.

The site chosen for this biggest and most fateful summit meeting of World War II was Yalta, on the Black Sea shore, in the Soviet Union's liberated Crimea. On February 4, Roosevelt, Churchill, and Stalin gathered with their staffs in palaces that once were used by vacationing czars but which by then were in a sorry state, due to the German occupation. The palaces themselves were still standing, but the rest of Yalta had been destroyed. (Roosevelt was outraged by this "reckless, senseless fury" of the Nazis, as he was later to report to Congress.) Indeed, the Soviet government had to requisition furniture, chambermaids, and waiters from Moscow's principal hotels and hastily dispatch them to the Crimea in order to make its guests comfortable.

The agenda covered the world, but it began with the country where the war began, Poland. Speaking for the West, Roosevelt's Secretary of State James Byrnes declared, "Our objective is a government in Poland both friendly to the Soviet Union and representative of all the democratic elements of the country."

Participants at the Yalta Conference sit for a formal portrait (opposite). Behind the Big Three are the diplomats, Anthony Eden of Great Britain, Edward Stettinius of the United States, Alexander Cadogan of Great Britain, Vyacheslav Molotov of the Soviet Union, and Averell Harriman of the United States. According to Roosevelt's critics, he gave away too much to Stalin at Yalta. According to his defenders, he got the best deal he could for Poland and other central European nations.

DEFEAT of GERMANY
December 1944–May 1945

⟵ U.S. forces   ⟵ Allied forces

✳ major fighting   ■ concentration camp

0   50   100

North Sea

DENMARK

• Copenhagen

• Flensburg

• Kiel

• Rostock

Hamburg
3 May

Bremerhaven

Lübeck

Wismar

Schwerin

Schwerin •

Stettin •

Emden

Oldenburg

Ravensbrück ■

**NETHER-
LANDS**

Bremen
26 April

Elbe

CAN. FIRST

Hanover
1 April

Stendal •

Berlin
22 April-2 May

BR. SECOND

Brunswick

Potsdam

Amsterdam •

Münster in
Westfalen

Osnabrück •

Luckenwalde •

Frankfurt an

Utrecht •

Arnhem •

U.S. NINTH

Magdeburg •

Wittenberg •

Oder

Nijmegen •

Düsseldorf
2 March

Kassel
4 April

*HARZ
MTS.*

Halle •

Torgau •

Gör

Antwerp •

Lippstadt •

Dresden •

Line 7

Cologne
7 March

Liége •

Aachen •

Erfurt •

Buchenwald ■

Leipzig •

Chemnitz •

ORE MTS.

BELGIUM

Bonn •

U.S. FIRST

Eisenach •

Line 7 May

BOHEMIAN FOREST

Namur •

Remagen

U.S. THIRD

8-19 March

25 Dec.

Rochefort •

St-Vith •

Coblenz •

Hof •

Prague •

Bastogne •

Mainz •

Coburg •

Frankfurt am-Main •

Main

Pilsen
6 May

CZEC

Vianden •

Rhine

GERMANY

Budweis •

Martelange •

LUX.

Worms •

Nuremberg
20 April

Trier
2 March

Regensburg •

Metz •

Mannheim
29 March

Danube

U.S. SEVENTH

Mautha

Verdun •

Line 15 Dec.

Nancy •

Stuttgart
22 April

Linz
5 May

Strasbourg •

Dachau ■

Munich
30 April

Moselle

Ulm •

Colmar 3 Feb.

FRENCH FIRST

Salzburg
4 May

Mulhouse •

Berchtesgaden
4 May

AUST

Basel •

Innsbruck
3 May

FRANCE

Graz •

• Bern

SWITZERLAND

*Brenner
Pass*

• Dijon

ALPS

U.S. FIFTH

BR. EIGHTH

ITALY

YUG

As this map illustrates, the Allies were pouring enormous forces into Germany in the first months of 1945. Berlin was the number one prize. The Soviets got there first, primarily because Eisenhower refused to engage in a race for Berlin, which he feared would cause a hundred thousand casualties "for a prestige objective." Instead, once over the Rhine and after the Ruhr encirclement was complete, he stopped the U.S. Ninth Army along the Elbe River and sent his main striking forces south, to cross over the Austrian Alps before the Nazis could set up a defensive position there.

Roosevelt meets with his principal advisers at Yalta: (from left to right) John Winant, U.S. Ambassador to Great Britain; Edward Stettinius; and Harry Hopkins. Administration policy was first of all to hold the Big Three together until Hitler's defeat was final. Roosevelt hoped to hold it together after peace came, and to bring genuine freedom to the nations of central and eastern Europe liberated by the Red Army. These turned out to be incompatible goals.

It was an impossible program. Any democratic government in Poland would be anti-Soviet. Stalin knew this and made it clear to Churchill and Roosevelt. At Yalta, he told them, "For the Russian people, the question of Poland is not only a question of honor but also a question of security. Throughout history, Poland has been the corridor through which the enemy has passed into Russia. Poland is a question of life and death for the Soviet Union." He insisted on boundary changes that gave the Russians gains in eastern Poland while moving Poland's western border to give Poland Silesia, Pomerania, and East Prussia. From six to nine million Germans would be forced out.

As to the Polish government, Stalin had broken with the Polish government-in-exile in London over the Katyn Forest massacre, and just before going to Yalta he had recognized the so-called Lublin government, a Soviet puppet he had created in 1943. Churchill and Roosevelt tried to retrieve the situation by insisting on free elections and a broadly based Polish government that would include major figures from the London government. They believed that they had achieved a miracle when Stalin agreed to "free and unfettered elections as soon as possible on the basis of universal suffrage and secret ballot," and also to "reorganize" the Polish government by bringing in Poles from London.

When Roosevelt reported to Congress on Yalta, he stressed Stalin's promise of free elections and thus fed soaring American expectations about the shape of postwar Europe. The liberated nations would be democratic, with a market economy. But before the year was out it was obvious that Stalin had only given a face-saving formula to Roosevelt. He had no intention of carrying out his agreements. Throughout the vast stretches of east and central Europe occupied by the Red Army, Stalin suppressed freedom of speech, assembly, religion, and the press through his satellite governments. Not until fifty years after Yalta did the Poles get to hold those free elections.

As a result, the American people felt a sense of betrayal. Amazingly, many of them blamed Roosevelt. Senator Joseph R. McCarthy of Wisconsin later charged that Roosevelt had committed treason when he "gave" Poland to Stalin. Such charges were nonsense. There was nothing Roosevelt or Churchill could do to force Stalin to live up to his word, or in any other way to influence his behavior in Poland. Power is the man on the spot with the gun in his hand. In Poland, that "man" was in the Red Army. That was the essential fact. Thus was Poland freed of Hitler only to get Stalin in the saddle.

At Yalta, a major aim of Roosevelt was to get the Soviet Union involved in the war against Japan. In return he was prepared to make concessions to Stalin in Manchuria. Roosevelt's critics later charged that he had sold out Chiang Kai-shek and the Nationalist Chinese just as he sold out Poland, but in truth there was nothing Roosevelt could do to hold back the Red tide in northern Asia, any more than he could move the Red Army out of Poland. No one could argue with Stalin's fundamental premise (as he put it to Tito): "This war is unlike all past wars. Whoever occupies a territory imposes his own social system. Everyone imposes his system as far as his army can advance." And, westward into Europe, eastward into Asia, he was resolved to impose the Communist system.

At Yalta, the Big Three ratified previous agreements made between the foreign ministers about the shape of postwar Germany. These agreements divided Germany into four zones of occupation (the Big Three plus France), with Berlin inside the Soviet zone but divided into four sectors. Although they could not agree on a fixed amount of reparations to be extracted from Germany by the Soviets, it was accepted that Germany would provide labor as well as funds for reconstruction.

Appended to these accords were three secret understandings. The British, Americans, and Soviets agreed to exchange each other's liberated prisoners and—more cynically—to repatriate each other's civilians as they were rounded up in Germany. This, of course, meant a Western obligation to send back to the Soviet Union many thousands of deserters and political refugees, most of them to certain death. The second secret understanding arranged a voting formula with a veto for permanent members in the Security Council of the proposed United Nations. In the third secret understanding, the Soviet Union formally promised to enter the war with Japan "in two or three months after Germany has surrendered."

Men of XV Corps, Seventh U.S. Army, stand atop a captured 274-millimeter railroad gun, April 10, 1945. This monster could hurl a 300-pound shell more than twenty kilometers.

While the political leaders talked in Yalta, their armies squeezed Germany ever tighter. Everywhere Hitler exhorted his troops to stand fast; everywhere they were overwhelmed. In the west, Hitler had an opportunity to pull his troops back behind the Rhine River, blow up all the bridges, and dare the Allies to cross. Instead, he ordered "no retreat," which gave Eisenhower's artillery and infantry an opportunity (gleefully seized) to kill Germans west of the Rhine. By the end of February, the Allied armies were closing the Rhine from its mouth to its source. At Cologne, and elsewhere, as Eisenhower's men got to the river, the Germans blew up the bridges.

South of Cologne, however, on March 7, when the U.S. Ninth Armored Division closed on the massive Ludendorff Bridge at Remagen, to the amazement of the Americans it stood intact. In one of the most daring actions of the war, GIs dashed across the bridge in the face of intense machine-gun fire, even as the Germans tried to blow it up, and took the bridge intact. The Allies were across the Rhine. Eisenhower rushed reinforcements to the bridgehead, and Hitler was furious. He set up a special court-martial to try the officers in charge of the bridge, and four of them were executed. He then fired Rundstedt and replaced him with Kesselring, who later said: "Never was there more concentrated bad luck at one place than at Remagen."

From then on, the German collapse accelerated on all fronts. In northern Italy, the U.S. Fifth and British Eighth armies launched a new spring offensive against the twenty-six German divisions that were holding a line along the Po and the passes leading northward into Austria. British troops north of Remagen got over the Rhine, as did Patton's troops to the south.

To the east, meanwhile, by April 13, the Soviet juggernaut had taken Vienna. Three days later, far to the north, it began to storm in force across the Oder River. By April 21, Zhukov reached the outskirts of Berlin, and the European war's last great battle started. Marshal Ivan Konev in his memoirs recalled that he and Zhukov had been summoned to the Kremlin on April 1 and told that "the Anglo-American command was preparing an operation aimed at capturing Berlin and with the object of capturing it before the Soviet Army." Stalin then turned to his two greatest marshals and asked: "So who's going to take Berlin then, we or the Allies?"

Somewhere in Germany, March 26, 1945, Eisenhower, Patton, Bradley, and Hodges share one of the lighter moments of the war in Europe. To the victor belongs the smiles— their armies were over the Rhine.

GIs of the Third Armored Division, U.S. First Army, advance through the ruins of Cologne, March 8, 1945. The towers of the famous cathedral stand undamaged. St. Paul's in London also survived despite widespread destruction around it. Some said its endurance was the result of divine intervention. Others said it was a tribute to how well medieval craftsmen built their cathedrals.

Artillery from the U.S. Seventh Army—155-millimeter howitzers—blasts a German observation post, March 13, 1945. By this stage of the war one of the strengths of the U.S. Army was its coordination between infantry and artillery. Forward observers called back to the batteries, either by telephone or radio, giving the coordinates of a target. When the shells began to hit, the observers called back corrections. Then the artillery blasted away. Such "directed fire" could be devastating.

Meanwhile, from their Rhineland bridgehead, the Allies swept northward to encircle and reduce the Ruhr, Germany's industrial heartland. Concentrating on speed and low casualties, the Supreme Allied Commander Eisenhower conducted the campaign like a chess champion. His Ninth and First armies joined east of the Ruhr and captured that sprawling complex of factories and four hundred thousand German troops. His Sixth Army Group swung southward toward Switzerland and on to the Austrian border. The Twelfth Army Group ground eastward to the Elbe, for a meeting with the Soviets.

At this junction, Churchill pressed Eisenhower to provide Montgomery's British troops with sufficient fuel and ammunition to drive across the north German plain to Berlin. He wanted to get to the city before the Red Army got there. He told Eisenhower that the Soviets were about to liberate Vienna, adding, "If they also take Berlin, will not their impression that they have been the overwhelming contributor to our common victory be unduly imprinted in their minds?" He stated that he deemed it best that Allied and Soviet troops "shake hands as far east as possible."

But Eisenhower thought it madness to send his forces dashing toward Berlin when there was little, if any, chance that they would arrive before the Red Army got there. Eisenhower also wanted a clearly recognizable demarcation line as the armies closed in from east and west, so that when his men met the Soviets there would be no incidents of friendly fire exchanges. And he

The Americans just kept coming. U.S. Army tanks roll across the Ludendorff Bridge at Remagen, March 7, 1945 (above). In one of the great feats of arms in the war, men from the U.S. Ninth Armored Division captured the bridge intact. They were lucky—the wire leading to the Germans' demolitions had been cut by a stray bullet—but they were also very good and very brave troops.

The U.S. Army enters Dusseldorf, Germany, April 17, 1945 (right). More than 300,000 Germans in the Ruhr pocket had just surrendered, and the city was open to its conquerors. It thus escaped the worst of the destruction that came down on most cities along the Rhine, especially Cologne, just to the south.

Standing amid advancing U.S. Seventh Army troops, an old German woman, in despair, surveys the hopeless wreckage of her home, March 27, 1945. The rule of thumb for the Americans was: if a place is defended, blast it; if it surrenders, let it be.

wanted to get Patton's Third Army into the Austrian Alps before the Germans could create a redoubt in the mountains. He therefore informed Stalin that he would halt the western armies when they reached the Elbe River. Churchill continued to press him to go farther east; finally Eisenhower wired his superiors to say, "I am the first to admit that a war is waged in pursuance of political aims, and if the Combined Chiefs of Staff (CCS) should decide that the Allied effort to take Berlin outweighs purely military considerations in this theater, I would cheerfully readjust my plans and my thinking so as to carry out such an operation." He was not willing to risk the lives of a hundred thousand or more men for no military gain. The CCS did not change his orders.

Nuremberg, the city where Hitler held his great Nazi Party rallies, lies in ruins, April 1945. Eisenhower commented in a letter to his wife that he thought the Germans had seen enough high explosives to last them for a century.

Hitler threw German youth into the hopeless battle. In the famous photograph below, he is in his bunker, where he has just awarded the Iron Cross to Hitler Youth members for bravery in the Battle of Berlin. By this time Hitler felt that the German people had let him down and deserved to die, but he loved children, especially if they were wearing a Nazi uniform.

As the Americans, British, and Free French broke through the walls of Hitler's Third Reich, they discovered to their horror that even the most ghastly tales about Nazi atrocities were understatements. One after another they penetrated the unbelievable hells of Buchenwald, Dachau, and Bergen-Belsen, while the Soviets, approaching from the east, entered the death mills of Lublin-Maidanek and Auschwitz.

After he had seen his first concentration camp near the aristocratic town of Gotha, Eisenhower cabled Washington and London to send journalists and members of Congress and Parliament to Germany as soon as possible. "I felt," he later wrote, "that the evidence should be immediately placed before the American and British publics in a fashion that would leave no room for cynical doubt."

Back in the United States, meanwhile, on April 12, 1945, a tired and prematurely old Franklin Roosevelt was resting at Warm Springs, Georgia,

Americans from the Forty-fourth Infantry Division, U.S. Seventh Army, have just opened the gates at a German prison camp holding 6,000 Allied POWs, including 3,364 Americans, April 3, 1945. For these POWs the sight of GIs brought an indescribable joy.

when suddenly he complained: "I have a terrific headache." Two hours later, he was dead of a cerebral hemorrhage. His death was succinctly announced in the regular Army-Navy casualty lists: "Roosevelt, Franklin D., Commander in Chief, wife, Mrs. Anna Eleanor Roosevelt, the White House."

The shock was profound. In those pre-television days, the public saw little of the president, and few Americans realized how FDR had sacrificed his health for his nation. For most of the 12 million soldiers and sailors in the U.S. armed forces, Roosevelt was the only president they could remember. If he could be properly criticized for not doing enough to prepare America for the war, he must be praised as a great wartime leader. It was Roosevelt, more than any other individual, who shook the lethargy out of the American people; it was Roosevelt who set the quotas for industrial production, then rallied the people so that the goals were not just met but exceeded; it was Roosevelt who provided the leadership in the long, sometimes bitter struggle over strategy; it was Roosevelt who gave Marshall the support he needed, and Roosevelt who selected Eisenhower to command Overlord. In World War II no one man was indispensable—except Churchill in 1940–41 and Roosevelt thereafter.

His contribution was understood around the world. In the United States, the shock of his death was comparable to Lincoln's, and the grief as great. Churchill called Roosevelt's passing "a loss to the British nation and to the cause of freedom in every land." Chiang Kai-shek began a fast and meditation. The streets of Moscow were filled with weeping men and women. Goebbels telephoned Hitler with delight: "My Führer, I congratulate you! Roosevelt is dead! It is written in the stars that the second half of April will be a turning point for us." Hitler himself issued an order of the day describing Roosevelt as "the greatest war criminal of all times." And Harry Truman, a modest but decisive man, moved into the American seat of power to usher the world into the atomic age. Not until after he had taken the oath of office did he know about the Manhattan Project. "Boys," he told the press, "last night the whole weight of the moon and stars fell on me. Please pray for me."

Roosevelt died at Warm Springs with the assurance that his cause had won. Such was not to be the fate of the Axis dictators.

Mussolini was the first to go. By the end of April, as the Allies were approaching Milan and as partisans were swarming up to the Swiss border, the Duce took off northward with a few followers and his young mistress, Clara Petacci. On April 27, his little caravan was stopped by a partisan roadblock. Mussolini disguised himself in a German helmet and military overcoat, but he was recognized and seized. On April 28, near Lake Como, the Duce and his mistress were stood against a wall and shot. The bodies were trucked to Milan, kicked, beaten, and strung up by the feet in front of a gasoline station.

When Hitler received the news, the Battle of Berlin was raging all around him, though his chancellory was still defended against the Soviets. On April 29, he dictated his personal will and his political testament. He named Martin Bormann, the number two Nazi, as his executor and expelled Göring and Himmler from the party because of their disloyalty to his frenzied last-minute commands. He appointed Grand Admiral Karl Dönitz President of the Reich and Supreme Commander of the Armed Forces. He made a last appeal against "international Jewry" and then concluded: "I myself

Chief Justice Harlan Stone swears in Harry Truman as president of the United States at the White House, April 12, 1945. Mrs. Bess Truman is between the principals. Truman had been vice president for only three months and was almost overwhelmed by his new responsibilities, but he quickly rallied and took charge, starting with an affirmation that unconditional surrender remained Allied policy.

and my wife—in order to escape the shame of overthrow or capitulation—choose death." His wife was Eva Braun, whom he married the day before his suicide.

Hitler ordered that his favorite Alsatian dog be poisoned, and poison was distributed to his secretaries. Then, early in the morning of April 30, he shook hands with remaining members of his entourage and retired with Eva Braun. Goebbels, Bormann, and a few other Nazi bosses were left behind to send the final telegrams. About 3:15 that afternoon, Eva Braun, sprawled on a sofa, took poison. At 3:30, Hitler, seated at a table near her, shot himself in the mouth with a pistol. The corpses were taken into the chancellory garden by Bormann, Hitler's valet, and a surgeon, placed in a Russian shell hole, doused in gasoline, and burned. Goebbels had an SS orderly shoot him and his wife after she had poisoned their six children. Bormann disappeared without a trace.

By the time of Hitler's death, thousands of Berliners were scurrying from their besieged capital in an hysterical effort to avoid Soviet retribution, as, block by block, floor by floor, the troops of Zhukov and Konev bored through the burning city.

An officer with a German tank unit at Tempelhof airfield kept a diary which gives some faint idea of that last terrible fight:

We retreat again, under heavy Russian air attacks. Inscriptions on the house walls: "The hour before sunrise is the darkest," and "We retreat, but we are winning." . . . The night is fiery red. Heavy shelling. Otherwise a terrible silence. . . . Women and children huddling in niches and corners and listening for the sounds of battle. . . . Nervous breakdowns. The wounded that are not simply torn apart are hardly taken in anywhere. The civilians in their cellars are afraid of them. Too many of them [wounded soldiers] have been hanged as deserters.

On May 2, Berlin at last fell. The Red Army had suffered 300,000 casualties (10 percent of the attacking force and the highest Red Army casualties of the war) and Germany lost 125,000 Berlin civilians and between 150,000 and 200,000 military personnel. The Soviets gained the first somber sense of triumph, the first awesome sight of the ruins, the first parades under the pall of smoke. They had taken Berlin, but at a terrible cost to themselves as well as to Berlin. The rape, pillage, and looting that followed was very great, even by World War II standards.

For a few more days, disconnected fragments of the *Wehrmacht* thrashed about in isolated sectors between the Austrian Tyrol and Scandinavia. Bormann had sent Dönitz Hitler's last message saying: "Grand Admiral Dönitz: In place of the former Reich Marshal Göring the Führer appoints you as his successor. Written authority is on its way. You will immediately take all such measures as the situation requires." Dönitz, whom nobody bothered to tell that Hitler was dead, wired back: "My Führer! My loyalty to you will be unconditional."

The German radio announced that the Führer had died "fighting to his last breath against Bolshevism." It said nothing of suicide. Dönitz went on

In Berlin, April 1945, Red Army photographers crowd around the remains of Adolf Hitler. He had ordered his body cremated so that the Soviets wouldn't get it. Dental records and other remains made a positive identification possible.

GÖTTERDÄMMERUNG

Never before had a country come to such complete catastrophe as did Germany in the spring of 1945. Here are some scenes from the final days of the Third Reich.

Wherever the Red Army went, it brought rape and plunder. A German woman in Konigsberg, the capital of East Prussia, recalled that after she and her friends had been raped repeatedly, "We often asked the soldiers to shoot us, but they always answered: 'Russian soldiers do not shoot women, only German soldiers do that.'"

Ernie Leiser, a reporter for the GI newspaper *Stars and Stripes,* was one of the first Western journalists to reach Berlin. On May 5 he wrote, "Berlin today is a charred, stinking, broken skeleton of a city. It is impossible to imagine what it looked like before. It is impossible to believe that the miles of disemboweled buildings, of cratered streets, of shattered masonry once could have been the capital of greater Germany and the home of 4 million people. Only a handful of the 4 million still remain as the last clatter of machine-gun fire echoes through the hollow city. There are no factories left

Berlin in 1945 was a burned-out shell of a city. Nearly 600,000 homes were destroyed in the city by wartime bombing and street-to-street fighting. By the end of the war, it was estimated that the city would take forty years and billions of dollars to rebuild.

for them to work in, no shops, no theaters, no office buildings."

On the morning of May 7, the British journalist James Wellard was on the Elbe River, where he witnessed the following:

. . . . The last battle on the western front. . . . It was fought 200 yards from me between thousands of disorganized, hysterical, screaming Germans and the implacable, ruthless Russian tanks and infantry. . . . Russian mortar shells burst in the midst of German soldiers and civilians waiting to cross the Tangermunde Bridge to the American side of the Elbe, scores of women and children were killed or wounded. German soldiers pushed old women out of the boats in which they were trying to cross the river. German officers, stripped naked, paddled a rubber boat loaded with German soldiers. A German girl drowned in mid-stream after screaming for help. German soldiers swam the river in their vests, climbed up the west bank, and were sent straight to the prisoners' cages, still in their vests. German soldiers panicked and rushed in waves towards the river as Russian tanks burst out from the woods. . . . In the past five days 50,000 Germans have passed into our lines. . . . I stood at the broken bridge and watched paratroopers, generals, high-ranking staff officers, nurses, tankmen and Luftwaffe men run across wild eyed.

On V-E Day, the London *Evening News* summed up the situation in Germany: "More than 60 million Germans cooped in compounds, waiting in bread queues, wandering about and living aimlessly, have to be controlled." The *Times,* in its V-E Day editorial, described the situation: "In a score of great cities of Germany scarcely a building stands intact; the Russian armies have swept like an avenging hurricane over the shattered avenues and palaces of Berlin. In the factories . . . the wheels of industry have stopped. The fields are left untilled by the liberation of the foreign slaves upon whose labor German agriculture had come to depend. Famine and pestilence lower over Germany; only by the efforts of her conquerors can she hope to escape or moderate their ravages."

A woman carrying her possessions escapes from a burning building in Seigburg, Germany, April 13, 1945.

A Soviet soldier raises the Hammer and Sickle on the roof of the Reichstag, April 30, 1945 (left). The Battle of Berlin cost the Red Army some 300,000 casualties. Most Soviet soldiers thought it criminal to assault the surrounded city and sacrifice so many good men, some of whom had fought their way from Moscow to Berlin, but Stalin insisted.

American and Soviet army officers and war correspondents toast each other as they celebrate the meeting of U.S. and Red armies in Torgau, Germany, May 3, 1945 (below). The faces reflect the high hopes of the men and women of the frontline units for Soviet-American postwar relations. The woman in the middle is a United Press war correspondent, Ann Stringer.

An ecstatic crowd gathers in Moscow, May 8, 1945. Across Europe, V-E Day was the signal, in Winston Churchill's words, for the greatest outburst of joy in the history of mankind. Everywhere people were deliriously happy.

the air to regret the "hero's death" of Hitler. He publicly hinted at a desire to arrange accommodation with the Western Allies against "the advancing Bolshevik enemy." On May 5, Admiral Hans von Friedeburg sought an eleventh-hour deal at Eisenhower's headquarters in Rheims while German forces in northwest Germany, Holland, and Denmark were already capitulating.

Friedeburg hoped to stall negotiations long enough to bring the maximum number of troops and refugees westward, eluding the Red Army's grasp before the fighting ceased. Eisenhower, however, threatened to close the entire Allied front against such refugees unless there was an immediate, total cease-fire.

The actual surrender came at 2:41 A.M., May 7, 1945, in a modest schoolhouse at Rheims. Friedeburg, Field Marshal Alfred Gustav Jodl, and his aide, Major General Wilhelm Oxenius, signed the terms. Eisenhower refused to attend in person. Instead he sent British, French, Soviet, and American emissaries to accept unconditional surrender of all German forces to both the Western Allies and the Soviet Union, together and simultaneously. When the brief ceremony ended, Jodl said with much difficulty: "With this signature, the German people and armed forces are, for better or worse, delivered into the victor's hands." The Allied representatives made no comment. The Germans were then conducted to Eisenhower's office. The Supreme Commander asked if they understood what they had signed. "Ja," said Jodl. The next day, at Soviet insistence, the ceremony was repeated in Berlin, where Zhukov signed for the Soviet Union. May 8 thus became the historical V-E Day.

The German surrender was, in Churchill's phrase, "the signal for the greatest outburst of joy in the history of mankind." London, Paris, New York, Moscow, the entire world, save for Japan and Germany, rejoiced. There was dancing in the streets, rockets and burb guns firing into the air, sirens howling, lights beaming from every window. Lights! This was the release from the blackout that had covered Europe, except only Switzerland, for the previous five years. In Moscow, crowds swarmed into Red Square, brushing aside police reinforcements. A thousand guns fired thirty rounds each to signalize "complete and total victory." The announcement came long before dawn, and thousands of people poured into the streets wearing everything from pajamas to fur coats. The crowd stayed on and on and grew ever larger. Soviets gathered in front of the British and American embassies, and whenever a foreigner was spotted, he was gently plucked up by a hundred hands and passed along with cheers. George Kennan, U.S. chargé d'affaires, made a speech from the embassy balcony, where the Red banner hung beside the Stars and Stripes. Roars went up: "Long live Truman!" "Long live Roosevelt's memory!" "Long live the great Americans!"

Churchill was making his way to the House of Commons on May 8, 1945, to announce the final victory, when he got caught up in the celebration. His people had been at war with the Germans longer than anyone else. For a year the British had been the only ones standing up to Hitler. It was Churchill who had inspired them, and it was to Churchill they turned in the moment of triumph.

In New York, Washington, Chicago, Los Angeles, and across the land, Americans celebrated. President Truman made a radio broadcast to remind people of the tasks ahead: "We must work to bind up the wounds of a suffering world—to build an abiding peace, a peace rooted in justice and in law. We can build such a peace only by hard, toilsome, painstaking work—by understanding and working with our Allies in peace as we have in war."

Already the process had begun. From April 25 onward, the nations of the world held a conference in San Francisco to create the United Nations. Until June 26, less than two months after the German surrender and shortly before the first nuclear device was exploded in secret, the principals conferred. They debated the "fundamental human rights" to which they would henceforth dedicate themselves, rights including "social progress and better standards of life" and "the equal rights of men and women." At the insistence of a Republican member of the United States delegation, Senator Arthur H. Vandenberg of Michigan, one word was added to the list—"justice."

Americans, too, had cause for celebration. All across the United States, people poured out onto the street on V-E Day, like these New Yorkers on Wall Street, May 8, 1945 (opposite). Above, U.S. troops crowd on board the *Queen Mary* on their way home from Europe. Three men rotated sleeping time in one bed. Many of these troops were not heading home, however; they were going to be transported across the United States and sent into the Pacific theater for the final assault on Japan.

THE END OF THE RISING SUN

The last year of the war in the Pacific was the worst year, for both sides. It was waged with a barbarism and race hatred staggering in scope, savage almost beyond belief, and catastrophic in consequence. Each side regarded the other as subhuman vermin. Atrocities abounded, committed by individuals, by units, by entire armies.

The Japanese government, and the U.S. government, characterized the enemy peoples as beasts, roaches, rats, monkeys, and worse in a campaign put out to the masses by government propaganda agencies, using the crudest formats (movies, radio, and press geared to a third-grade reading level). The aim was to teach soldiers and civilians alike to hate the enemy and regard all Americans (or Japanese) as animals to be feared, attacked, and exterminated. It worked. One American veteran recalled, "We had been fed tales of these yellow thugs, subhumans, with teeth that resembled fangs. If a hundred thousand Japs were killed, so much the better. Two hundred thousand, even better." It was a war without mercy.

It was also a war that saw sweeping maneuvers covering vast distances. Even before the mop-up had ended on Leyte in the Philippines, MacArthur sent Lieutenant General Walter Krueger's Sixth Army on a long, hooking loop through Surigao Strait, the Mindanao Sea, and on to Lingayen Gulf and Luzon, key to the whole Philippines archipelago. On January 9, 1945, some sixty-eight thousand Americans began clambering ashore on the vulnerable Lingayen beaches in what became the largest United States land campaign of the Pacific War. (More American forces were engaged on Luzon than in either Africa or Italy.)

Krueger's objective was Manila, the national capital and a magnificent port. He was opposed by an impressive army under General Yamashita,

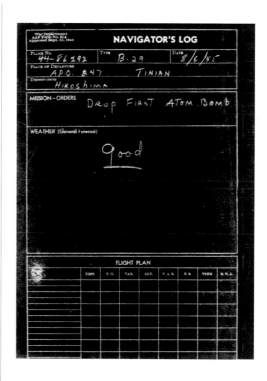

A mushroom-shaped cloud rises above Hiroshima (opposite) after the first atomic bomb was dropped on Japan by Colonel Paul Tibbets's B-29, the *Enola Gay*, on August 6, 1945. Above, the navigator's log for *Enola Gay*'s flight records the momentous event.

563

Manila burns as the battle rages, February 1945. The Japanese destroyed everything in a frenzy of looting, pillaging, and killing. The city suffered terribly for more than a month.

comprising 250,000 men divided into three groups. But despite their size and dispositions, Yamashita's troops had already been weakened by harassing guerrilla attacks and steady United States air bombardment, and they were unable to stop Krueger. By January 31, the Americans had moved deep into the central plain and had expelled the Japanese to the mountainous north and east. They prepared for the final drive on Manila, timed to coincide with an Eighth Army drive across the base of the Bataan Peninsula, which had begun with landings at San Antonio Bay on the twenty-ninth.

On February 3, the U.S. First Cavalry Division reached the outskirts of the capital, but it took twenty-nine days to complete the occupation against desperate house-to-house resistance. When Manila finally was freed on

March 4, several Japanese units on Luzon remained in effective condition, and Yamashita continued fighting from stronghold pockets until the very end of the war.

As they withdrew from Manila and other places, the Japanese were guilty of—in the words of Manuel Acuna Roxas, who became president of the Philippines in 1946—"unbelievable and vengeful sacking. . . . In every large city, in hundreds of smaller municipalities, and even in barrios, most of the habitable dwellings were destroyed; schools had been sacked and gutted; bridges over the principal rivers blown up; telephone and telegraph lines disrupted, radio stations dismantled, and all the government buildings . . . in ruins. All the inter-island vessels were sunk or taken away by the Japanese. No commercial aircraft remained. Streetcars and buses were destroyed or stolen. Railroads were bombed into uselessness and most of the rolling stock gone. Most of the precious work animals were eaten or killed."

Two weeks after returning to the rubble of Manila, where he had spent so many years, MacArthur was back on Corregidor. He issued an order: "Hoist the colors and let no enemy ever haul them down." At last, on July 5, he was able to announce that the campaign was over. In the Philippines the Americans had eliminated some 450,000 Japanese troops.

In the central Pacific theater, meanwhile, some six weeks after the landings in the Philippines, the U.S. Marines swung into action at tiny Iwo Jima. D-day was February 19. Only 775 miles from Honshu, a main island of Japan, the barren, volcanic island of Iwo Jima was of particular importance to the B-29 offensive. It was being used by the Japanese as a radar warning station and as a base for fighter interceptors. Once captured, its three airfields could be employed by P-51 Mustangs to provide fighter escort for the huge B-29s as they flew the thousand-mile return trip to their bases in the Marianas to the south. Iwo Jima could also serve as an emergency landing field for damaged B-29s on their homeward flight.

The eight square miles of Iwo Jima were defended by more than twenty thousand Japanese. The island had been well prepared with extensive mine fields, lengthy underground tunnels, and communications systems protected by artillery fortified with concrete made from the island's black volcanic ash.

Japanese guns remained silent as the Iwo Jima landings began on February 19, but an unforeseen difficulty immediately appeared. Men coming ashore sank to their calves in volcanic ash, and the armored amtracks were unable to climb from the beach up a high terrace of the loose black stuff. Then Japanese guns began to boom. The marines moving inland were pinned down by an enemy they could not see; low hummocks of sand were the tops of pillboxes, with their gun slits only a few inches above ground. When tanks came ashore, they were blasted by hidden antitank guns. Battleships and smaller warships offshore did magnificent work destroying enemy positions, but in most cases they had to be rooted out by men in yard-by-yard advances with flamethrowers and demolition charges.

The marines took Iwo by crawling forward on their stomachs or behind tanks that bogged down in the volcanic ash. Men with rifles and flamethrowers fought their way from pillbox to foxhole, climbing the dominant defensive feature, rocky Mount Suribachi, where on February 23, after three days

These two dead marines on the Gamen rocks of Iwo Jima were among the first to be killed on the godforsaken island on February 19, 1945. Joe Rosenthal, a photographer for the Associated Press, took the picture.

of furious combat, the marines hoisted the Stars and Stripes and photographer Joe Rosenthal of the Associated Press took one of the war's most famous pictures. To secure the island took a total of 26 days and 20,965 American casualties, including 6,821 dead. Lieutenant General Holland M. Smith commented succinctly: "The fighting was the toughest the marines ran across in 168 years." The price of Iwo Jima came high, but by the war's end, 24,761 B-29 crewmen had used its airfields for emergency landings.

By now the Pacific offensive was working like a one-two punch. On March 26, 1945, Lieutenant General Simon Bolivar Buckner's Tenth Army landed its Seventy-seventh Division in the Kerama Islands, west of Okinawa, principal center of the Ryukyu chain. The small islands were quickly subdued and became a seaplane base and anchorage for supply ships during the operation. At the same time, marines took the nearby Keise Islands, artillery was emplaced, and Okinawa, just eight miles away, came under direct attack.

Okinawa was only 700 square miles in size, but its strategic value was immense, because it was only 350 miles from Japan proper and had good harbor facilities with plenty of room to stage troops. It would provide an ideal jumping-off place for any invasion of Japan. This island was the site of the war's last amphibious assault. Vice Admiral Richmond Turner had elab-

On Iwo Jima's exposed slopes (left), the men of the Fifth Marine Division got pounded by Japanese artillery as they inched their way forward toward Mount Suribachi, hidden in the background by smoke from the battle (below). The Japanese made strongholds out of caves. Flamethrowers (bottom) were used extensively to root them out.

Japan's last desperate weapon was her young men, flying obsolete planes on suicide missions. The USS *Saratoga*, (CV-3) off Iwo Jima, has just been hit by a kamikaze attack, February 21, 1945 (left). The attack caused 123 deaths and tremendous damage to the *Saratoga*. Still the grand old carrier was able to steam out of the area and undergo repairs. A year and three months later, she was sunk in the atomic bomb tests at Bikini atoll.

Marines pour ashore from LSTs at Iwo Jima, March 3, 1945 (below). There was little resistance at the beach, but inland the Americans ran into dug-in Japanese troops who fought until they were out of ammunition and food—and then struggled on with their bayonets and teeth.

orated the actual operations plan for Okinawa's capture on February 9, ten days before the Iwo Jima landing. He arranged concentric invasions by forces under himself, Spruance, Mitscher, and Buckner (who commanded seven army and marine divisions).

General Mitsuru Ushijima, Okinawa's commander, had more than one hundred thousand men and three thousand aircraft at his disposal, plus the kamikazes. The kamikaze attack had become an integral part of Japanese tactics after its successful tryout at Leyte Gulf, where it sank an escort carrier and damaged others. From then on, Allied seamen came to know suicide pilots well. Kamikaze attacks during the Lingayen Gulf operation were very effective, sinking four Allied vessels and damaging forty-three. At Iwo Jima, suicide planes sank an escort carrier and hurt five other ships, including two carriers. Kamikaze tactics were well suited to the Japanese character and to the empire's desperate military situation. Almost all of Japan's top pilots were dead, and most of her first-line planes had been destroyed. But an obsolete plane was just as effective when loaded with explosives, and a young man could quickly be taught enough flying to get a plane to the Allied fleet and then dive it into a ship.

American and British seamen underwent their most fearsome trial by suicide planes during the Okinawa campaign. They were within close range of the airfields on the Japanese home islands, and both the invasion fleet and the fast carrier force were hit again and again. Thirty ships were sunk, and though none was larger than a destroyer, 368 were damaged, including carriers and battleships, some put out of action for months. Almost 5,000 U.S. Navy men were killed.

Joe Rosenthal's famous photograph of the marines raising the flag over Mount Suribachi (opposite) won him a Pulitzer Prize. Above, a chaplain celebrating mass on Mount Suribachi gives the communion wafer to a marine who is about to return to battle.

As the campaign progressed, tactics to cope with the suicide planes were developed. Transports and aircraft carriers were the preferred and most vulnerable targets, so the navy tucked them inside a circle of battleships and cruisers, with battleships surrounding the whole, while U.S. fighter planes flew outside the fleet to meet and disrupt if not destroy the kamikazes before they could get close to their targets.

At the same time, the Japanese were having difficulty finding young men willing to kill themselves. Many returned from their mission saying they had been unable to find the Allied fleet. But enough others kept boring in, regardless of their own fate, to make the kamikaze attacks a nightmare for the U.S. Navy. And the "divine wind" made those who were already at work on plans for the invasion of the home islands fearful, because they knew the Japanese had thousands of kamikazes waiting—plus human-guided torpedoes and kamikaze patrol boats packed with explosives.

First Okinawa had to be taken. The landing began at 8:30 A.M., April 1, Easter Sunday. During the first hours of the invasion the Americans were surprised to find almost no opposition on the beaches. In fact, there seemed

Kamikaze pilots drink their last sake before flying off to their deaths (top), then receive their briefings and orders (above, right, and opposite top and bottom). Not all of the pilots died; some returned to base to report that they could not get through the screen of U.S. fighter planes protecting the fleet. And not all were genuine volunteers. Although very few kamikazes got through to their prize targets—the aircraft carriers—enough did to cause great destruction and loss of life. Admiral Halsey said that the Japanese suicide aircraft was "the only weapon I feared in the war." During the battles for the Philippines, Iwo Jima, and Okinawa, the Japanese sent 2,257 aircraft on organized kamikaze attacks, of which 936 returned to base, unsuccessful. They sank 30 combat ships and damaged some 300 others, and killed an estimated 3,000 men on board ships and injured about twice that number. More U.S. sailors were killed or injured and more U.S. naval vessels were sunk or damaged by kamikazes off Okinawa between April and June 1945 than in the Japanese attack on Pearl Harbor.

A kamikaze takes off. After the war Admiral Nimitz declared, "Nothing that happened during the war was a surprise, absolutely nothing except the kamikaze tactics toward the end; we had not visualized these." The Japanese also developed suicide submarines called *kaiten*.

to be little opposition anywhere. Five hours after the first marines were ashore, they had captured one vital airstrip and not a shot had been fired.

If everything seemed to be going much too easily, it was because Ushijima had pulled back to the southern part of the island. The Japanese Army had finally learned a lesson that would have benefitted Rommel in Normandy; if you tried to stop the invasion at the beach, you subjected yourself to the overwhelming fire of U.S. battleships, cruisers, and destroyers. Conceding the beach and building fortifications inland was the most effective way to resist. Ushijima had decided on a defense in depth design. Five days elapsed while the marines muttered that Okinawa was "the screwiest damned place in the Pacific." Then the Japanese struck. On April 6 and 7, nearly 700 enemy aircraft, including some 350 kamikazes, pounded the beachheads and U.S. task forces assembled offshore.

The first five hours of the battle that was designed to smash the American invaders of Okinawa took a toll of six U.S. ships and 135 kamikaze pilots. The Japanese committed their largest battleship, the 72,908-ton *Yamato*, without air cover and with fuel enough for only a one-way trip—it was a kamikaze battleship. On April 7, despite its screen of eight destroyers and the light cruiser *Yahagi*, it was sunk in less than two hours—along with four destroyers and the *Yahagi*. Japanese losses from the *Yamato* alone were 2,500 men. And the Imperial Fleet was gone.

The land conquest of Okinawa proceeded in a series of pushes, by a combined army-marine force of 300,000 men. The army first reduced the northern defenses and then turned southward. The ultimate and most fiercely defended position was in the ancient city of Shuri, a center of pre-Chinese and pre-Japanese culture. Japanese troops hid everywhere, but

A 40-millimeter battery shoots at the enemy on an unidentified carrier during a kamikaze attack (right); a light carrier, the *Santa Fe*, comes to the aid of the carrier *Franklin*, which has been hit by a Japanese plane (below). The *Franklin* was partially abandoned, then reboarded by its crew and sailed to the States for repairs.

most of all in the caves that covered the island. It was not possible for the GIs and marines to simply bypass the caves and push on, because the Japanese would emerge at their backs and subject them to withering fire. American flamethrowers proved to be the only weapon that could either force Japanese soldiers out of their caves or kill them.

Even with flamethrowers, American losses were right at the edge of being unacceptable. Altogether the army, navy, coast guard, and marines suffered 49,200 casualties. This was the heaviest American toll of the war in the Pacific. People at home looked at the casualty list and shuddered. They began to ask, Isn't there another way to bring the Japanese to surrender, not only for the sake of American lives but for the Japanese too? When the last strongpoint on Kiiyama Peninsula fell, 110,071 Japanese were dead, nine for every American. General Buckner was among the Americans killed.

Before dawn on June 22, Ushijima and his principal subordinate, Lieutenant General Cho, knelt in full-dress uniform before their headquarters cave and cut out their entrails. They had fought on in a hopeless situation, dooming tens of thousands of young Japanese and Americans to senseless deaths, then tried to absolve themselves through suicide. Many of their men did the same; of the 100,000 troops on the island when the campaign began, only 7,500 surrendered, and many of them were wounded men who were too

A 20-millimeter gun crew on an unidentified cruiser off the Philippines follows the flight path of an oncoming plane (opposite). American defense against kamikazes began with an outer ring of fighters, who shot down the Japanese planes or forced them to break formation; destroyers surrounding the fleet then brought the Japanese under anti-aircraft fire; next came the cruisers and battleships, bristling with guns. Nevertheless, a few Japanese pilots managed to penetrate to the heart of the fleet, the carriers.

The artist Mitchell Jamieson's *Ack-Ack at Sunset* (below) captures one aspect of the Okinawa battle: The landings were virtually unopposed by Japanese infantry—they retired to the island's fortified areas inland—but then there was an all-out air attack, followed by the most costly of all the Pacific battles.

South
China
Sea

Hedo •
13 April 1945

Ie Shima
17-21 April

Motobu
Peninsula
20 April

Aha •
19 April 1945

16 April 1945 Minna

Bise Kouri

• Tako

Yagachi

Sesoko

Nago

• Taira

15 April 1945

U.S.
Fifth
Fleet

OKINAWA

• Kin
Line 4 April 1945

Yontan

main U.S.
landings
1 April

U.S.
Tenth
Army

Hagushi

Kadena

Pacific
Ocean

Kuba

Line 4 April 1945

Kakazu Ridge

Tsugen

• Naha

• Shuri

10 April 1945

OKINAWA
1–21 April 1945

kamikaze attack

Japanese airfield

Mabuni
21 June

diversionary
U.S. "landings"
1 & 2 April

0   5   10   15

Okinawa had to be taken before the assault on the home islands of Japan could begin. The heaviest fighting was in the fortified southern end of the island.

weak to kill themselves. This bespoke a fanaticism never seen previously, a willingness on the part of Japan's military dictators to commit national suicide rather than to surrender. On any rational basis, they should have surrendered after the fall of the Philippines, absolutely after the fall of Okinawa.

Japan still held a huge empire on the Asian continent, stretching from the Dutch East Indies northward to Manchuria, including Saigon and Seoul, Peking and Nanking, Hong Kong and Singapore. But these vast populations held in thrall by the Japanese were more a hindrance than a help to them. The Japanese Empire stretched far beyond the Japanese ability to police or profit from it.

At home, meanwhile, the nation was helpless. It could not contest control of the skies, which were open to the American B-29s. It could not contest control of the seas. It could only inflict death and destruction in a hopeless cause, which was exactly the course the Japanese military decided on.

The Japanese decision to fight to the death endangered the nation in another way: when the war in Europe ended, the Soviets were sure to turn their attention eastward. As disaster loomed over Germany, it became increasingly necessary for Japan to keep ground forces opposite the Soviet-Japanese border. As early as the spring of 1945 the Japanese General Staff had begun plans for defense against a Soviet attack. At Yalta, Roosevelt had promised Stalin the Kuril Islands and southern Sakhalin (which had been lost to Japan in 1905), as well as Soviet privileges in Chinese ports and railways, in return for the Soviet Union going to war with Japan. On April 5, 1945, Molotov informed the Japanese embassy in Moscow that the Soviet Union was denouncing its Neutrality Pact because the situation had "radically changed." On May 15, Tokyo annulled its alliance with a German state that had ceased to exist. But the gesture was meaningless; it was quite apparent that a new front soon would open, at a most disastrous moment for the emperor.

While Tokyo alerted its Manchurian army, it was facing accumulating difficulty in China itself. A 1944 offensive there had not succeeded in altering the strategic balance. Despite mutual recriminations, both Mao's Communists and Chiang's Kuomintang armies continued to nibble at areas occupied by a Japan that no longer had troops to spare. By early 1945, Mountbatten's forces had managed to open land communications between Burma and China. Mountbatten flew to Manila, where MacArthur promised to help prevent the Japanese from reinforcing their Singapore and Malayan garrisons. At Potsdam, Marshall authorized Mountbatten to assume over Siam (Thailand) whatever control he required and to plan for eventual operations in formerly Dutch Sumatra and in French Indochina, whose territory was thereby withdrawn from MacArthur's supervision.

The Japanese sought to stave off the reckoning by sending out vaguely worded messages to the Soviet Union exploring the possibility of negotiations. They were by no means ready to surrender, however; their fantasy was that they could trade some parts of their empire and hold onto others. When the Big Three victors met at Potsdam in July, Stalin told the British and Americans of these Japanese overtures. Truman then confided to Stalin the secret that the United States possessed a "new" bomb that could have a decisive effect on the war. But he avoided disclosing the weapon's full import. Stalin said he hoped Truman would use it with effect against the Japanese, and repeated his promise to declare war on Japan within three months of the end of the war in Europe—in other words by August 8.

By this time, Japan's most dreadful tribulations had begun. General Curtis LeMay had made of the Marianas a massive Superfortress base. Once he had assembled there three wings of long-range B-29s, he began a series of devastating raids against Japan's helpless main island cities. Starting in February 1945, employing a new bomb containing magnesium and jellied gasoline (napalm), bombers burned out factories, docks, urban areas, and Tokyo itself. Japan, with jerry-built wooden houses and jam-packed industrial centers, was particularly vulnerable to incendiary attack. LeMay made the most of the situation, reducing the armament and crews of his planes so they could carry a maximum weight of firebombs.

In March he dispatched 334 B-29s from Guam, Saipan, and Tinian on the most destructive single bombing mission ever recorded. It did more damage than even the dreadful atomic explosions that were to wipe out Hiroshima and Nagasaki.

The artist Dwight Shepler painted this detailed Okinawa battle scene, *Divine Wind*, to show a kamikaze attack on a heavy carrier at the carrier's most dangerous moment, when its decks were covered with fighters that had not yet gotten aloft.

On May 29, 1945, B-29 Superfortresses at 30,000 feet over the Japanese port city of Yokohama dropped ten tons of bombs from each plane. The B-29s had a maximum speed of 358 mph and carried a crew of eleven men. Its defensive armament consisted of eight 50-caliber machine guns and a 20-millimeter cannon. They were the biggest bombers of the war. By the summer of 1945, there were 1,500 of them in action in the Pacific out of a total production of 4,000 by the Boeing, Bell, and Martin companies.

On the night of March 9–10, just after midnight, the pounding of Tokyo started amid a high wind. Within half an hour, the resulting fires had flamed wholly out of control. A factory worker who took refuge in a school compound later described his experience:

The fires were incredible by now, with flames leaping hundreds of feet into the air. There seemed to be a solid wall of fire rolling toward the building. All the windows were closed to prevent sparks from pouring into the rooms and setting the school ablaze. . . . Many peo-

ple were already gasping for breath. With every passing minute the air became more foul. . . . The noise was a continuing, crashing roar. The great bombers were still coming over Tokyo in an endless stream. . . . Fire-winds filled with burning particles rushed up and down the streets. I watched people—adults and children—running for their lives, dashing madly about like rats. The flames raced after them like living things, striking them down. They died by the hundreds right in front of me. Wherever I turned my eyes, I saw people running away from the school grounds seeking air to breathe. They

Only the largest and most modern buildings in Tokyo still stand, September 4, 1945. In 1940, Tokyo's population had been 7,350,000; at the end of the war it was 3,500,000. The first hit was the Doolittle raid in April 1942; the second raid took place on November 24, 1944; the biggest was on the night of March 9–10, 1945, when 334 B-29s struck with 1,665 tons of petroleum-based incendiaries. Some 97,000 people were killed, another 125,000 injured.

Emperor Hirohito inspects the damage. Only rarely did he leave the imperial palace, and he was never seen by the Japanese public. His role in the decision to begin the war and in its conduct is murky. At the end, with his country and people on the verge of total catastrophe, he took decisive action and ordered that the unendurable had to be endured. Only then did Japan surrender.

raced away from the school into a devil's cauldron of twisting, seething fire. The whole spectacle with its blinding lights and thundering noise reminded me of the paintings of Purgatory.

A Japanese newspaperman wrote: "The city was as bright as at sunrise; clouds of smoke, soot, even sparks driven by the storm, flew over it. That night we thought the whole of Tokyo was reduced to ashes." The fire department estimated that the raid killed 97,000 people, wounded 125,000, and left 1,200,000 homeless.

One by one Japan's cities were reduced: Tokyo, then Nagoya, Kobe, Osaka. Each devastation was so terrible that currents of heat were flung upward into the sky, tossing the vengeful airplanes and tearing helmets from the heads of their crews. In one 10-day blitz, the Superfortresses wholly flattened thirty-two square miles of Japan's four most important centers.

By April 6, MacArthur was given command of all U.S. Army forces in the Pacific and was directed, with Nimitz, the naval commander, to prepare for the war's final operations. This task was rendered far easier than the Joint Chiefs of Staff could foresee by the development of the atomic bomb.

Tentative manufacture of a bomb had been begun by General Groves's Manhattan Engineer District in 1942. At Los Alamos, New Mexico, research director J. Robert Oppenheimer established a laboratory to work on producing an atom bomb. However, until its actual testing in July 1945, no one could be certain that it would work. So secret was the project that only a handful of persons were even aware of its existence, and they did not include Harry Truman, then vice president. The day after Roosevelt died, Secretary of State James F. Byrnes told Truman of the coming experiment, but his first thorough briefing did not come until twelve days later, from Secretary of War Henry K. Stimson.

Pandora's terrible box opened at dawn, July 16, in the desert near Alamogordo, New Mexico. As the countdown ended, Oppenheimer, standing with Groves in a distant control station, shouted, "Now!" The assembled officers and scientists peered through their dark glasses at the auroral burst of flame, and Oppenheimer thought of two passages from the Hindu epic, Bhagavad Gita. One read: "If the radiance of a thousand suns were to burst into the sky, that would be the splendor of the Mighty One." The other: "I am become Death, the shatterer of worlds." A tremendous blast rushed out across the desert, and above it rose the first mushroom-shaped cloud.

It remained for Truman to decide if, how, where, and when this fantas-

Hamamatsu, a city of 130,000, was devastated by a B-29 raid. Because Japanese homes were built mainly of wood, their cities were particularly vulnerable to firebombs, which the B-29s dropped by the thousands in a deliberate effort to burn the cities to the ground. At the beginning of the war the United States had strongly opposed urban bombing; by the end the policy was to destroy all Japanese cities.

tic weapon should be employed. Twelve days before the test, Churchill had given the president British consent in principle to drop the bomb on Japan. Truman himself was to write in his memoirs: "Let there be no mistake about it, I regarded the bomb as a military weapon and never had any doubt that it should be used."

In July, Truman met with Churchill and Stalin at Potsdam, near war-ravaged Berlin (British elections were held during early July, and Churchill was defeated and replaced at the later Potsdam sessions by the new prime minister, Clement Attlee.) It was the last of the wartime conferences, and it accomplished little. Stalin was urged to make good on his promise to declare war on Japan, although some U.S. military men were now cooling to the idea. It was decided to settle the question of Poland's western boundaries later—an empty gesture, for the Poles had already moved into eastern Germany after evicting the Germans there and plainly meant to stay. At one point the Americans threatened to leave the conference because of Stalin's insistence on reparations so huge that they would have left Germany without enough to subsist on. But the most important event during the conference occurred elsewhere: President Truman received word that the first atomic test explosion at Alamogordo, New Mexico, had been successful. The president at once issued the Potsdam Declaration, a surrender ultimatum to Japan.

There was some discussion among American leaders on what preliminary warning should be addressed to Tokyo prior to employment of the two bombs already being assembled on Tinian. Undersecretary of State Joseph C. Grew urged that Japan be alerted to its danger with a message indicating no insistence on the emperor's abdication. Stimson echoed this view, but Byrnes opposed it, on the grounds that the Japanese would regard this as a concession and would convince themselves that the casualties their troops inflicted on the Americans on Okinawa had made the enemy fearful. And, Byrnes warned, one concession would lead to another, to the point that the war would end with negotiations, not unconditional surrender. So the only warning the Japanese got came on July 26, when Truman released the Potsdam Declaration. Two days later, Premier Suzuki announced that his government would ignore the demand that Japan surrender unconditionally or face complete destruction.

Lieutenant General Spaatz, by now the commanding general of the U.S. Army Strategic Air Forces in the Pacific, had been instructed to prepare to utilize the first of the two atomic bombs after August 3, weather permitting, against one of four cities: Hiroshima, Kokura, Niigata, or Nagasaki. Following Suzuki's action, this order was confirmed. A B-29 from the 509th Composite Group, with a specially trained crew commanded by Colonel Paul W. Tibbets Jr., was chosen for the first mission.

At 8:15 A.M., August 6, Tibbets released over Hiroshima a uranium bomb called "Little Boy." He reported later: "As far as I was concerned it was a perfect operation." On August 9, a plutonium bomb known as "Fat Boy" was dropped on Nagasaki. The destruction in each case exceeded the most careful extrapolations of scientists, and it was hours before the mushroom clouds, smoke, and flames had blown away sufficiently to permit adequate photo reconnaissance.

The casualty toll was staggering and, of course, fails to suggest the indescribable suffering incurred, but estimates claim—no one knows for certain—that from seventy to eighty thousand people were killed at Hiroshima and an equal number were injured, and that some forty thousand died at Nagasaki and about sixty thousand were injured.

Life came cheap in the world of 1945. The losses at Hiroshima and Nagasaki were not as great as German losses in Berlin or Dresden or Japanese losses in Tokyo. It was the inherent shock of the event—one plane, one bomb, one city—that overwhelmed people, not the fact that another Japanese city or two had been destroyed, with most of its people killed or wounded.

The Big Three shake hands at the last wartime summit meeting, at Potsdam, outside Berlin, July 1945. Truman had succeeded Roosevelt. While the conference was going on, the Tory Party lost in the British general election and Churchill gave way to Labor leader Clement Attlee—not, however, before giving British approval for the use of the atomic bomb.

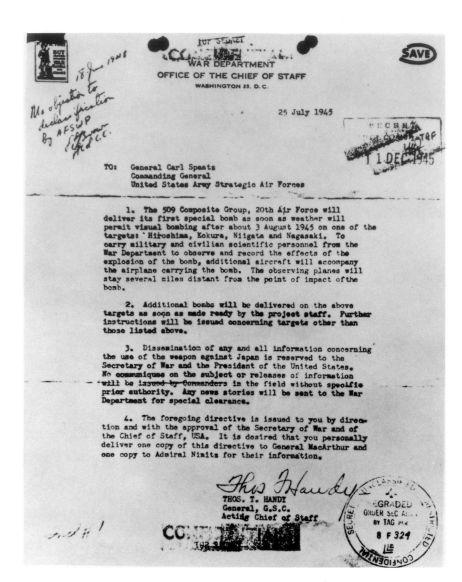

WAR DEPARTMENT
OFFICE OF THE CHIEF OF STAFF
WASHINGTON 25, D.C.

25 July 1945

TO: General Carl Spaatz
       Commanding General
       United States Army Strategic Air Forces

1. The 509 Composite Group, 20th Air Force will deliver its first special bomb as soon as weather will permit visual bombing after about 3 August 1945 on one of the targets: Hiroshima, Kokura, Niigata and Nagasaki. To carry military and civilian scientific personnel from the War Department to observe and record the effects of the explosion of the bomb, additional aircraft will accompany the airplane carrying the bomb. The observing planes will stay several miles distant from the point of impact of the bomb.

2. Additional bombs will be delivered on the above targets as soon as made ready by the project staff. Further instructions will be issued concerning targets other than those listed above.

3. Dissemination of any and all information concerning the use of the weapon against Japan is reserved to the Secretary of War and the President of the United States. No communiques on the subject or releases of information will be issued by Commanders in the field without specific prior authority. Any news stories will be sent to the War Department for special clearance.

4. The foregoing directive is issued to you by direction and with the approval of the Secretary of War and of the Chief of Staff, USA. It is desired that you personally deliver one copy of this directive to General MacArthur and one copy to Admiral Nimitz for their information.

THOS. T. HANDY
General, G.S.C.
Acting Chief of Staff

At right is the directive that ordered General Carl Spaatz to use the first "special bomb" on any one of four Japanese cities. Below, an early atomic bomb of the type called "Little Boy" and dropped on Hiroshima. It was 28 inches in diameter and 120 inches long. Weighing 9,000 pounds, its explosive power was the same as that of 20,000 tons of TNT.

The crew of the *Enola Gay* poses for a picture. Commander Paul Tibbets is standing fourth from the left. He was by reputation the best pilot in the Army Air Forces (he had been Eisenhower's pilot in England in 1942–43). The crew had been practicing for its single mission for almost a year.

Fifty years later, the American use of the atomic bomb in August 1945 remains one of the most controversial and emotional issues of the war. It was not necessary, one side says. The Japanese were licked and they knew it; all they sought was a guarantee that the emperor would remain on his throne. As the United States intended to retain the emperor in any case, because of fears of uncontrollable social upheaval otherwise, that guarantee should have been made.

Nonsense, say Truman's defenders. There is no indication the Japanese were prepared to quit; there is every indication they intended to fight one last glorious battle in defense of the homeland. Estimates of the casualties that would ensue ran very high, up to one million Japanese and American dead and injured.

In a sense the debate over the morality and wisdom of using the bombs is a generational dispute. Americans born before 1940, for the most part, cannot understand how anyone could be critical of Truman's decision. Americans born after 1945, the generations who grew up in the Cold War specter of the mushroom-shaped cloud, feel there must have been some better way to end the war.

It has to be doubted that there was another way, certainly none that would have had such an immediate impact. On August 8, right after the Hiroshima and two days before the Nagasaki bombs were dropped, the Soviet Union declared war

Survivors of the atomic bomb explosion in Hiroshima wait to receive first aid in the southern part of the shattered city, August 6, 1945. But 90 percent of the doctors, nurses, and medics had been killed or seriously injured and were unable to help. Exact figures are unknown, but some seventy to eighty thousand Japanese citizens were killed and an equal number wounded.

THE DECISION TO DROP THE BOMBS

In the summer of 1945, with their cities burning, their imports gone, their main armies now cut off on the Asian mainland, their people starving, incapable of reinforcing or supplying their fighting men, the military dictators in Japan still insisted on fighting. There was no indication that they would be willing to surrender on any terms. The awful casualties they inflicted and the heart-stopping casualties they suffered in the hopeless defense of Okinawa forced Americans to believe that the home islands would have to be invaded, overrun, and forced to submit.

Military leaders in the United States had to assume that the casualties in such a campaign would be horrendous. Colonel (later General and NATO commander) Andrew Goodpaster, of the War Department Operations Division, estimated one half million American casualties. He arrived at that figure by taking the number of Japanese troops on Okinawa and comparing it with the number defending Japan's home island, then calculating how many Americans on Okinawa the Japanese killed, and concluding that American

Of the 76,000 buildings in Nagasaki, 70,000 were damaged or totally destroyed. The bomb exploded 1,900 feet above Shima Hospital, near the center of the city. Within about eight-tenths of a mile around the hospital everything combustible ignited spontaneously. People vaporized. The surfaces of granite stones melted or split into thin layers. On some stones were imprinted the shadows of the vaporized.

casualties in an assault on the home islands would be twenty times the number on Okinawa. That estimate has been challenged as far too pessimistic, but not by anyone who had been in combat against the Japanese.

Those who argue the contrary assume that the Japanese military leaders were rational men who recognized that their cause was hopeless and were looking for a way to surrender with honor. That was not the case. Most Japanese officers wanted to go through with the final battle, some because they genuinely believed the American invaders could be defeated, but most because they considered it to be the last duty of the military, without which no subsequent surrender could be honorable. They were driven not by a view of what the situation required but by what they viewed as their code of honor.

This was made clear in the behavior of War Minister Korechika Anami, who came close to preventing the surrender. Even with the atomic bombing of two cities, even with Soviet entry into the war, Anami (and many others) wanted to fight the last battle. It was not just a question of their devotion to the emperor, it was also a question of their being disgraced or discredited. This was not noble heroism. The point of suicide as expiation for failure was that if the person who had failed had already paid with his life, there was no point to criticism by third parties.

And in truth the Japanese military had good reason to try to avoid criticism from the civilian population for they had, after all, recommended a war that they could not possibly win and carried it out with brutal disregard for the dictates of decency or the laws of war. So the code that required death in preference to surrender was the Japanese military's last recourse in the defense of their way of life.

It was not just the military who were ready to embrace national suicide. Prime Minister Suzuki was a hard-liner to an extraordinary degree. As late as August 12 he asserted in council that because the Allies were still insisting on Japanese disarmament there could be no alternative to continuing the war.

But Hiroshima and Nagasaki boxed the Japanese military into a corner from which they had no exit. They had no answer to the atomic bomb. They could not evade the fact that they were defeated and could offer no alternative to the government save a suicidal resistance, which the emperor refused to allow. The defection of the emperor from the militarist order of society and the possibility that the Imperial institution might survive as an organizing principle for a civilian-run government completed their isolation. With Hirohito's decision to surrender, the only alternatives open to the military were a revolt against the emperor (which would have shown the world the hypocrisy of their claim to being his most faithful servants) or mass suicide. A very few contemplated the first course, and some chose the second, but clearly the great mass refused either alternative and accepted the emperor's command to endure the unendurable. The war was over.

A Japanese POW in Guam bows his head after hearing Emperor Hirohito make the announcement of unconditional surrender, August 15, 1945.

on Japan and the Red Army swept through Manchuria and into Korea. The Soviets were preparing to invade the northern Japanese home islands. Had that happened, and it would have if the war had continued, Japan would have been divided like Germany, with a communist North Japan and a democratic South Japan.

The shock of the bombs brought about a swift denouement. Truman announced: "We are now prepared to obliterate rapidly and completely every productive enterprise the Japanese have above ground in any city." On August 10, Tokyo sued for peace on the basis of the Allies' Potsdam Declaration, but requested that Hirohito be retained as emperor. Truman agreed to some face-saving language.

The decision to surrender was reached at a final meeting of the Supreme War Council in the presence of the emperor. Hirohito said: "I cannot bear to see my innocent people suffer any longer." Following a lengthy discussion, Suzuki rose and quietly remarked: "Gentlemen, we have spent hours in deliberation without coming to a decision and yet agreement is not in sight. You are fully aware that we cannot afford to waste even a minute at this

Thousands of wounded in Hiroshima suffered, like this man, from radiation poisoning. A woman about a mile from the blast center remembered seeing people stark naked, their clothes in rags. "Their hair was stiff, ruffled out and burnt short," she said. "Their hands were so severely burned they could not move them. They were therefore forced to flee with their hands held out before them."

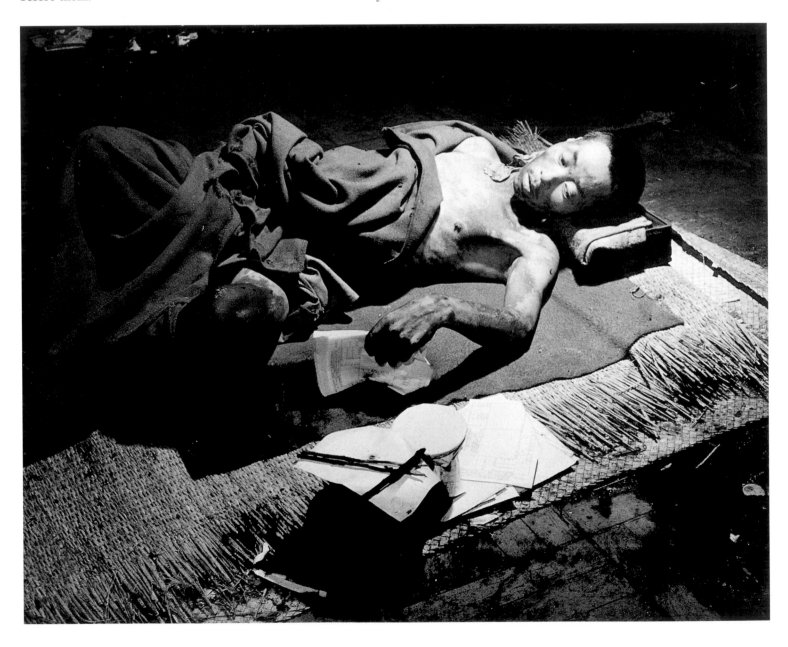

juncture. I propose, therefore, to seek the imperial guidance and substitute it for the decision of this conference." Hirohito indicated that Japan must accept the terms Truman offered. These terms stipulated that "from the moment of surrender the authority of the emperor and the Japanese government to rule the state shall be subject to the Supreme Commander of the Allied Powers." On August 15, in a taped radio message, his first direct voice communication with his people, the emperor informed them that the war was over and it was time to accept the unacceptable and endure the unendurable in order to "pave the way for a grand peace for all generations to come."

The Soviets spurned the announcement as "only a general statement on Japan's capitulation." They continued their brief but fierce offensive. The Kwantung Army surrendered August 22, but Soviet airborne troops and the Red Fleet moved on to Dairen and Port Arthur in Manchuria and seized southern Sakhalin and the Kurils. The Soviets captured 594,000 Japanese and killed some 80,000, against their own losses of 8,000 dead and 22,000 wounded. On August 28, meanwhile, American troops began a mass and unopposed landing on Japan's home islands, occupying all strategic centers.

There were several separate Japanese capitulations on widely separated fronts: China regained sovereignty over Inner Mongolia, Manchuria, Formosa, and Hainan; Britain reoccupied Hong Kong and accepted a formal Japanese surrender in Singapore on September 12. The crucial and historic act, however, that confirmed Imperial Japan's defeat took place aboard the 45,000-ton battleship, USS *Missouri*, on September 2, 1945, in Tokyo Bay. General MacArthur staged the event with a high sense of drama. Suzuki had resigned on August 15. The new premier, Prince Higashikuni, was able to avoid the capitulation ceremony for protocol reasons; he was the emperor's uncle. Instead, the one-legged foreign minister, Mamoru Shigemitsu, wearing striped pants and top hat, limped aboard the *Missouri* from a gig that flew the Stars and Stripes, accompanied by General Yoshijiro Umezu, representative of the General Staff.

The *Missouri*, flagship of the U.S. Pacific Fleet, was flying the same flag that had waved over the Capitol in Washington the day Pearl Harbor was attacked. Jammed together on the deck were masses of correspondents and Allied officers: British and Australians with scarlet bands on their caps and collars; Gaullist French with vivid decorations; Dutch with gold-looped emblems; Chinese in olive drab; Soviets in stiff shoulder-boards, headed by the obscure Lieutenant General Derevyanko, and Americans, garbed simply in plain suntans, the uniform MacArthur insisted upon, on the grounds that it was the uniform worn throughout the war.

After MacArthur opened the ceremony with a brief and generous address, Shigemitsu, with great dignity, signed two copies of the surrender document in Japanese and English. Umezu followed. Then MacArthur strode forward, bringing with him two high officers who had been rescued from Japanese POW camps: Lieutenant General Jonathan M. Wainwright, whom he had been forced to leave behind at Corregidor, and Lieutenant General Sir Arthur Percival, the loser of Singapore. MacArthur then signed, followed by Nimitz and the Allied delegates. The general, looking a generation younger than his years, said:

> We are gathered here, representatives of the major warring powers,
>   to conclude a solemn agreement whereby peace may be restored.

The photograph at right was taken in New York's Times Square on V-J Day. Neither the sailor nor the nurse has been positively identified. There are many who have said, "That's me." One woman who years later claimed to be the nurse said she had married the sailor, and she complained, "He doesn't kiss like that anymore!" Below is what Times Square looked like after the celebration.

The issues, involving divergent ideals and ideologies, have been determined on the battlefields of the world and hence are not for our discussion or debate. Nor is it for us here to meet, representing as we do a majority of the people of the earth, in a spirit of distrust, malice, or hatred. But rather it is for us, both victors and vanquished, to serve, committing all our peoples unreservedly to faithful compliance with the understandings they are here formally to assume. It is my earnest hope . . . that from this solemn occasion a better world shall emerge . . . a world dedicated to the dignity of man. . . . Let us pray that peace be now restored to the world, and that God will preserve it always. These proceedings are closed.

General MacArthur signs the surrender document on the battleship *Missouri* in Tokyo Bay, September 2, 1945.

CHAPTER 21

THE LEGACY

More people were killed in the Second World War than in any war in history, so it is inevitable that the most prominent symbol of the war is a mushroom-shaped cloud. The war left 53 million dead. The reality behind this figure is impossible to grasp, but it was there—young people, mostly, who died for causes that were not theirs, at ages when they had just begun to experience the fullness of life, leaving behind grieving parents, widows, children, friends. Millions more were crippled physically, condemned to lives in wheelchairs if they were lucky, to immobility if they were not. Other millions were damaged mentally by the experiences of combat, whether on the front lines or in bombed cities, doomed to live lives of anger, bewilderment, and confusion.

The Second World War left death, misery, destruction in its wake. Throughout much of the world, save the Western Hemisphere, in the summer of 1945, people wandered in the rubble, hungry, exhausted, terrified. The principal lessons of the war seemed to be that man's inhumanity to man knows no limit and that science is destined to provide mankind with the means of destroying the world. The two together portended that what already in 1945 was the worst century ever, would become even worse. And the political settlements made in Asia and Europe at the end of the war created problems that appeared to make World War III likely.

The Grand Alliance broke up with Hitler's suicide. He was the only man who could have brought the war about; his death finished it. Cold War replaced the hot war even as the smoke continued to rise from the smoldering ashes. Korea was divided against the will of the Korean people. Germany was divided against the will of the German people. Vietnam was handed back to the French colonial rulers against the will of the people and within

The American cemetery in Normandy sits on top of the bluff at Omaha Beach. Maintained by the American Battlefield Monuments Commission, the cemetery is widely regarded as one of the most beautiful sites in the world. Few Americans can visit it without crying.

599

The main street in Hiroshima is a scene of desolation in July 1947. The building standing in the right center is the Chuguko Press Building, which withstood the blast but was gutted inside. The flat terrain of the city made it especially vulnerable to the atomic bomb blast. No wooden buildings—the vast majority—survived.

less than a decade it too would be divided. And in each case the division split the countries into Communist dictatorships on the one side, anti-Communist regimes (and a democracy in West Germany) on the other. In those countries that were occupied by the Red Army, where one police state had replaced another, people had the additional burden of feeling that all the sacrifices of the past six years had been in vain. In China, a civil war raged.

But there was hope to be found in the ruins of war in those countries occupied by the United States. Whereas the Soviets took anything of value from their zones of occupation, the Americans set out to rebuild. In Germany, Eisenhower told his staff that the success of the occupation policies being imposed on the defeated nation could be judged only in fifty years. If after half a century the Germans had a stable, flourishing democracy, then the occupation could be considered a success. To bring that about, Eisenhower called in German reporters and told them that he wanted a free press in Germany, meaning that when he did something they disagreed with, it was their responsibility to criticize it in their newspapers. This invitation to criticize their conqueror came as a great surprise to reporters who had just emerged from twelve years of working for the Nazi propaganda machine. Eisenhower called in labor leaders and told them he wanted a free, independent labor movement. He told the schoolteachers they should teach their students that there were a number of legitimate points of view on various subjects and that they should learn to make up their own minds. To teachers who had worked for the Nazis for twelve years, the notion that schools should encourage independent thinking was astonishing.

No wonder that in September 1945 America's prestige had never been higher. The United States had provided the tools and the personnel to save Europe and the Soviet Union from Hitler and his Nazis. The United States had helped drive the Italians out of their African colonies and thrown the Japanese out of China, Indochina, the Dutch East Indies, the Philippines, Burma, and Korea. The United States had asked nothing for itself in return. Vietnamese communist leader Ho Chi Minh hailed the Americans as the true friends of the oppressed of the earth. So did such dissimilar men as Charles de Gaulle, Churchill, and on one occasion even Stalin himself. In a world full of hatred, death, destruction, deception, and double-dealing, the United States at the end of World War II was almost universally regarded as the disinterested champion of justice, freedom, and democracy.

Sixty-eight families, altogether 320 people, live in the burned-out bodies of buses in Tokyo, 1948. Virtually all the dwellings in Tokyo had burned to the ground. The Japanese, like the Germans, Soviets, Filipinos, Chinese, and so many others, faced the great challenge of rebuilding and much misery still to be endured.

The Germans rebuild with help from their conquerors, Berlin, 1950. The Marshall Plan provided $1.3 billion to West Germany between 1948 and 1951, from a total of $12 billion for Western Europe. The fear that prompted such expenditures was that all of Western Europe might be taken over by the Communists, through subversion, ballots, or the Red Army. The idea was to prime the pump, to give a hand up rather than a hand out, not food but fertilizer, not finished machinery but raw materials and credit. Having played a leading role in saving Europe from Hitler, General Marshall—by 1948 the Secretary of State—saved Western Europe from Stalin.

The truth was that the U.S. Army in northwest Europe liberated not only France, Belgium, Holland, and other conquered nations but it also liberated Germany. The difference between being occupied by the U.S. Army and the Red Army was, for nearly the next half century, apparent to all the world. In Asia, the horror of Japanese occupation was replaced in the Philippines by national independence, promised by the Americans before the war and delivered on July 4, 1946. In Japan, the Americans under General MacArthur's leadership emulated Eisenhower's actions in West Germany, bringing democracy and freedom to that nation, and in the process, liberating the Japanese people from their military dictators.

The American determination to lead in the reconstruction of Europe and to restore or create democratic regimes there was complete. It had many expressions, the best known and most important of which were the Marshall Plan, begun in 1947, and the creation of the North Atlantic Treaty Organization (NATO) to defend Western Europe from the Red Army. By 1953 West Germany had recovered its independence and joined NATO, meaning that less than a decade after the war the United States and Germany were allied with the nations of Western Europe in an anti-Soviet alliance. Stalin responded by creating the Warsaw Pact. Once again, as in 1939, Europe was re-arming, entering into antagonistic alliances, bluffing, threatening, rattling sabers.

But the Cold War never became hot. This was partly due to the presence of nuclear weapons, which continuously grew in explosive power through the 1950s, as the rockets grew bigger and more accurate. Fear of the consequences of a nuclear holocaust deterred U.S. and Soviet leaders from ever using their arsenals. Perhaps more directly to the point, the leaders of the world in the period 1945 to 1985 could all remember World War II. They had seen what the conventional weapons of that day could do in the way of strewing death and destruction. This memory was perhaps the chief reason deterrence worked and World War III never happened.

No statesman in 1939 was reckless enough to say that this war was being fought to end war, as Wilson had said in 1917. But for the rest of the half century after World War II no wars involving two of the major powers were fought. Japan, once blindly aggressive, hardly maintained an armed force. The Red Army held onto what it had gained in 1945 but never went beyond that point. The Germans, who had brought war to the Continent twice in the first four decades of the century, had learned the lesson the victors in World War I already knew: the costs of war in the twentieth century greatly exceed any potential gains.

That is another way of saying that change brought about by a peaceful political process is in every way superior to attempted change brought by force. And change swept Europe in the last decade of the century as the Cold

A display of Ajax missiles is lined up at Fort Bliss, Texas, 1958. The arms race of the Cold War was by far the most expensive and dangerous arms race in history. The arsenals were built at a cost of uncountable billions of dollars and rubles. They were capable, by the 1970s, of killing every American and every Soviet forty times over. It is almost incomprehensible that men could have gone so mad. And yet, it worked. The arsenals did deter. Fifty years after the end of World War II, the two sides were dismantling large parts of their arsenals, the first genuine disarmament in world history.

War came to an end. Eventually, the Soviet state imploded. Finally, the Poles got to elect their own government. Independence came to the various republics of the old Soviet Union, as to the satellites. A new world was emerging, with only a divided Korea left as a World War II problem. The century came to an end with democracy triumphant in Europe and in the Americas, in Japan, in the Philippines, and elsewhere in Asia (although not in China). Few would have dared in 1945 to predict that the world would avoid World War III, that the United States would survive the Cold War as the only superpower, that everywhere—even in the Soviet Union—people would say that if there was to be only one superpower, thank God it is the United States, that democracy and freedom would be prevalent over so much of the world, and most of all that it would be possible once again to believe in progress in human affairs. In 1945, in the aftermath of two world wars in one generation, it was impossible to believe in progress.

This belief in the possibility of progress is widely felt a half century later because the world's totalitarian ideologies have been thrown into the ash can of history. The single most important result of World War II was that the Nazis were crushed, the Japanese militarists were crushed, and the Italian Fascists were crushed. Surely justice has never been better served. And the Cold War completed the process, by throwing Soviet-style Communism into the same ash can.

East German border guards look on passively as a West Berlin man pounds away at the Berlin Wall (opposite), November 11, 1989. The hated wall was completely gone within a few days of the photograph. Workers jump off a toppled statue of Lenin in Riga, Latvia, August 25, 1991 (above). The disappearance of the wall and the bringing down of Lenin are symbolic of the legacy of a half-century of Communist dictatorship in Berlin, East Germany, and all the countries overrun by the Red Army in 1945. Thus has the most destructive century in history approached its end.

A German soldier returns home, Frankfurt, 1946.

ACKNOWLEDGMENTS AND SELECTED BIBLIOGRAPHY

ACKNOWLEDGMENTS

This edition of *The American Heritage New History of World War II* would not have been possible without the vision of David G. McCullough, who was the creator and editor of the first edition of the book.

Many individuals contributed their time and expertise in creating this new edition and are mentioned here: Thank you to Richard Snow, Frederick Allen, and Barbara Strauch of American Heritage for their guidance and expertise; Dinah Dunn for getting the process going; Marianne Cohen for her copy editing; Amy Chisam for proofreading; and Cathy Hemming, Cindy Achar, Erin Boyle, and Roni Axelrod of Penguin Putnam for their support of the project.

SELECTED BIBLIOGRAPHY

Many new quotes added by Dr. Ambrose are from interviews with enlisted men from World War II. Most of these interviews and oral histories, such as those with Lieutenant Dave Nagel, Captain Dan Villani, and Lieutenant John Morris in chapter 14 and that with Dwight D. Eisenhower in chapter 17 are now libraried at the Eisenhower Center at the University of New Orleans. The following books contain the anecdotes and quotations that appear in the text captions and sidebars, and are recommended for those readers interested in pursuing their study of War World II:

CHAPTER 1: THE DESCENT INTO HELL

Keegan, John. *Second World War*. New York: Viking Penguin, 1990.

Weinberg, Gerhard L. *A World at Arms: A Global History of World War II*. Cambridge: Cambridge University Press, 1994.

CHAPTER 2: BLITZKRIEG

Churchill, Winston S. *The Gathering Storm*. New York: Houghton Mifflin Company, 1948.

Hastings, Max. *Bomber Command*. New York: Dial Press/J. Wade, 1979.

Liddell Hart, Basil Henry. *History of the Second World War*. New York: Putnam, 1971.

Shulman, Milton. *Defeat in the West*. New York: E.P. Dutton Company, 1948.

CHAPTER 3: ENGLAND ALONE

Churchill, Winston S. *The Grand Alliance*. New York: Houghton Mifflin Company, 1950.

Dupuy, R. Ernest and Trevor N. Dupuy. *The Harper Encyclopedia of Military History: From 3500 B.C. to the Present*. New York: HarperCollins, 1993.

Murrow, Edward R. *This Is London*. Edited by Edward Bliss Jr. New York: Alfred A. Knopf Inc., 1967. The excerpt on pages 94–5 is reprinted by permission of the publisher.

CHAPTER 4: ARSENAL OF DEMOCRACY

Cohen, Stan. *V for Victory: America's Home Front During World War II*. Missoula, Montana: Pictorial Histories Publishing Co., Inc., 1991.

CHAPTER 5: JAPAN STRIKES

Ambrose, Stephen E. "War on the Home Front." *Timeline* Magazine (Ohio Historical Society, n.d.).

Prange, Gordon W., in collaboration with Donald M. Goldstein and Katherine V. Dillon. *At Dawn We Slept: The Untold Story of Pearl Harbor*. New York: Penguin Books, 1982.

CHAPTER 6: WAR AT SEA

Barnett, Correlli. *Engage the Enemy More Closely: The Royal Navy in the Second World War*. New York: Norton, 1991.

Blair, Clay. *Silent Victory: The U.S. Submarine War Against Japan*. Philadelphia: Lippincott, 1975.

Churchill, Winston S. *Their Finest Hour*. New York: Houghton Mifflin Company, 1949.

CHAPTER 7: THE DESERT WAR

Liddell Hart, B. H., ed. *The Rommel Papers*. New York: Harcourt, Brace and Company, 1953.

CHAPTER 8: THE WAR IN THE SOVIET UNION

Ambrose, Stephen E. *Band of Brothers: E Company, 506th Regiment, 101st Airborne from Normandy to Hitler's Eagle's Nest*. New York: Simon & Schuster, 1993.

Clark, Alan. *Barbarossa*. New York: William Morrow and Company, Inc., 1965.

CHAPTER 9: THE POLITICS OF WORLD WAR

Ambrose, Stephen E. *Pegasus Bridge: June 6, 1944*. New York: Simon & Schuster, 1985.

Churchill, Winston S. *The Hinge of Fate*. New York: Houghton Mifflin Company, 1950.

Ismay, General Lord. *The Memoirs of General Lord Ismay*. New York: Viking Press, Inc., 1960.

Orfalea, Gregory. *Messengers of the Lost Battalion*. New York: Simon & Schuster, 1997.

CHAPTER 10: THE SECRET WAR

Lewin, Ronald. *Ultra Goes to War*. London: Hutchinson, 1978.

Masterman, J. C. *The Double-Cross System in the War of 1939–45*. New Haven: Yale University Press, 1972.

CHAPTER 11: COUNTERATTACK IN THE PACIFIC

Kurzman, Dan. *Left to Die: The Tragedy of the USS Juneau*. New York: Pocket Books, 1994.

Spector, Ronald. *Eagle Against the Sun: The American War with Japan*. New York: Vintage Books, 1985.

The flag-drapped body of a U.S. major rests atop the ruins of St. Croix Church in St. Lô, France.

CHAPTER 12: ITALY

Churchill, Winston S. *Closing the Ring.* New York: Houghton Mifflin Company, 1951.

Clark, General Mark. *Calculated Risk.* New York: Harper & Row, Inc., 1950.

CHAPTER 13: OVER THERE

Colby, John. *War from the Ground Up: The 90th Division in WWII.* Austin, Texas: Nortex Press, 1991.

Egger, Bruce, and Lee Otts. *G Company's War.* Tuscaloosa: University of Alabama Press, 1992.

Mauldin, Bill. *Up Front.* New York: Holt, Rinehart and Winston, Inc., 1945.

Pyle, Ernie. *Brave Men.* New York: Holt, Rinehart and Winston, Inc., 1944.

CHAPTER 14: THE AIR WAR

Richards, Denis and Hilary St. George Saunders, *Royal Air Force, 1939–1945.* Vol. II. London: H.M. Stationery Office, n.d.

CHAPTER 15: THE HOME FRONTS

Goodwin, Doris Kearns. *No Ordinary Time: Franklin and Eleanor Roosevelt: The Home Front in World War II.* New York: Simon & Schuster, 1994.

Lee, Ulysses. *The Employment of Negro Troops.* Washington, D.C.: Office of the Chief of Military History, 1966.

CHAPTER 16: THE HOLOCAUST AND OTHER ATROCITIES

Fussell, Paul. *Doing Battle: A Memoir.* New York: Little Brown, 1996. The excerpt on pages 437–8 is reprinted by permission of the publisher.

Reid, Patrick. *Escape from Colditz.* Philadelphia: J. B. Lippincott, 1953. The excerpt on pages 446–7 is reprinted by permission of the copyright holder, HarperCollins, New York.

Reitlinger, Gerald. *The Final Solution: The Attempt to Exterminate the Jews of Europe, 1939–1945.* New York: Barnes, 1961.

CHAPTER 17: ASSAULT ON FORTRESS EUROPE

Ambrose, Stephen E. *D-Day: June 6, 1944: The Climactic Battle of World War II.* New York: Simon & Schuster, 1994.

Bradley, Omar N. *A Soldier's Story.* New York: Henry Holt and Company, 1951.

Eisenhower, Dwight D. *Crusade in Europe.* Garden City, N.Y.: Doubleday and Company, Inc., 1948.

Hastings, Max. *Overlord: D-Day and the Battle for Normandy.* New York: Simon & Schuster, 1984.

MacDonald, Charles. *Time for Trumpets.* New York: Da Capo Press, 1969.

CHAPTER 18: CLOSING IN ON JAPAN

Cowdrey, Albert E. *Fighting for Life: American Military Medicine in World War II.* New York: Free Press/Maxwell Macmillan International, 1994.

Josephy, Alvin M. *The Long and the Short and the Tall.* New York: Alfred A. Knopf, Inc., 1946. The excerpt on pages 507–8 is reprinted by permission of the publisher.

Litoff, Judy Barrett, and David C. Smith. *We're in This War, Too.* New York: Oxford University Press, 1994.

CHAPTER 19: SMASHING THE THIRD REICH

Ambrose, Stephen E. *Eisenhower: Soldier, General of the Army, President-Elect 1880–1952.* New York: Simon & Schuster, 1983.

Tully, Andrew. *Berlin: Story of a Battle.* New York: Simon & Schuster, Inc., 1963.

CHAPTER 20: THE END OF THE RISING SUN

Caidin, Martin. *A Torch to the Enemy.* New York: Ballantine Books, 1960.

PICTURE CREDITS

We would like to particularly thank the following individuals for their help with the art and photos: Stan Cohen, who was very generous with his time and energy and has an amazing collection of WWII memorabilia; David Williams, who was extremely helpful with his picture research in Great Britain and Europe; and Norman Currie of Corbis-Bettmann and Vanessa Weiman of American Heritage, who always graciously allowed us to descend on their photo archives with little warning.

ABBREVIATIONS
AH: American Heritage Picture Collection, New York
AP/WW: AP/Wide World Photos, New York
CB: Corbis-Bettmann, New York
IWM: Imperial War Museum, London
LC: Library of Congress, Washington, D.C.
MDC: Mondadori Documentation Center, Milan/New York
NA: National Archives, Washington, D.C.
SF: Sovfoto, New York
USHMM: United States Holocaust Memorial Museum, Photo Archives, Washington, D.C.

FRONT MATTER
i NA. **ii–iii** NA. **iv–v** NA. **vi–vii** IWM. **viii–ix** UPI/CB. **x** NA. **xi** UPI/CB.

CHAPTER 1
xii CB. **1** LC. **2** CB. **3** Staatliche Museen zu Berlin, Preussischer Kulturbesitz Nationalgalerie. **4** Bottom left: NA, neg. #111-SC-1251. **4–5** State Historical Society of Wisconsin, neg. #WHi (X3) 23019. **6** Top: AP/WW; bottom: UPI/CB. **7** Left: CB; right: NA, neg. #208-PU-93Y-5. **8** UPI/CB. **9** UPI/CB. **10** LC. **11** UPI/CB. **12–13** UPI/CB. **13** Captured German Paintings, U.S. Army. **14** UPI/CB. **15** MDC. **16** Both: UPI/CB. **17** Both: UPI/CB. **18** Bottom left: LC. **18–19** LC. **19** Bottom right: LC. **20** LC. **21** UPI/CB. **22** NA, neg. #131-UFA-201. **23** NA, neg. #BD2-GAP-218-D-22. **24** Top: NA; bottom: Captured German Paintings, U.S. Army. **25** UPI/CB. **26** Left: AP/WW; right: Novosti/CB. **27** Courtesy of The Mariners' Museum, Newport News, VA. **28** UPI/CB. **29** Both: UPI/CB. **30** Top left: NA, neg. #306-NT-1322A-44; top right: UPI/CB; bottom right: NA. **31** AP/WW. **32** Magnum Photos, Inc., New York, NY, © 1996 Robert Capa. **33** Top: UPI/CB; bottom: Museo Nacional Centro de Arte Reina Sofia, Madrid. **34** Top left: CB; top right: Bilderdienst Süddeutscher Verlag, Munich; bottom right: UPI/CB. **35** NA, neg. #208-AA 175QQ-Z. **36** AP/WW. **37** U.S. Army. **38** Top: LC; bottom: NA, neg. #242-JRB-26-38. **39** NA.

CHAPTER 2
40 AP/WW. **42–3** AH, updated by Steven Jablonoski. **44** UPI/CB. **45** UPI/CB. **46** Top: U.S. Army; bottom: NA, neg. #208AA-294-R-1. **47** MDC. **48** UPI/CB. **49** LC. **50** UPI/CB. **51** UPI/CB. **52** AP/WW. **53** © Hulton Getty Picture Collection Ltd., London. **54** © Hulton Getty. **56** CB. **57** AP/WW. **58** MDC. **59** AP/WW. **60–1** NA, neg. #208-PR-10L-3. **62** Left: AP/WW. **62–3** Top: AP/WW; bottom: MDC. **63** Right: NA. **64** Top: MDC. **64–5** © Hulton Getty. **65** Right: Real War Photos, Indiana. **66–7** Archipel, Bibliothèque de Documentation Internationale Contemporaine, Paris. **69** NA, neg. #208-N-31904-FO. **70** Top left and bottom right:

UPI/CB; top right: MDC. **71** Both: UPI/CB. **72** UPI/CB. **73** AP/WW. **74** NA, neg. #208-N-39860-fa. **75** Top: NA, neg. #242-EB-7-46; bottom: NA, neg. #242-EB-7-44.

CHAPTER 3
76 UPI/CB. **78** IWM, neg. #H 3589. **80** AP/WW. **81** MDC. **82** Top: IWM, neg. #HU 1185; bottom: IWM, neg. #C 465. **83** MDC. **84** UPI/CB. **85** Top: MDC; bottom: © The Paul Nash Trust, collection of IWM. **86** IWM, neg. #D 1568. **87** IWM, neg. #HU 1129. **88–9** IWM, neg. #HU 651. **89** Bottom right: NA, neg. #306-NT-3173V. **90** AP/WW. **91** © The Hulton-Deutsch Collection, London. **92** IWM, neg. #HU 3053. **93** NA. **95** UPI/CB. **96–7** © Hulton-Deutsch. **99** Top: © Ullstein, Berlin; bottom: courtesy of AH. **100** NA, neg. #208-AA-132L-1. **101** MDC. **102** © Ullstein. **103** UPI/CB. **104–5** New Zealand National Archives. **106** AP/WW. **107** AP/WW.

CHAPTER 4
108 Courtesy of FDR Library, Hyde Park, NY. **109** Courtesy of Stan Cohen and the Miracle of America Museum, MT. **111** Top: Lawrence Radiation Laboratory, Berkeley, CA; bottom: CB. **112** Top: CB; bottom: AP/WW. **113** All: Courtesy of Stan Cohen and the Miracle of America Museum. **114** Both: FDR Library. **115** UPI/CB. **116** Clarksburg Engraving Co., Courtesy of Clarksburg-Harrison Public Library, WV. **117** Top: CB; bottom: UPI/CB. **118** Margaret Bourke-White, *Life* Magazine © Time Inc. **120–1** FDR Library. **123** Courtesy of Stan Cohen.

CHAPTER 5
124 NA. **125** Courtesy of Stan Cohen and the Miracle of America Museum. **126** NA, neg. #80 G 30549. **127** Top: NA, neg. #208-PU-199R-1; bottom: AP/WW. **128** Both: NA (Navy). **129** Top: NA (Navy); bottom: AH, updated by Steven Jabolonski. **130** Top: NA (Navy); bottom: NA, neg. #80-G-32543. **131** Top left: NA; top right: FDR Library; bottom right: CB. **132** UPI/CB. **133** UPI/CB. **134** LC. **135** Top right: NA; bottom: LC; top left: NA. **136** Captured Japanese Paintings, U.S. Air Force. **137** Office of Military History, U.S. Army, Washington, D.C. **138** Top: CB; bottom: NA, neg. #80-G-178990. **139** Top: Captured Japanese Records, U.S. Army; bottom: NA, neg. #80-G-179029. **140** MacArthur Memorial, Norfolk, VA. **141** Both: MacArthur Memorial. **142** U.S. Air Force. **144–5** AH, updated by Steven Jabolonski. **146** MacArthur Memorial. **147** AP/WW. **148** Top left: Special Collections, U.S. Military History Center; bottom right: Defense Dept. (Marine Corps). **149** U.S. Army (Signal Corps). **150** Top: Captured Japanese Records, U.S. Army; bottom: MacArthur Memorial. **151** AH, updated by Steven Jabolonski. **152** U.S. Air Force. **153** NA, neg. #80-G-41197.

CHAPTER 6
154 IWM, neg. #A 15365. **156–7** AH, updated by Steven Jabolonski. **158** U.S. Destroyer Operations in WWII, © Naval Institute. **159** UPI/CB. **160** IWM neg. #A 4. **161** NA. **162** Captured German Paintings, U.S. Army. **163** Top: MDC; bottom: Steven Jabolonski. **164** AP/WW. **165** FDR Library. **166** Collections of the Naval Historical Center, Washington, D.C. **167** NA. **168** Top: Bundesarchiv, Coblenz; bottom: AP/WW. **169** U.S. Coast Guard. **170** IWM, neg. #A 6872. **171** Top: LC; bottom: Oregon Histori-

cal Society. **172** Top left: unknown credit; center: NA. **172–3** IWM. **173** Center: U.S. Army, OCMH; right, from top to bottom: NA; U.S. Air Force; NA; AP/WW. **174–5** AP/WW. **177** Both: NA. **178** U.S. Coast Guard. **179** Top: U.S. Coast Guard; bottom: U.S. Air Force. **181** NA. **182** U.S. Navy. **183** NA.

CHAPTER 7

184 U.S. Army Art Collection. **186** IWM, neg. #E 1591. **187** NA. **188** Bottom: IWM. **188–9** AH, updated by Steven Jabolonski. **189** Bottom: IWM, neg. #E 18640. **190** NA. **191** All: NA. **192** IWM, neg. #CNA 710. **193** Top: IWM, neg. #AX 99B; bottom: IWM, neg. #A 8168. **194** IWM neg. #E 15299. **195** NA. **196** MDC. **197** Both: Robert Capa, Magnum Photos, Inc., NY. **198** IWM, neg. #E 18832. **199** AH, updated by Steven Jabolonski. **200** MDC. **202** NA, neg. #111-SC-152176. **203** UPI/CB. **204** Top: IWM, neg. #NA 30; bottom: Courtesy of Eisenhower Center, KS. **205** U.S. Army. **206** Top: IWM, neg. #13313; bottom: MDC. **207** Real War Photos. **208** Courtesy of Eisenhower Center. **209** AH, updated by Steven Jabolonski. **210** NA, neg. #111-SC-172107. **211** Courtesy of Eisenhower Center. **212** IWM, neg. #NA 1815. **213** MDC.

CHAPTER 8

214 NA, neg. #AA-328HH-13. **215** U.S. Center for Military History. **216** SF. **217** SF. **218** NA. **218–9** AH, updated by Steven Jabolonski. **220** SF. **221** © Ullstein. **222** Bottom left: NA. **222–3** © Ullstein. **223** © Ullstein. **224** SF. **225** Novosti Press Agency. **226–7** All: Courtesy of AH, by Dennis Knight. **228–9** NA, neg. #306-NT-1208M-6. **229** NA. **230** NA. **231** NA. **232** MDC. **233** © Ullstein. **234** UPI/CB. **234–5** Tretyakov Gallery, Moscow. **236** Bundesarchiv, Coblenz. **237** SF. **238** SF. **240** Arthur Grimm, © Ullstein. **241** State Russian Museum. **242** Top: Novosti/CB; bottom: SF. **243** SF. **244** LC. **245** Both: SF. **246** AP/WW. **247** SF. **248–9** MDC. **249** AH, updated by Steven Jabolonski. **250** SF. **251** NA, neg. #208AA-33ZQQ-1. **252–3** MDC. **254–5** SF. **256** Fotokhronika Tass/SF. **257** Captured German Paintings, U.S. Army. **258** NA, neg. #208AA-329G-1. **259** Tretyakov Gallery, Moscow.

CHAPTER 9

260 Courtesy of Stan Cohen and the Miracle of America Museum. **261** FDR Library. **262** AP/WW. **264** UPI/CB. **265** NA. **266** Top right: IWM; bottom right: FDR Library; bottom left: NA. **267** MDC. **268** NA. **269** U.S. Army. **270–1** LC. **272–3** UPI/CB. **274** NA. **275** MDC. **276** Top: Courtesy of Stan Cohen and the Miracle of America Museum; bottom: NA. **277** U.S. Air Force. **278** NA. **279** NA. **280** UPI/CB. **281** All: UPI/CB. **282** Top: FDR Library; bottom: Eisenhower Library. **283** AP/WW.

CHAPTER 10

284 UPI/CB. **286** UPI/CB. **288** All: Erich Lessing/Art Resource, NY. **289** Top: AP/WW; bottom right: Lawrence Berkeley National Laboratory; bottom left: Los Alamos National Laboratory. **290** Both: UPI/CB. **291** The Nuclear Waste Documentary Project, Oak Ridge, TN. **293** Deutsches Museum, Munich. **294** From top to bottom: U.S. Air Force; U.S. Air Force; UPI/CB; UPI/CB. **295** NA, neg. #242-GAP-33H-2. **296** Courtesy of Barbara Eachus, Cambridge, MA. **297** Top: NA; bottom: Collections of the Naval Historical Center. **298** IWM, neg. #LD 4719. **299** LC. **301** Both: IWM. **302** From *Scientists Against Time*, by James Phinney Baxter III, in the public domain. **303** U.S. Air Force.

CHAPTER 11

304 Courtesy of the Navy Art Collection. **306** AP/WW. **307** Top: U.S. Marine Corps; bottom: Australian War Memorial, neg. #027017. **308** U.S. Defense Department, Washington, D.C. **309** U.S. Marine Corps. **310** NA. **311** Springer/CB. **312** Top: U.S. Army; bottom: U.S. Marine Corps. **313** U.S. Army. **314** AH, updated by Steven Jabolonski. **315** MacArthur Memorial. **316** U.S. Coast Guard. **317** NA. **318** NA. **320** NA. **320–1** MacArthur Memorial. **322** CB. **323** Top left: U.S. Defense Department; top right: U.S. Army; bottom: NA. **324** NA. **325** NA. **326** U.S. Defense Department. **327** Top: Army Time-Life Collection, Defense Department; bottom: U.S. Navy. **328** U.S. Army. **329** LC. **330–1** U.S. Air Force. **331** U.S. Army. **332** Top: NA; bottom: UPI/CB. **334–5** AH, updated by Steven Jabolonski. **336** U.S. Navy. **337** NA.

CHAPTER 12

338 U.S. Army. **340** MDC. **341** Top: Real War Photos; bottom: MDC. **343** AH, updated by Steven Jabolonski. **344–5** U.S. Army. **346** AP/WW. **347** AP/WW. **348** Top: AH, updated by Steven Jabolonski; bottom: U.S. Coast Guard. **349** IWM, neg #NA 8676. **350** MDC. **351** U.S. Army. **352** LC. **353** U.S. Army. **354–5** George Silk, *Life* Magazine © 1944 Time Inc. **355** U.S. Army. **357** Top: Bilderdienst Süddeutscher Verlag; bottom: MDC. **358** U.S. Army. **359** U.S. Army. **360** U.S. Army. **361** Both: NA. **362** Top right: U.S. Army; bottom left: reprinted with permission, Bill Mauldin, © 1944, Bill Mauldin. **363** UPI/CB.

CHAPTER 13

364 NA. **365** All: Courtesy of Stan Cohen and the Miracle of America Museum. **366** Top: NA; bottom: U.S. Navy. **367** Top: UPI/CB; bottom: reprinted with permission, Bill Mauldin, © 1944, Bill Mauldin. **368** Top left: Courtesy of Stan Cohen and the Miracle of America Museum; top right: CB; bottom: reprinted with permission, Bill Mauldin, © 1944, Bill Mauldin. **369** UPI/CB. **370–1** UPI/CB. **371** Right: *Forbes* Magazine Collection. **372** Both: reprinted with permission, Bill Mauldin, © 1944, Bill Mauldin. **373** Both: reprinted with permission, Bill Mauldin, © 1944, Bill Mauldin. **374** NA. **375** NA. **376** UPI/CB. **377** U.S. Coast Guard. **378** Left: reprinted with permission, Bill Mauldin, © 1944, Bill Mauldin. **378–79** Dmitri Kessel, *Life* Magazine © Time Inc. **380** Both: reprinted with permission, Bill Mauldin, © 1944, Bill Mauldin. **381** Top left: U.S. Army; bottom right: Courtesy of Stan Cohen.

CHAPTER 14

382 NA. **383** NA. **384–5** AH, Dennis Knight. **385** Top: IWM. **386** Captured German Art, Department of U.S. Air Force. **387** Top: AH, Dennis Knight; bottom: AH, Herb Borst. **388** Courtesy of the *Illustrated London News*. **389** IWM, neg. #MH 5591. **390** © Ullstein. **392–3** AH, updated by Steven Jabolonski. **393** Top: AP/WW; bottom: U.S. Air Force. **394** U.S. Air Force. **395** All: U.S. Air Force. **396** U.S. Air Force Art Collection. **397** All: U.S. Air Force. **398** Top: NA, neg. #80-G-471763; center: Courtesy of AH; bottom: U.S. Air Force. **398–9** NA, neg. #80-G-268190. **399** Top: NA, neg. #80-G-312900; bottom right: U.S. Air Force. **400** U.S. Air Force. **401** AH, Herb Borst. **402–3** UPI/CB. **404** Courtesy of Tony Vaccaro Photography, NY. **405** Both: AH, Dennis Knight. **406** U.S. Air Force. **407** UPI/CB. **408** U.S. Air Force. **408–9** AH, Dennis Knight. **410** U.S. Air Force. **411** U.S. Air Force.

CHAPTER 15

412 NA. 413 All: Courtesy of AH. 414 Left: Courtesy of FDR Library; right: NA, neg. #171-G-12A-8. 415 Both: NA. 416 Center left: Springer/CB; center right: CB; bottom: Springer/CB. 416-7 Penguin/CB. 417 Top right: Springer/CB; bottom right: Springer/CB; bottom left: CB. 418 UPI/CB. 419 Courtesy of FDR Library. 420 Both: Photographs and Prints Division, Schomburg Center for Research in Black Culture, The New York Public Library, Astor, Lenox and Tilden Foundations. 421 Photographs and Prints Division, Schomburg Center for Research in Black Culture, The New York Public Library, Astor, Lenox and Tilden Foundations. 422 UPI/CB. 423 Top: NA; bottom: Photographs and Prints Division, Schomburg Center for Research in Black Culture, The New York Public Library, Astor, Lenox and Tilden Foundations. 424 LC. 425 LC. 426 LC. 427 All: NA. 429 U.S. Center of Military History. 431 Top: NA: bottom: UPI/CB. 432 Novosti/CB. 433 UPI/CB. 434 IWM, LD 923. 435 UPI/CB.

CHAPTER 16

436 IWM. 437 Janka Rosenzweig, courtesy of USHMM. 438 UPI/CB. 439 Courtesy of the Navy Art Collection. 440 IWM. 441 American Jewish Joint Distribution Committee, courtesy of USHMM. 442 Bottom left: George Kadish, courtesy of USHMM; top right: AP/WW. 443 Clockwise from top left: KZ Gedenkstatte Dachau, courtesy of USHMM; Karl Bonhoeffer-Nervenklinik, courtesy of USHMM; Nordrhein Westfalisches Hauptstaatsarchiv; NA, courtesy of USHMM. 444 Terezin Memorial Museum, courtesy of USHMM. 445 Top: Central State Archive of Film, Photo and Phonographic Documents, courtesy of USHMM; bottom: NA, courtesy of USHMM. 446 NA. 447 Both: NA. 448-9 SF. 449 Bottom left: KZ Gedenkstatte Dachau, courtesy of USHMM; bottom right: Courtesy of USHMM. 450 Left: Arnold Kramer, courtesy of USHMM; right: Jewish Historical Museum of Yugoslavia, courtesy of USHMM. 451 Top: Yad Vashem Photo Archives, courtesy of USHMM; bottom: Thomas Veres, courtesy of USHMM. 452 NA, courtesy of USHMM. 453 Bottom left: Courtesy of Stan Cohen and the Miracle of America Museum; bottom: NA, courtesy of USHMM. 454 LC, courtesy of USHMM. 455 Top: KZ Gedenkstatte Dachau, courtesy of USHMM; bottom: NA, courtesy of USHMM. 456 Left: YIVO Institute for Jewish Research, courtesy of USHMM; right: IWM. 457 Top: IWM, neg. #NYP 76247; bottom: NA, courtesy of USHMM. 458 Top: NA, courtesy of USHMM; bottom left: UPI/CB; bottom right: CB. 459 U.S. Army.

CHAPTER 17

460 IWM, neg. #LD 3924. 462 Frank Scherschel, Life Magazine © Time Inc. 463 AH, updated by Steven Jabolonski. 464 AP/WW. 465 U.S. Army. 466 U.S. Army, OCMH. 467 Bottom left: © Ullstein; top right: U.S. Army. 468 Warren Josephy Collection. 469 Captured German Records, NA. 470 Top: IWM; bottom: NA. 471 Courtesy of the Navy Art Collection. 472-3 IWM, neg. #TR 1662. 473 Right: IWM, neg. #BU 1181. 474 NA. 475 Top: U.S. Coast Guard; bottom: NA, neg. #26-G-2343. 476-7 NA, neg. #26-G-2517. 478 Center: IWM; bottom: U.S. Army. 478-9 IWM, neg. #A 23938. 479 Center: IWM, neg. #B 5114;

bottom: U.S. Coast Guard. 480 Top: U.S. Army; bottom: IWM, neg. #B 5144. 480-1 U.S. Army. 481 Top right: NA; bottom left: U.S. Army. 482 U.S. Army. 483 IWM, neg. #LD 4285/6. 484 AP/WW. 485 Bottom left: Bayerische Staatsbibliothek, Munich; top right: © Ullstein. 486 Bayerische Staatsbibliothek. 487 NA, neg. #208-P4-154B-2. 488 U.S. Army. 489 AH, updated by Steven Jabolonski. 490-1 U.S. Air Force. 492 U.S. Army. 493 Top: AP/WW; bottom: NA. 494-5 U.S. Army. 496 Ralph Morse, Life Magazine © Time Inc. 497 AP/WW. 498 © Canadian War Museum, photography for CWM by William Kent. 499 © Canadian War Museum, photography for CWM by William Kent. 500 U.S. Army. 501 U.S. Army. 502 AH, updated by Steven Jabolonski. 503 U.S. Army. 504 U.S. Army. 505 U.S. Army.

CHAPTER 18

506 U.S. Coast Guard. 507 LC. 509 U.S. Army. 510-1 U.S. Coast Guard. 512 Both: U.S. Navy. 513 U.S. Navy. 514 All: U.S. Navy. 515 All: U.S. Navy. 517 UPI/CB. 518 Courtesy of the Navy Art Collection. 519 NA. 520 Defense Department. 522-3 Defense Department. 525 Top: NA; bottom: CB. 526 NA. 527 Top: UPI/CB; bottom: U.S. Air Force. 528 NA, neg. #11-SC-407101. 529 MacArthur Memorial. 530 MacArthur Memorial. 531 U.S. Coast Guard.

CHAPTER 19

532 U.S. Army. 533 IWM, neg. #LD 5257. 535 IWM, neg. #94506. 536-7 AH, updated by Steven Jabolonski. 538 U.S. Army. 540 U.S. Army. 541 Eisenhower Center, KS. 542-3 U.S. Army. 544 U.S. Army. 545 Both: U.S. Army. 546 Top left: U.S. Army. 546-7 U.S. Air Force. 548 Bottom left: Bayerische Staatsbibliothek. 548-9 U.S. Army. 551 U.S. Army. 552 AP/WW. 553 MDC. 554 CB. 555 NA. 556-7 Novosti/CB. 557 Bottom: UPI/CB. 558 Itar-Tass/SF. 559 UPI/CB. 560 UPI/CB. 561 NA.

CHAPTER 20

562 LC. 563 MDC. 564 MacArthur Memorial. 566 AP/WW. 567 Top: Defense Department; middle: U.S. Marine Corps; bottom: NA, neg. #80-G-427849. 568 Top: U.S. Navy; bottom: U.S. Coast Guard. 569 Top: U.S. Army; bottom: NA, neg. #80-G-399059. 570 U.S. Marine Corps. 571 NA, neg. #208-N-38632. 572-3 All: U.S. Naval Institute. 574 U.S. Naval Institute. 575 Top: NA, neg. #80-G-413915; bottom: U.S. Navy. 576 NA. 577 Courtesy of the Navy Art Collection. 578 Steven Jabolonski. 579 Courtesy of the Navy Art Collection. 580-1 AP/WW. 582-3 AP/WW. 584 MDC. 585 AP/WW. 587 IWM, neg. #BU 9195. 588 Top: Courtesy of AH; bottom: U.S. Air Force. 589 MDC. 590-1 AP/WW. 592 George Silk, Life Magazine © Time Inc. 593 NA. 594 MDC. 596 Both: NA. 597 U.S. Army.

CHAPTER 21

598 UPI/CB. 600 UPI/CB. 601 UPI/CB. 602 UPI/CB. 603 CB. 604 Reuters/CB. 605 Reuters/CB.

BACK MATTER

606 Courtesy of Tony Vaccaro Photography. 608 UPI/CB.

American, 260–261, 563
anti-Mussolini, 342, 346
Chinese, 329
deferred gratification and, 428
German, 275–277
Japanese, 430, 563
Navy, 311
of Nazi Party, 11–14
Soviet, 275–277, 432–433
Propaganda leaflets, 277
Proximity fuze, 299, 302
Public opinion, control of, 275–277
Purple decryption machine, 297
Purple Heart valley, 359
Pyle, Ernie, 369, 372, 377

Qattara Depression, 195
Queen Mary, 561
Quezon, Manuel, 527
Quincy, meeting of Roosevelt and
Ibn Saud aboard, 275
Quisling, Vidkun, 53, 72
Quonset hut, 378–379

Rabaul, 306, 322–323, 520
Allied plans to isolate, 315
Army Air Corps attacks on, 319
Rabi, Isidor Isaac, 289
Racism, in wartime United States,
420, 421–423
Radar
in attack on Saipan, 512
British invention of, 79
German and Japanese versions
of, 297–298
operation and continued value
of, 297–298
value of, 81, 84, 171
Radford, Rear Admiral Arthur W.,
508
Radio, 275–276
Radio beams, in Battle of Britain,
298–299
Radio newsmen, 95
Radios, in American households,
414–415
Raeder, Admiral Erich
shipbuilding program of, 158
submarine production increases
urged by, 167
Rafty, Tom, 440
Rajputa, sinking of, 168
Rangoon, 329
Rapallo, Treaty of, 3
"Rape of Nanking," 438
Rapido River, 356, 357, 362
Rationing
in Great Britain, 433
in Japan, 430–432
Reagan, Ronald, 416–417
Recent Guests of Japan (Backus), 439
Reconnaisance aircraft, 386
Recruits, American, 365–367
Red Army, 214–215. *See also* In-
fantry, Soviet; Soviet Union
advance toward Germany of, 504
in Allied strategies, 201
arrival in Berlin of, 552–553,
554–555, 556–557

casualties in, 225, 228
crossing of the Vistula by,
533–534
German atrocities against, 445
German underestimates of
strength of, 225
incompetence of, 217
invasion of Finland by, 48–51
lack of mechanical skills of, 366
at Leningrad, 232
at Moscow, 233–238
occupation of Eastern Europe
by, 538–540
planned German destruction of,
216–217
postwar gains of, 603
revenge against German Army
by, 430
revitalization of, 258–259
at Stalingrad, 247, 249, 250–251
Stalin's purges of, 37
weaknesses of, 51, 218–219
Red Ball Express, 226
Red Cross, 368, 369
Reid, Captain Pat, 446–447
Regensburg, Allied bombardment
of, 391–392
Reich Central Security Office
Heydrich as chief of, 448–449
Reichenau, Field Marshal Walther
von, in the Ukraine, 239, 241
Reichstag, Soviet flag above, 556–557
Reifenstahl, Leni, 11–14
Religion, in the Soviet Union, 230,
231–232
Remagen, 540, 541, 545
Rentenmark, 3, 22
Republic, sinking of, 173
Repulse, sinking of, 139, 142
Resistance movements, 72–73, 87, 92
espionage tools used by, 288
in France, 230
in Greece, 102
in Poland, 230
in the Soviet Union, 230
Rest after Battle (Neprintsev), 259
Retreat, May 1940 (Delpech), 66–67
Reuben James, sinking of, 165–166
Reuter, Ernst, 428
Reykjavik, 164
Reynaud, Premier Paul, 71
appeal to Roosevelt by, 110
resignation of, 68–69
Rhine, Allied crossing of, 498–499,
540, 541
Rhineland
Allied bombardment of, 391
German invasion of, 22–23
Ribbentrop, Joachim von
division of Romania by Ciano
and, 92–93
German-Soviet nonaggression
pact and, 37, 38
German-Soviet partition of
Poland by, 45–48
with Molotov in bombardment
of Berlin, 387
Richards, Albert, 460–461
Rimini, 346
Rivalries, among troops in differ-
ent services, 316–317, 380

Rjukan, Norway, heavy water plant
at, 287, 290, 291–292
Road to Morocco (film), 416
"Roaring Twenties," 16
Robertson, Angus, 516–517
Robinson, 2nd Lt. Edward, 420–421
Roccomanofin, Mark Clark and
Gerald Templar at, 349
Rochefort, Commander Joseph
cryptanalysis by, 297
"Rock, the", 146, 148–149
Rockets. *See also* Bazooka; Hand-
held rockets; Katyusha
rockets; V-2 rockets
wartime use of, 384
Rockwell, Norman, 412–413
Rokossovski, Konstantin, 259, 534
Romania
establishment of Communists
in, 534
German-Soviet nonaggression
pact and, 37
Hitler's "military mission" to, 98
partition of, 92–93
Rome
Allied bombing of, 346
Allied liberation of, 362–363
American troops in, 369, 381
Mussolini's takeover in, 25
Rome-Berlin Axis, formation of, 25
Rommel, Field Marshal Erwin,
164, 190–191. *See also*
Afrika Korps
African desert campaigns of, 209
on American troop quality, 366
on the D-Day invasion, 482
D-Day preparations of, 466
death of, 191, 485
on El Alamein, 211
in desert campaigns, 186–200,
206–207
in German takeover of Italy, 352
invasion of the Low Countries
under, 59
during Operation Fortitude,
300–301, 463–464
promotion to field marshal of,
192
removal from Italy to France, 356
victory at Tobruk by, 192
Roosevelt, Anna Eleanor, 550
Roosevelt, Franklin Delano, 15, 16,
55, 266
advisers of, 262
alliance with Stalin, 217, 220
in Allied propaganda, 342
on American productivity, 426
Atlantic defense outlined by, 165
campaign against Wendell
Willkie, 113–114
after Casablanca conference
and in Tunis, 282
Chiang Kai-shek's influence on,
327, 329, 333
on the D-Day invasion, 482
death of, 549–551
defeat of Herbert Hoover by, 20
defense of the Philippines, 125
dislike of de Gaulle by, 267–268,
269
economic reforms of, 20

Einstein's letter on the atomic
bomb to, 110, 111, 286
Eisenhower picked to head
Overlord by, 282, 461–462
friendship with Churchill of,
261
the Holocaust and, 452
isolationism of, 23–25, 59, 66
MacArthur ordered to Australia
by, 143, 146
meetings with Churchill, Stalin,
and Chiang, 263–265
meeting with Churchill, 119,
120–121
meeting with Churchill and
Chiang, 268–269
meeting with Churchill at
Casablanca, 265, 267–268,
270–271
Pacific strategy of, 148–149
Pearl Harbor address to
Congress by, 128, 131, 132
Pearl Harbor myths concerning,
127–128
plans for Overlord by, 461–462
political leadership of, 277,
280–283
postwar goals of, 534
production goals set by, 425
rearmament of America
initiated by, 110
relocation of Japanese-Americans authorized by, 134, 421
on strategic bombing, 384
at Teheran Conference,
264–265, 269, 272–274
wartime strategy of, 263
at Yalta Conference, 264–265,
534–535, 538–540
Roosevelt, Quentin, death of, 4
Roosevelt, Theodore, 4
Rosenthal, Joe, 566,
photograph of flag-raising on
Mount Suribachi, 566,
570–571
"Rosie the Riveter," 418–419, 420
Rostov, siege of, 241
Rotterdam, mass bombing of,
55–56, 59–61, 384
Roundup (Allied cross-Channel invasion of Europe), 201
cancellation of, 265
Roxas, Manuel Acuna, 565
Royal Air Force (RAF)
aid to Norway from, 53
Battle of Britain and, 79–87
bombing of Germany by, 401
at El Alamein, 196, 200
harassment of Germany by,
387–388
raids against Germany by, 94
in Southeast Asia, 139
Spitfire used by, 384–385
V-1s intercepted by, 483–484
versus *Bismarck*, 161
withdrawal from France of, 59
Royal Navy
aid to Norway from, 53
Battle of Britain and, 79
in Battle of the Atlantic,
154–169, 171–173

German defenses and, 394, 397
opposition to tactical bombing by, 401
Spanish civil war, 31–32
Special Operations Executive, anti-Nazi activities of, 87, 92
Speer, Albert, 68, ordnance production increases under, 428
Speidel, General Hans, on Montgomery, 194
Speidel, Lt. General Hans, on the D-Day invasion, 482
Spitfire, 81
Spitfire Mk Vb, 384–385
Sprague, Rear Admiral Clifton, in Battle for Leyte Gulf, 524, 525
Springfield rifle, 117
Spruance, Admiral Raymond, 508
in Battle of Midway, 180
island hopping by, 319
in Ryukyu campaign, 569
at Saipan, 512
Sri Lanka. See Ceylon
SS gangs, brutal treatment of Russian people by, 228
St. Paul's Cathedral, 92
bombardment around, 88–89
Stafford, Jo, 368
Stagg, Captain, 470
Stalags, 446
Stalin, Marshal Joseph, 20, 26, 201, 266, 277
address to Russian people by, 220, 224
aggression in Eastern Europe by, 74
alliance between Hitler and, 215
alliance with Roosevelt and Churchill, 217, 220
annexation of Baltic nations by, 92
atrocities ordered by, 438–439
concentration camps of, 440
consolidation of power by, 25
control of Middle Eastern oil fields and, 274
evacuation of Moscow ordered by, 233, 236
German annexation of Czechoslovakia and, 36–37
German-Soviet nonaggression pact and, 37–39
informed of Overlord by Roosevelt, 461–462
meeting with Harry Hopkins, 118
meetings with Roosevelt and Churchill, 263–265
mobilization of Russia against Germany by, 432–433
Polish patriots suppressed by, 533–534
postwar consolidation of power by, 602–603
postwar goals of, 534
at Potsdam Conference, 578–579, 586–587
reaction to German invasion of Russia, 217
Red Army takeover of Berlin ordered by, 541

relations between Churchill and, 263–265
requests for American aid by, 118–119
rule extended over Eastern Europe by, 539
strategies to defeat Germany, 232–233
support of Chiang Kai-shek by, 327
at Teheran Conference, 264–265, 269, 272–273, 274
unconditional surrender guarantee and, 268, 270
wartime politics of, 261, 263
at Yalta Conference, 264–265, 534–535, 538–540
Stalingrad. See Battle of Stalingrad
Stalin-JS tank, 258–259
Stalin Line, 217
Stars and Stripes, 372, 554–555
Stauffenberg, Lt. Colonel Count Klaus von, 484–486
Steinbeck, John, 369
Stettinius, Edward, 280, 534–535, 538
Stewart, Colonel James, 398–399
Stilwell, General Joseph
in Burma, 139, 142, 328
dealing with, 516, 520
debate with Chennault over Burma campaign, 333
dislike of Chiang Kai-shek by, 326, 329
Ledo Road opened by, 328–329
versus Chiang Kai-shek at Cairo, 268, 274
Stimson, Henry, 71, 280, 281
on bombing of Dresden, 407
denunciation of Japanese aggression by, 27–28
peacetime draft and, 112
Stimson Doctrine, 27–28
Stirling bomber, 386, 391
Stockell, Lt. Charles
on army medicine, 518
Strategic bombing, 384, 386, 388, 391–392, 394–397, 400, 401, 402, 404–411
Strategic Bombing Survey, United States, on the German armed forces, 428
Street fighting, in Stalingrad, 250–251
Stringer, Ann, 557
Stuka Ju-87 dive-bomber, 22, 116, 387, 388–389
in North African campaign, 206
use in blitzkrieg warfare of, 44, 45, 46
use in invasion of France of, 56
Submarines, American
in attack on Saipan, 512
in Battle for Leyte Gulf, 524
in Japanese waters, 336, 337
wartime role of, 337
Submarines, German, 158
in Battle of the Atlantic, 165–171, 167, 173
heavy losses of, 171

invincibility of, 149
shipping casualties from, 167, 169, 170, 171
snorkels for, 292
undeclared war against, 119
wartime importance of, 155, 158
wolf-pack tactics of, 170
Sudetenland, giveaway of, 32–33
Suez, German raids on, 186–187
Suez Canal, 185, 187
Suicide charges, 326
Japanese, 507–508, 520
Sulfa drugs, 518, 519
Sullivan brothers, 310–311
at Guadalcanal, 306, 308
Sullivans, The (destroyers), 311
Sullivans, The (film), 311
Sultan, Lt. General Daniel I., 520
Sulzberger, C. L.
in Prague, 32–33
in Yugoslavia, 98
Sumatra, 578
Summit conferences, 269
Surigao Strait, 524, 563
Suwannee, kamikaze attack on, 525
Suzuki, Prime Minister, 594–595
Swastika, 1
Sweating in the Mission (Pleissner), 326–327
Sweden, aid to Finland from, 50–51
Swimming tanks, 464
Sword Beach, invasion of France at, 467, 478–479
Syracuse, 342
Syria, 107

T-34 tank, 117, 231
American and German tanks and, 227
surprise appearance of, 225
Tactical bombing, 401
Taffy Three, 524, 525
Tanks and mechanized vehicles, American, 197, 226–227
bulldozers, 320–321
in D-Day invasion, 464–465
Deuce and a Half truck, 226
DUKW "Duck" amphibious vehicle, 226, 341, 464, 518
flail tanks, 464
Jeep, 226, 359
LVTs (amtracks, amphibious tractors), 319
quantities produced, 227
Sherman tank, 226–227, 373
swimming tanks, 464
Tanks and mechanized vehicles, British
Churchill tank, 227
Crusader tank, 187, 189
quantities produced, 227
Tanks and mechanized vehicles, German, 200, 227
at Kursk, 250
on the Lower Dnieper River, 244
Mark IV tank, 22–23
Panther tank, 227
Panzer tank, 198, 216, 225
quantities produced, 227

Tiger tank, 117, 227, 250
in the Ukraine, 222–223
use in blitzkrieg warfare of, 44, 45, 46
use in invasion of France of, 56
Tanks and mechanized vehicles, Italian, 187
Tanks and mechanized vehicles, Japanese, 227
Tanks and mechanized vehicles, Soviet
KV-2 tank, 258–259
numbers deployed, 230–231
quantities produced, 227
Stalin-JS tank, 258–259
T-34 tank, 117, 225, 227, 231
Tarawa, 318–319, 324, 326
Taylor, General Maxwell, surrender of Italy organized by, 346–347, 349
TBD-1 Douglas Devastator, 180–181
Tedder, Sir Arthur, 393, 471
Teenagers
in Battle of the Bulge, 501
German use of, 548
Teheran Conference, 264-265, 269, 272–273, 274, 461–462
Television, as a radar spinoff, 298
Teller mines, 467
Tempelhof airfield, 552–553
Templar, General Gerald, 349
Tennessee, sinking at Pearl Harbor, 127, 130
Terauchi, Field Marshal Hisaichi
defense of the Philippines by, 521
withdrawal from the Philippines of, 529
Terror bombing, 84, 390–391
of Dresden, 406–407
Terrorism, Nazi, 276, 428
Thailand, Japanese invasion of, 139
Theresienstadt, concentration camp at, 444
Thermopylae, 98
Third Reich. See Germany
Thirty Seconds over Tokyo (film), 416
Thoma, General Ritter von, capture of, 198
Thornton, Sgt. Wagger, 361
wartime heroism of, 278–279
Thrace, 98
Tibbets, Col. Paul, 589
atomic bombardment of Hiroshima by, 562–563
Tiger tank, 117, 227
at Battle of the Bulge, 501
at siege of Kursk, 250
Timoshenko, Marshal Semyon Konstantinovich, 216–217
defense of Smolensk by, 225, 228
recapture of Rostov by, 241
replacement of Budenny by, 233
Russian defense against Germany organized by, 217
Tinian
delivery of atomic bomb to, 311, 586
seizure of, 516
Tito, Marshal
Big Three support of, 269